CHANGING VIEWS

AUTHOR:

Joan Nelson, Ph.D.

Professor of Education, State University of
New York at Binghamton, Binghamton, New York

SENIOR CONSULTANT:

Harold L. Herber, Ed.D.

Professor of Education, Syracuse University
Syracuse, New York

CONSULTANTS:

Donna Alverman

Reading Consultant, East Syracuse-Minoa
School District, Syracuse, New York

Doris Taylor, Ed.D.

Assistant Director, Language Arts/Reading
Dallas Independent School District
Dallas, Texas

Director of Reading: *Sandra Maccarone*

Associate Editor: *Eleanor Franklin*

Editorial Assistant: *Jacqueline Turner*

Editorial Consultants: *Editorial Options, Inc.*

Designed by: *Thomas Vroman Associates, Inc.*

Production Director: *Barbara Arkin*

Production Manager: *Teresa Kluk*

Cover Design: **Thomas Vroman Associates, Inc.** Illustrators: Melanie Arwin, pp. 255, 459-462; Irving Barnett, pp. 260-261; Ray Burns, pp. 123-128; Renee Daily, pp. 218-228; Diane DeGroat, pp. 182-183; Marian Ebert, pp. 373-410; Richard Ferraro, pp. 436-443; Joy Troth Friedman, pp. 66-79; Joe LeMonnier, pp. 38-43, 45-46, 48, 177, 352-353, 359-361, 452; Roger Long, pp. 204-205, 332-336; Dick Loomis, pp. 179, 263-266; Frank Mayo, pp. 413-433; Michael O'Reilly, pp. 230-231, 243-251; Sue Parnell, pp. 22-33, 47, 117-119, 185, 276-277, 315-319, 366; Mark Passmore, pp. 44, 197-199, 351, 355-357, 455; Robert Pennell, p. 314; Albert John Pucci, pp. 161-172; Nancy Schill, pp. 305-307; Clyde Sibel, pp. 50-55, 235-238. 370; Jerry Smath, pp. 137-153, 281-301.

Photo Credits: Dennis Stock, Magnum, cover and p. 1; The Bettmann Archive, pp. 18-19; Herbert Lanks, Monkmeyer, pp. 60-61; Museum of New Mexico, Ben Wittick Photo, p. 85; Culver Pictures, p. 86 (top); Smithsonian Institution, p. 86 (bottom); Brown Brothers, p. 87; Smithsonian Institution, p. 89; Museum of New Mexico, p. 96; Murray Greenberg, Monkmeyer Press Photo, p. 97; Courtesy of Trica Consultants, p. 102; Wide World Photos, p. 106; London Daily Express, Pictorial Parade, p. 107; Wide World Photos, p. 109 (top); Photo Trends, p. 109 (bottom); Drawing by Alan Dunn, © 1960. The New Yorker Magazine, Inc., p. 115; J. Messerschmidt, Bruce Coleman, pp. 132-133; Wide World Photos, p. 187; Burk Uzzle, Magnum, p. 188; Culver Pictures, p. 189; Ken Regan, Camera 5, p. 191; Erich Hartmann, Magnum, p. 192; Brown Brothers, p. 203 and 205; Wide World Photos, p. 206; Waring Abbott, Sygma, p. 207; N.A.S.A., pp. 212-213; Drawing by Alan Dunn, © 1962. The New Yorker Magazine, Inc., p. 241; Russ Kinne, Photo Researchers, pp. 272-273; The Saturday Evening Post Company, 1975, p. 321; Reprinted from THROUGH HISTORY WITH J. WESLEY SMITH by Burr Shafer by permission of the publisher, Vanguard Press, Inc. Copyright, © 1960 by Burr Shafer. Copyright renewed, 1977 by Burr Shafer, p. 322 (top); Drawing by Alan Dunn, © 1967. The New Yorker Magazine, Inc., p. 322 (bottom); © 1962 The Curtis Publishing Company, Cartoon by Roland Michaud, p. 323; Flip Schulke, Black Star, pp. 326-327; The Bettmann Archive, p. 341; The Bettmann Archive, p. 345; George Holton, Photo Researchers, p. 346; The Bettmann Archive, p. 347; Brian Brake, Photo Researchers, p. 348; Peter B. Kaplan, Photo Researchers, pp. 398-399; Wide World Photos, p. 446.

American Book Company

New York   Cincinnati   Atlanta   Dallas   San Francisco

ISBN 0-278-45749-5

1   3   5   7   9   11   13   14   12   10   8   6   4   2

ACKNOWLEDGMENTS

Every reasonable effort has been made to trace the owners of copyright materials in this book, but in some instances this has proven impossible. The publishers will be glad to receive information leading to more complete acknowledgments in subsequent printings of the book, and in the meantime extend their apologies for any omissions.

To *Boys' Life* Magazine for "The Message" by Raboo Rodgers. Reprinted by permission of the author and *Boys' Life*, published by the Boy Scouts of America.

To Celestial Arts for "The Will." From *Chinese Folktales* by Louise and Yuan Hsi Kuo. Copyright © 1976 by Celestial Arts, Millbrae, California. Reprinted with permission of the publishers.

To Thomas Y. Crowell for Chapter 10 from *Harriet Tubman: Conductor on the Underground Railroad* by Ann Petry. Copyright © 1955 by Ann Petry. By permission of Thomas Y. Crowell.

To Curtis Brown, Ltd. for "The Pig," "The Rhinoceros," "The Panther," "The Sea Gull," "The Cobra" by Ogden Nash from *Verses from 1929 On*, published by Little, Brown and Company. Reprinted by permission of Curtis Brown, Ltd. Copyright © 1931, 1933, 1940, 1942, and 1956 by Ogden Nash; for "J.P. Sousa" by Adrien Stoutenburg from *American Tall-Tale Animals*, published by The Viking Press. Reprinted by permission of Curtis Brown, Ltd. Copyright © 1966 by Adrien Stoutenburg; and for "The Ugly Duckling" by A. A. Milne. Reprinted by permission of Curtis Brown, Ltd. Copyright 1941 by A. A. Milne.

To Doubleday & Company, Inc. for "Raymond's Run" from *Tales and Stories of Black Folks* by Toni Cade Bambara. Copyright © 1971 by Doubleday & Company, Inc. Reprinted by permission of Doubleday & Company, Inc.

To Farrar, Straus & Giroux, Inc. for "The Woods-Devil" from *Pride of Lions* by Paul Annixter. Copyright © 1960 by Hill and Wang (now a division of Farrar, Straus & Giroux, Inc.). Reprinted by permission of Hill and Wang.

To Philip George for permission to reprint "Battle Won Is Lost" from *Native American Arts #1*, published by the Institute of American Indian Arts.

To Hamish Hamilton, Ltd. for Chapters 15, 16, 17, and 18 from *Sing Down the Moon* by Scott O'Dell, © 1970 by Scott O'Dell, published by Houghton Mifflin Company.

To Harcourt Brace Jovanovich, Inc. for the excerpt from "My Great-Grandfather's Slaves" by Wendell Berry from *Openings*, copyright © 1965 by Wendell Berry, published by Harcourt Brace Jovanovich, Inc. Reprinted by permission of the publisher.

To Holt, Rinehart and Winston for Chapter 1 adapted from *Wounded Knee* by Dee Brown. Adapted for young readers by Amy Ehrlich. Copyright © 1970 by Dee Brown. Copyright © 1974 by Holt, Rinehart and Winston. Reprinted by permission of Holt, Rinehart and Winston, Publishers.

To Houghton Mifflin Company for "Perfect Number" by Isaac Asimov. From *More Words of Science* by Isaac Asimov. Copyright © 1972 by Isaac Asimov. Reprinted by permission of Houghton Mifflin Company; and for Chapters 15, 16, 17, and 18 from *Sing Down the Moon* by Scott O'Dell. Copyright © 1970 by Scott O'Dell. Reprinted by permission of the publisher, Houghton Mifflin Company.

To Alfred A. Knopf, Inc. for "Mother to Son" by Langston Hughes. Copyright 1926 by Alfred A. Knopf, Inc. and renewed 1954 by Langston Hughes. Reprinted from *Selected Poems of Langston Hughes*, by permission of Alfred A. Knopf, Inc.

To Laidlaw Brothers for an adaptation of "Probability" from *Growth in Mathematics* by B. H. Gundlach, copyright © 1974 by Laidlaw Brothers. By permission of Laidlaw Brothers, a Division of Doubleday & Company, Inc.

To Little, Brown and Company for "The Pig"—Copyright 1933 by Ogden Nash; "The Rhinoceros"—Copyright 1933 by Ogden Nash, first appeared in *The New Yorker*; "The Panther"—Copyright 1940 by Ogden Nash, first appeared in the *Saturday Evening Post*; "The Sea Gull"—Copyright 1940 by Ogden Nash, first appeared in *Harper's Bazaar*; "The Cobra"—Copyright 1931 by Ogden Nash.

To Edward W. Ludwig for permission to reprint "The Other Inhabitant" by Edward W. Ludwig from *Thrilling Science Fiction*, April, 1973.

To Macmillan Publishing Co., Inc. for Chapter 4 of *Call It Courage*. Reprinted with permission of Macmillan Publishing Co., Inc. from *Call It Courage* by Armstrong Sperry. Copyright 1940 by Macmillan Publishing Co.; renewed 1968 by Armstrong Sperry.

To Harold Matson Company, Inc., Agent/Associate: McIntosh, McKee & Dodds, Inc. for Chapter 1 from Dee Brown's *Bury My Heart at Wounded Knee* as adapted by Amy Ehrlich in *An Indian History of the American West*, © 1970 by Dee Brown, © 1974 by Holt, Rinehart and Winston. Reprinted by permission of Harold Matson Company, Inc.

To McGraw-Hill Book Company for "Where in the World Am I?: Latitude" and "Where in the World Am I?: Longitude" adapted from *Understanding Maps* by Beulah Tannenbaum and Myra Stillman. Copyright © 1969 by Tannenbaum and Stillman. Used by permission of McGraw-Hill Book Co.

To Roland Michaud for his Coast Guard cartoon which appeared in the March 4, 1962 issue of *The Saturday Evening Post*. © 1962 The Curtis Publishing Company.

To Lillian Morrison for "The Sprinters" by Lee Murchison (pseud.) from *Sprints and Distances* (T. Y. Crowell Co.). Copyright © 1965 by Lillian Morrison.

To New Directions Publishing Corp. for permission to reprint "The Secret" from *O Taste and See* by Denise Levertov. Copyright © 1964 by Denise Levertov Goodman. Reprinted by permission of New Directions.

To *The New Yorker* Magazine for permission to reprint the Alan Dunn cartoon of the Loch Ness hatchery, © 1960 *The New Yorker* Magazine; the Alan Dunn cartoon of the firemen in the tow-away zone, © 1967 *The New Yorker* Magazine; the Alan Dunn cartoon of the greenhouse shattered by the record-breaking flight, © 1962. *The New Yorker* Magazine.

To Plays Inc., Publishers for "An Imaginary Trial of George Washington" by Diana Wolman from *A Treasury of Holiday Plays for Teen-Agers* by A. S. Burack. Copyright © 1963 by Plays, Inc.

To Prentice-Hall, Inc. for portions of "Gravitation and Orbiting Objects," adapted from *Science in Action* by George K. Stone, copyright © 1964, Prentice-Hall, Inc. Adapted by permission of the publishers; and for permission to reprint an adaptation of pages 185-186 of *Teaching Reading in Content Areas*, second edition, by Harold L. Herber, copyright © 1978, 1970 by Prentice-Hall, Inc. Adapted by permission of Prentice-Hall, Inc.

To Quadrangle/The New York Times Book Co., Inc. for permission to adapt "A Magic Cabinet: The Illusion" and "The Reality" and "The Egg and the Handkerchief: The Illusion" and "The Reality" from *The Great Illusions Revealed and Explained* by David H. Charney © 1975 by Strawberry Hill Publishing Co., Inc.

To Random House, Inc./Alfred A. Knopf, Inc. for "Rocket Talk I" and "Rocket Talk II" by Harold L. Goodwin. Adapted by permission of Random House, Inc. from *All About Rockets and Space Flight* by Harold L. Goodwin. Copyright © 1964, 1970 by Harold L. Goodwin.

To Raboo Rodgers for "The Message" from the March 1977 issue of *Boys' Life*. Reprinted by permission of the author and *Boys' Life*, published by the Boy Scouts of America.

To Russell & Volkening, Inc. for Chapter 10 from *Harriet Tubman: Conductor on the Underground Railroad* by Ann Petry. Copyright © 1955 by Ann Petry. Published by Thomas Y. Crowell.

To Scholastic Magazines, Inc. for "Making Courage Visible," an adaptation of "Convictions" from the introduction to *By-Lines* by Elizabeth Levy. Reprinted by permission of Four Winds Press, a division of Scholastic Magazines, Inc. from *By-Line: Profiles in Investigative Journalism* by Elizabeth Levy. Copyright © 1975 by Elizabeth Levy.

To Scott, Foresman and Company for pronunciation key, grammatical key, and reduced key, from *Thorndike-Barnhart Intermediate Dictionary* by E. L. Thorndike and Clarence L. Barnhart. Copyright © 1974 by Scott, Foresman and Company. Reprinted by permission.

To Charles Scribner's Sons for "Finding Lost Numbers: The Mechanics" and "Finding Lost Numbers: A Practical Application," adapted from *Mathematical Magic* by William Simon. Reprinted by permission of Charles Scribner's Sons from *Mathematical Magic* by William Simon. Copyright © 1964 William Simon.

To Triangle Communications, Inc. for "Games" by Cheryl Curtis. Reprinted from *Seventeen®* Magazine. Copyright © 1978 by Triangle Communications, Inc. All rights reserved.

To Valen Associates for "The Runaway" by Felice Holman from *The Scribner Anthology for Young People*, copyright © 1976 by Charles Scribner's Sons.

To Vanguard Press, Inc. for the Burr Shafer cartoon of Queen Isabella and Christopher Columbus. Reprinted from *Through History with J. Wesley Smith* by Burr Shafer by permission of the Publisher, Vanguard Press, Inc. Copyright © 1950 by Burr Shafer. Copyright renewed, 1977 by Burr Shafer.

To The Viking Press for "The Open Window" by Saki (H. H. Munro) from *The Complete Short Stories of Saki* by H. H. Munro. Copyright © 1930, © renewed 1958 by Viking Press, Inc. All rights reserved. Reprinted by permission of Viking Penguin, Inc.; for "J. P. Sousa" by Adrien Stoutenburg. From *American Tall-Tale Animals* by Adrien Stoutenburg. Copyright © 1968 by Adrien Stoutenburg. All rights reserved. Reprinted by permission of Viking Penguin, Inc.; and for an excerpt from *The Summer of the Swans*. Adapted from *The Summer of the Swans* by Betsy Byars. Copyright © 1970 by Betsy Byars. By permission of The Viking Press.

Contents

one

two

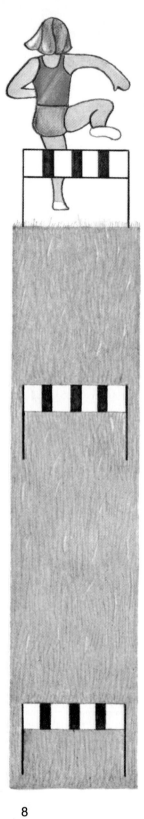

three

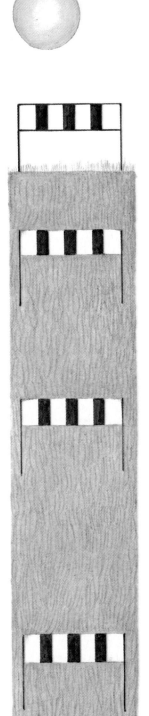

four

five

six

seven

Illusion and Reality

one

"Expectation creates reality out of illusion."

Do you understand this statement? Do you believe it? Reading the selections in this unit will help you understand the statement. You will have to decide for yourself whether or not you believe it.

Key Concepts

illusion   (a) something that deceives by creating a false impression;   (b) a false mental picture that may result from a misinterpretation of reality;   (c) something that is imagined.

reality   (a) a real object or fact; (b) something that exists whether or not people believe it does;   (c) something that is true or actual in contrast to what may appear to be.

Getting in Touch with Your Experiences

Have you ever had any of these experiences with illusion:
- Dreaming and then not being able to decide whether or not the events in the dream really happened?
- Being certain that "something" was following you on a dark night?
- Watching something happen that you knew couldn't happen?
- Seeing a figure change shape or position right before your eyes?
- Being told and believing that people are doing something different from what you see them actually doing.
- Thinking that people are different from what they really are because of special things they are wearing.

Talk about these experiences with your classmates. Share examples of each experience you have had.

Illusion and Reality in Magic

In discussing the different illusions that you have experienced, you probably discovered that different people have experienced the same kind of illusion and that the same people have experienced different kinds of illusions. There is one group of performers who make it their business to create illusions for their audiences. These performers are called magicians. Magicians create many kinds of illusions for people in their audience, but they also make certain that each illusion seems the same for everyone who is part of the experience.

The brief reading selection that follows is about one of these illusions. Read the selection for two purposes: (1) to find out what the illusion is; (2) to find out what possibly contributed to the illusion.

A Magic Cabinet: The Illusion

When the curtain rises, the magician brings a large, dark-colored cabinet to the center of the stage. The cabinet legs are a little longer than those of ordinary cabinets so that everyone can see underneath it. Nothing could slip from the cabinet to the stage beneath without being seen. The cabinet has two doors that are hinged on the sides. A bar separates the doors when they are closed.

The magician turns the cabinet around to show the audience that there is nothing unusual about the outside of the cabinet. He then asks some members of the audience to come up and examine the interior of the cabinet. They find it entirely empty. They can find no double bottom or any other hiding place.

After the witnesses examine the cabinet, they position themselves in different places around the stage. Some of them even agree not to watch the trick so that they can remain behind the cabinet to make certain that all possible escape routes are

covered. The cabinet is thus surrounded on all sides, and everyone is able to look under it. Fraud would seem impossible.

The magician's assistant then comes on stage and enters the cabinet. The magician closes the doors and a few moments later opens them again. Lo and behold! The cabinet is empty. The woman has disappeared.

The magician then closes the doors again and reopens them a few seconds later. The woman is seen again. She has reappeared. At the end of the trick, the witnesses examine the cabinet again and find nothing changed. They are justly amazed.

React to the Illusion

You have just read about an illusion created by a magician. What contributed to the illusion? Below are some statements. Decide which ones represent ideas that may have contributed to the illusion. Discuss your responses with others in your group and give evidence for your choices. Some statements can be supported or rejected by referring to the selection. Other statements will have to be accepted or rejected on the basis of your own experiences.

1. The woman could not escape out the back of the cabinet.
2. People who pay to see a magician perform expect to be fooled.
3. Using witnesses from the audience makes an illusion more believable.
4. The cabinet contained no hiding place.
5. The cabinet was examined before the woman disappeared and after she reappeared, but not in between.

Predict the Reality

Magicians can create the same illusion for many different people because they can predict or make guesses about human nature. You can usually predict how someone will react, what your grades will be, etc., by examining your past experiences with such things. The same thing can be done when you read.

Make some predictions about how the magic cabinet illusion is created. Using what you have just read and your own experiences, decide which of the statements below offer reasonable explanations. Share your reasons for accepting or rejecting all the statements.

1. The woman hides on a ledge on the back of the cabinet and cannot be seen when the magician opens the doors.
2. The woman unrolls a screen that is painted to look like the back of the cabinet. She stands behind it and seems to disappear.
3. The woman hides behind mirrors inside the cabinet so that the people see the inside of the cabinet reflected.
4. The magician has the power to actually make the woman disappear.

What other predictions can you make?

Now read about how the illusion was created. Discover the reality behind the illusion. Be sure to use the diagram as you read. It will help you understand where everything is and how the illusion is created.

A Magic Cabinet:
The Reality

The illusion is produced with mirrors. When the magician closes the cabinet doors, the woman pulls two mirrors—one from each side of the cabinet—toward her. In the diagram, these are represented by the lines CE and DF.

The mirrors are hinged at the corners, C and D. When they are swung toward the center, their edges rest against the center bar, B. They are then in the position shown by the dotted lines CB and DB.

When the magician reopens the doors, the spectators cannot see the woman because she is hidden behind the mirrors in area A. The interior of the cabinet, however, looks the same because the spectators see the image of each side reflected from the corresponding mirror. To them, this looks like the back of the cabinet. The illusion is perfect.

When the magician closes the doors, the woman swings the mirrors back against the sides at E and F. Then the magician opens the doors again, and the woman steps out. The spectators re-examine the cabinet and see nothing but the backs of the mirrors, which are covered with the same wood as the interior of the cabinet. The cabinet really is empty, and no one can figure out how the interior changed during the "disappearance" of the woman.

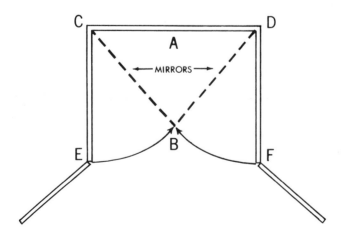

Now that you have read the reality, go back and review your predictions. How close did you come to guessing the reality?

Support Your Ideas

Here are several ideas that relate to illusion and reality. Decide which ones you can support *both* from the reading selections and from your own ideas and experiences. Discuss the reasons for your choices.

1. Witnesses are reliable only if they know what they are looking for.
2. Mirrors can reflect reality to create an illusion.
3. What you think you see may not be as accurate as what you really see.
4. When you check on only the beginning and ending of an activity, you may draw an inaccurate conclusion about what happened in between.

Make More Predictions

You have read about the magician's use of mirrors to create an illusion. Now you can read about his or her use of prestidigitation. From looking at the parts of the word, can you guess what kind of illusion prestidigitation involves? Each part has a meaning:

presti—fast or lively
digit—finger
ation—action or process

Now, can you tell what a prestidigitator is?

Read the description of the egg-and-handkerchief illusion which follows. Before reading the explanation of the reality, discuss the illusion with your classmates. Make some predictions about how the illusion is created. Then read the reality to see how well you predicted.

The Egg and the Handkerchief: The Illusion

In this illusion, an egg and a handkerchief change places. The prestidigitator shows the audience a basket of eggs. She breaks one to prove they are real. She places an egg in an eggcup. She covers both with a hat so neither the egg nor the eggcup can be seen.

Next, the prestidigitator picks up a small, silk handkerchief by one corner. She slowly gathers it into both of her hands so that it gradually disappears. When the handkerchief completely disappears from sight, the prestidigitator opens her hands. Surprise! Instead of seeing a handkerchief in her hands, the audience sees the egg.

The prestidigitator then lifts the hat to show the audience the handkerchief—in the eggcup. The two objects have changed places right before your very eyes! That's the illusion.

The Egg and the Handkerchief: The Reality

Real eggs are in the basket, and a real egg is broken. But the egg that is placed in the eggcup is not real. It is only half a wooden shell painted to look like a real egg. Only the upper half of the egg can be seen. Stuffed inside that half shell is a small silk handkerchief just like the one the prestidigitator rolls up in her hands. The half shell fits perfectly into the eggcup so that its bottom cannot be seen.

When the prestidigitator uses her left hand to cover the egg and eggcup with her hat, she quickly turns over the egg with her right hand. This action releases the handkerchief in place. The audience, of course, does not see this because it takes place under the hat.

As the prestidigitator picks up the handkerchief that is in sight on the table, she secretly picks up another false egg. This one is made of metal and has a small hole in one end. As she pretends to gather the handkerchief into her hands, she is actually pushing it into the hole in this egg. When the handkerchief is completely enclosed in the false egg, the prestidigitator opens her hands to reveal the egg—not the handkerchief. She then removes the hat to reveal the handkerchief that has been waiting for her.

That's the reality!

 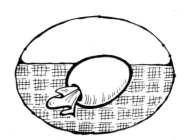

Confirm Your Predictions

Review the predictions you made before you read the reality of the illusion. How close did you come to predicting the reality?

Apply the Ideas

Here are some ideas that relate to both illusions. Decide which ones you can support both from the reading and from your own ideas and experiences. With your group, discuss the reasons for your choices.

1. Seeing is not always believing.
2. The illusion is more entertaining than the reality.
3. The hand is quicker than the eye.
4. Part of something is not necessarily the whole.

Illusion and Reality
in Literature

Magicians create illusions with their hands and with special equipment. Other people create illusions with words and active imaginations. As you read the story that follows, see if you can separate the reality from the illusion. The paragraphs are numbered to help you find information later on.

Expand Your Vocabulary

The story you are going to read was written by a British author who uses some words that may be unfamiliar to you. Some of the words he uses are listed below on the left. To check your understanding of those words, match each word on the left with its meaning on the right. Use the glossary if you need extra help.

1. endeavor   a. approaching
2. sufficient   b. illness
3. self-possessed   c. residence
4. engulf   d. to try
5. treacherous   e. enough
6. imminent   f. to swallow up
7. scarcity   g. possibility
8. prospect   h. self-assured; confident
9. infirmity   i. dangerous
10. habitation   j. shortage

As you read the story, notice how the context supports the meaning.

The Open Window   by Saki (H.H. Munro)

1   "My aunt will be down presently, Mr. Nuttel," said a very
self-possessed young lady of fifteen; "in the meantime you must
try and put up with me."

2   Framton Nuttle endeavored to say the correct something
which should duly flatter the niece of the moment without unduly
discounting the aunt that was to come. Privately he doubted more
than ever whether these formal visits on a succession of total
strangers would do much toward helping the nerve cure which
he was supposed to be undergoing.

3   "I know how it will be," his sister had said when he was
preparing to migrate to this rural retreat; "you will bury yourself
down there and not speak to a living soul, and your nerves will
be worse than ever from moping. I shall just give you letters of
introduction to all the people I know there. Some of them, as far
as I can remember, were quite nice."

4   Framton wondered whether Mrs. Sappleton, the lady to
whom he was presenting one of the letters of introduction, came
into the nice division.

1   "Do you know many of the people round here?" asked the niece, when she judged that they had had sufficient silent communion.

2   "Hardly a soul," said Framton. "My sister was staying here at the rectory, you know, some four years ago, and she gave me letters of introduction to some of the people here."

3   He made the last statement in a tone of distinct regret.

4   "Then you know practically nothing about my aunt?" pursued the self-possessed young lady.

5   "Only her name and address," admitted the caller. He was wondering whether Mrs. Sappleton was in the married or widowed state. An undefinable something about the room seemed to suggest masculine habitation.

1   "Her great tragedy happened just three years ago," said the child; "that would be since your sister's time."

2   "Her tragedy?" asked Framton; somehow in this restful country spot tragedies seemed out of place.

3   "You may wonder why we keep that window wide open on an October afternoon," said the niece, indicating a large French window that opened onto a lawn.

4   "It is quite warm for the time of year," said Framton, "but has that window got anything to do with the tragedy?"

5   "Out through that window, three years ago to a day, her husband and her two young brothers went off for their day's shooting. They never came back. In crossing the moor to their favorite snipe-shooting ground, they were all three engulfed in a

treacherous piece of bog. It had been that dreadful wet summer, you know, and places that were safe in other years gave way suddenly without warning. Their bodies were never recovered. That was the dreadful part of it." Here the child's voice lost its self-possessed note and became falteringly human. "Poor aunt always thinks that they will come back someday, they and the little brown spaniel that was lost with them, and walk in through that window just as they used to. That is why the window is kept open every evening till it is quite dusk. Poor dear aunt, she has often told me how they went out, her husband with his white mackintosh over his arm, and Ronnie, her youngest brother, singing 'Bertie, why do you bound?' as he always did to tease her, because she said it got on her nerves. Do you know, sometimes on still, quiet evenings like this, I almost get a creepy feeling that they will all walk in through that window—"

1   She broke off with a little shudder. It was a relief to Framton when the aunt bustled into the room with a whirl of apologies for being late in making her appearance.

2   "I hope Vera has been amusing you," she said.

3   "She has been very interesting," said Framton.

4   "I hope you don't mind the open window," said Mrs. Sappleton briskly; "my husband and brothers will be home directly from shooting, and they always come in this way. They've been out for snipe in the marshes today, so they'll make a fine mess over my poor carpets. So like you menfolk, isn't it?"

5   She rattled on cheerfully about the shooting and the scarcity of birds, and the prospects for duck in the winter. To Framton it was all purely horrible. He made a desperate but only partially successful effort to turn the talk onto a less ghastly topic; he was conscious that his hostess was giving him only a fragment of her attention, and her eyes were constantly straying past him to the open window and the lawn beyond. It was certainly an unfortunate coincidence that he should have paid his visit on this tragic anniversary.

6   "The doctors agree in ordering me complete rest, an absence of mental excitement, and avoidance of anything in the nature of violent physical exercise," announced Framton, who labored under the tolerably widespread delusion that total strangers and chance acquaintances are hungry for the least detail of one's ailments and infirmities, their cause and cure. "On the matter of diet they are not as much in agreement," he continued.

7   "No?" said Mrs. Sappleton, in a voice that only replaced a yawn at the last moment. Then she suddenly brightened into alert attention—but not to what Framton was saying.

1   "Here they are at last!" she cried. "Just in time for tea, and don't they look as if they were muddy up to the eyes!"

2   Framton shivered slightly and turned toward the niece with a look intended to convey sympathetic comprehension. The child was staring out through the open window with dazed horror in her eyes. In a chill shock of nameless fear Framton swung round in his seat and looked in the same direction.

3   In the deepening twilight three figures were walking across the lawn toward the window; they all carried guns under their arms, and one of them was additionally burdened with a white coat hung over his shoulders. A tired brown spaniel kept close at their heels. Noiselessly they neared the house, and then a hoarse young voice chanted out of the dusk, "I said, Bertie, why do you bound?"

4   Framton grabbed wildly at his stick and hat; the hall door, the gravel drive, and the front gate were dimly noted stages in his headlong retreat. A cyclist coming along the road had to run into the hedge to avoid imminent collision.

1 "Here we are, my dear," said the bearer of the white mackintosh, coming in through the window; "fairly muddy, but most of it's dry. Who was that who bolted out as we came up?"

2 "A most extraordinary man, a Mr. Nuttel," said Mrs. Sappleton; "could only talk about his illnesses, and dashed off without a word of good-bye or apology when you arrived. One would think he had seen a ghost."

3 "I expect it was the spaniel," said the niece calmly; "he told me he had a horror of dogs. He was once hunted into a cemetery somewhere on the banks of the Ganges* by a pack of pariah dogs and had to spend the night in a newly dug grave with the creatures snarling and grinning and foaming just above him. Enough to make anyone lose their nerve."

4 Romance at short notice was her specialty.

* Ganges (gan′jēz′) a river in India.

Confirm the Reality

"The Open Window" closely combines both illusion and reality. Decide whether each statement below tells what really happened in the story. Be ready to support your answers with evidence from the story. The numbers following some of the statements show first the number of the page and then the number of the paragraph in which you might find the evidence.

1. Framton Nuttel had come to the country to cure his nerves. (29, 2)
2. Framton was an old friend of the Sappleton family. (30, 4–5)
3. A great tragedy had occurred in Mrs. Sappleton's life. (31, 1)
4. The niece said that Mr. Sappleton was lost while hunting. (31, 5)
5. Mrs. Sappleton believed her husband would return from hunting. (32, 4)
6. The niece was frightened by what she saw.
7. Framton ran from the house.
8. Mr. and Mrs. Sappleton were puzzled by Framton's actions.
9. The niece said that Framton ran off because he was afraid of dogs.

Interpret the Illusion

The illusion in the story depends on different people believing different things about the same event. Decide which statement(s) following each person's name describe(s) what he or she believed. Since more than one statement may be correct for each person, be sure you can find evidence from the story to accept or reject each.

1. The niece believed that:
   a. the hunters would return on time and come through the open window.
   b. Framton Nuttel would believe anything she told him.
   c. her aunt's actions would support the story she told Framton.
   d. her own actions could convince Framton that her story was true.
   e. illusion was more fun than reality.
2. Mrs. Sappleton believed that:
   a. Framton was a nervous and self-centered person.
   b. the hunters would return before dark.
   c. her niece would properly entertain Mr. Nuttel.
   d. Framton Nuttel had seen a ghost.
3. Framton Nuttel believed that:
   a. Mrs. Sappleton was out of touch with reality.
   b. all three of them had seen a ghost.
   c. the safest place for him was out of the house.
   d. the hunters' dog was out to get him.

Apply the Ideas

Below are some ideas that may relate to the story and to similar kinds of experiences. Work with your group to decide which ideas you can support from your own experiences and from the story.

1. People see what they expect to see.
2. The body will act on what the eyes see even though the mind doesn't believe.
3. What you don't know can't hurt you.
4. Ordinary events can be made extraordinary by the suggestions of a clever person.
5. An active imagination can always find a willing audience.
6. Nervous people are easily fooled.
7. The same event can be both illusion and reality.

Illusion and Reality in Perception

Thus far in this unit you have read how magicians and imaginative storytellers can lead people to confuse illusion with reality. In this section, you will see how your own eyes and mind create illusions as you look at particular arrangements of lines and figures.

Review Your Vocabulary

Before you read about optical illusions, look at the pairs of words below. You probably know most of them from your studies. To be sure, discuss the words in each pair with your group. Then decide whether the words have similar meanings or opposite meanings. Use the glossary if you need help.

parallel—converging   receding—approaching
visual—optical   converging—diverging
perspective—outlook   bulge—swell
vertical—horizontal   extended—prolonged

OPTICAL ILLUSIONS

Look carefully at the three parallel lines in Figure 1 below. Do they appear to be the same length? Use a ruler to be sure.

Now look at the parallel lines after other lines have been added to them in Figure 2. Do they seem the same length to you? If not, which seems longest? Which seems shortest?

Fig. 1

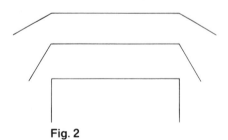

Fig. 2

Show this second set of lines to three or four other people. Do they see the lines as being the same or different in length? Let them check their impressions with a ruler.

Most people see the lines as being different in length, with the top line being the longest and the bottom one the shortest. What they—and you—are experiencing is an *optical illusion.*

An optical illusion is visual perception that has to be corrected when more information is added. In other words, your eyes and brain tell you one thing about what you are seeing, but when you find out more about what you are looking at, you discover that it is not what you thought it was.

Take a look at Figure 3. As you study it, decide which statements describe what you seem to see. Don't do any measuring until after you make your decisions.

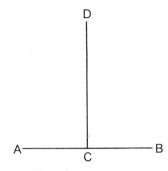

Fig. 3

1. Line AC is the same length as line CB.
2. Line AB is the same length as line CD.
3. Point D on line CD seems to be farther away from you than point C.

Use a ruler to check the reality of what you see. Number 3, of course, cannot be proven one way or the other by measuring.

Draw Some Conclusions

Which of the following conclusions would you support? What is your evidence?

1. A line that is divided seems shorter than a line that is undivided.
2. A line that is undivided seems shorter than a line that is divided.
3. When one line seems close to you and a second line seems to move into the distance, the second line looks longer than the first.

Check your conclusions with this information:

Most people see line CD as being longer than line AB for two reasons. First, line CD is not divided and line AB is divided. A line that is not divided looks longer than a line that is divided. Second, most people see a drawing in perspective; that is, they see some parts of the drawing as being close to them and other parts as being off in the distance. Because of this habit, most people see line AB as being close to them and line CD as moving into the distance. This also gives the illusion that line CD is longer than line AB.

more OPTICAL ILLUSIONS

Following are more figures that can create optical illusions for most people. Look at both figures carefully. Then read the statements about them that follow. Discuss the statements and decide which ones describe what you seem to see. Don't do any measuring until you get to number 8.

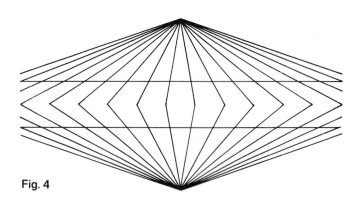

Fig. 4

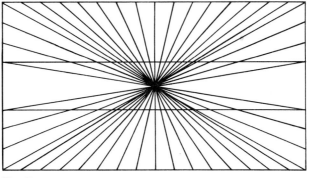

Fig. 5

1. In Figure 4, the points where the lines come together (converge) at the top and bottom seem farther away than where the lines connect between the horizontal lines.
2. In Figure 4, the horizontal lines do not seem parallel; they seem to dip toward each other at the center.
3. In Figure 4, the horizontal lines seem to curve as though they are going around a circle.
4. In Figure 5, the point where the lines converge between the horizontal lines seems farther away than where the lines spread apart.
5. In Figure 5, the horizontal lines do not seem parallel; they seem to curve away from each other at the center.
6. In Figure 5, the horizontal lines seem to curve as though they are going around a circle.
7. In Figure 4, we seem to be on the outside of something, looking in.
8. In Figure 5, we seem to be on the inside of something, looking out.

Draw More Conclusions

Which of the following conclusions would you support? Discuss the evidence you find with your group.

1. When lines come together (converge) at a point in the center of a figure, the center seems far away.
2. When lines spread apart (diverge) in the middle of a figure, the middle seems closer to you.
3. When lines converge between horizontal lines, the horizontal lines seem to curve away from you.
4. When lines diverge between horizontal lines, the horizontal lines seem to curve toward you.

Check your conclusions against this information:

With Figure 4, most of us (without realizing it) construct a visual image of a figure that bulges toward us in the center. It recedes from us above, below, and at the sides. In this image, the horizontal lines seem to be on the surface of the figure. They too bulge toward us and toward each other in the center and away from us and away from each other at the sides. Even if you blot out the drawing above and below the horizontal lines, the image cannot be changed easily into one in which the lines are parallel.

With Figure 5, most of us construct an image of a figure receding toward the point where the converging lines meet. In this image, the horizontal lines again seem to be on the surface of the figure. As a result, they seem closer together at the sides and farther apart nearer the point where the converging lines meet. Most people cannot change this image without blotting out all the converging lines.

Check—With New Information

Now that you have seen how your perception can make lines move forward and backward, examine each of the following figures. Try to see each illusion suggested.

Fig. 6

1. The white shape is a wide-mouth vase.

2. The dark shapes are silhouettes.

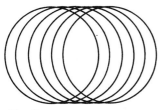

Fig. 7

1. A hollow tube runs from left to right.

2. A hollow tube runs from right to left.

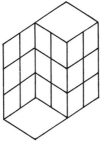

Fig. 8

1. Two solid figures are leaning against each other.

2. One solid figure has an extended side.

Fig. 9

1. The dark areas are tops of cubes.

2. The dark areas are bottoms of cubes.

Apply the Ideas

Now that you have examined some optical illusions, which of the following ideas can you relate to them? Be ready to share the reasons for your choices with your group.

1. Different people can see the same thing differently.
2. People believe only what they see.
3. What seems to be is not always what is.
4. Appearances can be deceiving.

Illusion and Reality in Graphic Aids

In your reading, you have discovered that people are surrounded by illusions. They need to be constantly alert to detect illusions and to recognize reality. You saw how this was true in the material about magicians and optical illusions. You also saw it, in a different way, in the story "The Open Window." Now you are going to read about another source of illusion—factual information.

Factual information is supposed to communicate reality. How can something factual be an illusion? Well, it depends on the way the facts are presented. There are many different ways to present factual information. It can be written out in sentence form or shown visually with line graphs, bar graphs, charts, or pictures.

Visual aids, such as graphs, are frequently the clearest way to present information. They do, however, leave more room for interpretation and thus allow for illusions to be created.

The following section presents a series of problems related to using graphic aids to show facts. Study the figures very carefully, keeping in mind their stated purpose. Try to separate the illusion from the reality. Notice the importance of paying attention to details when you read charts and graphs.

Line Graphs: Problem No. 1

Two coaches from different colleges wanted Ramona to play basketball for them. Ramona couldn't decide which college to choose. Ms. Fonie, the coach at Denim University, suggested that Ramona compare the season records of the two colleges. She could then choose the one that won the most games.

Ramona agreed to this idea. So Ms. Fonie briefly showed her the following line graphs. Figure 1 shows Denim University's record, and Figure 2 shows the other college's record.

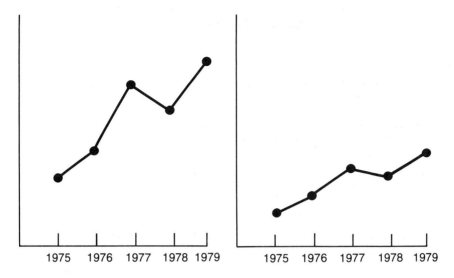

Fig. 1: Denim University   **Fig. 2:** Classy College

Ramona decided to go to Denim University. Later, when the coach at Classy College heard this, she went to see Ramona. After looking at the two figures, she said, "Hey, wait a minute. Something's missing!" Then she added some information and gave the graphs back to Ramona. Now they looked as they do in Figure 3 and Figure 4.

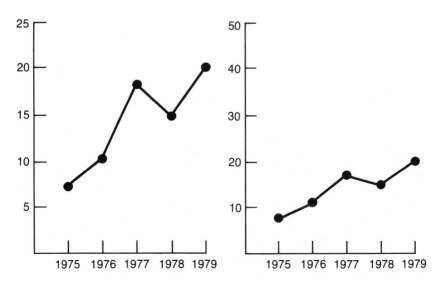

Fig. 3: Denim University   **Fig. 4:** Classy College

Ramona studied the graphs for a while. Then she said, "Well, I guess I can't make a choice on the basis of this information after all. I'm going to need more information before I can make up my mind."

1. What did Ramona discover?
2. What information did the coach from Classy College add to the figures?
3. What did you learn from Ramona's experience with these figures?
4. Later, Ramona said to her parents, "I had not realized how easily illusions could be created with graphs." Would you agree with her observations? Why?

Interpret the Illusion in Problem No. 1

Below are some ideas related to the line graphs in Problem No. 1. Decide which ones you can support with evidence from the problem.

1. Line graphs have to have two sets of information: one set along the vertical line (axis) and one set along the horizontal line (axis).
2. To get accurate information from line graphs, you have to examine each set of figures carefully and compare the information.
3. Illusions can be created in graphs by the way information is arranged.

44

Bar Graphs: Problem No. 2

XYZ Company has a savings plan to help their employees when they retire. It's called a pension plan. Each year the same total amount of money is put into the plan. But each year the company pays a higher percentage, and the workers pay a lower percentage.

Now the workers and the owners are talking about a new agreement. Each group believes it has given a lot already. A board will decide which group should increase its share.

Study the bar graphs that represent each group's share. Use the KEY so that you will know which bar represents which group.

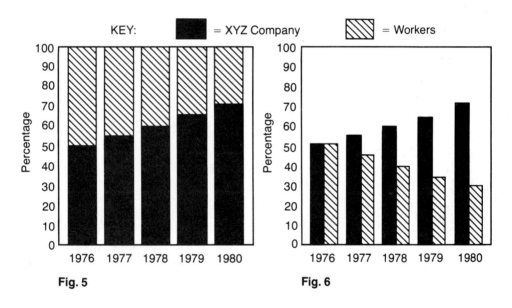

Fig. 5   Fig. 6

Interpret the Illusion in Problem No. 2

Answer the following questions about the bar graphs. Share your reasons for answering the questions as you do.

1. Which of the two figures will the workers show the board? Why?
2. Which figure will the owners show? Why?
3. What's the reality?
4. How is the illusion created?

More Line Graphs: Problem No. 3

Mr. Tightlip and Mr. Looselip are both being considered for promotion to sales manager. Their boss said that the decision between them would be made on the basis of their sales records for the first six months of the year.

Study the figures below that represent the sales figures. Try to find the illusion and the reality.

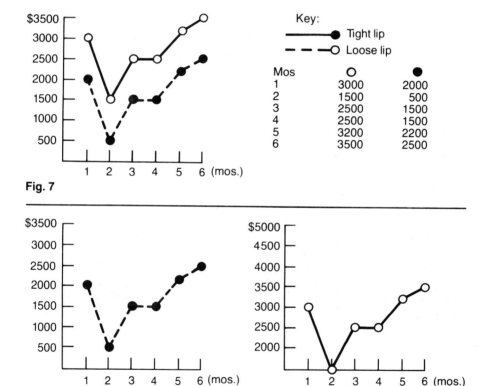

Fig. 7

Fig. 8

Analyze the Illusion in Problem No. 3

Answer the following questions about the information in the line graphs.

1. Which figure will Mr. Tightlip present to his boss? Why?
2. Which figure will Mr. Looselip present? Why?
3. What is the reality in the information?
4. What is the illusion? How is the illusion created?

Cartoons: Problem No. 4

Two communities are asking for money from their state government. What they get depends on what they already have. The more they have, the less they get. Community B gets twice as much as Community A.

Analyze the Illusion in Problem No. 4

Study Figure 9 and Figure 10. Which figure will Community B use in its presentation to the state? Why? Which figure will Community A use? Why? What is the illusion? How is the illusion created?

Community A   Community B

Fig. 9

Community A   Community B

Fig. 10

Maps: Problem No. 5

The president of Big B Bubble Gum Company called her national sales manager. She said, "I don't think we are doing as well as we should. Give me a report on the areas in which we have sales and those in which we have contracts. I want to see how your figures compare with mine."

Study the figures below. Which figure will the sales manager show the president? Which will the president show the sales manager? Why? What is the reality in these figures? What is the illusion? How is the illusion created?

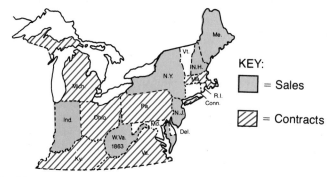

KEY:

⬛ = Sales

▨ = Contracts

Fig. 11

Fig. 12

Think about the use of charts, graphs, and pictures in creating illusions. Decide which of the following conclusions seem reasonable. Be sure to give reasons for your choices.

1. The same information can be presented in different ways.
2. Charts and graphs help give meaning to numbers.
3. Most people use information to their own advantage.
4. Numbers don't lie, but people can use them to make different impressions.
5. When interpreting charts, graphs, or pictures, don't depend on how they look; read to find out what they mean.

More Illusion and Reality in Literature

It's possible to experience an illusion and believe it's reality. It's also possible to experience reality and believe it's an illusion. Read the following story to see what Sam Harding experiences.

As you read the story, try to separate illusion from reality. Look for clues that show how each factor below affects the character's beliefs and behaviors.

1. strange environment
2. fear
3. loneliness
4. hope

The Other Inhabitant
by Edward W. Ludwig

1   Astro-lieutenant Sam Harding counted: one, two, three, four, five, six, seven, eight, nine, ten.

2   Then he screamed. It was a wild, ringing scream that knifed through the dark night and the soft, silent forest of Alpha III.

3   With a shiver of terror he closed his lips, but the scream did not die, not at once. It dissolved into a thousand-voiced echo that bounced from the tiny planet's gold-leafed cacti to the purple ravine, from the pock-marked mountain to the red-grassed valley, then faded at last.

4   Release of the scream relieved the terror within him. "Take it easy, lieutenant," he told himself. "Remember, an officer of the United Earth Space Corps has been thoroughly conditioned. He's mentally sound. He can't go psycho. So there's nothing following you. You're just lost in the forest, and you're tired and hungry. Don't imagine things."

5   A voice within his mind said, "But you heard it! Whatever it is, you felt it following you, hiding in the shadows, watching you. It *was* there."

6   He stood with his fists clenched, fighting with all his strength to conquer this fear, crush it, and thrust it from his consciousness.

1   "This is a gentle, kind planetoid. You've circled the whole surface in seven days and found no signs of carnivores, no indications of intelligent life. Nothing except lizards, birds, squirrel-things, moths, and insects. Plenty of water, wild fruit, berries, and nuts. And the point-four-seven gravity makes you feel like a kid of ten instead of a grizzled old space-dog of thirty-six. Except for the mountain and cactus country, this is paradise.

2   "And you've seen a hundred planets and planetoids. You know your worlds. There are no fire-breathing monsters here. There might be a lizard or a squirrel that'd be more scared than you are. But nothing more. Of course not. Certainly not."

3   The voice within him was silent. He sighed. The fear was gone. How silly he'd been! Imagine—counting to ten in order to calm himself and then screaming like an idiot. He chuckled and proceeded to make a bed of dry purple leaves. He threw his gaunt body down. Soon he was asleep.

4   He awoke as light from Alpha Centauri filtered down through a ceiling of purplish branches, casting gentle warmth upon his face. The sound of birds chirping drifted pleasantly down to him. He listened and smiled. Except for the purplish reflection of the leaves, it was almost like Earth.

5   "This," he murmured, "may be the day. Today they'll find me—Captain Hernandez and Sergeant Long. And this is the seventh day. Seven is a lucky number."

6   He rubbed his thin, bony hand over his face. His body

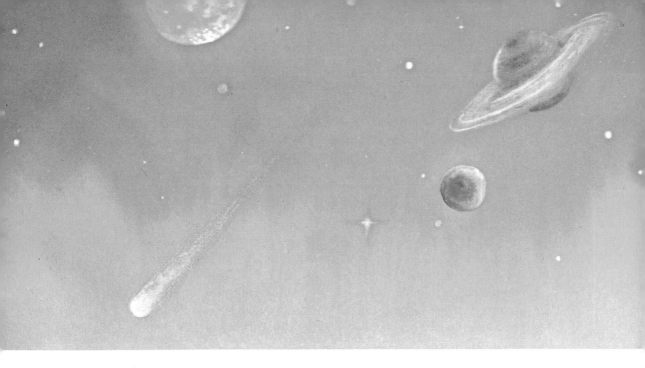

jerked. He rubbed his face again. What a beard he had! It was so
long! Not just a stubble, but a real beard! How could his whiskers
have grown so long in seven days? What kind of a planetoid
was this?

1   Seven. The number stuck in his mind. Seven days. *Or was it
seven weeks?*

2   He stared at the forest ceiling for a long time, frowning,
forcing himself to remember. Finally, he smiled.

3   "You were on a flight from Proxima Centauri with Juan
Hernandez as captain and Marla Long as engineer. You got
orders to go on to Alpha VII. The drive grids cracked over Alpha
III; you crashed. You and Juan and Marla camped for three days.
Then you decided to explore. You split up. You were supposed
to regroup in twenty-four hours. But you—you got lost. You've
walked for seven days, you've camped for three. You probably
didn't shave on the trip from Proxima. That's why your beard
is so long."

4   Reassured, he rose and breakfasted on cactus nuts and
berries that tasted like spiced apples, washing them down with
clear, cool spring water.

5   "Ah, that's better!"

6   He started to lie down when another memory slashed into
his consciousness. The Creature! The Creature that had been
following him these past nights, the invisible, nameless presence
that he had sensed but never seen.

1   "It doesn't exist," he told himself. "It was your imagination." The voice within said, "But suppose there *is* something, something alien and terrible, something no other space explorer has ever encountered. You must be ready."

2   He *would* be ready. He worked swiftly, gathering cactus limbs and piling them in a circular wall around the tiny clearing where he slept. He built his wall high and broad, and then he sought weapons.

3   He spied a large fallen branch that was like a cudgel. Excellent. The end, where it had splintered from a tree, was pointed and sharp, almost like the tip of a spear.

4   He gathered stones—small stones for throwing, large stones for crushing—in case the Creature attempted to break through his wall.

5   Abruptly, a shadow fell upon him. He tensed and stood motionless. The shadow deepened, and a coolness was in the air. Somehow the forest had changed. There was a silence. Even the bird twitterings had ceased.

6   His eyes darted sharply from side to side, searching for the cause of the shadow. Nothing was near him—nothing except the

silent trees, the black-hued berry shrubs, and the purplish fern foliage. He saw that the sky was darkening. It was evening. How quickly the day had gone!

1   He climbed over the mass of tangled cactus branches and squatted inside his fortress, with the pile of stones on his right, the cudgel on the left. He was ready.

2   A murmur arose in the heart of the forest as if a million elfin voices were calling, whispering, combining to form a somber chant. He thought, "It's the wind. That's all."

3   As the wind rose and darkness fell, something stirred within the forest. It was as if deep in the brooding night a giant heart had begun to beat and a giant body had been awakened.

4   Lieutenant Harding paled. A watery weakness was in his legs. His breath came rapidly. He wanted to run, to flee.

5   "You mustn't run!" his mind screamed. "You must stay here by the spring. If you run, you'll get lost again with no water. You must stay here till Captain Hernandez finds you. You must fight the Creature."

6   But what was the Creature? What manner of thing could it be?

7   Whatever it was, it seemed to be coming closer. The wind, over there to the right, seemed more than wind. The trees swayed and rustled with an abnormal, alarming restlessness. The sudden coolness seemed more than the coolness of evening. It was a chilling, alien coolness that belonged in a dark, forgotten tomb.

8   Then, unexplainably, a realization came to Harding. The Creature was hideously ugly, wildly insane, and incredibly ancient. And it was coming closer, settling down upon him like a great cloud.

9   He forgot his cudgel and his stones. He crashed his way out of the wall of branches, arms flailing, screaming. He ran.

10   He ran through the black forest, cactus arms tearing at his naked shoulders like sharp-nailed fingers. He stumbled across thick-grassed ravines, scrambled down rocky mountainsides, falling, tumbling.

11   Always, the Creature remained at his heels, constant as the night.

12   He paused to catch his breath. A soft pale light fell upon his face. The twin moons of Alpha III appeared above the tops of the mountains.

13   Harding gasped. Not more than ten feet (about three meters) before him lay the rocket. Finally, thank God, he'd found the rocket. He began to shout. "Captain Hernandez! Sergeant Long! Captain—" His words froze.

1   No, *this* was not the rocket. This was a hollow, pitted, rusted shell of a rocket. It was a metallic skeleton filled with grass and covered with rust. The air of the planetoid couldn't have oxidized rocket steel in only seven days. Or was it seventy days? Or—

2   No, this was not his rocket. His face saddened. One year, a long, long time ago, another rocket had crashed here and other space explorers had perished. But there was no time now to think about the rocket. The Creature was still here, lurking in the shadows, waiting.

3   Suddenly it seemed as if there were a humming in the ravine, like the insect murmur of electricity through a power line. It seemed to be the sound of a living thing: its strange breath, slow movement, and pulsing heart all combined to form a single sound that was the surge of alien life.

4   He whirled and ran back to the dark protection of the forest.

5   He kept running until he fell exhausted. He lay panting with his hands thrust before him. His fingers dug into the soft cushion

of grass as if to pull his body another inch forward, another inch, away from the stalking Creature.

1   Abruptly, he became defiant. He was weary of running, weary of this crazed night flight. Why not face the Creature? Death itself could be no worse than constant terror.

2   He rose with his face hard and his eyes wide.

3   "Come out, whoever you are! I'm not afraid!"

4   No answer.

5   He stood silently for a while. Then he saw that he was standing near the edge of a pit. A chill crept down his spine. An eerie realization again came to his mind. This must be the home of the Creature!

6   He sank to his knees and crawled forward until his hands slipped out from beneath him and dangled in the air. He was at the edge of the pit. Cautiously, his heart pounding, he peered over the edge into the blackness. He saw a faint but definite movement, and he knew the Creature was here.

1   A pale pink glow crept into the forest. The planetoid's moons were rising above the tips of the trees.

2   Suddenly, the moonlight fell upon the Creature.

3   Harding stared, his gaze frozen. The monstrosity glared back at him. It was hideously ugly, wildly insane, and incredibly ancient—a hundred years old, maybe a thousand. A shock of long white hair covered its skull, straggling down past sunken cheeks and bare bony shoulders. Its eyes, set deep within black hollows, were wide and red and insane. The mouth was twisted in an idiotic grimace that revealed rotten teeth. Its flesh was wrinkled and dry like that of a mummy.

4   Harding tried to scream, but his voice, like his body, was paralyzed. The Creature seemed to hold him, draining life from his body.

5   He thought, "I am going to sleep, because if things like you exist, I do not want to live. I am going to sleep forever, and I will be free of you forever."

6   His eyes closed, and a great silence hung over the forest.

7   As his withered hand relaxed, it disengaged a small pebble which tumbled down the bank shattering the mirrorlike surface of the forest pool.

Confirm the Reality

Read the statements that follow and decide which ones reflect reality as presented in the story. With your group, discuss your reasons for accepting or rejecting each statement. Be ready to provide evidence from the story to support your decisions. A few page and paragraph numbers are given in parentheses to help you find the information for making decisions.

1. Sam Harding and two other space explorers crashed on Alpha III. (51, 3)
2. Alpha III was a small planetoid with at least two moons. (49, 7; 53, 12)
3. Alpha III had short days and low gravity pull. (49, 7; 52, 6)
4. Alpha III was inhabited by many strange and dangerous animals.
5. Sam talked to himself to keep his fears under control.
6. Sam thought his beard was long because he hadn't shaved on the trip.
7. Sam believed that he had been lost on Alpha III for seven days.

8. Sam believed that a hideous old monster was closing in on him.
9. Sam ran from the forest and found an old rusted shell of a rocket.
10. Sam finally faced the creature in the pit and decided it would be better to die than to live with the hideous creature.

Interpret the Illusion

First, discuss the factors on page 49 that may have contributed to Sam Harding's illusions. Then read the statements below and decide which ones are reasonable explanations of what happened in the story. Be sure you can provide evidence from the story to support your decisions.

1. The strangeness of the environment of Alpha III caused Sam to lose track of time.
2. For Sam to believe he would be rescued, he had to believe he had been lost only a short time.
3. Sam rejected or explained away all evidence that he had been lost more than seven days.
4. Sam was really running away from the realization that he had been on Alpha III for a very long time.
5. Captain Hernandez, who had grown old and ugly, was following Sam around and finally frightened him to death.
6. The cactus nuts that Sam ate caused him to have illusions.
7. Sam created the illusion of a monster because he couldn't face reality.
8. Sam finally faced his monster and was frightened to death.

Do you think Sam recognized the monster or do you think he died without realizing what the monster was?

Apply the Ideas

Discuss the statements below and decide which ones you can accept or reject on the basis of the story *and* your own experiences.

1. Refusal to accept the truth about oneself can make one create a world of illusion to live in.
2. Fear creates its own monsters.
3. Illusion is sometimes safer than reality.
4. It is difficult to recognize your enemy in yourself.

FOLLOW-THROUGH

In this unit on illusion and reality, you have read about:
1. illusions created by magicians;
2. an illusion created by a young girl with a lively imagination;
3. illusions created by visual perception;
4. illusions created by the presentation of factual information; and
5. an illusion created by belief in it.

Below are some ideas that have to do with illusion and reality. Decide which of the five illusions you have read about *would* or *would not* support each of the ideas. Be ready to give reasons for your choices and evidence from the readings.

1. Seeing is believing.
2. Your mind does not always believe what your eyes tell you.
3. Ordinary events can be made to seem extraordinary with a little imagination.
4. Perception shapes reality and creates illusions.
5. Expectation creates reality out of illusion.

Putting Your Knowledge to Work

Create your own illusions. Following are some ideas for activities to allow you to demonstrate your understanding of illusions and reality. Choose one or more that you'd like to do. It might be fun to work in groups for some of the activities.

1. Put on a magic show for your classmates. The following books will help you learn the tricks of the trade.

   Cobb, Vicki. *Magic . . . Naturally! Science Entertainments and Amusements.* Philadelphia: J. B. Lippincott Company, 1976.

   Lamb, Geoffrey. *Mental Magic Tricks.* Nashville: Thomas Nelson, Inc., 1972.

   Severn, Bill. *Magic in Mind: Mental Magic Tricks.* New York: Henry Z. Walck, Inc., 1974.

2. Construct a miniature illusion box on the same principles as the magic cabinet. You will need two small mirrors the same size and some heavy cardboard for the box.

3. Write a story in which real happenings are used to create an illusion, as in "The Open Window."

4. Find and demonstrate for your classmates more optical illusions. Most encyclopedias have examples of such illusions. In addition, here are some books from which you can get more information:

Froman, Robert. *Science, Art, and Visual Illusions.* New York: Simon and Schuster, Inc., 1970.

Kettelkamp, Larry. *Tricks of the Eye and Mind: The Story of Optical Illusion.* New York: William Morrow and Co., Inc., 1974.

Simon, Seymour. *The Optical Illusion Book.* New York: Four Winds Press, 1976.

5. Create an illusion with factual information. Make your football or basketball team record look better than it really is. Or, find examples of illusions created with information in newspapers, magazines, television ads, and so on.

6. Write a radio play and present it to your classmates. Try to create illusions with your voices and sound effects.

Here are some books dealing with illusion and reality that you might find interesting:

Babbitt, Natalie. *Tuck Everlasting.* New York: Farrar, Straus and Giroux, Inc., 1975.
The Tuck family reveals the secret of eternal life to ten-year-old Winnie Foster.

Courlander, Harold and George Herzog. *The Cow-Tail Switch and Other West African Stories.* New York: Holt, Rinehart and Winston, Inc., 1947.
This classic collection of folktales includes "The Messenger to Maftam," a story about a man who cannot tell a lie.

L'Engle, Madeleine. *A Wrinkle in Time.* New York: Farrar, Straus, and Giroux, Inc., 1962.
Meg, Charles, and Calvin are "tessered" through space to a strange planet to search for Meg and Charles's father.

Norton, Andre. *Knave of Dreams.* New York: The Viking Press, 1975.
Ramsay Kimble finds himself in the middle of political chaos—in another world and in another body.

Phipson, Joan. *The Way Home.* New York: Atheneum Publishers, 1973.
Three children survive an automobile accident and find themselves transported to the time of the dinosaurs.

Towne, Mary. *Goldenrod.* New York: Atheneum Publishers, 1977.
Babysitter Goldenrod "travels" with the children to any place on the globe that begins with a *G*.

Fact and Fiction

two

The words *fact* and *fiction* are opposites, but very often, it is difficult to sort out fact from fiction. Fictional material sometimes includes a lot of fact, and factual material sometimes includes a bit of fiction.

Key Concepts

fact   (a) something known to be true or to have really happened;   (b) something said or supposed to be true;   (c) reality;   (d) an actual event;   (e) truth.

fiction   (a) works of literature involving imaginary people or happenings;   (b) something made up or imagined;   (c) something that has no basis in reality;   (d) a fabrication.

Getting in Touch with Your Experiences

In the books you have read in school and elsewhere, you have come across many different kinds of material—some fact, some fiction. It is very important to be able to separate the fact from the fiction in what you read.

Following are some terms that describe different kinds of written material. Each of the terms is usually associated with either fact or fiction. For example, a *novel* is a long fictional story about a group of characters and a series of events in their lives. A *journal* is a daily factual record of experiences. Discuss each of the remaining terms with your group and decide whether it describes material that is fact or fiction.

novel	article	story
journal	myth	folktale
report	play	biography
fable	document	history

As you discussed whether the kinds of written material are usually fact or usually fiction, you probably recognized that very few are completely one or the other. Folktales are clearly fiction, and history is supposed to be pure fact. In between the two extremes you can find many different combinations of fact and fiction. How much of each is in the other depends on the kind of material that is being written and whether the author's purpose is to inform or entertain.

Discuss with your group any experiences you have had in reading the various types of written material on the list. List specific examples of literature you have read and decide how much fact and how much fiction was contained in each.

The selections in this book include many different kinds of material. As you read them, decide whether each is mostly fact, mostly fiction, or some combination of the two.

Fact and Fiction
in Literature

By the middle of the 1800's, most people in the United States believed that their country was destined to include all the land from the Atlantic Ocean to the Pacific Ocean. To achieve this destiny, however, they had to take the land away from the various American Indian nations who had lived on it for centuries.

As the settlers tried to take over the land, the different American Indian groups resisted. The United States government tried to persuade the native peoples to give up their land peaceably. It promised them money and other lands to replace what they were giving up. In many cases, however, the money was not paid and the land on which they were resettled was so poor that they could not survive on it. Conflict broke out, and many people were killed. The American Indians were finally forced off their lands.

The selection you will read next is about one such incident in which a Navaho tribe was forced off its lands. The novel from which it was taken, *Sing Down the Moon,* is historical fiction. Some of the events described in it actually happened, but they are described through the eyes of a fictional character who tells the story as she sees it. To make the story more believable and more personal, the author uses the words *I* and *me* to relate the events from the point of view of one of the characters.

Set Your Purposes

To understand and enjoy this story, you should do two things as you read.
1. Decide what information is important in the story. Look for information that tells what is happening, how people are feeling, and what people are thinking.
2. Decide how all the information fits together and what ideas are created from the information.

The story is divided into two sections. After each section, there will be some statements that will help you identify the important information in that section. At the end, there will be some statements to help you decide how the information in the story fits together to form ideas.

Sing Down the Moon

by Scott O'Dell

Sing Down the Moon is a story told through the eyes of a fourteen-year-old Navaho girl named Bright Morning. Bright Morning's clan lives in the area around the Canyon de Chelly,[1] where they farm the land, hunt, and raise sheep. They are happy but live in fear of the American soldiers from Fort Defiance who have threatened to burn down their village if they break the peace.

One day Bright Morning and her friend Running Bird are captured by Spanish slavers and sold as household servants. After escaping, they are met by Tall Boy and Mando, two young men from their village. In a fight with the Spaniards who have been following them, Tall Boy is shot in the arm and never regains the use of it.

Life returns to normal in the village until the soldiers come and tell the Navahos that they must leave the Canyon de Chelly. The Navahos know that they cannot win a battle with the soldiers, but they do not want to give up their land permanently. So they move to a mesa overlooking the canyon. They believe that this will trick the soldiers into thinking they have gone and that the soldiers will then leave them alone to return to their village. At the beginning of this selection, the Navahos are watching the soldiers from their hiding place on the mesa.

1   In the morning guards were set again at the head of the trail. Running Bird and I crawled to our places near the piñon[2] tree and crouched there as the sun rose and shone down on the camp of the Long Knives.[3] Other lookouts hid themselves along the rim of the mesa, among the rocks and brush.

2   Nothing had changed in the night. There were the same number of tents among the trees and the same number of horses tethered on the riverbank.

3   Our hogans[4] were deserted. No smoke rose from the ovens or the fire pits. There was no sound of sheep bells.

[1] de Chelly (de shā′) a canyon in northern Arizona.
[2] piñon (pin′yen *or* pē′nyōn) a low-growing pine with edible seeds.
[3] Long Knives   a term the Navahos used for American soldiers.
[4] hogan (hō′gän′) traditional form of house used by the Navahos.

1   The camp of the Long Knives was quiet until the sun was halfway up the morning sky. Men strolled about as if they had nothing to do. Two were even fishing in the river with long willow poles. Then—while Running Bird and I watched a squirrel in the piñon tree, trying to coax him down with a nut—I saw from the corner of an eye a puff of smoke rise slowly from our village. It seemed no larger than my hand. A second puff rose in the windless air and a third.

2   "Our homes are burning!"

3   The word came from the lookout who was far out on the mesa rim, closest to the village. It was passed from one lookout to the other, at last to me, and I ran with it back to our camp and told the news to my father.

4   "We will build new homes," he said. "When the Long Knives leave we will go into the forest and cut timber. We will build hogans that are better than those the soldiers burned."

5   "Yes," people said when they heard the news, "we will build a new village."

6   Tall Boy said nothing. He sat working on his lance, using his teeth and one hand, and did not look up.

7   I went back to the piñon and my father went with me. All

our homes had burned to the ground. Only gray ashes and a mound of earth marked the place where each had stood. The Long Knives were sitting under a tree eating, and their horses cropped the meadow grass.

1   My father said, "They will ride away now that they have destroyed our village."

2   But they did not ride away. While we watched, ten soldiers with hatchets went into our peach orchard, which still held its summer leaves. Their blades glinted in the sunlight. Their voices drifted up to us where we were huddled among the rocks.

3   Swinging the hatchets as they sang, the soldiers began to cut the limbs from the peach trees. The blows echoed through the canyon. They did not stop until every branch lay on the ground and only bare stumps, which looked like a line of scarecrows, were left.

4   Then, at the last, the Long Knives stripped all the bark from the stumps, so that we would not have this to eat when we were starving.

5   "Now they will go," my father said, "and leave us in peace."

6   But the soldiers laid their axes aside. They spurred their horses into a gallop and rode through the cornfield, trampling the green corn. Then they rode through the field of ripening beans and the melon patch, until the fields were no longer green but the color of the red earth.

1   "We will plant more melons and corn and beans," my father said.

2   "There are no seeds left," I said. "And if we had seeds and planted them they would not bear before next summer."

3   We watched while the soldiers rode back to their camp. We waited for them to fold their tents and leave. All that day and the next we watched from the rim of the mesa. On the third day the soldiers cut alder poles and made a large lean-to, which they roofed over with the branches. They also dug a fire pit and started to build an oven of mud and stones.

4   It was then we knew that the Long Knives did not plan to leave the canyon.

5   "They have learned that we are camped here," my father said. "They do not want to climb the cliff and attack us. It is easier to wait there by the river until we starve."

6   Clouds blew up next morning and it began to rain. We cut brush and limbs from the piñon pines and made shelters. That night, after the rain stopped, we went to the far side of the mesa where our fires could not be seen by the soldiers and cooked supper. Though there was little danger that the soldiers would attack us, my father set guards to watch the trail.

7   We were very careful with our jars of water, but on the sixth day the jars were empty. That night my father sent three of us down the trail to fill the jars at the river. We left soon after dark. There was no moon to see by so we were a long time getting to the river. When we started back up the trail we covered our tracks as carefully as we could. But the next day the soldiers found that we had been there. After that there were always two soldiers at the bottom of the trail, at night and during the day.

8   The water we carried back lasted longer than the first. When the jars were nearly empty it rained hard for two days and we caught water in our blankets and stored it. We also discovered a deep stone crevice filled with rainwater, enough for the rest of the summer. But the food we had brought with us, though we ate only half as much as we did when we were home in the village, ran low. We ate all of the corn and slaughtered the sheep we had brought. Then we ground up the sheep bones and made a broth, which was hard to swallow. We lived on this for two days and when it was gone we had nothing to eat.

9   Old Bear, who had been sick since we came to the mesa, died on the third day. And that night the baby of Shining Tree died. The next night was the first night of the full moon. It was then that my father said that we must leave.

1   Dawn was breaking high over the mesa when we reached the bottom of the trail. There was no sign of the soldiers.

2   My father led us northward through the trees, away from our old village and the soldiers' camp. It would have been wiser if we had traveled in the riverbed, but there were many who were so weak they could not walk against the current.

3   As soon as it grew light we found patches of wild berries among the trees and ate them while we walked. The berries were ripe and sweet and gave us strength. We walked until the sun was overhead; then, because four of the women could go no farther, we stopped and rested in a cave.

4   We gathered more berries and some roots and stayed there until the moon came up. Then we started off again, following the river northward, traveling by the moon's white glow. When it swung westward and left the canyon in darkness we lay down among the trees. We had gone no more than two leagues[5] in a day and part of a night, but we were hopeful that the soldiers would not follow us.

5   In the morning we built a small fire and roasted a basket of roots. Afterward the men held council to decide whether to go on or to stay where we were camped.

6   "They have burned our homes," my father said. "They have cut down the trees of our orchard. They have trampled our gardens into the earth. What else can the soldiers do to us that they have not already done?"

7   "The Long Knives can drive us out of the canyon," my uncle said, "and leave us to walk the wilderness."

8   At last it was decided that we stay.

9   We set about the cutting of brush and poles to make shelters. About mid-morning, while we were still working on the lean-tos, the sound of hoofs striking stone came from the direction of the river.

10   Taking up his lance, Tall Boy stepped behind a tree. The rest of us stood in silence. Even the children were silent. We were like animals who hear the hunter approach but from terror cannot flee.

11   The Long Knives came out of the trees in single file. They were joking among themselves and at first did not see us. The leader was a young man with a red cloth knotted around his neck. He was looking back, talking to someone, as he came near the place where Tall Boy stood hidden.

[5] league (lēg)   a unit of distance equal to 2.4 to 4.6 miles (4 to 7 kilometers).

1   Tall Boy stepped from behind the tree, squarely in his path.
Still the leader did not see him.

2   Raising the lance, Tall Boy quickly took aim and drew back,
ready to send it toward the leader of the Long Knives. He had
practiced with the lance before we came down the mesa, time
after time during all of one day, trying to get used to throwing it
with his left hand. With his right hand he had been the best of all
the warriors. It was with a lance that he had killed the brown
bear beyond Rainbow Mountain, a feat of great skill.

3   But now, as the iron-tipped weapon sped from his grasp,
it did not fly straight. It wobbled and then curved upward, struck
the branch of a tree, and fell broken at the feet of the soldier's
horse.

4   The horse suddenly stopped, tossing its head. Only then did
the soldier turn to see the broken lance lying in front of him. He
looked around, searching for the enemy who had thrown it. He
looked at my father, at my uncle, at me. His eyes swept the small
open space where we stood, the women, the children, the old
people, all of us still too frightened to move or speak.

1   Tall Boy, as soon as he had thrown the lance, dodged behind the tree where he had hidden before, backed away into the brush and quietly disappeared. I saw his face as he went past me. He no longer looked like a warrior. He looked like a boy, crushed and beaten, who flees for his life.

2   The rest of the Long Knives rode up and surrounded us. They searched us one by one, making certain that no one carried a weapon, then they headed us down the canyon.

3   We passed the ruined fields of beans and corn and melons, the peach trees stripped of their bark and branches, our burned-out homes. We turned our eyes away from them and set our faces. Our tears were unshed.

4   Soon we were to learn that others bore the same fate, that the whole nation of the Navahos was on the march. With the Long Knives at their backs, the clans were moving — the Bitter-Water, Under-His-Cover, Red-House, Trail-to-the-Garden, Standing-House, Red-Forehead, Poles-Strung-Out — all the Navahos were marching into captivity.

Identify the Information

The author of *Sing Down the Moon* describes how real events affected fictional characters. Both factual and fictional information are important to understanding the story. To see how well you understood the information, read each statement below. Decide if it is accurate according to the part of the story shown by the page and paragraph numbers after the statement. Discuss the evidence you find to support your decisions.

1. The Navahos sent lookouts, to watch the American soldiers. (65, 1)
2. The soldiers burned down the Navahos' village. (66, 2)
3. Bright Morning's father remained hopeful that the soldiers would leave so that his people could return to their lands. (66, 4)
4. The soldiers left the Navahos' peach trees and crops alone. (67, 2–6)
5. The Navahos realized that the soldiers planned to stay and to starve them out. (68, 4–5)
6. The Navahos found enough water to last the summer, but they ran out of food. (68, 8)
7. The Navahos left the mesa but could not travel far because many of their people were too weak. (69, 2–4)

8. Tall Boy killed the leader of the soldiers and escaped. (70, 2–3; 71, 1)
9. The soldiers captured the Navahos and marched them into captivity. (71, 2–4)
10. None of the Navahos shed a tear as they were driven past their destroyed village and crops. (71, 3)

Make Some Predictions

Before you read the rest of Bright Morning's story, make some predictions about what you think will happen next. Some of your predictions should be based on the facts you know about the history of the American West. Discuss your reasons for deciding whether or not each of the following statements is a reasonable prediction. Add any other predictions you would like to make.

1. The American soldiers will let the Navahos go as soon as they drive them out of the Canyon de Chelly.
2. Tall Boy and other Navaho warriors will attack the soldiers and free their people.
3. The American soldiers will take the Navahos to a nearby fort where the Navahos will be fed and clothed.
4. Many Navahos will die on a long walk to a distant land where the soldiers are taking them.
5. Bright Morning will marry an American soldier, and she and her family will be allowed to return to the Canyon de Chelly.

Now read the next selection to see how accurate your predictions were. Remember to try to separate the facts from the fiction.

more from
Sing Down the Moon

1   The sky was gray and the air smelled of bitter winds. The Long Knives drove us along the river and through the portals of the canyon. Like sheep before the shepherd, we went without a sound.

2   By noon on that day snow fell out of the gray sky. A sharp wind blew against us. The Long Knives made camp in a wooded draw and told us to do likewise. We stayed there in the draw until the snow stopped, until two days had gone. Then on the third morning we set off again.

1   My father asked one of the Long Knives where they were taking us. The soldier said, "Fort Sumner." He pointed southward and that was all.

2   On that day we met Navahos from Blue Water Canyon, more than fifty of them. They came down from their village, driven by the Long Knives. Their clothes were ragged and all were on foot. Most of them were old men and women, but one girl about my age was carrying two young children on her back. They were heavy for her and I asked if I could help her carry one of them.

3   The girl's name was Little Rainbow. She was small but pretty like a flower and her children, a boy and a girl, looked like flowers too, with their round faces and big dark eyes. She gave me the girl and I made a sling and carried her on my back the rest of that day.

4   Toward evening we came upon another band of Navahos. There were about a hundred of them, a few on horses. They belonged to the Coyote Clan and had been on the trail for a week, prodded along by five soldiers.

5   We lighted fires that night and had a gathering. The Long Knives left us alone, but we could see them watching us from the trees while we chanted our songs and our prayers. Little

Rainbow came and we sat together in the grass, playing with
the children. She took the girl with her when she went off to
sleep, but in the morning gave her back to me.

1. Sometime in the night, Tall Boy slipped into our camp and
lay down by the fire. We found him there in the morning, his
clothes torn and his feet bare and bleeding. He ate the mush I
brought to him but would not talk. He had the same shamed look
about him that I had seen when he fled from the Long Knives,
his lance lying broken upon the ground.

2. The trail led south and eastward across rough country and
we went slowly because of the old people. We had two wagons
with good horses but they were not enough to carry all those
who needed help. We made scarcely a league during the whole
morning.

3. At noon two large bands of Navahos overtook us. They
were mostly men, some of them wounded in a fight with the
Long Knives. They went by us with their eyes on the ground,
silent and weaponless.

4. That afternoon we saw many bands of Navahos. They came
from all directions, from the high country and from the valleys.
It was like a storm when water trickles from everywhere and
flows into the river and the river flows full. This was the way the
trail looked as night fell, like a dark-flowing river.

5. Little Rainbow did not come for her child when we camped
that night and I asked my mother what I should do.

6. "There is nothing to do," she said.

7. My sister said, "You were foolish to take the child. You
have enough to carry without her."

8. "We will find the girl tomorrow," my mother said, "or she
will find us. In the meantime she knows that her child is safe."

9. We did not find her the next day. Tall Boy went out looking
at sunrise, but soon returned, saying that a soldier had threatened
him. The soldier told him to go back to his clan and not to
wander around or someone would shoot him.

10. All day as we trudged eastward I looked for Little Rainbow.
I asked people I did not know if they had seen her. Everyone
shook their heads. In a way I was glad that I did not find her.
I was carrying three rolled-up blankets and a jar filled with corn-
meal. It was a heavy burden even without the girl. But she was
good all the time, making happy sounds as the two of us went
along.

11. As on the day before, Navahos by the hundreds came out of
the mountains and forests to join us.

12. The river flowed slower now and many old people began to

falter. At first, the Long Knives rode back and forth, urging them on if they lay down beside the trail. But so many fell that afternoon when the cold wind blew from the north that the soldiers did not take notice anymore, except to jeer at them.

1   The march went on until dusk. Fires were lighted and people gathered around them. Our clan said little to each other. We were unhappy and afraid, not knowing where we were driven.

2   "The soldiers tell me that it is a place of running water and deep grass," my father said. "But it lies a long walk to the east."

3   He said this every night as we huddled around the fire. I think he believed it. He wanted us to believe it, too.

4   "Cast your eyes around," he said. "You will see many people sitting beside their fires. They are hungry but not starving. They are cold but they do not freeze. They are unhappy. Yet they are alive."

5   "We are walking to our deaths," my mother said. "The old die now. The young die later. But we all die."

6   Tall Boy stared at the fire, saying nothing. He had said little since that day when he tried to throw his iron-tipped lance and had failed. The Navahos, his people, were captives of the Long Knives and there was nothing he could do to free them. Once he

had been haughty, his wide shoulders held straight, his black eyes looking coldly at everyone. I wished, as I sat there beside him, that he would act haughty once more.

1   My sister took the little girl from my lap, where she was sleeping. "She is heavy," Lapana said.

2   "No wonder," my mother answered. "She eats a lot, as much as I do almost. And food is scarce. Every day there will be less until there is none."

3   I took the child back and wrapped her in a blanket and lay down with her in my arms.

4   The fire died away and I could see the stars. I wondered what the little girl's name was. She was like a flower, like a flower in a spring meadow. I gave her that name—Meadow Flower—as she lay beside me.

5   The north wind was cold, and far off among the trees the horses of the Long Knives were restless.

6   A new moon showed in the west and grew full and waned and still we moved on.

7   The hills and the piñon country fell behind. There were few streams anymore. When we came to water we drank deeply and filled our jars to the brim. The land was covered with gray brush and rolled away so far that it hurt the eyes to look.

8   By this time there were thousands of Navahos on the march. We spread out along the trail for miles, each clan keeping to itself by command of the soldiers, who rode at the head of the column and at the rear. At night the Long Knives posted guards near all the Indian fires.

9   We now had six wagons, each drawn by two horses. At first they carried only water and flour and blankets, but as old people grew lame or sick the supplies were taken out of the wagons to make room for them.

10   For those who died, we scooped out shallow holes in the frozen earth and laid them there, putting rocks on the graves to keep the wild animals away.

11   My grandmother was the second old woman to die. Somehow she got herself out of the wagon where she had been riding

and stumbled off into the brush. She lay down and pulled a blanket over her head. She wanted to die and drove us away when we tried to help her.

1   Food grew scarce. The soldiers sent some of the young Navahos out to kill deer and buffalo, but hunting was not good.

2   People began to eat their pets and from then on I never let my black dog out of sight. Before I went to sleep at night I put a leather rope around his neck and tied it to my wrist, as I had at the crone's hut.

3   In the beginning I fed the little girl first, which did not please my mother or my sister. When food ran low I fed her from my share so they could not complain. My back got very sore from the sling I carried her in. Tall Boy fashioned a carrying board from brush and pieces of cloth. This made my load seem lighter.

4   The country changed during the next moon. The flatlands rolled up into hills and we crossed many draws where water ran. Grass was springing everywhere, which helped us feed our starving horses. Every afternoon rain fell and our clothes never dried out from one day to the next.

5   It was about this time that the little girl became ill. We had a chant for her one night. Then the medicine man went over her from head to foot with his gentle hands. He drove away some of the evil spirits so that she smiled and was better.

6   A large band of Navahos came straggling down upon us. They were ragged and hungry and many were sick. Many, they said, had died on the trail. They came from the rim rock country far to the west. Now the line of people struggling along stretched from one horizon to the other. In the daytime flocks of buzzards followed us and at dusk coyotes sat on the hills and howled.

1   Spring came overnight, with fleecy clouds and larks soaring from the grass. It made us happy to know that winter was behind us. Then there was word that we were only two suns march from the end of the trail, from a place near Fort Sumner.

2   The place was called Bosque Redondo[6] and we reached it at noon of the third day. It was in a bend of a big looping river, flat bottomland covered with brush.

3   We were on a small rise when we looked down upon it first. My mother had not cried since we left our canyon. But she cried now as she stood there and looked down upon this gray country that was to be our home.

4   I planned to go out in search of the little girl's mother the next morning after we reached Bosque Redondo. But the child woke me before dawn with her cries, so I minded her all day and sent Running Bird to look for her mother. She came back about dark, not having found her. That night the medicine man came and touched the little girl and we had a sing.

5   The night was half over and I was sitting beside the fire with the little girl in my arms. She held one of my fingers tight in her small fist and I was singing a song to her about a bird in a pine tree. I sang another song to her and another before I was aware that she was no longer listening, that she had died quietly in my arms.

6   In the morning I went out to search for her mother. I went to hundreds of lean-tos and fires and when night came I lay down in the brush and went to sleep, wondering what I could say when I found her.

7   In the morning I started out again. A young man told me that he had seen the girl I described to him and she was living on the bank of the river near a tree, which he pointed out. It was far away and it took me until noon to make my way through the hundreds of people working to make shelters for themselves.

8   I saw her before I reached the river and she saw me. We ran toward each other through the thick brush.

9   There was an open place covered with pale grass and we both stopped as we came to it and looked at each other.

10   It was a short time that we stood there yet it seemed long. Then I went over to her and put my hand in hers. I could not think of anything to say, but I did not need to. She had been crying and I knew that her other child had died too. We put our arms around each other and stood together in the spring sun without speaking.

[6] Bosque Redondo (bosk'ri don'dō)

78

Identify the Information

As you saw after reading the first part of this story, both factual and fictional information are important to your understanding of the story. To check your understanding of the information in the second part of the story, read each statement below. Decide if it is accurate according to the part of the story shown by the page and paragraph numbers following the statement. Discuss the evidence you find to support your decisions.

1. It began to snow shortly after the soldiers drove the Navahos out of the canyon. (72, 2)
2. Bright Morning met Little Rainbow and offered to take care of one of her children. (73, 2)
3. Clans of Navahos from different areas were brought together on the march. (73, 4; 74, 3–4; 74, 11)
4. Tall Boy returned, still proud of his accomplishments. (74, 1)

5. Travel was slow because many Navahos were not fed or clothed properly for a long walk in bad weather. (74, 2)
6. Because food was scarce and the weather was bad, many Navahos became sick and died on the march. (74, 12; 76, 9–11; 77, 1)
7. Bright Morning's mother and father both believed that the Navahos would survive the trip and make a new home for themselves. (75, 2–5)
8. The long walk of the Navahos lasted through the winter and into the spring. (72, 2; 78, 1)
9. The Navahos were taken to Bosque Redondo, a desolate area near Fort Sumner. (78, 1–2)
10. Little Rainbow's children would never see their new home because they both died on the long walk. (78, 5; 79, 5)

Make Some Generalizations

Writers of historical fiction frequently create a character to represent particular kinds of people or groups of people. That way they can tell how a historical event affected different people by making up a story about how that event affected one person who represents a whole group. Below are the names of some of the fictional characters from *Sing Down the Moon*. Match each with the group of people he or she represents. Find evidence from both selections to support your answers.

1. Bright Morning
2. Tall Boy
3. Bright Morning's father
4. Bright Morning's mother
5. Little Rainbow

a. the young Navaho mothers who lost their children on the long walk, despite all their efforts to keep them alive
b. the Navahos who remained hopeful and wanted to believe that everything would work out for the best in the end
c. the rebellious young warriors who tried to fight back but were defeated
d. the survivors who took one day at a time, making the most of what they had and accepting what they did not have or could not change
e. the pessimistic Navahos who knew that they were doomed but who accepted their fate, knowing that they were powerless to change it

Interpret the Ideas

The author of *Sing Down the Moon* combined fact with fiction to present certain ideas about how the Navahos had been treated. Below are some statements of ideas that may or may not be interpreted from the excerpts. By combining information and ideas from both parts of the story, decide which statements you can accept or reject. Be sure to give evidence from the selection to support your answers.

1. The Navahos did not understand why they were being driven out of their homeland.
2. The Navahos did not care enough about their land to cry when they were driven out of it.
3. The American soldiers had little regard for the Navahos as people and even less regard for their property.
4. The Navahos deserved to be removed from their land because they did not care about it enough to fight for it.
5. Some Navahos followed the soldiers willingly because they believed that they would be treated fairly.
6. Starving people who have been defeated in battle, who have seen their homes and crops destroyed, and who have been driven out of their homeland find it difficult to fight back.
7. Many Navahos were more concerned about helping the less fortunate than they were about saving food and water for themselves.
8. The sight of Bosque Redondo destroyed any hope that some Navahos had of being given a decent place to live.
9. The death of Meadow Flower at the first sign of spring was the author's way of foreshadowing trouble for the Navahos.

Expand Your Reading

If you would like to know the rest of Bright Morning's story, read *Sing Down the Moon* by Scott O'Dell (Boston: Houghton Mifflin Company, 1970).

Fact and Fiction
in History

The same events can be reported as fact or as fiction. *Sing Down the Moon*, which you just read, is a fictional story about an actual event in American history. It contains historical facts even though it is presented as fiction. The selection you will read next is a factual presentation of the same historical event. As you read, you will want to compare the two presentations to see how they are alike and how they are different.

Expand Your Vocabulary

Since the next selection describes events that took place during a specific period in history, it is important to understand the words the author uses. Check your understanding of some of those words by matching the words on the left with their meanings on the right. Use the glossary if you need help.

1. nomad	a. someone who fights on the same side as another
2. treaty	
3. ally	b. a settlement in which both sides give up something
4. Civil War	
5. Bluecoat	c. the act of giving up or yielding
6. Graycoat	d. a Union soldier in the Civil War
7. reservation	e. a person who wanders from place to place
8. campaign	
9. surrender	f. a reward given for a specific purpose
10. bounty	g. a written agreement between two groups
11. truce	h. a tract of land set aside for "Indians"
12. compromise	i. an agreement to quit fighting temporarily; a cease-fire
	j. a Confederate soldier in the Civil War
	k. a series of military operations
	l. the war between the Union (North) and the Confederacy (South) in the United States (1861–1865)

Set Your Purposes

The excerpt from *Wounded Knee*, which you will read next, is part of an "Indian History of the American West." It is different from most historical accounts of the period which describe the events as they affected the United States government and the settlers who moved West. In *Wounded Knee*, the author tries to present the other side of the picture—the American Indians' story. He has "tried to fashion a narrative of the conquest of the American West as the victims experienced it."*

Wounded Knee uses many quotations from people who lived during the period. Some of the quotations come from official government documents. You will see these sources in footnotes when you read the excerpt. Other quotations come from records of treaty councils and other formal meetings. These are not footnoted because they are not official documents.

The quotations in the selection were made by people who witnessed the events. Since people bring all their own experiences and beliefs into everything they see and do, no two people see the same thing the same way. When they describe events, they describe them from their own point of view and express their own opinions in the process. Opinions are not necessarily fiction, but they are not necessarily facts either. As you read the selection, be aware of the places in which people are expressing their opinions. You will have to read carefully to determine when fiction may creep into the facts.

As you read, there are three things that you should do. You practiced doing the first two when you read the selection from *Sing Down the Moon.* Review those now and note how the third step brings everything together for you.

1. Decide what information is important. Look for things that tell what is happening and how people feel about it.
2. Decide how all the information fits together and what ideas are created from the information.
3. Think about other things you have read and other ideas you have had that relate to what you are reading. Examine the ideas from all the sources to see how they fit together. Then decide

---

* Dee Brown, Introduction to *Bury My Heart at Wounded Knee: An Indian History of the American West* (New York: Holt, Rinehart and Winston, 1970), p. xvi.

what new ideas can be formed by putting all the other ideas together. See if those new ideas can be put to use in your own life.

The selection that you will read is divided into two sections. After each section, there will be some statements that will help you identify the important events and the order in which they occurred. At the end, there will be some statements to help you interpret the ideas from the information. Finally, there will be an activity to help you form new ideas based on both the factual and fictional accounts of the same event and other things you have read and experienced.

The Long Walk of the Navahos

by Dee Brown, adapted by Amy Ehrlich

1   The Navahos were a large tribe who lived in the dry and rugged country of the Southwest. Unlike most western Indians, they had been fighting Spanish-speaking white people for 250 years before the Americans began to come into their territory.

2   By the 1850's, however, most Navahos had taken the Spanish white people's road and were leading a settled existence, cultivating the land and raising animals. Some bands of the tribe had grown wealthy as herders and weavers. Other Navahos continued as nomads, raiding their old enemies—the Pueblos, the Mexicans, or members of their own tribe.

3   When the troubles with the new English-speaking white people began, Manuelito,[1] a prosperous herder, was head chief. He had been chosen by an election of the Navahos held in 1855. Manuelito and other leaders made treaties with the Americans. "Then the soldiers built the fort here," Manuelito remembered, "and gave us an agent who advised us to behave well. He told us to live peaceably with the whites; to keep our promises. They wrote down the promises, so that we would always remember them."[2]

4   Manuelito tried to keep the promises in the treaty. But after the soldiers came and burned his hogans and killed his livestock because of something a few wild young Navahos had done, he grew angry at the Americans. He and his band had been wealthy, but the soldiers had made them poor. To become ricos[3] again, they must raid the Mexicans to the south. For as long as anyone could remember, the Mexicans had been

[1] Manuelito (man'wə lēt'ō)
[2] U.S. Congress. 49th. 1st session. House of Representatives Executive Document 263, p. 14.
[3] ricos (rē'kōz) members of the influential and wealthy clan from which leaders were chosen.

Manuelito (1818-1894) and his Wife, Juana *(Museum of New Mexico; Ben Wittick Photo)*

raiding Navahos to steal their young children and make slaves of them. And for as long as anyone could remember, the Navahos had been retaliating with raids against the Mexicans.

1   After the Americans came to Santa Fe and called the country New Mexico, they protected the Mexicans because they had become American citizens. The Navahos were not citizens because they were Indians. Whenever there were raids, soldiers would punish the Navahos for stealing from the Mexicans. No Mexicans were ever punished for stealing from Indians. It all seemed an angry puzzle to Manuelito and his people.

2   The first fort the Americans built in the Navaho country was in a grassy valley at the mouth of Canyon Bonito.[4] They called it Fort Defiance and put their horses out to graze on pastureland long prized by Manuelito's band. Because there were no fences, the Navahos' livestock strayed onto the pastures. One morning some soldiers rode out of the fort and shot all the animals belonging to the Navahos.

---

[4] Bonito (bə nēt′ō)

1　To replace their dead horses and mules, the Navahos raided the soldiers' herds. The soldiers in turn began to attack bands of Navahos. Finally Manuelito and his ally Barboncito[5] built up a force of more than a thousand warriors and attacked Fort Defiance. They were determined to wipe it off the face of their land. They did not have adequate weapons to do so. But, by the time the Navahos pulled back into the hills, they were satisfied they had at least taught the soldiers a good lesson.

2　The United States Army, however, considered the attack a challenge to the flag over Fort Defiance, an act of war. For a whole year, soldiers led by Colonel Edward Canby chased Manuelito and his warriors through the Chuska[6] Mountains but were unable to catch them. In January 1861, a meeting was held between Manuelito and other *rico* leaders and Colonel Canby. The Indians wanted to

Major General E. R. S. Canby

return to their crops and livestock and readily signed a new peace treaty. This time they hoped to be left alone.

3　After the winter meeting, there were several months of friendship between the soldiers and the Navahos. A second fort, called Fort Wingate, had been built, and the Navahos went there often to trade. The custom of having horse races between the Navahos and the soldiers started. All the Navahos looked forward to these contests and on racing days hundreds of men, women, and children would dress in their brightest costumes and ride their finest ponies to Fort Wingate. One September morning there was a special race scheduled between Manuelito and a soldier lieutenant. Their horses jumped off together but in a few seconds Manuelito lost control of his pony, and it ran off the track. Soon everyone could see that Manuelito's bridle rein had been slashed with a knife.

Barboncito (1820-1871)
Smithsonian Institution

---

[5] Barboncito (bär'bən sēt'ō)　　[6] Chuska (chüs'kə)

1   Angry at the trickery, the Navahos stormed after the judges—who were all soldiers—and demanded that the race be run again. The judges refused and slammed the fort's gates shut in their faces. When a Navaho tried to force his way in, he was shot dead. The soldiers then opened fire on the Navahos, shooting and bayoneting innocent men, women, and children.

2   That massacre occurred on September 22, 1861. It was a long time before there was friendship again between white people and Navahos.

3   Rumors had been reaching the Indians of a big war somewhere to the east, a war between the Americans of the North and the South. At first it seemed to the Navahos that they were far away from the white people's Civil War. But in 1861 an army of Confederate Graycoats had marched into New Mexico and fought big battles with the Bluecoats along the Rio Grande.[7] Kit Carson, the Rope Thrower, was a leader of the Bluecoats. Most of the Navahos knew of Rope Thrower Carson and trusted him because he had always talked truthfully to Indians. They hoped to make peace with him when he was finished with the Graycoats.

4   In the spring of 1862, however, many more Bluecoats came marching into New Mexico from the west. Their general, James Carleton, wore stars on his shoulders and was much more powerful than Carson. He and his soldiers camped along the Rio Grande Valley, but they had no one to fight because all the Graycoats had fled into Texas.

5   The Navahos soon learned that Star Chief Carleton had a great hunger for their land. "A princely realm," he called it, "a magnificent pastoral and mineral country." Since he could not find any Graycoat soldiers, he began looking around for Indians to fight. The Navahos, he said, were "wolves that run through the mountains" and had to be tracked down.

6   Star Chief Carleton had prepared the Bosque Redondo reservation on some worthless land far away in the Pecos.[8] If all the Indians could be moved there, the territory which they occupied would be open for settlement by American citizens. In April 1863, Carleton arranged a meeting with several *rico* leaders. He told them that the only way they could prove they wanted peace would be to take their people to live on the reserva-

Christopher "Kit" Carson

[7] Rio Grande (rē'ō grand' *or* rē'ō gran'dē) river flowing through the southwestern part of the United States.

[8] Pecos (pā'kəs)

tion. To this Barboncito replied: "I will not go to the Bosque. I will never leave my country, not even if it means that I will be killed."

1   On June 23, Carleton set a deadline for surrender. Any Navahos who still refused to go to the Bosque Redondo by July 20 would be hunted down. July 20 came and went, but no Indians volunteered to surrender.

2   In the meantime Carleton had ordered Kit Carson to march his troops to Fort Wingate to prepare for a war against the Navahos. Carson was reluctant. He had enlisted to fight Confederate soldiers, not Indians, and he tried to resign from the Army.

3   Kit Carson liked Indians. In his days as a trader, he had lived with them for months without seeing another white person. But since then things had changed in New Mexico. Carson had discovered that there was room at the top even for a rough mountain man who could hardly read or write. The land he had claimed for a ranch and the respect of people like Carleton had come to mean more to him than old friendships with Indians. So in the summer of 1863, Carson withdrew his resignation and went to Fort Wingate to make war against the Navahos.

4   Though they respected Carson as a fighter, the Indians were unafraid. It was their land they were defending, and they knew its every canyon, cliff, and mesa. Their stronghold was Canyon de Chelly. Cutting westward for thirty miles (about fifty kilometers) from the Chuska Mountains, the canyon had red rock walls that rose a thousand feet (about 300

meters) or more. At wide places inside the canyon, the Navahos grazed sheep and goats, or raised corn, wheat, fruit, and melons. They were especially proud of their peach orchards, carefully tended since the days of the Spaniards.

5   When they learned that Carson had over a thousand soldiers, the Navaho chiefs reminded their people of how in the old days they had driven the Spaniards from their land. "If the Americans come to take us, we will kill them," the chiefs promised.

6   Late in July Carson moved up to Fort Defiance, renamed it for the Indians' old enemy Canby, and began his campaign against the Navahos. He knew that they would stay well hidden and that the only way to conquer them was to destroy their crops and livestock—to scorch their earth. But he did not move quickly enough for General Carleton. On August 18, the general decided to "stimulate the zeal" of his soldiers by offering money for every Navaho horse, mule, and sheep brought into Fort Canby.

7   Since the soldiers did not get paid very much, the bounty offer did stimulate them. Some of the soldiers even extended it to the few Navahos they were able to kill. To prove their soldierly abilities, they began cutting off the knot of hair fastened by a red string which the Navahos wore. The Navahos could not believe that Kit Carson approved of scalping, which they considered a barbaric custom started by the Spaniards. (The Europeans may or may not have brought scalping to the New World, but the Spanish, French, Dutch, and English colonists made the custom popular

Navajo Tribe Delegation to U.S. Government
Smithsonian Institution

by offering bounty money for the scalps of their enemies.)

1   Pushed by General Carleton, Carson accelerated his scorched-earth program. By autumn he had destroyed most of the herds and grain between Fort Canby and Canyon de Chelly. On October 17, two Navahos appeared under a truce flag at Fort Wingate. One of them was El Sordo,[9] who had been sent by his brothers Delgadito[10] and Barboncito and their 500 followers. Their food supply was gone, El Sordo said; they had only piñon nuts to eat. They were almost without clothing and blankets and too afraid of soldiers' hunting parties to build fires for warmth. They did not want to go far away to the Bosque but would build hogans near Fort Wingate, where they would always be under the eyes of the soldiers as peaceful Indians.

2   But when the compromise offer was sent to General Carleton, he refused it. Under no conditions would he allow the Navahos to remain in their own country. A new gold strike

[9] El Sordo (el sôrd'ō)   [10] Delgadito (del'gäth ēt'ō)

had made it far too valuable. In a memo to the War Department asking for more soldiers, Carleton had clearly stated his intent "to whip the Indians and to protect the people going to and at the mines. . . . Providence has indeed blessed us . . . the gold lies here at our feet to be had by the mere picking of it up!"[11]

1   The Navahos who had offered to make peace were shown no mercy. They could either surrender and go to the Bosque Redondo or hold out, risking starvation, freezing, or death at the hands of Kit Carson's soldiers. Burdened with suffering men, women, and children, Delgadito surrendered. Barboncito, El Sordo, and many of the warriors waited in the mountains to see what would happen to their people.

2   It was then that General Carleton ordered Carson to invade Canyon de Chelly and kill or capture the Navahos there. After one false start, the soldiers finally marched out of Fort Canby on January 6, 1864. Six inches (about fifteen centimeters) of snow lay on the ground, the temperature was below freezing, and the journey was slow.

3   A week later the first group of soldiers entered the east end of the canyon. From rims and ledges, hundreds of half-starved Navahos hurled stones, pieces of wood, and Spanish curses upon their heads. But they could not stop them. The soldiers marched straight through, burning hogans, destroying food supplies, capturing the women and children, and killing any Navahos who got within range of their guns. On January 14, they linked up with Carson's men who had made camp at the western end. The entire canyon had been taken without a major fight.

4   That evening three Navahos approached the soldiers under a truce flag. Their people were starving and freezing, they told Carson. They chose to surrender rather than to die. "You have until tomorrow morning," Carson replied. "After that time my soldiers will hunt you down." Next morning, sixty starved and ragged Navahos arrived at the camp and surrendered.

5   Before returning to Fort Canby, Carson ordered complete destruction of everything the Navahos had grown in the Canyon—including their fine peach orchards, more than five thousand trees. The Navahos could forgive the Rope Thrower for fighting them as a soldier, even for making prisoners of them, but the one act they never forgave him for was cutting down their beloved peach trees.

6   During the next few weeks, as news of the soldiers' victory at Canyon de Chelly spread through the hidden camps of the Navahos, the people lost heart. "We fought for that country because we did not want to lose it," Manuelito said afterward. "We lost nearly everything. . . . The American nation is too powerful for us to fight. When we had to fight for a few days we felt fresh, but in a short time we were worn out and the soldiers starved us out."[12]

[11] U.S. Congress. 39th. 2nd session. Senate Report 156, p. 139.
[12] U.S. Congress. 49th. 1st session. House of Representatives Executive Document 263, p. 15.

Sequence the Events

Now that you've read the first selection from *Wounded Knee,* you can see how important it is to follow the sequence of events. The statements below describe some of the major events in the selection, but they are not in order. With your group, discuss the statements and decide the order in which they should be arranged. Page and paragraph references are given to help you find some of the events. Then, write the numerals *1–12.* Next to each numeral, write the letter of the event that belongs in that position and the page and paragraph numbers you used to determine the sequence.

a. Led by Manuelito, the Navahos attacked Fort Defiance and then hid in the mountains. (86, 1)

b. The Civil War moved westward into New Mexico where Kit Carson and the Bluecoats fought the Graycoats, forcing them into Texas.

c. American soldiers burned the Navahos' hogans and killed their livestock over the pranks of a few young Navahos.

d. Most Navahos in the Southwest were wealthy farmers and herders when they signed the first peace treaty with the Americans who moved into their territory.

e. The Americans took away the Navahos' pastureland to build Fort Defiance and then killed Navaho livestock that strayed onto it. (85, 2)

f. When there was no food left, two Navaho representatives went to Fort Wingate and offered a compromise that would keep them from going to the reservation at Bosque Redondo.

g. After hiding in the mountains for a year, Manuelito and his followers signed a treaty with Colonel Canby and returned to live peaceable with the Americans.

h. The Navahos who were starving and freezing in the Canyon de Chelly were finally forced to surrender.

i. Because there were no Graycoats in the area, General Carleton decided to fight the Navahos and take away their land.

j. Knowing that the Navahos were weak from hunger and cold, American soldiers invaded the Canyon de Chelly from both sides, killing and capturing Navahos.

k. General Carleton prepared a reservation at Bosque Redondo and told the Navahos to go there if they wanted peace.

l. Kit Carson killed all the Navahos' livestock and destroyed their crops because he knew that was the only way to defeat them.

Expand Your Vocabulary

Finding relationships among word meanings is almost as important to understanding what you read as finding relationships among the ideas. Before you read the next selection from *Wounded Knee,* check your understanding of some of the words the author uses. For each set of words below, decide which word does not belong. Then decide how the other three are related to one another. Work with your group and share your reasons for your decisions. Use the glossary if you need help with any word meanings.

1. departure   exodus   attack   migration
2. gallantly   cowardly   bravely   heroically
3. fate   destiny   future   respect
4. minimum   pittance   abundance   trifle
5. respect   admiration   criticism   regard
6. authorized   exiled   entitled   licensed
7. endure   destroy   tolerate   suffer
8. superintendent   warrior   commander   supervisor

In the first selection from *Wounded Knee,* you read about the events leading up to the capture of the Navahos in the Canyon de Chelly. In the next selection, you will find out what happened to them afterward. As you read, remember to pay attention to the sequence and to separate the fact from the fiction when people are expressing their opinions.

The Story of Defeat

1   By early spring of 1864, 3,000 Navahos had surrendered and come in to the two forts, Fort Canby and Fort Wingate. They had been forced to do so because of the lack of food and severe winter weather, but conditions at the forts were no better. The army gave out only small amounts of food, and the very old and the very young began to die.

2   During March, the Long Walk of the Navahos to the Bosque Redondo was set in motion. It took place in three stages. The Navahos had the strength to bear freezing weather, hunger, and the hard three-hundred-mile (about 480 kilometers) journey, but they could not bear the homesickness, the loss of their land. They wept and hundreds of them died before they reached their cruel destination.

3   An officer in command reported, "On the second day's march, a very severe snowstorm set in which lasted for four days with unusual severity, and occasioned great suffering amongst the Indians, many of whom were nearly naked and of course unable to withstand such a storm." This march reached the Bosque on May 11, 1964. "I left Fort Canby with 800 and received 146 en route . . . making about 946 in all. Of this number about 110 died."

4   Throughout that long hard winter, Manuelito and Barboncito had stayed with their people in the mountains, still determined not to surrender. Late in April, Manuelito came out of hiding for a meeting with the commander of Fort Canby. He told the soldier chief that his people wished to stay near the fort, plant their grain crops, and graze their sheep as they had always done.

5   "Why must we go to the Bosque?" Manuelito asked. "We have never stolen or murdered and have at all times kept the peace we promised General Canby." He added that his people feared they were being collected at the Bosque so that soldiers could shoot them down as they had after the horse race at Fort Wingate in 1861. The soldier chief assured him that this was not so, but Manuelito said he would not surrender his people and disappeared once more.

6   In September, Manuelito heard that his old ally Barboncito had been captured in the Canyon de Chelly. Now he, Manuelito, was the last of the *rico* holdouts, and he knew the soldiers would be looking everywhere for him.

7   During the autumn, Navahos who had escaped from the Bosque Redondo began returning to their homeland with frightening tales of what was happening to the people there. It was an ugly and barren land, they said. The soldiers pushed them with bayonets and herded them into

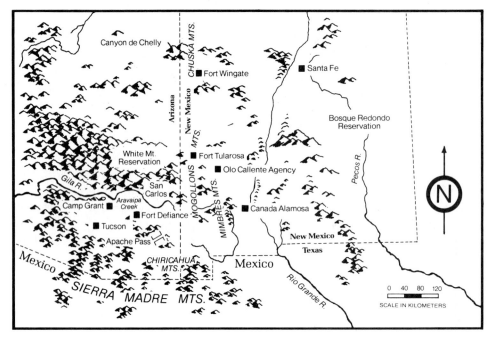

Map showing regions involved in *The Long Walk of The Navahos*

adobe[13]-walled areas where the soldiers were always counting them and putting numbers down in little books. The soldier chiefs promised them clothing and blankets and better food, but their promises were never kept. All the trees had been cut down so that only roots were left for firewood. To shelter themselves from rain and sun, they had to dig holes in the sandy ground and cover them with mats of woven grass. They lived like prairie dogs in burrows. Because they were so crowded, disease had begun to strike down the weaker ones. It was a bad place, and although escape was difficult, many were risking their lives to get away.

1   Ignoring the Indians' suffering, Star Chief Carleton described the place to his superiors in Washington as "a fine reservation . . . there is no reason why they [the Navahos] will not be the most happy and prosperous and well-provided-for Indians in the United States. . . . At all events . . . we can feed them cheaper than we can fight them."

2   And no supporter of Manifest Destiny ever used that philosophy more smugly than he did:

3   The exodus of this whole people from the land of their fathers is not only an interesting but a touching sight. They have fought us gallantly for years on years; they have defended their mountains and their stupendous canyons with a heroism which any people might be proud to emulate; but when, at length, they found it was their destiny, too, as it had been that of their brethren,

---

[13] adobe (ə dō'bē) brick made of sun-dried earth and straw.

tribe after tribe, away back toward the rising of the sun, to give way to the insatiable progress of our race, they threw down their arms, and, as brave men entitled to our admiration and respect . . . we will not dole out to them a miser's pittance in return for what they know to be and what we know to be a princely realm.[14]

1   Manuelito had not thrown down his arms, however, and he was too important a chief for General Carleton to ignore. In February 1865, Navaho runners brought Manuelito a message from the Star Chief, a warning that he and his band would be hunted to the death unless they came in peaceably before spring. "I am doing no harm to anyone," Manuelito told the messengers. "I will not leave my country. I intend to die here." But he finally agreed to talk with some of the chiefs who were at the Bosque Redondo.

2   In late February, six Navaho leaders were released from the Bosque to meet with Manuelito and propose the terms for his surrender. The weather was cold and the land was covered with deep snow. After embracing his old friends, Manuelito led them back into the hills where his people were hidden. Only about a hundred people were left of Manuelito's band; they had a few horses and a few sheep. "Here is all I have in the world," Manuelito said. "See what a trifling

amount. You see how poor they are. My children are eating palmilla[15] roots." After a pause he added that his horses could not travel to the Bosque just then. One of the Navaho leaders, a man named Herrero Grande,[16] replied that he had no authority to extend the time for him to surrender. Manuelito wavered. He said he would surrender for the sake of the weak and the sick. Finally he declared flatly that he could not leave his country.

3   "My God and my mother live in the West, and I will not leave them. . . . Nor could I leave the Chuska Mountains. I was born there. I shall remain. I have nothing to lose but my life, and *that* they can come and take whenever they please, but I will not move. I have never done any wrong to the Americans or the Mexicans. I have never robbed. If I am killed, innocent blood will be shed."

4   Herrero Grande said to him: "I have done all I could for your benefit; have given you the best advice; I now leave you as if your grave were already made."[17]

5   But in spite of Herrero Grande's warning and General Carleton's continuous pursuit, Manuelito managed to avoid capture all through the spring and summer of 1865. Freedom, even with so much danger, was better than a life of imprisonment.

6   Late in the summer, Barboncito and several of his warriors escaped

---

[14] Senate Report 156, pp. 144, 157, 162–67, 174, 179, 183–84, 259–60. Lynn R. Bailey, *Long Walk* (Los Angeles: Westernlore, 1964), pp. 164–66. Document in Lawrence C. Kelly, *Navajo Roundup* (Boulder: Pruett, 1970). William A. Kelleher, *Turmoil in New Mexico, 1846–1868* (Santa Fe: Rydal Press, 1952), p. 441.

[15] palmilla (päl mē′ yə)   [16] Herrero Grande (ā rā′rō grand′ā)

[17] Senate Report 156, pp. 221-22.

from the Bosque Redondo; they were said to be far away in Apache country. So many Navahos were leaving the reservation now that General Carleton posted permanent guards for forty miles (about sixty-five kilometers) around. In August the general ordered the post commander to kill every Navaho found off the reservation without a pass.

1   When the Bosque's grain crops failed in the autumn of 1865, the Army gave the Navahos meal, flour, and bacon which had been condemned as unfit for soldiers to eat. Deaths began to rise again; so did the number of attempted escapes.

2   Although General Carleton was being criticized now by New Mexicans for conditions at the Bosque Redondo, he continued to hunt down Navahos. At last, on September 1, 1866, the chief he wanted most—

Manuelito—limped into Fort Wingate with twenty-three beaten warriors and surrendered. They were thin and hungry, dressed in rags. One of Manuelito's arms hung useless at his side from a wound. A short time later Barboncito came in with twenty-one followers and surrendered for the second time. Now there were no more war chiefs.

3   Ironically, only eighteen days after Manuelito surrendered, General Carleton was removed from command of the Army's Department of New Mexico. The Civil War, which had brought Star Chief Carleton to power, had been over for more than a year now, and the New Mexicans no longer wanted him in their territory.

4   When Manuelito arrived at the Bosque, a new superintendent was there, A. B. Norton. The superintendent examined the soil on the

General James H. Carleton

Cagallo Lake, New Mexico

reservation and said no grain could be grown on it; he examined the water and said it was unhealthy. The reservation, Norton added, had cost the government millions of dollars. He recommended that the reservation be abandoned and that the Navahos be permitted to return to their land.

1   For two years officials from Washington came through the reservation to observe the conditions there. Some were truly sympathetic to the Navahos; some were mainly concerned with cutting down the costs.

2   "We were there for a few years," Manuelito remembered. "Many of our people died from the climate. . . . People from Washington held a council with us. . . . We promised to obey the laws if we were permitted to get back to our own country."

3   But before they could leave, the chiefs had to sign a new treaty (June 1, 1868) which began: "From this day forward all war between the parties to this agreement shall forever cease."

4   The Navahos were eager to be off. Manuelito said:

> The nights and days were long before it came time for us to go to our homes. The day before we were to start we went a little way towards

97

home, because we were so anxious to start. We came back and the Americans gave us a little stock and we thanked them for that. We told the drivers to whip the mules, we were in such a hurry. When we saw the top of the mountain from Albuquerque we wondered if it was our mountain, and we felt like talking to the ground, we loved it so, and some of the old men and women cried with joy when they reached their homes.[18]

And so the Navahos returned to the land they had been so painfully torn away from. When the new reservation lines were made, much of their best pastureland was taken away for the white settlers. Life would not be easy. They would have to struggle to endure. But bad as it was, the Navahos would come to know that they were among the more fortunate of the western Indians. For the others, the ordeal had just begun.

[18] House of Representatives Executive Document 263, p. 15.

Sequence the Events

The statements below describe the major events from the second selection of *Wounded Knee,* but they are not in order. With your group, discuss the statements and decide the order in which they should be arranged so that they describe the events in correct sequence. Page and paragraph references are given to help you find two of the events. On a separate sheet of paper, write the numerals *1–12*. Next to each numeral, write the letter of the event that belongs in that position and the page and paragraph numbers you used to determine the sequence.

a. Six Navaho leaders from the Bosque Redondo tried to persuade Manuelito to surrender, but he still refused. (95, 2)

b. Crop failure and unfit food at the Bosque Redondo caused the number of deaths and the number of escapes to increase.

c. The new superintendent of the Bosque Redondo, A. B. Norton, found the soil and water there unfit and recommended that the Navahos be allowed to return home.

d. When they returned home, the Navahos discovered that much of their best pastureland was not given back to them.

e. The Navahos were forced to walk 300 miles (480 kilometers) from the fort to the Bosque Redondo. (93, 2)

f. After being attacked in the Canyon de Chelly, about 3,000 Navahos surrendered to the Americans.

g. General Carleton posted permanent guards around the Bosque Redondo and gave them orders to shoot any Navahos found off the reservation without permission.

h. Shortly after Manuelito surrendered for the first time, Barboncito surrendered for the second time.
i. General Carleton was removed from command of the Bosque Redondo.
j. The New Mexicans criticized General Carleton for the conditions at the Bosque Redondo.
k. After several years of government inspections and bad living conditions, the Navahos signed a new peace treaty and were allowed to return to their lands.
l. Barboncito, his followers, and many other Navahos escaped from the Bosque Redondo.

Interpret the Facts

Read the statements below. Decide which ones can be accepted or rejected by the facts presented in the article. With your group, discuss the evidence you find to accept or reject each statement.

1. The Navahos were driven off their land because it was valuable, not because they had done anything wrong.
2. The Navahos were properly paid for their land.
3. The United States government interpreted the Navahos' defense of their land as the acts of an enemy.
4. The Navahos were happy and prosperous on the reservation.
5. The soldiers showed admiration and respect for the Navahos they had defeated.
6. General Carleton believed that he was justified in treating the Navahos badly because the end result, getting their valuable land, was good for his own people.
7. The Navahos who didn't surrender to their enemy were considered courageous by their own people but stubborn by their enemy.
8. The Navahos could expect no kindness from the soldiers who had been ordered to kill them.
9. The Bosque Redondo was an unfit place for people to live.
10. General Carleton was eventually punished for his actions.

Now look back over the statements you rejected. Were any of them presented as facts by anyone quoted in the article? Discuss your answers and your reasons with your group. Notice that the author depends on the reader to separate the fiction from the fact.

Apply the Ideas

Below is a list of some fictional characters from *Sing Down the Moon* and the names of some real people from *Wounded Knee.* For each statement following the list, decide which persons or characters would agree with it. Work with your group and be ready to give reasons for your decision.

Sing Down the Moon (Fictional)	*Wounded Knee* (Factual)
Bright Morning	Manuelito
Bright Morning's father	Kit Carson
Bright Morning's mother	Superintendent Norton
Tall Boy	General Carleton

1. Freedom, no matter how dangerous, is better than imprisonment.
2. We would rather die for what we believe in than live without pride.
3. We will do whatever we have to do; we cannot be blamed.
4. If we want to get ahead, we have to obey orders regardless of how we may feel personally.
5. When hope is gone, life is not worth living.
6. We don't understand why we must give up what is ours to please those who already have more than we do.
7. If we are to fulfill our destiny, we must have room to expand.
8. We cannot be expected to remain content in places where it is impossible for us to survive.

Expand Your Reading

If you would like to know more about what happened to the Navahos and other American Indian groups, read *Wounded Knee: An Indian History of the American West* by Dee Brown, adapted for young readers by Amy Ehrlich from *Bury My Heart at Wounded Knee* by Dee Brown (New York: Holt, Rinehart and Wilston, Publishers, 1970, 1974).

Fact and Fiction
in Legends

Science involves finding answers to questions people have about their world and their experiences. The answers are not easily found. Because people need to have answers, they sometimes make up answers that are based more on fiction than on fact. The scientist's job is to find out what *is* fact and what *is* fiction.

The article you will read next describes some of the attempts made to answer one question that people have been asking for many centuries: Is it true that a monster exists in the inland waters of Scotland called Loch (Gaelic for "lake") Ness? Scientists have joined the search to determine what is fact and what is fiction in the reports of the monster's existence. How soon they will find the answers is, of course, a mystery, but this article may help clarify the mystery in your mind.

Set Your Purposes

Scientific material may appear in several different forms. It may be very detailed, with charts, graphs, numbers, and figures. It may be less detailed but still contain special vocabulary and lists of objects or events. It may also be fairly general, with background information and summaries of information so that it reads almost like a story. The article you will read next is such a scientific article.

Regardless of the form it takes, scientific material can be read with the same three purposes as literature or social studies. Briefly, to refresh your memory, those purposes are: (1) decide what information is important; (2) decide what ideas can be formed by fitting the information together; (3) decide what new ideas can be formed by combining the information and ideas with other things you have read or experienced.

As you read, make use of the headings in the article to help you organize the information. After reading the article, you will have the opportunity to discuss the ideas that relate to the article and to other things you have read or experienced.

The Search for the Loch Ness Monster

Does this look like the home of a monster?

In the beautiful highlands of northern Scotland lies a long, narrow, and very deep body of water. That body of water, called Loch Ness, has become famous for what may—or may not—live in its depths. Loch Ness is the home of a "maybe-monster," affectionately known as Nessie by those who are inclined to believe that she exists.

The Mysterious Loch

If Nessie exists in fact, Loch Ness would make an ideal home for her. The loch is 24 miles (about 39 kilometers) long and about a mile (about one and a half kilometers) wide. The average depth is 433 feet (about 130 meters), with the deepest spots more than 900 feet (about 275 kilometers). On the average, that's twice as deep as the North Sea.

The water at the bottom of the loch is about 42°F. (60°C.). Though the water never freezes, it is too cold for people to swim in comfortably.

Despite the cold waters, there are enough trout, salmon, and arctic char in the lake to provide food for a family of monsters. Furthermore, the waters of the lake are murky from tiny bits of peat floating in it, providing ideal protection for a seemingly shy sea monster.

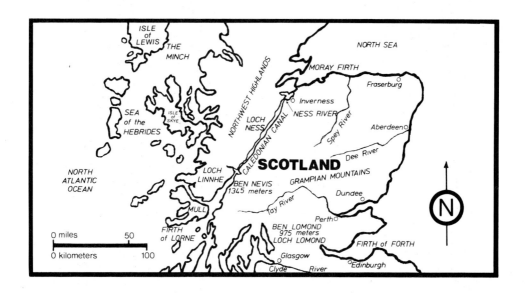

Nessie's Many Faces

For more than 1,400 years, sightings of a mysterious creature swimming in the depths of Loch Ness have been reported. Descriptions of the creature vary, but certain characteristics stand out. The monstrous animal is reported to have a small head, a very long neck, and a humped body. Its length, depending on which witness you believe, may be from 20 to 60 feet (about 6 to 18 meters). The animal moves quickly through the water and, according to some witnesses, it sometimes leaves the lake and lurches clumsily on land. Because of its many surface sightings, it is thought to be an air breather.

Some describe Nessie as a big worm, others as a long-necked seal, a snake, an eel, a giant frog, or a sea cow. She has also been described as a living plesiosaur,[1] a marine reptile of ages long past.

Monster Mania

It's not really strange to think of a monster living in a deep lake somewhere in the world. Since the beginning of time, people have been frightened, but fascinated, by monsters. The ancient Greeks had their famous story of the Minotaur, the half-man/half-beast that fed on young people. Other ancient people believed in fire-breathing dragons, sometimes fierce and sometimes friendly.

More recently, people claim to have sighted another kind of monster—a manlike creature that inhabits the

---

[1] plesiosaur (plē′sē ə sôr′)

vast, snowy regions of North America. According to reports, his footprints are so huge that people have named him Bigfoot.

Bigfoot bears a striking similarity to another manlike monster that has been reported in the mountainous regions of Asia. This monster is called the Abominable Snowman. Mountain climbers claim to have seen him. Estimates of his size vary, too, depending on the person reporting the sighting.

None of these monsters have been proven to exist, yet many people believe in them. Obviously the people who have seen the monsters believe in them. Others believe because of what they have heard. They think it reasonable that there may be creatures in remote parts of the world that have not been identified yet.

It is only recently that the giant squid of ancient sea tales has been confirmed as a living creature. And the coelacanth,[2] a primitive fish thought to be extinct for millions of years, was discovered alive and well and living off the coast of Africa.

There are many people, on the other hand, who feel that seeing is believing. They don't believe that the monsters exist and will not be con-vinced without scientific evidence. And that's just what scientists and scholars are trying to find.

Early Sightings

St. Columba, an Irish missionary in Scotland, first sighted a "fearsome beastie" in Loch Ness in the year 565. He commanded the animal to return to the depths, and that's apparently what it did. It was not heard from again for a thousand years—at least not as far as recorded history is concerned.

Rumors about monsters in the vicinity persisted, however. There is a 1570 record of a "monstrous fish" in Lochfyne. A map from 1653 refers to a "fish without fin" in Loch Lomond. A story recorded in 1773 told of a "sea horse from Loch na Mna." In 1815 the famous writer, Sir Walter Scott, mentioned a "monster long reported to inhabit Cauldshields Loch."

Meanwhile back at Loch Ness, the monster had not been forgotten. In 1802, a farmer reported seeing a large animal with short, stubby legs swim toward him. In 1880, a diver was inspecting a shipwreck under water when he spotted a huge "froglike" creature resting on one of the many rock shelves in the loch.

---

[2] coelacanth (sē′lə kanth′)

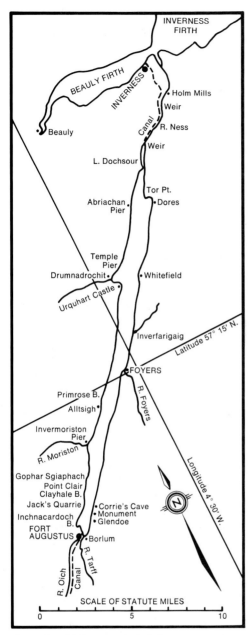

Fig. 1 Loch Ness and Vicinity.

The man vowed never to dive in Loch Ness again.

Many residents of the area apparently just accepted the legend of the monster without trying to find out what it might be. They simply warned their children to stay away from any strange creatures they might run into along the shores of the loch. And, of course, parents may have found it useful to have a monster in the neighborhood ready to pounce on misbehaving children.

Stories of the monster were generally limited to the people living near the lake. Loch Ness was isolated in a remote area of Scotland. Its high steep sides made it difficult for people to approach it. There were no roads and no means of transportation. All that changed in the 1920's, however, when a road was built along the lake.

Spreading the News

The completion of the road brought more travelers to the area, and the number of sightings greatly increased. Nessie began to achieve worldwide fame.

In July of 1933, Mr. and Mrs. George Spicer were driving along the new road on their way to London. Suddenly they saw a strange creature stumble across the road near the loch. It had a long, thin neck, much the size of an elephant's trunk. The head was small, the body thick, and it moved on four flipperlike feet. It appeared to be 25 to 30 feet (about 7 to 9 meters) long and was carrying something in its mouth—perhaps a young animal. The Spicers called it a "loathsome sight."

That year and the next, others claimed to have seen the creature swimming about in the loch making the waters "froth and foam."

As the sightings increased, the newspapers gave full publicity to each report. Although none of the reports could be supported by evidence, some were obviously hoaxes. In one instance, a group of children used an umbrella stand made from the hind leg of a hippopotamus to leave a series of mysterious tracks by the lake. Other hoaxes cast doubt on all the reports.

Then, in 1934, newspapers published a photograph taken by Dr. R. Kenneth Wilson, a London surgeon. The picture, which showed what appeared to be a long-necked animal swimming in Loch Ness, seemed authentic. The surgeon himself would say only that he had seen the head of a strange animal. He never expressed belief in the existence of a monster. But his photograph created a new interest in Nessie and revived attempts to solve the mystery.

Solving the Mystery

The first efforts to solve the mystery were anything but scientific. Shortly after the appearance of Dr. Wilson's photograph, Rupert Gould, an

Loch Ness Monster (Dr. Kenneth Wilson)

The "Loch Ness Monster"

officer in the British Navy, began interviewing all the people who reported seeing the creature. He filled two books with the descriptions they provided and with his own ideas about the monster's existence. Many similar books appeared after his, but none offered concrete evidence of the monster's existence other than the number of sightings and the credibility of the witnesses.

Interest in the monster lagged during the years of World War II. Then, in 1951, interest was stimulated again by a photograph showing three dark humps above the waters of Loch Ness. The photographer, Lachlan Stuart, claimed that he saw the monster's head but that it disappeared below the surface just as he snapped the picture. Doubters insisted that the picture was a fake. The person who developed it, however, said it was not a fake and had the negative as proof.

Electronic equipment developed in World War II began to play a part in the search for the monster. Sonar is designed to locate and determine the size and shape of objects under water by sound waves. In 1954, the sonar on a fishing vessel recorded what seemed to be a large animal about 120 feet (about 39 meters) off the bottom of the loch. The company that made the equipment stated that a large animal could have made that kind of recording on their equipment.

In 1960, Tim Dinsdale, an aeronautical engineer, filmed the movement of something swimming in Loch Ness. The film was examined by the British Joint Air Reconnaissance Intelligence Center. The only conclusion they reached was that something large, and probably alive, was in the water.

Dinsdale also re-examined the first picture of the monster. He discovered that there were two sets of ripples on the surface of the water. One set was made by the neck as it moved through the water. The other set seemed to be made by some part of the body well behind the neck. Mr. Dinsdale thought this might be a hump on the back of the creature. He estimated it to be 25 to 30 feet (about 7 to 9 meters) long. It was his opinion that the ripples would be almost impossible to fake.

No one has shown more persistence in the search for Nessie than Dr. Robert Rines, an American patent lawyer and president of the Academy of Applied Sciences in Boston. Since 1969, Dr. Rines has organized search teams to try to find scientific evidence for Nessie's existence. In 1970, using sonar, he tracked large moving bodies in the water. In 1972 and 1975, he combined sonar with elaborate underwater photography equipment, including powerful strobe lights, in an attempt to get pictures of the moving objects. Equipment was set to go off automatically and photograph anything that came within range of the cameras. The 1972 expedition yielded an indistinct picture of a large mass with flipperlike appendages. In 1975, the floating camera recorded what has been interpreted as a whole body shot of a Ness creature and a close-up of the head.

The photos are very indistinct because of the murky, peat-filled waters. Computer analysis, however, clarified the photos and supported Rines' contention that he had a picture of the Loch Ness monster. Rines' photographs were published in journals throughout the world, stirring up a great deal of controversy in the scientific community.

Believers and Nonbelievers

Opinions about Nessie's existence differ as much as

**Nessie's Fin, they say—
Dr. Robert H. Rines released this photo
which he said showed the fin of
the Loch Ness monster**

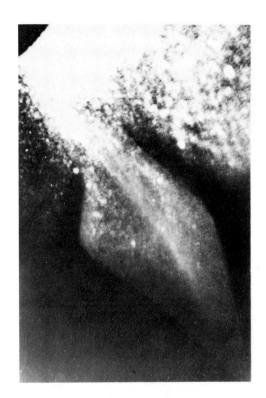

**Full Body Shot of the Loch Ness
Monster taken by
Dr. Robert H. Rines**

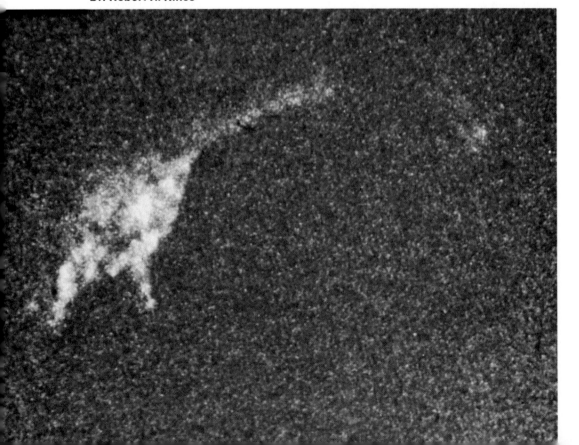

the descriptions of Nessie. Some experts from the British Museum of Natural History claim of Rines' photographs that "none of the photographs is sufficiently informative to establish the existence, far less the identity, of a large living animal in the Loch."

Sir Peter Scott, a respected British naturalist, disagrees with the British museum experts. He is convinced that Nessie exists; in fact, he believes there may be a whole herd of Nessies.

George Zug, a curator at the Smithsonian's National Museum of Natural History, also believes in Nessie. He studied the computer-refined photographs taken by Rines and could distinguish a flippered creature in them.

Opinions of the local citizens differ as much as the opinions in the scientific community. Some inhabitants of the area have never seen Nessie; others tell of numerous sightings.

Alex Campbell, a local water bailiff and newspaper reporter, first sighted Nessie in 1934. He says that he saw a huge neck rising from the water and then "a small head that kept turning nervously." A passing trawler frightened Nessie away. Since then, he has spotted Nessie seventeen more times.

A local priest and local police officers also tell of sightings. The lake looked like a "pot of boiling water," said Sergeant Donald Nicholson, when he spotted Nessie.

Even though stories of a monster have attracted many tourists to the Loch Ness area, it is probably incorrect to think that local residents have played up the Nessie story for commercial interests. There are, of course, many tourists each summer who come to scan the lake for a glimpse of the fabulous monster. But most tourists go to see the incredibly beautiful and unspoiled countryside that surrounds the lake. With the exception of a single "Monster-Burger" wagon and a few litter baskets, the 25 miles (about 40 kilometers) of lake road have remained quiet, wooded, and peaceful. In fact, during most of the year, the lake road is practically deserted because superhighways, many miles to the east, carry traffic to Inverness, bypassing the lake area.

Souvenirs, such as Nessie statues, T-shirts, posters, and the like, can be purchased in Inverness, a small city north of Loch Ness. The lake area itself, however, remains virtually untouched.

Continuing the Search

In the summer of 1976, **National Geographic** sent underwater photographers and divers to the loch. Together with Dr. Robert Ballard of the Woods Hole Oceanographic Institution, they made a thorough investigation of parts of the lake. Among the items found on the lake bottom were shoes, bottles, and teakettles—and what was thought to be the skeleton of a sea monster. Unfortunately the "skeleton" turned out to be a log.

Another 1976 expedition was sponsored by the **New York Times**. Lures were set to attract Nessie. The investigators set up strobe lights to catch Nessie's eye. They also sent out sounds of fish in distress to attract Nessie's ear and set out several species of dead fish to stimulate Nessie's appetite. The investigators waited patiently, but no signs of the sea monster appeared.

The photographs taken to date, using the most advanced equipment, have convinced some of Nessie's existence but leave others in doubt. Even the advanced sonar equipment has produced only the information that something large is swimming in the lake. The mystery continues.

Loch Ness has not yet given up its secret. Whether Nessie is a creature of fact or fiction remains to be seen. The search goes on, but there are many people who hope that evidence, pro or con, will never be found. They feel that the world can ill afford to lose one of its most enduring mysteries.

Find the Information

Check to see how well you focused on important information in each section of the article. Read each statement below and decide whether or not it is correct according to the information in the article. The headings in parentheses after each statement identify the section of the article in which the information may be found. With other members of your group, discuss the evidence you find to determine whether or not each statement is accurate.

1. It is difficult to hide anything in Loch Ness because its waters are shallow and clear. (The Mysterious Loch)
2. There is little agreement about what the Loch Ness monster looks like. (Nessie's Many Faces)
3. Throughout history, people have always been interested in monsters. (Monster Mania)

4. Science has shown that there is some basis in fact for some creatures thought to be fiction. (Monster Mania)
5. Sightings of a monster in Loch Ness were reported in 565, 1802, and 1880. (Early Sightings)
6. Newspaper publicity about sightings made the monster in Loch Ness known all over the world in the 1930's. (Spreading the News)
7. No one ever tried to trick people into believing that the monster really existed. (Spreading the News)
8. People always believe what they see in photographs. (Spreading the News; Solving the Mystery; Believers and Nonbelievers; Continuing the Search)
9. Rupert Gould wrote two books about the Loch Ness monster and proved its existence beyond any doubt. (Solving the Mystery)
10. Electronic equipment has played an important part in recent attempts to determine whether or not the monster really exists. (Solving the Mystery)
11. Robert Rines used sonar along with underwater photography equipment to get pictures of the monster. (Solving the Mystery)
12. The only people who believe in the Loch Ness monster are the local citizens. (Believers and Nonbelievers)
13. Despite the publicity surrounding the monster, the area around Loch Ness has remained quiet and unspoiled. (Believers and Nonbelievers)
14. Everyone has given up trying to solve the mystery of the Loch Ness monster. (Continuing the Search)

Interpret the Ideas

Besides finding important information as you read, you have to see how the information fits together to form ideas. The statements that follow express ideas that may or may not be supported by information from the articles. Decide which ones can be supported by the article and discuss the evidence for your decisions.

1. Opinion is divided over whether or not the Loch Ness monster really exists.
2. The mystery of the monster has been good for the tourist business near Loch Ness.
3. No one cared whether or not there was a monster in Loch Ness until newspapers made the possibility known.

4. Some stories about the monster are thought to be fiction.
5. Some evidence about Nessie's existence is thought to be fact.
6. The photographs taken by Robert Rines prove that a monster lives in the Loch.
7. There is no final proof that Nessie does exist.
8. There is no final proof that Nessie does not exist.

Apply the Ideas

In addition to identifying important information and ideas contained in an article, you can also ask yourself how those ideas relate to other experiences you have had or read about. Below are some ideas about how people react to reports such as those about the Loch Ness monster. Decide which statements you can support both from the article about Nessie and from your own experiences with similar stories. Discuss the reasons for your decisions.

1. People believe what they see, not what they don't see.
2. Facts can spoil good fiction.
3. There is very little in life that is known for certain.
4. Mystery makes life interesting.
5. Science cannot always separate fact from fiction.
6. Good mysteries make good business.

Make Some Speculations

In this unit on fact and fiction, you have seen how a person's point of view can affect what he or she sees as reality. Take the point of view suggested in each item below and answer the questions as you think the person would. Discuss the reasons for your answers with others in your group.

1. If you were a citizen living near Loch Ness and had never seen the monster, would you believe it to be fact or fiction?
2. If you were a merchant near Loch Ness, would you want the mystery to be solved? Why or why not?
3. If you were a scientist, would you try to solve the mystery of the Loch Ness monster? If not, why not? If so, what steps would you take?
4. Do you believe the Loch Ness monster to be fact or fiction? Why?

Fact and Fiction in Cartoons

Most people express their ideas through words. But some people express their ideas in pictures. These pictures sometimes take the form of *cartoons*. Cartoons are an artist's humorous way of expressing an idea, usually related to some event. In "reading" cartoons, you should follow these steps.

1. Study the drawing to notice as much of the detail as you can. Ask yourself questions about the details: Is the emphasis on people, places, objects, or events? Who is doing what, when, where, and why? Do some things in the cartoon look unusual? Faces? Body positions? Size?
2. Search your memory to see if you have read, heard, or seen anything that is related in some way to the cartoon.
3. Decide what ideas related to the people or the events in the cartoon the cartoonist is trying to communicate.

Analyze the Cartoon

Study the cartoon on page 115. Then discuss the answers to the following questions.

1. Who are the men in the cartoon?
2. Where are the men in the cartoon?
3. What do the men seem to be doing?
4. What is strange about what the men are doing?
5. Why do you think the men are doing it?
6. How does what the men are doing relate to what you've read, heard or seen before?
7. Do you agree with the cartoonist's idea? Why or why not?

Fact and Fiction
in Mathematics

The article you will read next contains facts about different kinds of numbers in mathematics. Most people consider mathematics a tool for work, not an opportunity for fun. Read to find out how both ancient and modern mathematicians have had fun searching for a certain kind of number and how modern technology is adding to the fun.

Expand Your Vocabulary

Mathematics is a very specialized branch of learning that uses words as they are not commonly used. For example, would you normally use the word *perfect* to describe a number? The next selection does! Below are some other words that you will encounter as you read the selection. The mathematical meanings of the words are important to understanding the article. Although the words are explained in the article, knowing what words to look for will help you. Use the glossary if you have any difficulty understanding the words as you read.

integer	abundant	formula
factor	deficient	computer

Read for Different Purposes

Mathematics usually puts a great deal of information into a few words and examples. Furthermore, it builds one idea on top of another. While reading mathematics, it is useful to have a pencil and paper close by. This enables you to jot down important ideas or check examples as you read them. Remember to use these techniques as you read about the different kinds of numbers mathematicians have found.

PERFECT NUMBER

by Isaac Asimov

The ancient Greeks enjoyed playing games with numbers, and one of them was to add up the factors of particular integers. For instance, the factors of 12 (not counting the number itself) are 1, 2, 3, 4, and 6. Each of these numbers, but no others, will go evenly into 12. The sum of these factors is 16, which is greater than the number 12 itself, so that 12 was called an *abundant number*. The factors of 10, on the other hand, are 1, 2, and 5, which add up to 8. This is less than the number itself, so 10 is a *deficient number*.

But consider 6. Its factors are 1, 2, and 3, which add up to the number itself. The Greeks considered 6, therefore, a *perfect number*. Throughout ancient and medieval times, only four different perfect numbers were known. The second was 28, the factors of which are 1, 2, 4, 7, and 14. The third and fourth perfect numbers are 496 and 8,128. The fifth perfect number

1 + 2 + 3 = 6

was not discovered till 1460, and the name of the discoverer is not known. It is 33,550,336.

There are no practical uses for the perfect numbers; they are merely a mathematical curiosity. Mathematicians, however, are curious and have worked out formulas that will yield perfect numbers if certain conditions are met. If even the fifth perfect number is over thirty million, those still higher are, you can well imagine, terribly tedious to work out.

The break came with the development of computers during and after World War II. To demonstrate what computers could do, one could set them to work solving formulas for perfect numbers. By now, twenty-one perfect numbers are known. The twenty-first perfect number, worked out in 1971, is a number with twelve thousand and three digits.

Such a number has no more practical use than any smaller perfect number, but wouldn't the Greeks have been astonished if they could have seen it!

Confirm the Facts

Discuss the following statements with your group and decide whether or not each statement contains facts presented in the article. Be ready to provide evidence from the article to support your decisions.

1. Ancient Greeks enjoyed playing number games.
2. The factors of the number 12 are 1, 2, 3, 4, and 6 because each of these numbers can be divided evenly into 12.
3. The factors of the number 10 are 1, 2, 3, and 5.
4. The sum of the factors of the number 12 is 16, and the sum of the factors of the number 10 is 8.
5. The number 12 is called an *abundant number* because the sum of its factors is greater than the number itself.
6. The number 10 is called a *deficient number* because the sum of the factors is less than the number itself.
7. The number 6 is called a *perfect number* because its factors (1, 2, and 3) add up to the number itself.
8. Until 1460, only three perfect numbers were known.
9. Computers have discovered many practical uses for perfect numbers.
10. Computers make it possible to find perfect numbers that would have astonished the Greeks.

Interpret the Ideas

Did you write down important information and work the examples as you read the selection? If so, you should be able to see how the facts relate to other numbers and ideas. Work with your group to decide which of the following statements contain information or ideas that are accurate according to the article. Be ready to give reasons for your decisions.

1. The factors of any number are those numbers that can be divided evenly into it.
2. The number 8 is a deficient number.
3. The number 14 is a deficient number.
4. The number 16 is an abundant number.
5. The number 18 is an abundant number.
6. The number 20 is a deficient number.
7. The number 22 is a deficient number.

8. Modern mathematicians are similar to ancient mathematicians; they also like to have fun with numbers.
9. Perfect numbers are quite rare.
10. It seems that there are more *deficient* numbers than *abundant* ones.

Apply the Ideas

The statements below represent ideas related to the article. With your group decide which ones you agree with based on information in the article and on ideas and information you have learned elsewhere. Be sure to discuss the reasons for your decisions.

1. A problem does not need to be practical to be interesting.
2. Playing with number facts is as interesting to mathematicians as playing with ideas is to cartoonists.
3. Different people have different definitions of perfection.
4. Perfection is very rare.
5. Facts can be as interesting as fiction.

Facts Stranger Than Fiction

When you compare fact and fiction, you may discover that real events can be as unusual as imaginary stories. In fact, Lord Byron, a poet, said, "Truth is . . . stranger than fiction."

Relate Titles to Articles

The next selection consists of several short articles and pictures that sound like fiction but are really fact. None of the articles has a real title. Match each of the titles below with Title A, B, C, D, E, F, or G.

> *Royalty to the Rescue*
> *No Turns*
> *Explosive Pacifist*
> *Traveling Trees*
> *Old Faithful*
> *Suspended Animation*
> *Stored Energy*

Titles of short articles are sometimes like headings in long informational articles. If you ask yourself *what, why,* and *how* questions about the title, you can usually get a good idea about what information you can expect to find in an article with that title. For example, with the title "Royalty to the Rescue," you might ask yourself these questions:

1. What (or who) was rescued?
2. Why did royalty go to the rescue?
3. How was something (or someone) rescued?

Ask yourself questions about what kind of information you would expect to find in an article with each of the titles listed. Then read the articles to find out which ones answer which questions. Give each article a title from the list that relates to the information in it.

After you have read the articles and made your own decisions, compare them with those made by others in your group. Discuss the questions you used and the reasons for your choices. If you like, make up other titles you think would be appropriate for the articles.

Strange As It Seems

by Elsie Hix

(TITLE A)

Year after year a dedicated Swedish chemist worked to find a substance which, when mixed with nitroglycerine, would make explosives safer to handle without weakening their force. He had a personal as well as scientific reason to pursue his search, because his own brother had been killed when a can of nitroglycerine accidentally exploded. The oily liquid had been responsible for so many disasters that its manufacture had finally been outlawed by many countries.

While experimenting with a new formula one morning, the doctor broke a test tube and gashed his finger. He was daubing the wound with collodion, a coating solution of gun-cotton dissolved in ether-alcohol, when the idea struck him—mix collodion with the nitroglycerine! This was the answer. The new mixture, called blasting gelatine, was not only as safe to handle as dynamite, but it was also one-and-a-half times more powerful! In fact, so powerful was this new explosive that it paved the way for a whole new era in construction and engineering. Mines were opened up, roads were built, and canals were cut at a speed once believed impossible. It had another use, also—death and destruction in warfare. Its inventor had believed that the power of his new explosive would so awe the military mind that it would actually be a deterrent to war. Instead it became a weapon that brought death to millions of soldiers and civilians.

The wound a Swedish chemist suffered resulted in an explosive that literally rocked the world. Blasting gelatine brought much to its inventor: fantastic profits from its wartime manufacture, heartaches and ideals, and an enduring fame throughout the world. For the scientist was Dr. Alfred B. Nobel, founder of the Nobel Peace Prize—strange as it seems!

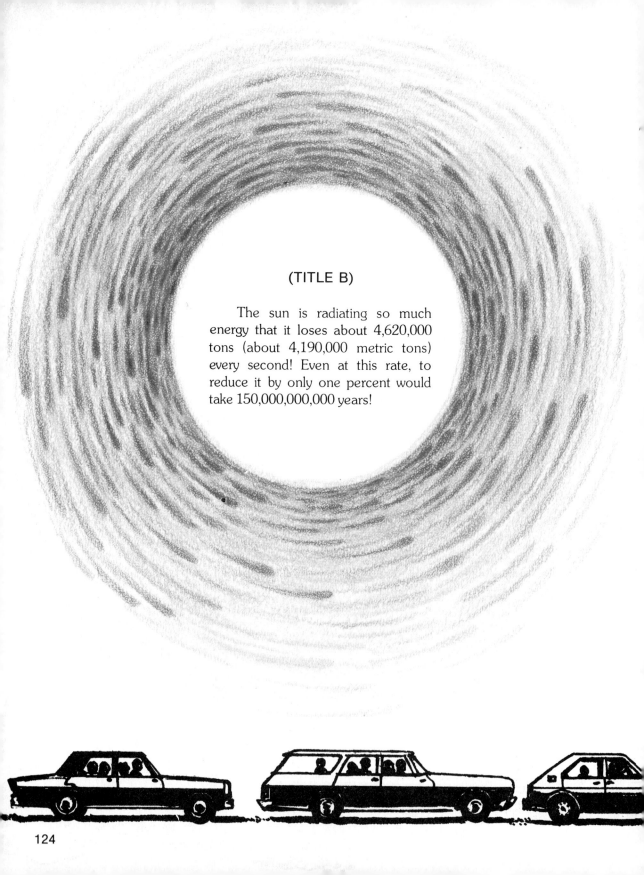

(TITLE B)

The sun is radiating so much energy that it loses about 4,620,000 tons (about 4,190,000 metric tons) every second! Even at this rate, to reduce it by only one percent would take 150,000,000,000 years!

(TITLE C)

California's famed tourist attraction, the stately, awe-inspiring giant redwood, might be described as "the tree with the itchy foot"—for it is not even a native Californian, strange as it seems.

These trees, among the largest and oldest of all living things, migrated to California from the Arctic. There they grew eons ago, just as enormous in height and girth as they are today. But the warmer climate drew them southward although it took some seventy-five million years to complete the move.

Carried by birds, rodents, and vagrant winds, their seeds traveled thousands of miles in a mass migration from what is now the northernmost tip of Alaska to California, their last stand. Only the hardiest of seeds survived—a few strays that visited Europe soon became extinct. But those that made it to California put down roots, grew into luxuriant forests, and became camera subjects for the hundreds of thousands of tourists who visit California's giant redwoods each year.

(TITLE D)

You can travel around the world by water in one continuous straight line! (60th Parallel, South Latitude)

(TITLE E)

The notice at the entrance of Greyfriars' Churchyard in Edinburgh, Scotland, was clear and legible: **Dogs Not Admitted.** But for fourteen years it was successfully violated by two fellow conspirators—a kindly caretaker and a small, shaggy Skye terrier named Bobby.

Bobby and his master, farmer John Gray, were familiar sights in Edinburgh. Every Wednesday after a visit to market and exactly as the time-gun boomed one o'clock, the two would enter Traill's Dining Room for their midday meal, a frugal lunch for Gray, and a bun for Bobby.

Then in 1858, the schedule was interrupted. Farmer Gray died. Three days after the funeral exactly at one o'clock, Traill found himself looking into a pair of beseeching canine eyes. Bobby got his bun and disappeared.

126

This was repeated for several days until Traill's curiosity got the better of him. He followed the small terrier as he left and raced to his master's grave. There he remained each day, fair or foul, despite the efforts of dog-loving townspeople to give him a new home. The graveyard caretaker, while sympathetic, tried to enforce the Dogs Not Admitted notice. But Bobby's devotion and fidelity were so great that the caretaker provided Bobby with a shelter close to the grave to protect him from bad weather.

Then, after nine years, Bobby was arrested as a vagrant because he had no license. The restaurant keeper appeared in court with Bobby. He was released by merciful justice. But just to make sure the law could not touch him, Lord Provost William Chambers paid Bobby's fee each year and presented him with a brass-plated collar inscribed *"Greyfriars' Bobby from The Lord Provost, 1867, Licensee."*

After that, Greyfriars' Bobby was allowed to keep his lonely vigil undisturbed. He never varied his mealtime. Each day he left the graveyard as the gun roared one o'clock to pick up his bun and take it back to eat at his master's side. He must have been a hardy little dog, for he lived until 1872, having kept to his solitary post for fourteen long years. He was buried in Greyfriars', of course, in a flower bed near John Gray's tombstone.

(TITLE F)

"A rolling stone gathers no moss," but there is one living animal that does gather moss—the three-toed sloth of South America. This slowest-moving member of the animal kingdom is so inactive that moss actually gathers on its body and turns it green—strange as it seems!

Most of the sloth's life is spent motionless, hanging upside down from a limb. And that is the way its hair grows. Long and coarse, the strands form receptacles for the damp jungle algae which turn the brown fur a mossy green. Actually this moss helps the animal survive because it serves as a perfect camouflage against the leafy trees and hides the sloth from the jungle's swift-moving hunters. The sloth would have little chance of survival on the ground. With long, curved claws hooked over the limb of a leafy tree, it spends the long hot hours during the day drowsing and eating. Inch by inch,

it strips the leafy limbs bare and crawls slowly down the trunk to find a new dining spot, but only at night.

In addition to looking rather like a vegetable, the sloth is a strict vegetarian. Running out of its favorite leaf is about the only thing that will make a sloth move. Then its appetite may even goad the animal into swimming a stream to reach a juicy succulent. It will also goad it into fighting to keep the tree all to itself. The sloth is lazy and prefers to be alone, but it will tolerate its own relatives!

(TITLE G)

Amelie, queen of Portugal (1889-1908), plunged fully clothed into a raging surf to save the life of a drowning fisherman! Her bravery was acclaimed in every European capital.

The articles you just read presented many unusual facts about different people and things. The questions you used to help you figure out the titles for the articles should also help you recall the details related to the subjects of the articles. The numbered items below represent the subjects of the articles; the lettered items, the details. Match each detail with the subject it relates to. Most subjects will have more than one detail. With your group, discuss the evidence you find to match the items.

1. Dr. Alfred B. Nobel
2. the sun
3. giant redwood trees
4. a ship
5. Bobby
6. a sloth
7. Queen Amelie

a. Greyfriars' Churchyard
b. moss growing on its body
c. saving a drowning man
d. handling dynamite safely
e. from Alaska to California
f. daily vigil
g. 60th Parallel, South Latitude
h. hanging upside down
i. radiating energy
j. peace prize
k. tourist attraction
l. swimming fully clothed

In the articles, you read about some very unusual people and things. How different do you think their ideas would be from yours? Read the statements that follow. Decide which ones you and the subjects of the articles would agree or disagree with. You will, of course, have to imagine what the nonhuman things like the giant redwoods and the sloth might think—if they could think. Be sure to discuss the reasons for your decisions with others in your group. Also discuss any experiences you may have had with any of these ideas.

1. There's no sense moving if you're content where you are.
2. When you are trying to help someone, speed is of the utmost importance.
3. Loyalty can be carried to extremes.
4. No matter how good your intentions are, people can take your ideas and use them destructively.
5. Nature works in funny ways.
6. You have to be strong and healthy to survive.

FOLLOW-THROUGH

Pulling It All Together

In this unit on fact and fiction, you have read about:

1. a Navaho girl and her family being driven from their homes;
2. the facts related to the Navahos being driven off their land;
3. a monster that is believed to be both fact and fiction;
4. a cartoon that attempts to explain the existence of the monster;
5. mathematical facts that are fun;
6. facts about real events and people that are as strange as fiction.

At the beginning of this unit, you discussed several types of literature that are related to fact and fiction. You have seen how different things affect what people perceive as fact or fiction. Facts may be presented as fiction or as a person's point of view. Fiction may be pure fantasy or mostly fact.

As you read, it is helpful to evaluate how much of the material is fact and how much is fiction. The following scale will help you visualize how materials may be rated in terms of fact and fiction. At one end of the scale is Pure Fiction (-3); at the other end is Pure Fact ($+3$); and the midpoint value is 0. The numbers are only a means of identifying points on the scale. As you move from the Pure Fiction end toward the midpoint, you will find more and more facts added to the fiction. As you move from the Pure Fact end toward the midpoint, you will find more and more fiction being added to the fact.

The excerpt from *Sing Down the Moon,* for example, is realistic fiction that contains many facts. Therefore, it would be placed on the fiction side of the scale between -1 and 0.

Pure Fiction		midpoint			Pure Fact	
-3	-2	-1	0	$+1$	$+2$	$+3$

Sing Down the Moon

Work with your group to decide where on the scale you would place each selection you have read so far in this book. Discuss how much fact and fiction is contained in each selection as the basis for rating it.

With your group discuss the statements below. Decide which ones are *supported* or *rejected* by what you have learned about fact and fiction.

1. Fact can be stranger than fiction.
2. Fact and fiction have nothing in common.
3. Too much fiction in fact makes fact fiction.
4. Reading fiction is more fun than reading fact.

Putting Your Knowledge to Work

Following are some ideas for activities that give you opportunity to use what you have learned about fact and fiction. Choose one or more that you would like to do alone or with a group.

1. Read about some groups of people who have been forced out of their homes by governments. Each of the following books tells about events that really happened. The first one is historical fiction; the other two are autobiographies.

   Moskin, Marietta. *I am Rosemarie.* New York: The John Day Company, 1972.

   Frank, Anne. *Anne Frank: The Diary of a Young Girl.* Garden City, N.Y.: Doubleday and Co. Inc., 1967.

   Houston, Jean Watatsuki and James D. Houston. *Farewell to Manzanar.* Boston: Houghton Mifflin Company, 1973.

2. Have a classroom debate on the Loch Ness monster, with one side trying to prove it is fact and the other trying to prove it fiction.
3. Prepare a book about other mysterious monsters and events that may be fact or fiction. You might want to do research on UFO's, the Bermuda Triangle, or Bigfoot.

Here are some books based on fact and fiction you might enjoy:

Beatty, Jr., Jerome. *From New Bedford to Siberia.* Garden City, N.Y.: Doubleday and Company, Inc., 1977.
This fictionalized biography tells about Daniel Hall who jumps ship on the coast of Siberia with winter approaching.

de Trevino, Elizabeth Borton. *I, Juan de Pareja.* New York: Farrar, Straus and Giroux, Inc., 1965.
The life of the black slave who served Velazquez is described in this biographical fiction.

Hirsch, S. Carl. *Theater of the Night.* Chicago: Rand McNally and Company, 1976.
Facts, theories, and myths, about dreams are explored.

Konigsburg, E. L. *Father's Arcane Daughter.* New York: Atheneum Publishers, 1976.
Is Caroline really Father's long-lost daughter, or is she an imposter only after his money?

Lampman, Evelyn Sibley. *Cayuse Courage.* New York: Harcourt Brace Jovanovich, Inc., 1970.
The fictionalized facts of the Whitman Massacre in the Oregon Territory are told.

Courage and Cowardice

three

FOCUS

> *"Courage is resistance to fear, mastery of fear—not absence of fear."*
>
> —Mark Twain

This quotation makes a statement about courage. Read the selections in this unit to see if you find support for this statement.

Key Concepts

courage   strength of mind to venture, persevere, and withstand danger, fear, or difficulty.

cowardice   (a) lack of courage to face danger; (b) shameful fear.

Getting in Touch with Your Experiences

Listed below are words that have something to do with courage, but each suggests a slightly different kind of courage. With your group, discuss the differences among the words. Then, drawing on your own experiences and ideas, describe actions that represent each kind of courage.

perseverance	bravery	heroism
boldness	fortitude	will power
nerve	daring	gallantry
chivalry	guts	determination

Following are some descriptions of people who acted with courage. With your group, discuss each description and decide which kind of courage the person displayed.

- The soldier risked his own life to help a friend who was wounded in battle.
- Mrs. Whiley distracted the bear long enough for her children to get safely inside the house. Then she, too, ran for cover.
- To publicize her new act, the acrobat set up a tightrope between the World Trade Centers and walked across it.

Courage and Cowardice
in Literature

The selection you are going to read is from the novel *Call It Courage.* It is the story of a fifteen-year-old Polynesian boy named Mafatu[1] who lives on the island of Hikueru[1] in the South Pacific. When he was three years old, Mafatu was caught in a hurricane with his mother, who died saving him. Mafatu grows up fearing the sea and everything connected with it. Because the people of Hikueru worship courage and make their living from the sea, they ridicule and shun Mafatu. Mafatu's only friends are his dog Uri and an albatross, Kivi.

Mafatu finally decides that he can no longer live among people who scorn him. He sets out with Uri to prove his courage by sailing to the islands to the south. A storm strikes, stripping the canoe of its sail and mast and Mafatu of his food and weapons. Mafatu and Uri drift helplessly for several days until Kivi leads them to an island. Mafatu's canoe is wrecked on the reef surrounding the island, but he and Uri swim safely to the island.

After exploring the island, they discover that it is uninhabited but that it is periodically visited by the "eaters-of-men." As this excerpt begins, Mafatu is planning how he will survive and escape from the island before the "eaters-of-men" return.

Anticipate the Ideas

The selection is divided into three parts; each part corresponds to a test of courage that Mafatu must pass. As you read each part, keep in mind the ideas about courage and cowardice that you discussed.

The first section describes some of the many things Mafatu does to survive on the island and prepare to escape from it when necessary. At the end of this section, you will be asked to identify some of the things he does and to put them in correct sequence.

---

[1] Hikueru (hē′kü′ə rü)

Trouble with Sharks: The First Test

From *Call it Courage* by Armstrong Sperry

The very next morning Mafatu set about building his canoe. He had banked his fire the night before in the natural shelter of a cave, and he resolved never to let the sparks die out. For it was altogether too difficult to make fire with the firestick, and it required too much time. In Hikueru, for that reason, the fires were always kept burning, and it was the special charge of the younger members of a family to see that fuel was ever at hand. Woe unto the small child who let the family fires go out!

While his breakfast roasted in the coals, the boy cleared the brush away from the base of the great *tamanu*.[2] There was no wood better for canoe building than this. It was tough, durable, yet buoyant in the water. Mafatu could fell his tree by fire and burn it out, too. Later he would grind an adze out of basalt for the finished work. The adze would take a long time, but he had made them often in Hikueru, and he knew just how to go about it. The boy was beginning to realize that the hours he had spent fashioning utensils were to stand him now in good stead. Nets and knives and sharkline, implements and shell fishhooks—he knew how to make them all. How he had hated those tasks in Hikueru! He was quick and clever with his hands, and now he was grateful for the skill which was his.

The fire crackled and snapped about the base of the *tamanu* tree. When at length it had eaten well into the trunk, Mafatu climbed aloft and crept cautiously out upon a large branch that overhung the beach. Then taking firm hold of the branches above his head, he began to jump up and down. As the fire ate deeper into the trunk, the tree began to lean under the boy's weight. With a snap and a crash, it fell across the sand. As it fell, Mafatu leaped free of the branches, as nimbly as a cat.

"That's enough for today, Uri," he decided. "Tomorrow we'll build our fires down the trunk and start burning it out. When the eaters-of-men come, we will be ready!"

In the meantime there were many other things to do: a fish trap of bamboo, a net of sennit,[3] a fishhook, too, if only he could find some bone. And while the canoe was building, how could

---

[2] *tamanu* (tə mä′nü) a tree that yields hard, light wood.
[3] sennit (sen′ət) braided cord or fabric.

Mafatu get out to the distant reef to set his trap, unless first he made a raft of bamboo?

The boy decided that the raft was of first importance. He chose a score or more of fine bamboos as large around as his arm, felling them by fire; then he lashed them together with strips of *purau*[4] bark, making a sturdy raft of two thicknesses. It would serve him well until his canoe should be finished.

As he worked, his mind returned again and again to the wild pig he was determined to kill. How could he go back to Hikueru without a boar's-tooth necklace? Why, that necklace was almost as important as a canoe! For by that token his tribe would know his

[4] *purau* (pü′rou) a tree that yields light, tough wood.

strength and courage. When the day came that he should leave this high island, he would sail to the north and east. Somewhere in that quarter lay the Cloud of Islands, the great Tuamotu Archipelago[5] which extends across a thousand miles (about 1,600 kilometers) of ocean and ten degrees of latitude. Within those reef-spiked channels floated Hikueru, his homeland. . . . There was no doubt in his mind that he would find it; for Maui,[6] who had led him safe to this shore, would someday guide him home again. But first, Mafatu knew, he must prove himself worthy. People should never again call him Mafatu, the Boy Who Was Afraid. And Tavana Nui should say with pride: "Here is my son, come home from the sea."

Kivi, the albatross, came and went on his mysterious errands, emerging out of blue space, vanishing into it again. At sundown, regularly, the white bird came wheeling and circling, to alight clumsily on the beach almost at Mafatu's side, while Uri pranced about and greeted his friend after his own fashion. As for Uri, he was having the time of his life; for there were countless sea birds nesting along the shore to be chased and put to rout; and wild goats and pigs in the mountains to make life exciting enough for any dog.

Mafatu had discovered a mulberry tree. He stripped off the bark and removed the inner white lining. Then he wet the fiber and laid it upon a flat stone and set about beating it with a stick of wood. The fiber spread and grew thinner under the persistent beating. The boy added another strip, wet it, and beat it into the first one; then another and another. Soon he had a yard of "cloth" to serve as a *pareu*.[7] It was soft and white, and now at last he was clothed.

"Before I go home I will make a dye of *ava*[8] and paint a fine design on my *pareu*," the boy promised himself. "I must not go back ill-clothed and empty-handed. My people must know that I have conquered the sea and made the land serve me as well."

The days passed in a multitude of tasks that kept Mafatu busy from dawn till dark. His lean-to grew into a three-sided house with bamboo walls and a thatch of palm leaves. The fourth

---

[5] Tuamotu Archipelago (tü′ ə mō′tü är′kə pel′ə gō) a body of water in the South Pacific with many scattered islands.

[6] Maui (mou′ē) god of fishermen.

[7] *pareu* (pär′ē ü′) a wraparound skirt or loincloth.

[8] *ava* (äv′ə) a fruit-bearing shrub.

wall was open to the breezes of the lagoon. It was a trim little house and he was proud of it. A roll of woven mats lay on the floor; there was a shelf in the wall with three bowls cut from coconut shells; bone fishhooks dangled from a peg; there was a coil of tough sennit, many feet long; an extra *pareu* of tapa[9] waterproofed with gum of the *artu*[10] tree, for wet weather. All day long the wind played through the openings in the bamboo walls, and at night lizards scurried through the thatch with soft rustlings.

One morning, wandering far down the beach, Mafatu came upon a sheltered cove. His heart gave a leap of joy; for there, white-gleaming in the sun, was all that remained of the skeleton of a whale. It might not have meant very much to you or to me; but to Mafatu it meant knives and fishhooks galore, splintered bone for darts and spears, a shoulder blade for an ax. It was a veritable treasure trove. The boy leaped up and down in his excitement. "Uri!" he shouted. "We're rich! Come—help me drag these bones home!"

His hands seemed all thumbs in his eagerness; he tied as many bones as he could manage into two bundles. One bundle he shouldered himself. The other Uri dragged behind him. And thus they returned to the campsite, weary, but filled with elation. Even the dog seemed to have some understanding of what this discovery meant; or if not, he was at least infected with his master's high spirits. He leaped about like a sportive puppy, yapping until he was hoarse.

Now began the long process of grinding the knife and the ax. Hour after long hour, squatting before a slab of basalt, Mafatu worked and worked, until his hands were raw and blistered and the sweat ran down into his eyes. The knife emerged first, since that was the most imperative. Its blade was ten inches (about twenty-five centimeters) long, its handle a knob of joint. It was sharp enough to cut the fronds of coconut trees, to slice off the end of a green nut. *Ai,*[11] but it was a splendid knife! All Mafatu's skill went into it. It would be fine weapon as well, the boy thought grimly, as he ground it down to a sharp point. Some sea robber had been breaking into his bamboo trap, and he was going to find out who the culprit was! Probably that old hammerhead shark who was always cruising around. . . . Just as if it owned the lagoon!

---

[9] tapa (tap'ə) the bark of the paper mulberry tree from which cloth is made.
[10] *artu* (är'tü) a tree that yields heavy, green resin.
[11] *ai* (ä'ē) an interjection.

Fishing with a line took too long when you were working against time. Mafatu could not afford to have his trap robbed. Twice it had been broken into, the stout bamboos crushed and the contents eaten. It was the work either of a shark or of an octopus. That was certain. No other fish was strong enough to snap the tough bamboo.

Mafatu's mouth was set in a grim line as he worked away on his knife. That old hammerhead—undoubtedly *it* was the thief! Mafatu had come to recognize it; for every day when the boy went out with his trap, that shark, larger than all the others, was circling around, wary and watchful. The other sharks seemed to treat the hammerhead with deference.

Hunger alone drove Mafatu out to the reef to set his trap. He knew that if he were to maintain strength to accomplish all that lay ahead he must have fish to add to his diet of fruit. But often as he set his trap far out by the barrier reef, the hammerhead would approach, roll over slightly in passing, and the cold gleam of its eye filled Mafatu with dread and anger.

"Wait, you!" the boy threatened darkly, shaking his fist at the *ma'o.*[12] "Wait until I have my knife! You will not be so brave then, *Ma'o.* You will run away when you see it flash."

But the morning that the knife was finished, Mafatu did not feel so brave as he would have liked. He hoped he would never see the hammerhead again. Paddling out to the distant reef, he glanced down from time to time at the long-bladed knife where it hung about his neck by a cord of sennit. It wasn't, after all, such a formidable weapon. It was only a knife made by a boy from a whale's rib.

Uri sat on the edge of the raft, sniffing at the wind. Mafatu always took his dog along, for Uri howled unmercifully if he were left behind. And Mafatu had come to rely upon the companionship of the little yellow dog. The boy talked with the animal as if he were another person, consulting with him, arguing, playing when there was time for play. They were very close, these two.

This morning as they approached the spot where the fish trap was anchored, Mafatu saw the polished dorsal of the hated hammerhead circling slowly in the water. It was like a triangle of black basalt, making a little furrow in the water as it passed.

"*Aiá,*[13] *Ma'o!*" the boy shouted roughly, trying to bolster up

[12] *ma'o* (mä'ō')   [13] *aiá* (ä'ē ä') an interjection.

his courage. "I have my knife today, see! Coward who robs traps —catch your own fish!"

The hammerhead approached the raft in leisurely fashion; it rolled over slightly, and its gaping jaws seemed to curve in a yawning grin. Uri ran to the edge of the raft, barking furiously; the hair on the dog's neck stood up in a bristling ridge. The shark, unconcerned, moved away. Then with a whip of its powerful tail, it rushed at the bamboo fish trap and seized it in its jaws. Mafatu was struck dumb. The hammerhead shook the trap as a terrier

might shake a rat. The boy watched, fascinated, unable to make a move. He saw the muscles work in the fish's neck as the great tail thrashed the water to fury. The trap splintered into bits, while the fish within escaped only to vanish into the shark's mouth. Mafatu was filled with powerless rage. The hours he had spent making that trap— But all he could do was shout threats at his enemy.

Uri was running from one side of the raft to the other, furious with excitement. A large wave sheeted across the reef. At that second the dog's shift in weight tipped the raft at a perilous angle. With a helpless yelp, Uri slid off into the water. Mafatu sprang to catch him, but he was too late.

Instantly the hammerhead whipped about. The wave slewed the raft away. Uri, swimming frantically, tried to regain it. There was desperation in the brown eyes—the puzzled eyes so faithful and true. Mafatu strained forward. His dog. His companion. . . . The hammerhead was moving in slowly. A mighty rage stormed through the boy. He gripped his knife. Then he was over the side in a clean-curving dive.

Mafatu came up under his enemy. The shark spun about. Its rough hide scraped the flesh from the boy's shoulder. In that instant Mafatu stabbed. Deep, deep into the white belly. There was terrific impact. Water lashed to foam. Stunned, gasping, the boy fought for life and air.

It seemed that he would never reach the surface. *Aué*,[14] his lungs would burst! . . . At last his head broke water. Putting his face to the surface, he saw the great shark turn over, fathoms deep. Blood flowed from the wound in its belly. Instantly gray shapes rushed in—other sharks, tearing the wounded hammerhead to pieces.

Uri—where was he? Mafatu saw his dog then. Uri was trying to pull himself up on the raft. Mafatu seized him by the scruff and dragged him up to safety. Then he caught his dog to him and hugged him close, talking to him foolishly. Uri yelped for joy and licked his master's cheek.

It wasn't until Mafatu reached shore that he realized what he had done. He had killed the *ma'o* with his own hand, with naught but a bone knife. He could never have done it for himself. Fear would have robbed his arm of all strength. He had done it for Uri, his dog. And he felt suddenly humble with gratitude.

[14] *aué* (ou'ē) an interjection.

Surviving on an uninhabited island is a difficult task that requires planning. Mafatu set certain priorities to accomplish what he needed to do to survive. Following are some statements that describe some of the things Mafatu did and did not do. First, identify the statements that are accurate according to the story. Second, rearrange the accurate statements so that they present the information in the same sequence as it is given in the story.

a. Mafatu makes a raft and a trap from bamboo trees.

b. Mafatu makes cloth for a pareu from the bark of a mulberry tree.

c. Mafatu draws a map of the island.

d. Uri falls into the water with the shark.

e. Mafatu faces the shark that has been robbing his trap.

f. Kivi catches fish and gives them to Mafatu and Uri.

g. Mafatu expands his house with bamboo and palm leaves.

h. Mafatu discovers the skeleton of a whale and makes many tools from the bones.

i. Mafatu fells a tamanu tree to use for a canoe.

j. Mafatu kills the shark to save Uri.

k. Mafatu vows never to let his fire die out.

Anticipate the Ideas

Mafatu passed the first test of courage—he fought the shark to save his dog. How do you think Mafatu felt afterward? Do you think that proving himself courageous one time will make Mafatu more courageous or better prepared for the second test? Read the next section to find out what Mafatu's second test is and whether or not he passes it. As you read, look for details that relate to all the different things Mafatu does to fill his days and prepare for his journey home.

Trouble on Land: The Second Test

Now the adze was completed. Thus the canoe, too, was beginning to take finished shape. It was fifteen feet (about four-and-a-half meters) long, three feet (about one meter) deep, and scarcely a foot (about thirty centimeters) wide. Often as he worked, the boy would pause to stand off and admire his craft. It was a beautiful canoe! How proud his father would be. . . . Alas that it was such slow work.

When the hull had been hollowed out, it must be smoothed off with the adze and caulked with *artu* gum. Then a mast must be made of *pukatea*,[15] straight and true; a sail woven from pandanus.[16] And there was rigging to be made of sennit, tough and strong as wire. The craft would have been finished sooner if only there were not so many things to interfere. Every day, for example, Mafatu climbed the plateau to his lookout. He had not missed one day since he arrived at the island. He knew that when the eaters-of-men came they would sail by day; they would have to

---

[15] *pukatea* (pük′ə tā′ə) a tree having light-colored wood that is soft, but strong.
[16] pandanus (pan′dān′əs) a screw pine tree.

beat against the prevailing wind. It would take them many hours to come from Smoking Island. Mafatu would be able to see them from his lookout long before they arrived. If only he could be ready before they came! He must, he must! But that trip up the mountain every day took so much precious time. His canoe would have been finished days ago, but for that.

"Today I will not go," the boy thought, as his adze whirred and chipped. "It takes too long."

Then he sighed and laid down the adze. Caution was the better part of wisdom. He picked up his shining spear with its new shaft and turned toward the trail that led to the high plateau. Uri leaped ahead, his nose keen-pointed to the ground.

This day as Mafatu climbed the rough trail through the jungle, he was preoccupied, lost in his thoughts. His mind was not in this business at all: he was thinking about the rigging of his canoe, planning how he could strengthen it here, tighten it there. Some instinct of danger must have made him pause, warning him to beware. There it was—just a rustle in the undergrowth. Scarcely louder than an insect's hum. The boy drew up tense and listening. Uri had dashed off on some wild-goose chase of his own. The boy stood rooted, alert. He saw it then: a wild boar with lowered head. Eyes red with hate. The flash of its wicked tusks.

The animal pawed the ground suddenly. Its grunting snort broke the stillness. Mafatu knew a blind impulse to turn and run. Then he drew a deep breath and shouted out a challenge: *"Puaa viri!*[17] Wild pig! I, Mafatu, have come to kill you!"

The boar charged. Over the ground it tore. Foam flew back from its tusks. The boy braced himself. He met the charge with a perfectly timed thrust of the spear. The boar impaled itself, shoulder-deep, upon the spearhead.

Mafatu was thrown off balance, sent spinning headlong. Over and over he rolled. He leaped to his feet in a panic, defenseless. But the boar toppled, gave a convulsive shudder, lay still.

Mafatu was struck dumb. He had killed a wild pig! For a second he could not grasp the wonderful truth of it. Then he leaped wildly into the air, shouting: *"Aué te aué!*[18] I have killed the *puaa!* Do you hear me, Tavana Nui? I, your son, have killed a boar! Ho! Ha!"

Uri came leaping out of the jungle and barked himself hoarse at sight of the pig.

"A fine one you are!" Mafatu joked at his dog. "Where were you when I needed you? Off chasing butterflies, that's you! Was it for this I saved you from the teeth of the *ma'o?* I've a mind not to give you one mouthful of *puaa.*"

Uri hung his head and dropped his tail, then brightened as Mafatu laughed joyously. "Foolish one! Here—drag your share."

The boy made a rule sled of bamboo and loaded the heavy animal onto it. Then he hitched a stout liana[19] about Uri's neck, and the dog threw his weight into the task. The two started home in triumph with their burden, Mafatu singing at the top of his lungs a lusty song of blood and battle. He was all Polynesian now, charged with the ancient fierceness of his race. Victory coursed like fire through his veins. There was nothing he would not have dared! Nothing he feared! *Aiá,* but life was good!

When they reached the campsite, Mafatu built up a roaring fire and set a pile of stones to heat. While the stones were heating, the boy cleaned the pig at the water's edge, then stuffed its empty belly with succulent *ti*[20] leaves and red bananas. When at last the oven stones were white and smoking, Mafatu dragged the pig back to the fire and rolled it upon the hot *umu.*[21] Then he covered it with layer upon layer of plantain leaves—dozens of them—to hold in the steam and to allow the pork to cook

---

[17] *puaa viri* (pou'ä vē'rē)   [18] *aué te aué* (ou'ē tə ou'ē)   an interjection.
[19] liana (lē än'ə)   a climbing plant that roots in the ground.
[20] *ti* (tē)   a tree with varicolored leaves.   [21] *umu* (ü'mü)   a roasting pit.

through slowly. Uri leaped about, sniffing at the delicious odors, barking his delight. Pork! After weeks of fish and fish and fish, how good it would taste! Besides, fish was not good for dogs. Too many bones. Kivi, no meat eater, looked on calmly, wondering what all this disturbance was about; the bird was content with a coconut that Mafatu split open for him, that he might join in the feast.

Mafatu's mouth fairly watered in anticipation. But even as he settled back to await the feast, his hands were busy: the sun gleamed brightly on the curving tusks that already he was making into a necklace. They formed almost a complete circle and were as white as bleached coral. *Aué!* How his people's tongues would chatter when they saw this fine necklace! Even Grandfather's had been no finer.

A strange picture on that lonely beach under the palms: a pig roasting on a fire; a boy lean and brown and whip-strong, making a boar's-tooth necklace; a prancing yellow dog; a calm, wide-winged albatross pecking at a coconut.

Mafatu slipped the necklace about his throat, and he could fairly feel its magic charging him with strength! He pulled the oven stones away from the *umu,* and there lay the pig, golden, glowing, done to a turn. Rich juices ran in little rivulets down its sides. And as Mafatu ate, one thought alone filled his mind, overshadowing even his enjoyment of this rare feast: soon, soon now he would be ready. He had killed the *ma'o.* The *puaa,* too. His canoe would soon be completed. And then—then he would return to Hikueru!

Mafatu does not get lonely on the island because there are many things to keep him busy. The numbered items below refer to the main activities that fill up Mafatu's time in the second part of the story. The lettered items are statements based on the story. Decide to which activity each statement relates. Since some statements may relate to more than one activity, be sure to discuss your reasons for making the associations as you do.

1. Mafatu's preparations for leaving
2. Mafatu's everyday survival
3. Mafatu's thoughts and feelings
4. Mafatu's fight with the boar

a. The canoe was beginning to take finished shape.
b. How proud his father would be.
c. Then a mast must be made of *pukatea,* straight and true; a sail woven from pandanus.
d. Every day, for example, Mafatu climbed the plateau to his lookout.
e. Caution was the better part of wisdom.
f. Some instinct of danger must have made him pause, warning him to beware.
g. Mafatu knew a blind impulse to turn and run.
h. He met the charge with a perfectly timed thrust of the spear.
i. The boy made a rude sled of bamboo and loaded the heavy animal onto it.
j. Victory coursed like fire through his veins.
k. The sun gleamed brightly on the curving tusks that already he was making into a necklace.
l. Mafatu slipped the necklace about his throat, and he could fairly feel its magic charging him with strength.
m. Soon now he would be ready. He had killed the *ma'o.* The *puaa,* too.

Mafatu has faced—and passed—two severe tests of his courage. He now feels ready to return home. Unknown to him, however, he faces still another test. Read this section to find out what the third test is and whether or not Mafatu passes it as well as he passed the others.

Pay attention to the events that lead up to the third test, the third test itself, and the events that follow it. Also look for the details that describe how Mafatu's previous tests have affected his opinion of himself and of courage.

Trouble in the Deep: The Third Test

The canoe was finished. Mafatu lashed the tough *purau* outrigger into place with hands that trembled. The woven sail was complete and ready; the rigging strong as wire. There—it was all over! The boy could hardly wait to get his craft into water.

Placing logs under the curving stem, he gave a shove and a push. The canoe stirred, moved forward, quick with life. Another shove and the craft slid into the lagoon. And there it floated lightly, easily as a gull poised for flight. Mafatu stood back and surveyed it with shining eyes. He could hardly believe that all these weeks of labor were at an end. Suddenly he was quiet. With lifted head he offered up the prayer with which all ships were launched at Hikueru:

> "Taaroa,[22] Mighty One!
> My thanks to you
> In this task completed.
> Guide it on your back
> To safe harbor.
> Taaroa, *e!*"

The boy leaped into the stern, picked up the paddle, and ran up the sail. Uri sprang into the bow, yelping for very joy. Kivi

---

[22] Taaroa (tə arʼō ə)   a Polynesian god.

sailed far overhead on widespread wings. The breeze caught the
sail, swelled it to a golden curve. The outrigger leaned at a sharp
angle and sped ahead toward the distant reef. Spray flew back
from the prow, and Mafatu's heart beat high. He let out the sheet,
wrapped the sennit rope around his foot, and gripped the steering
paddle with both hands. He was filled with pride in his canoe.
Never had he been as happy as in this moment.

Out toward the black reef, closer and closer the canoe
skimmed on a wide arc of speed. It was late afternoon and the

sun was setting in a blaze of glory, but the boy was reluctant to turn back. He knew that he should have climbed to the lookout that morning. This was the first day he had neglected that duty. But the temptation to complete his canoe had been too great. Tomorrow at daybreak he would climb the plateau for the last time. And then—and then Hikueru!

As the little craft skimmed out toward the barrier reef, the thunder of the surf increased in volume to an overwhelming sound. Waves, born far south in the Antarctic ice fields—the home of all waves—broke their backs upon this coral rampart. Gathering far out, they charged the reef: sea horses with flinging manes of foam. The surf shot skyward, and above its mist sea gulls swooped and darted. The reef thunder no longer filled Mafatu with unease. He had lived too close to it these past weeks. Out here, half mile (about 800 meters) from shore, detached from all security of the land, he had come to believe that at last he had established a truce with Moana,[23] the Sea God. His skill against the ocean's might.

The boy skirted along the edge of the reef, lowered his sail, and dropped overboard the lump of coral which served as anchor. Then he took out his fishline and baited the hook with a piece of crab meat. He wanted to enjoy to the full this new sensation of confidence in himself, this freedom from the sea's threat. He looked back at the land fondly, but without longing. The high peak, purple in the waning light, stood somber against the sky. The valleys were shadowed with mystery. All these weeks he had lived close to this island and been grateful for its bounty. But he had been born on an atoll—a low island—and all his life had been spent in the spaciousness of open sea and windswept palms. There was something gloomy and oppressive in this high island. The reef—this was a part of his heritage. The sea, at last, was as much his element as the land.

The realization flooded through him in a warm tide of content. He lowered his fishline, fastened it to the midthwart, and looked deep down into the clear water. He saw a scarlet rock-cod materialize, hang in the shadow of the canoe, motionless save for the slight movement of its gills. With a sudden flip of the tail, it vanished.

How fantastic was that undersea world! The boy saw branching staghorn corals, as large as trees, through which jellyfish floated like a film of fog. He saw shoals of tiny mullet, miniature

[23] Moana (mō ä'nä)

151

arrowheads—the whole school scarcely larger than a child's hand. A conger eel drew its ugly head back within a shadowy cavern.

Here beside the wall of reef Mafatu's bamboo fish trap hung suspended; before he returned to shore he would empty the trap. It had been undisturbed since the hammerhead was killed, and each day had yielded up a good supply of mullet or crayfish or lobsters. Here the wall of living coral descended to the lagoon floor. Its sides were pierced with caves of darkness whose mystery the boy felt no desire to explore. Far below, perhaps forty feet (about twelve meters), the sandy floor of the lagoon was clear and green in the dappled light. A parrot fish emerged from the gloom, nibbled at Mafatu's bait, then vanished.

"*Aué!* These fish must be well fed. My piece of crab meat does not tempt them."

The boy decided to give it up and content himself with the fish in the bamboo trap. He leaned over the gunwale and pulled it up out of water. Through the openings in the cage he could see three lobsters, blue-green and fat. What luck! But as he dragged the heavy, wet trap over the gunwale, the fiber cord that fastened his knife about his neck caught on an end of bamboo. The trap slipped. The cord snapped. The knife fell into the water.

With dismay the boy watched it descend. It spiraled rapidly, catching the sunlight as it dropped down, down to the sandy bottom. And there it lay, just under the edge of a branching staghorn. Mafatu eyed it uncertainly. His knife—the knife he had labored so hard to shape. . . . He knew what he ought to do: he should dive and retrieve it. To make another knife so fine would take days. Without it he was seriously handicapped. He *must* get his knife! But . . . .

The reef wall looked dark and forbidding in the fading light. Its black holes were the home of the giant *feké*[24]—the octopus. . . . The boy drew back in sudden panic. He had never dived as deep as this. It might be even deeper than he thought, for the clarity of the water confused all scale of distance. The knife looked so very near, and yet . . . There it lay, gleaming palely.

The boy gazed down at it with longing. He remembered the morning he had found the whale's skeleton, the first one he had ever seen. Surely Maui, God of the Fishermen, had sent the whale there to die for Mafatu's use! The long hours that had gone into the making of the knife . . . It had saved Uri's life, too. And now Uri, in the bow of the canoe, was looking at his master with eyes so puzzled and true.

[24] *feké* (fə kē′)

152

Mafatu drew a deep breath. How could he abandon his knife? Would Maui (the thought chilled him) think him a coward? Was he still Mafatu, the Boy Who Was Afraid?

He leaped to his feet, gave a brave hitch to his *pareu*. Then he was overside in the water. He clung for a moment to the gunwale, breathing deeply. Inhaling, then releasing the air in a long-drawn whistle, he prepared his lungs for the pressure of the depths. Many times he had seen the pearl divers do it. In the canoe lay a coral weight fastened to a length of sennit. Mafatu took this weight and held the cord in his toes. With a final deep breath he descended feet-first, allowing the weight to pull him downward. At about twenty-feet (about six meters) he released the weight, turned over, and swam for the bottom.

Here the water was cool and green. The sunlight filtered from above in long, oblique bands. Painted fish fled before him. He saw a giant *pahua,*[25] a clam shell, five feet (about 150 centimeters)

[25] *pahua* (pə hü′ə)   giant clam.

across and taller than he: its open lips waiting to snap shut upon fish or human. Green fronds waved gently as if in some submarine wind. A shadow moved above the boy's head, and he glanced upward in alarm: only a sand shark cruising harmlessly. . . . An eel, like a cold waving ribbon, touched his leg and was gone.

The knife—there it lay. How sharp and bright it looked. Now the boy's hands were upon it. He seized it and sprang upward toward the light.

In that second a whiplash shot out from a cavern at his back: a lash like a length of rubber hose. The boy caught the flash of vacuum cups that lined its under surface. Panic stabbed him. The *feké*—the octopus! Another lash whipped forth and encircled his waist. It drew taut. Then the octopus came forth from its den to face and kill its prey.

Mafatu saw a purplish globe of body, eyes baleful and fixed as fate; a parrot-mouth, cruel and beaked, that worked and wabbled. . . . Another whiplash encircled the boy's leg. The knife— Desperately Mafatu stabbed for one of the eyes. Then darkness clouded the water as the octopus siphoned out its venom. There in submarine gloom, a boy fought for his life with the most dreaded monster of the deep. He could feel the sucking pressure of those terrible tentacles. . . . His wind was almost gone.

Blindly Mafatu stabbed again, this time for the other eye. The blow, so wildly driven, went true. The terrible grip relaxed, slacked. The tentacles grew limp. Then Mafatu was springing upward, upward, drawn up toward light and air and life.

When he reached the canoe, he had hardly enough strength to cling to the gunwale. But cling he did, his breath coming in tearing gasps. Uri, beside himself, dashed from one end of the canoe to the other, crying piteously. Slowly strength returned to the boy's limbs, warmth to his chilled soul. He dragged himself into the canoe and collapsed on the floor. He lay there, as in a trance, for what seemed an eternity.

The sun had set. Dusk was rising from the surface of the sea. Mafatu struggled upright and peered cautiously over the side of the canoe. The inky water had cleared. Down there, forty feet (about twelve meters) below, the octopus lay like a broken shadow. The white cups of its tentacles gleamed dully in the watery gloom. With sharkline and hook the boy fished up the *feké*'s body. As he dragged it into the canoe, one of the tentacles brushed his ankle. Its touch was clammy and of a deathly chill. Mafatu shuddered and shrank away. He had eaten squid and small octopi ever since he was born, but he knew that he could not have touched a mouthful of this monster. He raised his spear and plunged it again and again into the body of his foe, shouting aloud a savage paean of triumph. A thousand years of warrior-heritage sounded in his cry.

Once more Maui had protected him! What to do with the *feké?* The boy decided that he would cut off the tentacles; they would dry and shrink, but they would be still of prodigious size, and the people of Hikueru would say: "See, Mafatu killed the *feké* single-handed. *Aué te aué!*"

Dusk, almost in an instant, deepened into night. As Mafatu turned the nose of his canoe toward shore, the first stars were appearing, bright and close and friendly. There was the Southern Cross, pointing toward the end of the world. . . . The lagoon was a black mirror dusted with starshine. Far below in the dark waters, illuminated fish moved and had their being: meteors, galaxies, constellations under the sea. The boy saw a line of light, narrow as a blade, as the rare *pala*[26] flashed away in its everlasting quest. A sand shark, phosphorescent ghost, darted after the *pala*— seized it in a swirl of luminous mist. The mist faded slowly. It was blood. Mysterious life forces were completing their cycle in those dark depths, even as on the earth and in the air above. This sea—no more to be feared than earth or air: only another element for humans to conquer. And he, Mafatu, had killed the *feké*. *Aué te aué!*

As he dipped his paddle with a swinging rhythm, the rhythm of his thoughts swung in unison: "Tomorrow I shall start home! Tomorrow, tomorrow! *Aiá!*"

The very thought of it set him aquiver. "Tomorrow, tomorrow!" He had been here so long. . . .

He dragged the canoe up on the beach, placed the logs under the curving stem so that he might launch it easily on the morrow. He would never need to climb the high plateau to the lookout again. Let the eaters-of-men come!

As Mafatu waited for his supper to cook, he set about preparing for his homeward journey; he would start at daybreak with the ebbing tide. He would be ready. He filled bamboo containers with fresh water, sealed them with leaves that were gummed into place, watertight and secure. Then he stored them carefully in the canoe. He prepared a *poi*[27] of bananas and sealed it, like-

[26] *pala* (pal′ə)
[27] *poi* (pō′ē)   food made of mashed ripe bananas or pineapples to which coconut cream is usually added.

wise, into containers; there it would ferment and sour and become delicious to the taste. Then he picked a score or more of green drinking nuts and flung them into the canoe. And as he trotted back and forth across the beach and his supper steamed on the fire, one thought alone, like an insistent drum beat, echoed in the boy's heart: "Tomorrow I shall start home! Tomorrow, tomorrow!"

Never again need he hang his head before his people. He had fought the sea for life and won. He had sustained himself by his own wits and skill. He had faced loneliness and danger and death, if not without flinching, at least with courage. He had been, sometimes, deeply afraid, but he had faced fear and faced it down. Surely that could be called courage.

When he lay down to sleep that night, there was a profound thankfulness in his heart. "Tavana Nui," he whispered, "my father—I want you to be proud of me."

He fell into a heavy, dreamless sleep.

Before dawn he was awakened by a sound of measured booming, like the beating of a supernatural drum. Thump-thump THUMP! Thump-thump THUMP! It rose above the thunder of the reef, solemn and majestic, filling the night with thunder.

Instantly awake, listening with every sense, Mafatu sat upright on the mats. Far out on the reef the seas burst and shot upward like sheeted ghosts in the moonlight. There it came again: Thump-thump THUMP! Thump-thump THUMP! Steady as a pulse, beating in the heart of darkness. . . .

And then Mafatu knew. The eaters-of-men had come.

Sequence the Events

Mafatu had very little time to think about whether or not his courage was being tested in the first two episodes. In this episode, however, he is forced to put his own courage to the test. The statements below relate to Mafatu's last test. Divide the statements into three categories by deciding: (a) which represent actions or ideas that *lead up to* the test; (b) which represent actions or ideas that *actually were* the test; (c) which represent actions or ideas that *resulted from* the test. Then arrange the events within each category so that they tell the story in correct sequence. Be ready to give evidence to support your decisions.

1. Mafatu slept soundly until the drums awoke him.
2. Mafatu decided to go after his knife because he thought Maui was testing his courage.
3. Mafatu felt confident that he had made his peace with the sea.
4. Mafatu stabbed the octopus and swam for the surface.
5. Mafatu finished the canoe and took it on a test run.
6. Mafatu was captured by the octopus.
7. Mafatu's knife fell to the bottom of the lagoon.
8. Mafatu recovered the body of the octopus and cut off its tentacles.
9. Mafatu finished his preparations to return home.
10. Mafatu dove to the bottom of the lagoon and retrieved the lost knife.

Interpret the Ideas

Mafatu's courage was tested in all three sections of the story. Following are some ideas that may or may not relate to that testing. Decide which statements you can support with evidence from all three parts of Mafatu's story. Be ready to give reasons for your decisions.

1. Mafatu believed that if he could prove he was courageous to himself, then he could prove it to his father and to his people.
2. Being courageous was more important to Mafatu than staying alive.
3. Mafatu did not plan his tests of courage; they just happened.
4. If Mafatu gets home safely, he will be able to show evidence for only two of his three tests.

5. Activities that were only boring chores at home became the activities that made it possible for Mafatu to survive on the island.
6. Mafatu wanted to return home more to escape his enemies than to prove his courage to his people.
7. Mafatu realized that a person can be afraid and still be courageous.
8. Mafatu realized that to accomplish a goal it is important to have a plan and to be well organized.

Apply the Ideas

Most people will never have their courage tested in the same way that Mafatu did. Even so, the story presents many ideas related to courage, to independence, and to proving something to oneself. Below are some of those ideas. Read them carefully. Decide which of these ideas you agree with; then decide if Mafatu would agree with you. Be ready to give evidence from your own experiences and from the story to support your decisions.

1. In any effort to please others, people usually please themselves as well.
2. One of the best feelings in the world is knowing that you have done a good job.
3. Nothing seems quite as beautiful as what you have made with your own hands.
4. Success does not come instantly; it takes time and effort.
5. Some things that you learn may have more value in the future than they do in the present.
6. It is possible to be proud of what you have accomplished without being boastful.
7. Courage builds confidence; confidence builds courage.
8. Survival comes from instinct; courage comes from education.
9. The first act of courage is always the most difficult.

Expand Your Reading

If you would like to know the rest of Mafatu's story, read *Call It Courage* by Scott O'Dell (New York: Macmillan Publishing Co., Inc., 1940).

More Courage and Cowardice in Literature

In the previous selection, you read about Mafatu, who found courage when he found himself. In the next selection, you will read about another young man who faces a similar struggle. The young man in "The Woods-Devil" is named Nathan, and his struggle takes place in a completely different setting and time period. As you read the story, see if you agree that Nathan's experiences are similar to Mafatu's.

Expand Your Vocabulary

The author of "The Woods-Devil" uses some words that may be unfamiliar to you. Some of these words are defined in context. Others are defined by footnotes. Many of them, including the ones listed below, are defined in the glossary. Following the list are sentences with a word missing from each. Work with your group to decide which word from the list goes in each blank. Be sure that the word you choose fits the meaning of each sentence. Use the glossary to help you with the meanings.

intermittently	antagonistic	implacable
indomitability	trepidation	furtively
stolid	inaccessible	inexorable
soughing		

a. The five starters on the team had played together for four years. They had won every game and had developed a sense of

_____ .

b. It had been raining on and off for days. The construction workers had become used to running indoors _____ to keep dry.

c. Not wishing to be caught, the fox sneaked _____ toward the hen house.

d. The girls were on opposite sides of almost every issue. They had been _____ toward each other for years.

e. The night was dark and the house deserted. Mark jumped at every sound until he realized that the _____ of the wind in the shutters was making the noise.

f. The child was _____ in his demands, never being satisfied with what he had or what he received.

g. The movement of the locusts through the field was _____, and they destroyed everything in their path.

h. Suddenly faced with almost certain death, the young woman was filled with fear and _____.

i. They lived in an _____ village, high on the mountain and far from any transportation.

j. His personality seemed to be rather flat and _____. He rarely showed any emotion.

Anticipate the Imagery

The author of "The Woods-Devil" also uses many words and phrases that help you to imagine what the character is seeing, hearing, or feeling. Here are some examples from the story:

1. "The slate-black clouds of winter had banked up in the north and west."
2. "His gaunt, unshaven face was etched with the memory of the pain he had endured . . ."
3. "The wind made hollow bottle noises down the chimney . . ."
4. "Something seemed to listen behind each tree and rock . . ."
5. ". . . a dark humped shape took form beneath the drooping boughs of a spruce . . ."

Which of the five quotations have to do with seeing? With hearing? With feeling? For each quotation, think of an experience of your own that may be similar to the one described. Share your experiences with others in your group. You will probably be surprised to find that your classmates have had many experiences similar to yours.

As you read the story, be sure to look for other descriptive phrases that appeal to your senses and help you imagine and experience what the character is experiencing.

THE WOODS-DEVIL

by Paul Annixter

1   For the four days since his father's accident, it had snowed intermittently. The slate-black clouds of winter had banked up in the north and west. They were motionless, changeless, remote, and ridged like banks of corrugated metal. For days during this north Maine winter, the only sun the family had seen had been a yellowish filter at midday that came in the cabin window like a thin sifting of sulphur dust.

2   Nathan was just bringing in the night's wood, enough short logs to burn till morning; with another pile of wood chunks beside the daubed clay fireplace, they would last the following day if need be. His face and ears burned from laboring in a temperature of thirty below Fahrenheit. He was dressed in brown linsey-woolsey; on his feet were shoes of heavy felt, stuffed with coarse, gray socks against the cold. A cap of worn coonskin crowned his shagbark hair that had not been cut in many weeks. He had reached the gangling age of fifteen and a half, when the joints are

all loose and clumsy. His lean face was drawn and pinched, the dark eyes sullen from overwork.

1   His mother sat darning a sock over an egg, rising now and then to stir the pot of mush or turn the cooking rabbit. His father lay in the cord bunk in the corner of the cabin, his injured leg raised high beneath the blankets. His gaunt, unshaven face was etched with the memory of the pain he had endured before the settlement doctor had come to set the broken bone. Worry showed in his black eyes turned up to the ceiling poles. Little food was left for the family—a bit of jerked venison in the smokehouse, a side of bacon, some beans, and meal. The Stemlines were true woodsies. They'd been eking along, waiting for the fur season. All that they ate, spent, and wore came from their traps and rifles.

2   Nathan went out for the final log, and the door creaked behind him on its crude hinges. The snow in the clearing was almost knee-deep. The forest surrounded it on all sides, broken only where a road cut a black tunnel through the balsams toward the settlement down to the south.

3   A sudden wind rose with the darkness. Nathan could hear it far off and high, a growing roar above the forest. Abruptly it snatched at the clearing, whirling the snow in eddies; the pine tops bent in rhythm. Because his impulse was to hurry in and close the door against it, Nathan stood for several minutes, his face straight into it, letting the cold and darkness and emptiness sink into him.

4   Indoors, he eased down his log and took off his sheepskin coat and cap, baring his mop of brown hair. He sat down beside Viney, his eight-year-old sister, playing with the endless paper people she cut out of the mail-order catalogue. The wind made hollow bottle noises down the chimney, and the driven snow made a dry *shish-shish* against the log walls.

5   "Listen to that," said Nathan's mother. "The Almanac was right. We're due for another cold spell. 'A stormy new moon. Keep a good fire,' Father Richard says for the ninth. 'Colder. Expect snow,' it says for the tenth."

6   Nathan's voice had a manly note. "It's getting colder all right, but it won't snow. It's too darned cold to snow. A fellow'd soon be stiff if he didn't keep working."

7   "Is the ax in?" his father asked.

8   "Yes." Nathan fetched it and put a keen, shining edge on it with the whetstone. Then he ran a greased rag through each of the rifle barrels. He could feel his father's approving gaze on his back as he sighted through each barrel into the firelight. "Bright's a bugle," he copied his father's invariable comment.

1   Then he sat waiting, his hands clasped tightly between his knees, for what he knew must come.

2   "Nathan," his father said presently, and the boy went over and stood doubtfully by the bunk. "Do you think you can cover the trapline tomorrow, son?"

3   "Yes, I guess I can."

4   He was prickling with trepidation. The wind shook the cabin door as he spoke, and he thought of all that lay up in the far pine valley—things to be felt, if not seen or heard.

5   "It's a long ways, I know, and it's mortal cold. . . ." His father's voice was drained and tired, and for a moment Nathan glimpsed the naked misery and worry in his mind. "But money's scarce, son. We've got to do what can be done."

6   "I don't mind the cold or the snow." Nathan stared down at his feet until that look should leave his father's face.

7   "I'll be laid up three, four weeks, maybe more. It's four days

since we laid out the line. Varmints may have got most of our catch by now. You've got to go, Nathan. If you start at daylight you can make the rounds and be back by night."

1   "Shucks, yes." Nathan forced a smile.

2   When he dared lift his eyes, he saw his father's face had hardened again in coping with the problem.

3   "You needn't try to bring in the catch," he said. "You can hang some of it on high boughs, then reset the traps. Main thing's to find what kind of range we got in there. Later on, you may have to spend a night in the valley. Think you'll be a-scairt to sleep alone in the deep woods?"

4   "Not me." Nathan's tone discounted all concern, but misgivings quickly crowded in. "Anyhow I'd have an ax and a rifle and plenty cartridges," he said.

5   His father managed a smile. "Might have to sleep in there once every week till I'm up again. So you'd best look at that log cache we built to store traps in. It's plenty big enough to sleep a man."

6   Pride filled Nathan. This was real man's work he was detailed to do.

7   "You'd best eat now and turn in early," his father said, "so's you can start at dawn."

8   "All right."

9   "You're a brave boy, Nathan," his mother said. "You're the provider for this family now. What a blessing it is you're big enough to cover the line while your father's down. Last year you could never have done it."

10   "He's near about as good as any man now," his father said. "Knows the woods and critters as well as I."

11   Young Nathan grew more stolid than usual, holding himself against the rushing tide of feeling. He wished he were all they said of him. Inside he was frightened whenever he thought of the Little Jackpine Valley where their trapline had been laid out. For three days the vision of the valley and what he had felt there had lurked before his mind's eye, filling him with dread, even when he tried to put his mind to something else.

12   Methodically, Nathan ate the man's share of food his mother set before him on the hewn-log table. Soon after, he climbed the sapling ladder to the small quarter loft where he slept. He lay quiet, pretending to sleep, but long after the lamp went out he was still grappling with his thoughts. Storm gripped the cabin. The snow crept up against the walls and the night was full of voices. Once far in the forest a wolf howled. Nathan's skin prickled and his two hands made fists underneath the blankets.

1   Now and again he could hear his father stirring and knew that he, too, was thinking the same thoughts.

2   Dawn had not yet come when Nathan descended the ladder. He built up the fire, made coffee, and ate a hurried breakfast. He took down his old wool sweater to wear under his sheepskin oat.

3   "Make sure you don't forget anything," his father said. "Have you got plenty of cartridges . . . matches? Belt ax? Bait?"

4   "Yes, Pa."

5   "Best take my rifle," his father said.

6   Nathan took down his father's finely balanced rifle with its curly walnut stock and held it proudly in his hands. It was a far better weapon than the old Sharps[1] Nathan usually carried.

7   "I wouldn't take the sled," his father was saying. "It's heavy, and I want you should be back by night. Be right careful, won't you, son?" he called, as Nathan lifted the latch.

[1] Sharps   a type of gun

1   The cold bit deep. It was scarcely light yet in the clearing. The storm had died down in the night, and there was no wind now, but the air cut Nathan's cheeks like a razor. It was colder than anything he had ever known.

2   After twenty minutes of tramping he thought of turning back. His face and hands were numbing; his joints seemed to be stiffening. Each breath was agony. He snatched up some of the hard, dry snow and rubbed it against his stiffened face till a faint glow of feeling came. Then he ran for a long way—beating his arms, one, then the other, against his body, shifting the rifle, till his thin chest was heaving. Again his face was like wood. He was terrified, but he would not give up, would not turn back.

3   He covered the three miles to the mouth of the Little Jackpine in a daze. He did not know what he could do with his numbed hands if he did find a catch in the traps; he could not even use the rifle if the occasion arose. He would have cried had he been a year younger, but at fifteen you do not cry. He started into the valley.

4   The Little Jackpine lay at the foot of old Shakehammer Mountain, and through it a small stream rushed and snarled like a wildcat, its bed choked with almost inaccessible jungles of windfalls. It was an appalling wilderness.

5   Both Nathan and his father could read the silent speech of place and time in the outdoors, and what the valley had said to them had been vaguely antagonistic from the first—almost a warning. Nathan remembered how they had threaded the valley bottom, in single file, silent. The breeze had droned its ancient dirge[2] in the treetops, but not a breath of it had stirred along the stream bed. The hiss of the water had created an intense hush.

6   He remembered how he had spat in the boiling waters to show his unconcern, but it hadn't done much good. Several times as they headed homeward, Nathan's father had stopped abruptly in his tracks to look behind and to all sides. "Queer," he had muttered. "A full hour past I had a right smart feelin' we were bein' watched and followed. I still got it."

7   "I had it, too, Pa," Nathan had said. "It's mighty fearsome back yonder, ain't it?"

---

[2] ancient dirge   a sad old song

1   "It ain't a bear." His father had evaded the question. "May be some young lynx cat, figurin' he'd like to play with us. A lynx is a tomfool for followin' humans."

2   They had backtracked to the top of a rise to look, but they saw nothing. Then the valley struck its first blow. A perfectly placed boulder that had lain poised for untold years had toppled at that exact moment to crush the older Nathan's leg as he scrambled down a rocky ledge . . .

3   Nathan passed the spot, but he did not pause. Something seemed to listen behind each tree and rock, and something seemed to wait among the taller trees ahead, blue-black in the shadows. After a while it felt warmer, perhaps because he was climbing. Then he came to the first trap and forgot wind, cold, and even fear.

4   A marten, caught perhaps two days before, lay in the set. Its carcass had been partially devoured, its prime pelt torn to ribbons as if in malice. Roundabout in the snow were broad, splayed tracks, but wind and sleet had partly covered them, so that their identity was not plain. But they told Nathan enough. Neither fox nor wolf had molested this trap, nor was it a bear. Nathan knew what it was, but he wasn't admitting it yet—even to himself.

5   He stood up, his eyes searching for a glimpse of a secret enemy, but the valley gave back nothing. Except for the soughing of the balsam boughs far overhead, the stillness was complete.

6   He moved on between the endless ranks of trees and again had the feeling of being watched. At intervals he stopped to glance back along his trail, but saw nothing. The trunks of the dark trees seemed to watch him as he approached, slipping furtively behind him as he passed.

7   The next trap had been uncovered and sprung, the bait—a frozen fish—eaten, and the trap itself dragged off into the brush and buried in the snow. It took nearly half an hour of floundering and digging to uncover trap and clog. Hard by was another set, and there Nathan saw a thing that made his skin crawl. The remains of a porcupine lay in the trap, and the creature had been eaten—quills, barb, and all. Blood from the jaws of the eater was spattered all around. Only a devil could have done that! Beneath a spruce he saw clearly the despoiler's trail—splayed, hand-shaped tracks like those of a small bear, each print peaked with fierce claw marks.

1   These were the tracks of a giant wolverine, the woods-devil, bane of all hunters and trappers.

2   For long minutes Nathan stood in the dusky shadows, fighting down his fear. He had heard about the evil fortune that fastens upon trappers molested by a wolverine. Then he thought of what awaited him at home—that stricken look on his father's face. His fear of that was greater than his fear of the valley.

3   He hung his sack of frozen bait on a high bough. Useless to reset any of the traps now, for the creature he was pitted against could smell cold steel, unbaited, through two feet of snow, and, in sheer deviltry, would rob and destroy whatever it prowled.

4   Nathan plodded on again, his chest hollow with hopelessness, not knowing what he could do.

5   The snow became deeper. One after another he came upon six more sets that had been robbed. Each had held a catch, and each ravaged pelt meant the loss of food and clothing to his family.

6   Then Nathan gave a whimpering cry. He had come to the seventh trap, and that one had contained treasure, a pelt worth a whole season's work to the Stemlines. This was a black fisher marten, always a trapper's prize. If only he could have carried home such a pelt on this first day of his rounds! How smoothed and eased his father's worried face would have become! But the woods-devil had destroyed it—an even more thorough job than on any of the others, as if he had sensed the value of this catch.

7   The boy whimpered again as he crouched there in the snow. Then anger flooded him, fought back the tears. He rose and began the endless plodding again, peering into every covert for the dark, skulking shape. He did not know the size of a wolverine. He'd never seen one. He recalled old Laban Knowles' tale of the wolverine that had gnawed his walnut rifle stock in two and scored the very rifle barrel. And Granther Bates told of a woods-devil that had killed his two dogs, then gnawed through a log wall to rob him of his grub cache.

8   It was afternoon when Nathan neared the farthest limit of the trapline. Of twenty-odd traps, only two had been unmolested. Abruptly he came upon a fresh trail in the snow: the same hand-shaped tracks and demon claws, no more than an hour old. Grimly he turned aside to follow their twisting course.

He was descending a steep, wooded slope, when on a sudden impulse he doubled back on his own tracks and plunged up the grade through deep snow. As he reached the crest, a dark, humped shape took form beneath the drooping boughs of a spruce—a ragged, sooty-black and brown beast, some three-and-a-half feet long, that lumbered like a small bear; it was lighter colored along its back and darker underneath, in direct contrast to all other forest beings. It saw him, and its green-shadowed eyes fixed on those of the boy beneath a tree some hundred feet away. The black jaw dropped open, and a harsh grating snarl cut the stillness. The utter savagery of this challenge sent a shiver through Nathan's body. His rifle flew up, and without removing his mitten he fired. The whole valley roared. In the same instant, the wolverine disappeared.

169

1   Nathan rushed forward, reloading as he ran. Under the spruce were several drops of blood in the snow, but the wolverine had vanished completely. Because of his haste and the clumsiness of his mittened hand, Nathan had only grazed the animal; he'd lost his one big chance.

2   Panting, stumbling, sobbing, the boy plunged along the trail, bent low, ducking under the drooping limbs of the trees, sometimes crawling on hands and knees. He saw other drops of blood. They gave him heart. He had a lynx eye, his father had often said. He would follow on to the very Circle if need be; he would not miss a second time. His one hope now was to settle with the beast for good and all.

3   The trail led down along the stream bed, twisting through tangles of windfalls, writhing masses of frost-whitened roots, and branches that seemed caught in a permanent hysteria. Twice he fell, but each time he thrust high the rifle as he went down, to keep the snow from jamming its snout. He plunged on again; he did know for how long or how far, but he was aware at last of the beginning of twilight. And the end of light meant the end of the trail. Victory for the enemy.

4   The way had grown steeper. He was coming to the narrow throatlatch[3] of the valley's head, a place where hundreds of great trees, snapped off by storm and snowslide from the slopes above, had collected in a mighty log jam, a tangle of timber, rock, and snow that choked the stream bed from bank to bank. Countless logs lay crisscrossed helter-skelter with two- and three-foot gaps between. The great pile was acre large, fifty feet high, rank with the odor of rotted logs and old snow.

5   Into this maze led the trail of the woods-devil. Nathan skirted the pile. The trail did not come out!

6   Trembling, he squeezed his way between two logs into the great jam. The wolverine might be fifty yards inside, but somehow it must be ferreted out. In and in Nathan wormed his body, pausing to watch, to listen, his rifle thrust carefully before him. Then down and down into the twisting chaos of dead and dying

[3] throatlatch   the area around the head of a valley

trunks, led by his nose, for the rank odor of the devil's den now filled the air. Coming upward from the very bottom of the jam, it was fouler than any skunk taint.

1   Nathan stopped short, his body tensing like a spring. To his ears came a harsh and menacing growl, but from which direction he could not tell. He waited but could see nothing. He loosened the safety on his rifle and wriggled forward again, and again the air was filled with that ominous challenge. This time it seemed to come from behind him. He whirled in panic, but there was nothing. His terror mounted. The creature must be watching him, and he could not see it. And might not there be *two* of them? Then a movement caught his eye, and he glimpsed a soot-dark shape in the lower shadows.

2   The boy wriggled on his belly along a slanting log, maneuvering for a shot through the intervening timbers. He braced himself, craning far downward. . . . Then in the very instant he took aim, he slipped on the snow-sheathed log. The gun roared; the shot went wild; and, as Nathan caught himself, the rifle slid from his ice-slick grasp. It clattered downward, striking against log after log before it lodged at the bottom of the jam, snout down in snow, its barrel clogged and useless.

3   In that instant all the craft that has made man master of the wild fell away, and Nathan was reduced to first principles. The wolverine clambered slowly upward. Inexorably it advanced upon him. He screamed at it, but there was no vestige of fear in the beast. Nathan's hand went to his light belt ax; he gave no ground.

4   With a panicking shout he leaned and swung at the low flat head, but missed because of hindering logs. He swung again and again, and the blade struck, but with no apparent effect, for the creature's advance never checked. Its small, implacable eyes shone blue-green.

5   It lunged suddenly for Nathan's dangling legs. He flung himself up and over the log, then slipped on the icy sheath, grasped desperately for another log, and slipped again to a point eight feet below. He flung around with a cry of desperation, expecting to meet open jaws, as the demon was almost upon him. But the

animal was sluggish. Its power lay in its indomitability—a slow, irresistible power.

1   In it came again, above him now. He stood upright, braced on two logs, to meet it. He was crying now, sobbing and unashamed.

2   He struck again, yelling with each blow of the belt ax, but hack and cut as he would, the beast bore in and in, maneuvering along the undersides of logs to avoid the ax blows.

3   Then as Nathan slipped again, he avoided the traplike jaws.

He fell to the bottom of the jam, biting snow as he screamed. He was on his feet again before the creature above released its claw hold and dropped upon him like a giant slug.

1   Flinging an arm up over his throat, he jerked back blindly. Spread saber claws tore open his heavy coat. Then the ax fell again, blow after blow with all his strength; he shouted with every blow. No longer cries of terror, but of war.

2   The thing would not die. The jaws clamped on Nathan's leg above the knee, and he felt his own warm blood. Then his hand found the skinning knife at his belt, and the blade sank into the corded neck—turned till the clamp of jaws released.

3   Nathan climbed up out of the abatis till half his body emerged from the top of the great jam, and there he rested—panting, spent. He whimpered once, but there were no tears now. Instinctively, his eyes lifted skyward. Overhead, as night drew on, a great rift appeared in the leaden canopy of cloud, and a few stars shone through. He fixed his eyes on the brightest star until chaos left him, then his vision steadied as if his head were higher than ever it had been before, in a realm of pure air. His brain was almost frighteningly clear.

4   The trickle of warm blood down his leg roused him. He pressed his heavy pants leg around his wound till he felt the bleeding stop. Painfully, he turned down into the maze of logs again and brought up the rifle. Then down again to struggle up-ward, dragging the woods-devil by its short and ragged scut. He laid it out on the snow and pulled out his bloody knife. He wasn't tired now, he wasn't cold, he wasn't afraid. His hands were quick and sure at the skinning; even his father had never lifted a pelt with smoother, defter hand. Darkness shut down, but he needed no light. There was no hurry. The head he cut from the body, leaving it attached to the hide.

5   He thought of the proud fancy that made the far northern Indians covet a garment made of a wolverine's skin. Oh, there would be talk in the cabin tonight; they would sit at the table long after their eating was done, as great folk were supposed to do. He'd recount all the details of the day and the fight before he brought his trophy in to show.

6   He rose at last and rolled up his grisly bundle, fur side out, and moved away through the blackness of the trees, sure of tread, for he had the still hunter's "eyes in the feet." Reflection from the snow gave a faint light. He was limping a bit.

7   Off in the black woods, a wolf howled dismally, and Nathan smiled. Never again would the night dogs make his skin crawl. Never again would he be afraid of anything above ground.

A whole chain of events led Nathan to his final victory; that is, one event caused a second event to occur, and that second event caused a third event, and so on. The event that makes something else happen is called the cause; the event that results from that cause is called the effect. The two events together are called a cause-and-effect relationship.

Following are pairs of items separated by a slanted (/) line. From your understanding of the story, decide whether the first item in each pair represents a cause that led to the effect suggested by the second item. Some of the cause-and-effect relationships are stated quite clearly in the story. Others can be found only by making inferences, that is, "reading between the lines." In either case, be ready to give evidence from the story to show why you accepted or rejected each possible cause-and-effect relationship. Page and paragraph refe.ences are given to help you find some of them.

Cause / Effect

1. rolling boulder / Pa's broken leg (167, 2)
2. dependency on trapping / low food supply (162, 1)
3. need to provide for family / action in spite of fear (166, 1–2)
4. Pa's broken leg / dependency on Nathan
5. struggle for survival / skill as a woodsman
6. anger at losses / stalking the enemy
7. loss or rifle / primitive battle
8. courage in face of danger / loss of fear
9. victory / confidence
10. confidence / peacefulness

Compare and Contrast Story Characters

Both Nathan and Mafatu were forced to struggle with their own fears. Both proved to be courageous when faced with danger. It is interesting to compare the two boys' experiences to how they were alike as well as how they were different.

Following are several ideas. For each statement, decide if the idea is true for Nathan or for Mafatu or for both or for neither. Be ready to support your decisions with evidence from both stories.

1. He was more afraid of his own fear than of anything else.
2. He was skilled in living off the land.

3. He wanted his father to be proud of him.
4. He mistook natural fear for cowardice.
5. He discovered his courage when fighting for his own life.
6. He saw himself as an adult when he overcame his fear.

What other similarities and differences do you see between Nathan and Mafatu?

Interpret the Imagery

Paul Annixter, the author of "The Woods-Devil," uses phrases and sentences that say a lot in just a few words. Read the following quotations from the story and be ready to explain what they mean and how they are related to the story action. The page and paragraph references will help you find the quotations in context.

1. ". . . misgivings quickly crowded in." (164, 4)
2. "Nathan's skin prickled, and his two hands made fists underneath the blankets." (164, 12)
3. "Both Nathan and his father could read the silent speech of place and time . . ." (166, 5)
4. ". . . Nathan was reduced to first principles." (171, 3)
5. "He fixed his eyes on the brightest star while chaos left him." (173, 3)

Apply the Imagery

As you read the story, you probably noticed how the author used descriptive words and phrases to help you imagine what the character was seeing, hearing, and feeling. Choose two or three descriptive phrases that you found were particularly effective. With your group, discuss how each phrase stirred your imagination. Then think of a similar experience of your own and write a paragraph about it using descriptive words that will help others know what you were seeing, hearing, or feeling.

The Biology of Courage
and Cowardice

Mafatu and Nathan faced physical dangers and threats to their lives, and they fought to survive. Each overcame the dangers he faced by acts of courage. Courage and cowardice are both related to fear. People respond to fearful situations differently: some with courage and some with cowardice. No matter which way they respond, their bodies are prepared for a response to danger or stressful situations in a special way. The article you will read in this section tells how the human body prepares itself for action in times of fear or stress.

Expand Your Vocabulary

The article contains some biology terms that may be unfamiliar to you. Before you read it, check your understanding by matching each word at the left with its meaning on the right. When you encounter the words in the article, notice how the context supports the definition. Use the glossary if you need extra help with the meanings.

1. gland
2. kidney
3. secrete
4. hormone
5. compound
6. bronchial
7. vessel
8. dilate
9. protrude
10. symptom

a. to produce and give off a substance
b. a cell or group of cells that secretes products in the body
c. a substance formed in glands that circulates and affects other glands
d. a vein or artery that carries body fluids
e. to stick out
f. a substance formed by the union of separate elements
g. relating to the respiratory system
h. a sign, indication
i. to make or grow larger
j. the organ at the back of the stomach that eliminates urine

THE BODY'S REACTION TO DANGER OR STRESS

Have you ever been startled by a loud noise or by someone appearing suddenly behind you on a dark night or by a snake in the grass? Do you remember the sudden, tight feeling in your chest, the way your heart started to pound, the way you seemed to breathe more rapidly? Such reactions occurred because you were frightened. Your brain sent a signal to a special gland in your body called the adrenal gland. Other parts of your body were involved, too, but the adrenal gland has a very special function. Let's see what it does and how it helps you react to fear or anxiety.

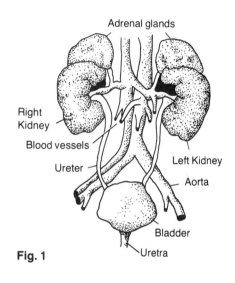

Fig. 1

The Adrenal Gland

The adrenal gland is located on top of your kidney (see Figure 1). Since you have two kidneys, you also have two adrenal glands. Each adrenal gland is divided into two parts: a cortex and a medulla (see Figure 2). The cortex forms the outer shell; the medulla forms the central core. Both the cortex and the medulla secrete hormones, but they have different functions.

The cortex produces more than forty different chemical compounds and hormones. All these things are essential to sustain life. The medulla secretes adrenalin (also called epi-

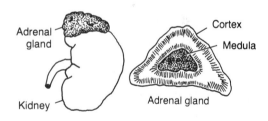

Fig. 2

nephrine), the hormone that prepares the body for emergencies. This article focuses on the adrenalin produced by the medulla and how it prepares the body to handle special situations.

Effects of Adrenalin

When you are suddenly faced with a dangerous or stressful situation, part of your brain instantly sends a signal to the adrenal gland, and all sorts of things begin to happen in your body. The medulla releases an extra amount of adrenalin into the bloodstream. The adrenalin is carried rapidly throughout the body, stimulating other glands and systems. Here are some of the things that happen almost instantly and simultaneously:

1. Adrenalin stimulates the liver, and the liver releases glucose into the bloodstream. Glucose is a form of sugar that gives instant energy to your body.
2. Your heart beats faster, and your digestion all but stops.
3. Your rate of breathing increases, and the bronchial tubes become larger to let more air into the lungs.
4. The spleen produces more blood cells which can carry oxygen throughout your body.
5. Some of your blood vessels expand and others contract. More blood is sent to the parts of your body that need extra strength to help meet the situation. Less blood is sent to those parts that are not so important during the emergency. For example, blood vessels in your skin contract, making you look pale; blood vessels in your muscles expand, allowing the energy (glucose) released by the liver and the oxygen supplied by the lungs to enter the muscles quickly so that they become tense and very strong.
6. The clotting time of the blood is decreased so that less blood is lost in case of injury.
7. Your eyes are stimulated to open wider than usual. The pupils dilate, and the eyeballs appear to protrude somewhat from their sockets. This allows more light to enter the eye so objects are more visible and vision is sharper.

Reactions to Fear and Danger

In response to fear or danger, your entire body is mobilized for action in an incredibly short time. The fear can be for your own safety or for the safety of others. There are many true stories of people who have performed amazing acts to save themselves or others from danger. People have lifted cars to free trapped victims. People have leaped very high fences—fences they were barely able to climb in normal circumstances—to escape from danger. There have been instances in which people have killed large animals with their bare hands to save themselves or others.

Adrenalin mobilizes the body for action in emergencies. It does not decide whether the stimulation results in "fight or flight." Each person responds to danger according to his or her own resources: knowledge, experience, ability, temperament. Whether a person stays and fights or runs away is often a matter of good judgment, not just an emotional response.

Reactions to Stress and Excitement

There is one more aspect about adrenalin to be considered. The adrenal gland responds to stress and excitement as well as to fear and danger. For example, when you are involved in some sort of contest that is very exciting, your brain signals the adrenal gland to release some adrenalin. The adrenalin stimulates various parts of your body the same way it does in a fear reaction. That stimulation is used to increase your performance in the contest. Athletes frequently experience this adrenalin stimulation when they are engaged in competition.

Return to Normal

How long does adrenalin stimulation continue? If it continued indefinitely, the body could destroy itself by its own strength and activity. But this does not often happen because a safety factor is built into the system. At the same time that the fear or excitement stimulates the medulla to secrete adrenalin, the brain signals the pituitary gland to release a substance called ACTH. This ACTH, in turn, acts on the cortex of the adrenal gland, causing it to release its hormones. These hormones are those that govern the normal function of various parts of the body: maintaining normal blood pressure, flow of blood to all vital organs, converting fat and protein into sugar. With these normal functions stimulated, the body begins to return to normal—to await another emergency.

The next time you find yourself in a dangerous or stressful situation and suddenly feel the symptoms of your body mobilizing for action, you will recall that your adrenal gland is working for you.

Analyze the Causes and Effects

Very few things in life happen without a reason. This is particularly true of the human body and its functions. All the changes that occur during adrenalin stimulation have a purpose. Listed in Part A are changes that occur in the body when adrenalin is released into the bloodstream. Listed in Part B are the results of those changes. Work with your group to relate the changes in Part A with their results in Part B.

PART A

1. Blood vessels in the skin contract.
2. The liver releases glucose into the bloodstream.
3. Breathing rate increases.
4. Blood clots more quickly.
5. The spleen produces more blood cells.
6. Eyes open wider and pupils dilate.
7. Heart beats faster.
8. Blood vessels in the muscles expand.

PART B

a. Instant energy is available to the body.
b. Less blood flows from a cut.
c. Bronchial tubes enlarge, admitting more oxygen to the lungs.
d. The skin turns pale.
e. More light enters the eye making vision sharper.

f. More oxygen is carried throughout the body.

g. Blood flows more quickly.

h. Muscles become strong and tense, enabling the body to perform actions of great strength.

Interpret and Apply the Ideas

Now that you have analyzed the causes and effects of adrenalin stimulation, see if you can interpret what they mean. Decide which of the following statements express ideas that could be supported by information in the article. Be ready to give evidence from the article to support your decisions.

1. The two parts of the adrenal gland perform the same function.
2. Your body works the same way to prepare you for danger, stress, or competition.
3. All the different parts of the body work together to prepare you to handle different situations.
4. The body can cope with anything as long as necessary.
5. If people could control their adrenal glands, they could become super-people.
6. Strength has to do with a person's body being prepared for action; courage has to do with what the person does with strength.
7. For every accelerator there has to be a brake.
8. It is harder to be afraid and do nothing than it is to be afraid and take some kind of action.

Courage and Cowardice in Poetry

You have read two stories about young men who overcame fear and an informational article about how the body prepares itself to cope with fear. In the next selection poetry is used to describe a very common fear.

Before you read the poem, notice how it differs from prose in the way it looks on the page: capitalization at the beginning of each line, short lines, stanzas separated by extra space. As you read the poem to yourself, notice the images the poet uses to describe the "narrow fellow" and her own responses to it. After reading the poem to yourself several times, take turns reading the poem aloud with the members of your group.

A Narrow Fellow

by Emily Dickinson

A narrow fellow in the grass
Occasionally rides;
You may have met him—did you not?
His notice sudden is.

The grass divides as with a comb,
A spotted shaft is seen;
And then it closes at your feet
And opens further on.

He likes a boggy acre,
A floor too cool for corn.
Yet when a boy, and barefoot,
I more than once, at morn,
Have passed, I thought, a whiplash
Unbraiding in the sun—
When, stooping to secure it,
It wrinkled, and was gone.

Several of nature's people
I know, and they know me;
I feel for them a transport
Of cordiality;

But never met this fellow
Attended or alone,
Without a tighter breathing
And zero at the bone.

Analyze the Imagery

Emily Dickinson uses uncommon words and phrases to describe common things and events. Decide which lines of the poem best fit each of the following descriptions. Be ready to read aloud the lines you choose for each item.

1. The poet's feeling toward most wildlife.
2. Where the "narrow fellow" likes to live.
3. The appearance and movement of the "narrow fellow" through the grass.
4. The body's adrenalin reaction to the "narrow fellow's" appearance.
5. The poet's childhood experience with the "narrow fellow."

Interpret and Apply the Ideas

What animal does "A Narrow Fellow in the Grass" describe? Can you think of phrases that describe other animals in the same way? Here are some examples:

A wide-eyed scholar hooting in the night.
A furry ball of mischief on the rug.

See if you can make up other descriptive phrases of animals as riddles for your group.

Compare the Poems

Emily Dickinson used descriptive phrases and formal language to tell about a fairly common fear. In the next poem, Langston Hughes uses different kinds of descriptive phrases and informal language to describe a kind of courage that people need in everyday life. Recall the different kinds of courage you discussed at the beginning of this unit. As you read the next poem to yourself, try to determine what kind of courage the poet is describing. Then take turns reading the poem aloud with your group. Notice the short lines and dialect as clues to reading the poem aloud.

Mother to Son

by Langston Hughes

Well, son, I'll tell you:
Life for me ain't been no crystal stair.
It's had tacks in it,
And splinters,
And boards torn up,
And places with no carpet on the floor—
Bare.
But all the time
I'se been a-climbin' on,
And reachin' landin's,
And turnin' corners,
And sometimes goin' in the dark
Where there ain't been no light.
So, boy, don't you turn back;
Don't you set down on the steps
'Cause you find it kinder hard.
Don't you fall now—
For I'se still goin', honey,
I'se still climbin',
And life for me ain't been no crystal stair.

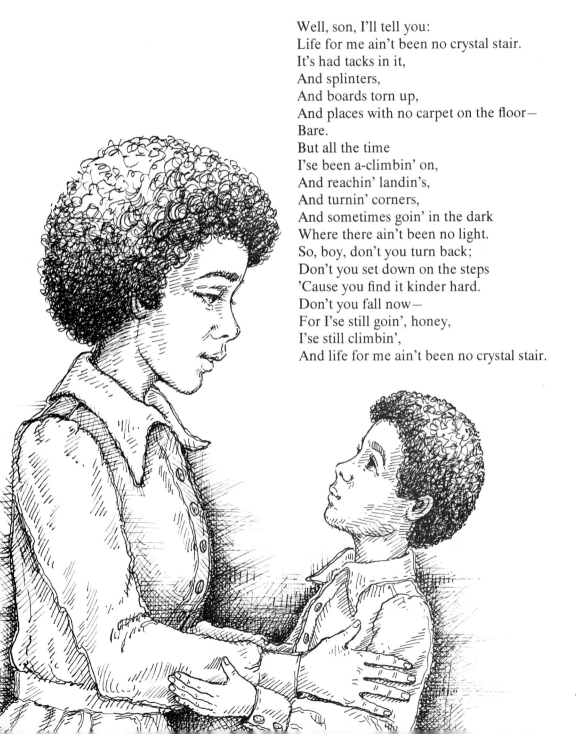

185

Analyze the Imagery

How did the poet's use of words like *tacks* and *splinters* add to your understanding of the poem? Listed in Column A are some ideas that Langston Hughes deals with in the poem. In Column B are some of the images he uses to describe those ideas. Match each image in Column B with the idea it describes in Column A. Since more than one image may be used to describe an idea, be sure to discuss your reasons for matching the ideas as you do.

Column A	Column B
1. life	a. no crystal stair
2. troubles/setbacks	b. set down on the steps
3. making decisions	c. fall
4. giving up	d. a-climbin' on
5. persevering	e. tacks
	f. turn back
	g. splinters
	h. still goin'
	i. reachin' landin's and turnin' corners
	j. boards torn up

Interpret and Apply the Ideas

Langston Hughes wrote his poem in the form of a mother giving advice to her son. But that advice might be applied to anyone. Decide which of the ideas below express advice the poet's mother would give. Give evidence from the poem to support your decisions. Then decide which advice you would accept or reject if you were the son. Discuss your reasons for accepting or rejecting each.

1. Life is full of obstacles that you have to overcome so that you can keep going.
2. When you meet a particularly difficult obstacle, take time to analyze it before going on.
3. Once you sit down and give up, you may never get up again to fight.
4. You have to have more courage to face a series of small obstacles or setbacks than to face a few big ones.

Courage and Cowardice in Real Life

Most people are not required to test their courage as Mafatu and Nathan were in the first two stories in this unit. They are, however, required to face everyday obstacles and setbacks, as suggested in the poem "Mother to Son." In this section, you will read four biographical sketches of real people who exhlbited courage in their everyday existence. As you read the sketches, think about the different kinds of courage you discussed at the beginning of this unit and what the people in the sketches did to exhibit courage.

Jill Kinmont

"Never say die" might well be Jill Kinmont's motto. Jill severed her spinal cord in a skiing accident at age nineteen. Despite losing almost all use of her arms and legs, the former Olympic hopeful built a new life for herself as a teacher.

In January 1955, Jill Kinmont seemed certain to make the United States Olympic ski team. Since age twelve, she had focused on this goal. Throughout high school in Bishop, California, she had competed at most Western ski areas, including Mammoth Mountain, Sun Valley, Aspen, Jackson, and Brighton. She had won both the women's and the junior national slalom championships before traveling to Alta, Utah, to compete in the pre-Olympic tryouts. As Jill says, "Skiing was it—everything—my world."

Jill's world collapsed on January 30 when she skied off the Alta run and landed helpless on the slope. Her fourth, fifth, and sixth cervical vertebrae were broken. For days, Jill hovered between life and death. By April, it became clear that she would be paralyzed from the shoulders down.

Jill underwent rehabilitation therapy with cheerful determination. She learned to write, to type, and to feed herself. Once she had mastered daily living skills, she enrolled in the University of California at Los Angeles, where she studied art, German, and English. After overcoming yet another personal tragedy, the death of her boyfriend in a plane crash, Jill graduated in 1961.

By this time, Jill had chosen a new career goal: teaching elementary school children. Officials at UCLA, however, rejected her application for admission to the graduate school of education because of her paralysis. But she persevered, working with children in the UCLA Clinic School. When her family moved to Seattle, Jill was able to fulfill her new dream. She attended the School of Education at the University of Washington and began her new life's work as a teacher.

Jill is as enthusiastic a teacher as she was a skier. She works tirelessly to improve educational opportunities for American Indian children in the state of California. She also has gotten married and worked as a consultant on the two movies that tell the story of her courage: *The Other Side of the Mountain, Part I and Part II.* The biography of Jill's life was also made into a book by the same title, written by E. G. Valens (New York: Harper and Row, Publishers, 1966, 1975).

Jill Kinmont with American Indian child

Babe Didrickson Zaharias

"The incomparable Babe" refers not only to the great American baseball player Babe Ruth, but also to his namesake Babe Didrickson Zaharias. The athletic Babe Didrickson Zaharias lived a champion and died a champion. Noted mainly for her skill as a golfer, Babe also set Olympic world records in the women's 80-meter hurdle and the javelin throw. She excelled in high jumping and broad jumping, basketball, baseball, tennis, bowling, sprinting, billiards, swimming and diving, the shot put, and the discus throw.

Mildred Didrickson acquired her nickname with her famous long ball in the local sandlot in Beaumont, Texas. Babe had closely studied the boys' baseball game and had practiced the techniques of the better players. After much persistence, she talked the boys into letting her join the team and soon built her reputation for hitting home runs.

Babe similarly studied the fine points of basketball. She became the highest-scoring member of her high school team. After high school, Babe joined the Employees Casualty Company of Dallas and competed in the Amateur Athletic Union Games as a member of the company team. Babe became high scorer for the team and was named to the women's All America basketball team in 1930 and 1931.

Training for the 1932 Olympics, Babe continued to show unusual athletic ability. She beat every track and field team entered in an Olympic elimination event in Evanston, Illinois. Two weeks later, she won gold medals in two of the three events she entered at the Olympics.

Ready for new athletic worlds to conquer, Babe discovered golf. She again worked hard to master the fine points of the game. In 1934, she entered her first tournament. A few months later, she won the Texas State Women's Championship.

Golf became the major sports activity in Babe's life. In fact, she spent her honeymoon playing golf exhibitions in Australia. She played golf throughout the United States in the 1940's, winning fifteen contests in a row. In 1947, she played the British Women's Amateur in Scotland and became the first American to win.

Babe first became aware that she was straining herself in 1948 when she developed an erratic pain in her left side. Her real problems, however, started in 1953 when she underwent an operation for cancer.

Although weakened by the operation, Babe made a comeback. She won the National Women's Open and the Tam O'Shanter All-America Tournament. She also won the Ben Hogan Trophy for overcoming a physical disability to go on and play winning golf.

Babe's cancer returned in 1955, and she spent the rest of her life in and out of the hospital. Between hospital visits, she played golf and supported cancer drives with the same persistence she first showed as a would-be athlete in Beaumont, Texas. Babe once commented, "I have to keep demonstrating that you can come back after being laid low by cancer and still do whatever you did before, and do it as well as before, too." Babe remained a champion until her death on September 27, 1956.

Stevie Wonder

Ask Steveland Morris and he'll tell you that blindness is not necessarily disabling. Steveland was born prematurely and totally without sight in 1950. He became Stevie Wonder — composer, singer, and pianist. The winner of ten Grammy awards, Stevie is widely acclaimed for his outstanding contributions to the music world.

As a child, Stevie learned not to think about the things he could not do, but to concentrate on the things that he could do. His parents encouraged him to join his sighted brothers in as many activities as possible. They also helped him to sharpen his sense of hearing, the sense upon which the visually disabled are so dependent.

Because sound was so important to him, Stevie began at an early age to experiment with different kinds of sound. He would bang things together and then imitate the sound with his voice. Often relying on sound for entertainment, he sang, beat on toy drums, played a toy harmonica, and listened to the radio.

Stevie soon graduated from toy instruments to real instruments. He first learned to play the drums, a present from the Detroit Lions Club. He then mastered the harmonica and the piano. He became a member of the junior church choir and a lead singer. In the evenings and on weekends, Stevie would play different instruments and sing popular rhythm and blues tunes on the front porches of neighbors' homes. Large groups of people would gather around and provide him with an appreciative audience.

One of Stevie's sessions was overheard by Ronnie White, a member of a popular singing group called The Miracles. Ronnie immediately recognized Stevie's talent and took him to audition for Berry Gordy, the president of Hitsville USA, a large recording company now known as Motown. The rest of Stevie's story is music history.

Stevie recorded his first smash hit "Fingertips" in 1962 at age twelve. Shortly after, he recorded his first album and took the first of many road trips. Stevie continued to develop his own musical style throughout his teenage years. He not only sang, but he also wrote and played the music which he produced. In 1971, when he turned twenty-one, he set up his own recording company as well as his own publishing company.

Stevie's incredible talents are reflected in the one-man albums he has produced. He continues to grow as an artist, entertaining millions of people with his talents.

Rachel Carson

A 1963 cartoon shows a praying mantis praying: "God bless Momma . . . and Poppa . . . and Rachel Carson!" Environmentalists today are likely to agree with the sentiment. Poet and scientist, artist and author, Rachel Carson was a gentle person who sparked a revolution with her book *Silent Spring*. In fighting against the poisoning of the earth, she took a stand that brought about a complete change in the average citizen's regard for the universe.

During her childhood, Rachel showed an interest in nature and in writing. She loved both books and the natural world. After high school, she enrolled in Pennsylvania State College for Women, intending to become a writer. She switched to biology, however, thereby setting the course of her life. Rachel went to Johns Hopkins University in Baltimore for further study and became a member of the zoology staff at the University of Maryland.

For fifteen years, Rachel worked for the United States Fish and Wildlife Service, writing and editing publications. Fortunately, her employer encouraged her to reach a larger audience. Rachel's poetic style of writing in three books about the ocean caught the imagination of the general reader. Her rare talent as both a physical scientist and a gifted writer earned her the National Book Award for *The Sea Around Us*.

Rachel's next book marked her as a leading conservationist and a crusader for the preservation of the natural environment. She began writing *Silent Spring,* knowing that she would be personally attacked and ridiculed. She continued writing despite the ill health that slowed her progress. Rachel knew the importance of what she was doing. Upon completing the book, she wrote to a close friend, "I have felt bound by a solemn obligation to do what I could —if I didn't at least try I could never again be happy in nature. But now I can believe I have at least helped a little."

Rachel Carson did more than help a little; she played a major role in the environmental revolution. Although both government and industry opposed her, specialists in public health, the press, and the public itself all supported her fight against the irresponsible use of insecticides. Her book eventually led the government to ban DDT.

Although Rachel Carson died of cancer in 1964, others are continuing her battle for a clean environment.

Find the Supporting Details

As you can see from reading the sketches, there are many different ways the people (subjects) displayed courage in their everyday lives. Below are the names of the subjects followed by a list of actions. Match the actions to the person(s) who displayed them. Since some actions may apply to more than one person, be sure you can find evidence from the sketches to support your answers. Also, recall the kinds of courage you discussed at the beginning of this unit. Decide which kind of courage is demonstrated by each action. Share your ideas with your group.

1. Jill Kinmont
2. "Babe" Didrickson Zaharias
3. Stevie Wonder
4. Rachel Carson

a. worked hard to become the best at whatever he/she did
b. took risks to become a member of the United States Olympic ski team
c. didn't give up after being rejected
d. made the most of what he/she could do without being discouraged about what he/she could not do
e. was subjected to a great deal of criticism for doing what he/she believed in
f. had to fight very hard to overcome prejudice against being the first to do something
g. continued to grow and expand his/her talents even after achieving success
h. inspired others to continue against terrific odds
i. developed one of his/her senses to overcome not having one

---

Interpret and Apply the Ideas

Now that you have analyzed the people and their actions, try to determine how they would feel about courage. Read each statement below and decide which person(s) would agree or disagree with it. Discuss the reasons for your choices and then decide which statements you agree with and give your reasons.

1. It's easy to be courageous when people are watching you.
2. Ordinary people exhibit courage by standing up for what they believe.
3. It's easier to overcome a disability that you are born with than one that is developed later in life.
4. Courage is persistence.
5. Most people don't think of themselves as being courageous; they simply do what they feel is right for them.

Courage and the Press

People may be courageous but never know it because they have never been in a situation that requires them to be courageous. Courage is not what you think you would do, but what you actually do in that situation.

Some people have their courage tested constantly because they have jobs that require courage. What jobs do you think of most frequently when you think of jobs that require courage? Fire fighters? Police officers? Miners? News reporters? You might not think of news reporting as a job that requires courage. But, as you saw in the biographical sketch of Rachel Carson, it does take courage to gather information and to use it to correct a wrong. News reporters must also frequently put themselves in dangerous situations to get good stories.

Journalists in the United States have a long history of having both the opportunity and the responsibility to be courageous in their reporting. The article you will read next discusses how and why they have both.

Use Headings to Locate Information

The article "Making Courage Visible" is divided into several parts. Each part has a heading that separates it from the other parts. Headings can help you sense the organization of the article. Knowing how an article is organized can help you find specific information quickly.

A good way to anticipate what information might be included under the headings is to turn the headings into questions. For example, the first heading in the article you will read next is "The Influence of Opinion." Using the interrogative *what,* you can change the heading into a question that would help you look for *information.* Thus, you could ask, "What is the influence of opinion?" or "What does opinion influence?"

You can also use the interrogative *why* to change the heading into a question that would help you look for *reasons.* Thus, you could ask, "Why does opinion influence?"

You can also use the interrogative *how* to change the heading into a question that would help you look for *operations* or *ways* things work. Thus, you could ask, "How does opinion influence?"

Changing headings into questions this way is a good study technique. Practice using the technique on the other headings in this article. Before you read each section, change the heading into three questions: a *what* question, a *why* question, and a *how* question. Then read that section to find the answers. Sometimes you may not find answers to all the questions, but that's all right. The technique itself helps you understand the article by raising *possible* questions. Not finding some answers is an answer of sorts because it tells you what the article does not present as well as what it does present.

Remember to use the *what, why,* and *how* questions before and after you read each section of the article.

Making Courage Visible

by Elizabeth Levy

The Influence of Opinion

The best reporters are not necessarily objective truth-seekers. They have definite opinions as to what is right and what is wrong. Without this ability to make judgments, they would never suspect that "something is wrong" with the official story.

The fact that investigative reporters hold strong opinions does not mean that they allow their opinions to interfere with the accuracy of their reports. Their opinions give them an edge, which enables them to believe less than anyone else. That edge also enables them to dig deeper than anyone else and keeps them going through a great deal of criticism and controversy. People who do not allow themselves to have strong opinions (or reporters who believe it is wrong even to have opinions) do not make good investigators. There is no fuel to feed the fire.

Freedom of the Press

Even though the best reporters are often those with strong opinions, they have to have something else. That something else has nothing to do with the personality of the journalist; it has to do with the freedom to investigate.

Freedom of the press is basically freedom of opinion. Being free to believe anything one wishes would be meaningless without freedom to put that belief down on paper. The writers of the United States Constitution knew they were taking a risk when they made freedom of the press an absolute. They knew from experience that freedom of the press meant a risk to the government in power, but they felt that freedom was worth the risk.

In fact, putting ideas down on paper was probably one of the causes of the American Revolution. The most opinionated reporter at that time was probably Tom Paine. Many thought he was a slightly mad troublemaker.

Arriving in the colonies at the end of 1775, Paine already held strong opinions about the situation there. He felt that monarchy was hateful, that George III was the worst monarch of all, and that revolution was the only answer. Taking up his pen, Paine wrote a pamphlet called *Common Sense*. In it, he laid out a tight case for independence, exposing George III as the "royal brute of Great Britain." Paine cited the benefits that would come to an independent America. He closed saying, "Freedom hath been shunted around the globe. Asia and

Africa have long expelled her. Europe regards her like a stranger, and England hath given her warning to depart. O receive the fugitive and prepare in them an asylum for all mankind!"

The circulation of Paine's pamphlet was enormous. Thousands of colonists caught the revolutionary fever from the words of Tom Paine.

Paine was never jailed for writing *Common Sense,* even though it supported rebellion. The king's soldiers would have locked him up if the American Revolution hadn't interfered.

The original Constitution did not include freedom of the press. However, many people realized that the Revolution might never have happened without people like Tom Paine and Sam Adams. Such people had the courage to write, even though they might be jailed. The founders discovered that they would not be able to get their Constitution ratified without a bill of rights granting absolute freedom of the press.

The First Amendment states that "Congress shall make no law . . . abridging the freedom of speech of the press." Those words are very clear. Congress is not allowed to make any law that restricts freedom of the press. Almost no other country has followed this example and granted freedom of the press. It didn't take very long for some people in America to regret that the First Amendment had ever been written.

In the twenty years after the founding of the nation, newspapers became political organs, backing one party or the other. There was a lot of name-calling and many ugly attacks on politicians by their opponents. As a result, people began to think that complete freedom of the press wasn't such a good idea after all.

The Sedition Act

The Federalists, who ran the government in 1798, passed a sedition act. This made it a crime to write anything "false, scandalous, or malicious" against the government. These words are very vague. Several editors were put in jail over the next few years. It became clear that the government could interpret the word *malicious* to its own advantage. Nothing could be printed if it displeased the authority in power. The name-calling might have been annoying, and even a little frightening, but the suppression of the press was even worse. In 1801, when Thomas Jefferson took office, the alien and sedition laws were not renewed.

Congress learned its lesson well. For the next 117 years, no further attempt was made to limit what journalists might or might not say.

The Muckrakers

Just at the beginning of the twentieth century, a new kind of journalist began to appear. The new journalists were not interested in just describing events. Nor were these journalists political hacks like those in the 1700's. These journalists were called "the muckrakers." They raked around the muck uncovering wrongdoings in American life. Their object was not to entertain; they wanted to reform.

The muckraking reporters led a wave of reform that hit many aspects of American life. Upton Sinclair wrote about the filthy conditions of the Chicago meat market, and laws were passed to have meat inspected by the federal government. Ida Tarbell exposed the tremendous power of Standard Oil, and new laws were passed limiting the power of the huge trusts. Lincoln Steffens exposed the evils and corruption in city governments, and many progressive reforms were passed. Journalists gained a new respect and a new power. It seemed that whenever they exposed a wrong, a law was passed to correct that wrong.

LOCAL GOVERNMENT REFORMS
ANTI-TRUST LAWS
FOOD & DRUG ADMINISTRATION

The Espionage Act

In 1918, when the United States became involved with overseas enemies, Congress passed the Espionage Act. This prohibited writing anything that might hurt the war effort. But how was the law to be interpreted? Was there any way to draw the line between threats to national security and legitimate criticism of government? Supreme Court Justice Oliver Wendell Holmes ruled that the press could be limited only if the "words used . . . are of such a nature as to create a clear and present danger that will bring about the substantive evils that Congress has a right to prevent."

This meant that the government had to prove a "clear and present danger." In 1972, for example, former president Richard Nixon told the attorney general to get a court order preventing *The Washington Post* and *The New York Times* from publishing the Pentagon papers. The government said its national security was in "clear and present danger." The Supreme Court ruled that since the Pentagon papers dealt with the past, there was no clear and present danger to foreign policy.

Libel and Slander Laws

In 1963, a landmark decision was made on Sullivan vs. *The New York Times*. The Supreme Court ruled that in cases involving public officials, no reporter or paper could be held liable for printing falsehoods if such falsehoods were the result of carelessness. If the reporter had meant to be malicious, then both the reporter and the paper were guilty of libel.

Debate still goes on over this ruling. Many feel that the Sullivan decision gives reporters too much freedom. Reporters no longer have to worry about being sued if they report a rumor that turns out to be a lie.

Many journalists think the Sullivan decision encourages healthy and much-needed criticism of government and politics of this country. They point out that the Sullivan rule applies only to public officials and that the ordinary citizen's privacy is still protected.

Protection of Sources

There is one "legal" limitation that still hangs over the heads of reporters. That concerns the reporter's right to protect his or her source of information. So far, the courts have not ruled definitely on whether or not a reporter can be ordered to name informants. Woodward and Bernstein's detecting of Watergate is a good example. Unless they had been able to guarantee not to name their sources, there might never have been accurate reporting of the Watergate break-in.

The law about whether or not a reporter has a right to "shield" sources is not clear. In 1972, the Supreme Court ruled that the First Amendment did not protect reporters against grand-jury questions. However, the Supreme Court was divided. Because of this, the ruling was to apply only to this one case. It was not to be taken as a general rule.

About twenty-five states now have "shield laws" which let reporters protect sources. Local judges, however, have sometimes ruled that these laws do not apply to certain information wanted. Many people have tried to get laws passed to protect reporters' sources. But so far they have not been successful.

Besides the legal forces that influence most reporters, what other demands or limitations are placed upon the journalist's freedom to question, to search, and then to print? One obvious restriction is the philosophy and judgment of the people who run either the newspaper or the television station. The views of stockholders, subscribers, and advertisers *do* matter to the managers of the news media and, in the end, to the reporter.

Fortunately, the news business is highly competitive. A story that hits sensitive nerves will probably sell a lot of newspapers or attract a lot of television viewers. The combination of legal freedom, courageous reporters and publishers, and the competitive nature of the news business have made American reporting the best in the world. Remarkably few reporters complain about being called off a good story. In fact, most editors complain that there are too few first-rate investigative reporters.

Analyze the Comparisons

When you changed headings into questions, you read for information and ideas. In this article, the author hints at, or *implies,* many ideas without stating them directly. To understand those *implied* ideas, you have to make inferences, or "read between the lines."

This author presents ideas "between the lines" by making implied comparisons. In most cases, the comparison is not stated but can be inferred from the information and ideas that *are* stated. The following activity will help you sense these implied comparisons.

Listed under the following article headings are pairs of words or phrases separated by a slanted line. Decide if the author suggests each comparison listed under each heading through information and ideas from that section. Be ready to give evidence from the article to support your decision.

The Influence of Opinion

1. fact/opinion
2. accuracy/inaccuracy
3. strength/weakness

Freedom of the Press

4. risk/safety
5. action without authority/authority without action
6. courage/safety
7. use/abuse

The Sedition Act

8. danger in vagueness/safety in preciseness
9. minor annoyance/major danger

The Muckrakers

10. inform/reform
11. a powerful few/a powerful public
12. abuse/conformity

Libel and Slander Laws

13. reporter/source
14. danger in caution/safety in risk
15. criticism/conformity

Protection of Sources

16. public/private
17. volunteering/ordering

Apply the Ideas

Courage and freedom of the press are related in many ways. Below are some statements that deal with *courage* and with the *press*. Decide which ones you can support from the article and from other sources.

1. Courage is shown in many ways other than the physical.
2. You can have freedom without showing courage but you can't keep it that way.
3. Rights must be protected because there is always someone ready to take them away.
4. A free society requires a free press.
5. A free press must be run by people with a need to find the truth and the courage to reveal it.

Courage and Investigative Journalists

Anticipate the Facts

Now that you have explored many ideas related to courage and freedom of the press, find out how some real investigative journalists put that freedom to work. Read the four biographical sketches in the next section to see how the investigative reporters exhibited courage. Pay particular attention to the character traits each needed to test his or her courage and how each took advantage of an opportunity to be responsible for protecting freedom.

Nellie Bly

Nellie Bly was one of the first women reporters. Born Elizabeth Cochrane in Pennsylvania on May 5, 1867, she took her pen name from the song written by Stephen Foster.

In 1885, she took her first job as a reporter. She was offered a position on the Pittsburgh *Dispatch* after writing a letter to the editor supporting women's rights. She began her investigative reporting by posing as a factory worker. From firsthand experiences, she then wrote an article about how difficult the life of a factory worker was, especially for a woman.

In 1887, she went to work for Joseph Pulitzer's New York *World*. To get another firsthand story, she pretended to go out of her mind. She was then committed to the mental hospital on Blackwell's Island in New York. After spending several days there, she got out and wrote her story. It exposed the appalling conditions in the hospital and led to an official investigation and eventual reforms. Nellie Bly also investigated and reported on women's prisons, free medical clinics, and bribery in the state legislature. All her newspaper reports led to various reforms.

Nellie Bly was a reporter for the New York *Journal* at the time of her death on January 27, 1922.

Ida Tarbell

Ida Tarbell was one of the first investigative reporters. She and other journalists wrote about the political, economic, and social wrongs in the early 1900's. President Theodore Roosevelt gave these writers the name "muckraker." Ida Tarbell accepted the title as a mark of honor, for she thoroughly researched her subjects and carefully documented her findings.

Ida Tarbell was born in Pennsylvania on November 5, 1857. Her schooling included a college education, which was unusual for a woman at that time. After graduating from Allegheny College, she became head of a private school, where she also taught eight subjects. When her contract expired, she began writing magazine and newspaper articles and books. She wrote biographies of Manon Roland (a leader of the French Revolution), Napoleon Bonaparte, and Abraham Lincoln. Her most famous work, however, was *The History of the Standard Oil Company*, an ex-

posé of the corrupt business practices of the oil industry.

When she began investigating the Standard Oil Company, she expected that her findings would fill about three articles. The first installment appeared in *McClure's Magazine* in November 1902. By the time she had finished her investigation, she had written eighteen installments, the last of which appeared in October 1904. The articles were later combined into a two-volume book of 554 pages. Her research was thorough and her information accurate. She exposed the company's power and the corrupt practices it followed to achieve that power. Because of her findings, the movement to end the powerful monopolies was greatly strengthened. In 1911, the Supreme Court of the United States won its case to break the Standard Oil Company monopoly.

Geraldo Rivera

Geraldo Miguel Rivera, award-winning television journalist and talk-show host, was born in New York City on July 3, 1943. He pursued his education through journalism and law schools and received degrees from the University of Arizona, Brooklyn Law School, and Columbia University.

Geraldo Rivera is well known for his compassionate investigative reports on WABC-TV *Eyewitness News*. He has done exposés of New York City's welfare hotels, the overpricing of prescription drugs, and drug abuse. In 1971, he received the Associated Press Broadcaster of the Year award for the program *Drug Crisis in East Harlem*. He received the award again in 1972 for the program *Migrants, Dirt Cheap*.

His most famous exposé however was done on the horrible conditions at Staten Island's Willowbrook State School. It is the world's largest institution for the mentally disabled. His investigation began when he and his camera crew gained access to one of the buildings. Geraldo's emotionally charged reports exposed the unsanitary conditions and neglectful, often abusive, treatment of the patients. He cried over what he discovered, and he made his viewers cry, too. The programs created a public plea for reform, and changes were made. Governor Nelson Rockefeller of New York restored $20 million to the school's slashed budget. The programs—*Willowbrook: The Last Great Disgrace* and *The Willowbrook Case: The People Versus the State of New York*—earned him the Scripps-Howard Award, an Emmy, and the Robert F. Kennedy Journalism Award.

Geraldo Rivera has continued working for the mentally disabled. He founded One-to-One, a charity that provides small group homes for the care of the mentally disabled in the community. He hosts huge outdoor festivals for the mentally disabled in New York City's Central Park. He also wrote a book about some of the courageous people he has met as an investigative journalist. It is called *A Special Kind of Courage* (New York: Simon and Schuster, 1976). As he himself says, "I make no pretense of objectivity. But I'm not just in the business of making people cry. I'm in the business of change."

Woodward and Bernstein

Robert Woodward and Carl Bernstein became famous for their investigative reporting of the burglary and illegal bugging of the Democratic National Committee's headquarters in the Watergate office building.

"There are only two similarities between me and Woodward, and the rest is all different," said Carl Bernstein. "One thing is that neither of us ever takes 'no' for an answer. And the other is that we usually made up our own assignments."

Bob Woodward got a late start as a reporter. After graduating from Yale, he served in the Navy. Then he went to Harvard Law School but dropped out. At the age of twenty-seven, he got his first newspaper job with the *Montgomery County Sentinel*. There he covered only local news, such as PTA and civic group meetings. A year later, Woodward began his career as an investigative reporter when he took a job with the *Washington Post*. After covering his scheduled assignments, Woodward did more work on his own time. He investigated frauds in Medicaid, prescription drugs, and meat pricing. He also investigated health and housing violations, narcotics smuggling, and police corruption.

Woodward's long hours paid off. He got more front-page stories with his by-line than any other *Post* reporter. He worked hard, followed the advice of his editors, and got his stories on the front page.

Carl Bernstein began his career as a reporter at age sixteen. He carried copy and ran errands at the *Washington Star*. By the age of nineteen, he was a full-fledged reporter and was hired by the *Washington Post*. Like Bob Woodward,

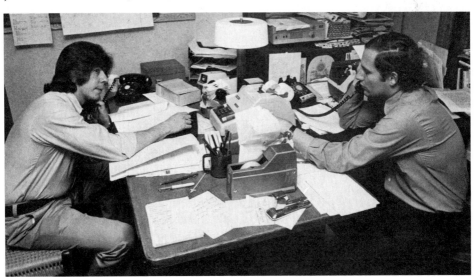

Left: Carl Bernstein   Right: Bob Woodward

he investigated such subjects as slum landlords, narcotics, fraudulent career schools, and corruption in police departments and in the courts. His methods of work, however, were completely different from Woodward's. Bernstein worked odd hours and did stories only on subjects that interested him. He took little advice from his editors or more experienced reporters and frequently disobeyed orders. He did, however, write front-page stories.

When the Watergate break-in was discovered, Bob Woodward was assigned to cover the story. Carl Bernstein was interested in the investigation and assigned himself to the story. Suspicious of the official story, they began a lengthy, painstaking investigation. They ran into opposition everywhere they turned. Nobody would talk to them. The few people who did talk made the reporters promise not to use their names because they were afraid of losing their jobs.

Even the *Washington Post* presented obstacles. The management tried to take Woodward and Bernstein off the investigation and would not print anything that had not been confirmed by two separate sources. After putting in full days at the office, Woodward and Bernstein spent their evenings interviewing everyone they could get hold of who might give them some information. By piecing together scraps of information, they linked the break-in to the White House. This eventually led to Richard Nixon's resignation from the presidency.

For their reporting, Bob Woodward and Carl Bernstein won the Pulitzer prize. The story of their investigative efforts was made into a book and a movie, both entitled *All the President's Men.*

Analyze the Character Traits

Journalists have had a very special place in American history since the Bill of Rights assured freedom of the press. The journalists you just read about exhibited courage to make that freedom work to benefit humanity. Listed below are the names of the investigative reporters from the selection. Also listed are character traits commonly associated with effective journalists. Discuss each journalist and decide which character traits he or she possessed. Be sure to give your reasons for assigning traits to the different reporters.

1. Nellie Bly
2. Ida Tarbell
3. Woodward and Bernstein
4. Geraldo Rivera

a. objectivity
b. persistence
c. ambition/drive
d. nerve/guts
e. compassion/concern

The statements below describe some of the actions taken by the investigative reporters. Decide first which reporter(s) the statement applies to and second which character trait is exhibited by the action. Since each statement may apply to more than one reporter and more than one character trait, be sure you can support your choices with evidence from the selections.

1. got committed to a mental institution in order to do firsthand reports on conditions there
2. overcame a great deal of opposition to expose corruption in government
3. wrote thorough and accurate exposés of corrupt business practices.
4. worked on stories that dealt with important issues on his/her own time
5. aroused the public to correct a wrong
6. thoroughly investigated the facts before reporting them
7. stood up against government and big business to fight for the "little person"

Apply the Ideas

Investigative reporters need special kinds of courage and other qualities to do their jobs effectively. Below are some ideas that relate those qualities to different situations that reporters confront. Decide which statements you agree or disagree with. Then decide which of the investigative reporters would agree with you. Give reasons from the selection and your own sources for your decisions.

1. It is more difficult to report a story accurately than it is to report it sympathetically.
2. The public needs to know when something is wrong before anything can be done to correct it.
3. If at first you don't succeed—try, try again.
4. The only way to do a good story is from firsthand experience.
5. Getting information for a story is easy because people are open and truthful with reporters so that they can see their names in print.
6. Reporters need more courage to fight a powerful organization than they do to put themselves in situations in which they might get hurt physically.

FOLLOW-THROUGH

In this unit on courage and cowardice, you have read about:

1. the courage shown by a young man as he proved to himself that he was not a coward;
2. the courage shown by a young man as he fought his worst enemy and won;
3. the way the body prepares for action, whether based on courage or cowardice;
4. how a common fear affected one person;
5. a special kind of courage needed to meet everyday obstacles;
6. how four real people found the courage to overcome obstacles in their own lives;
7. how the courage of news reporters makes a free press really free and really important.

Here are the people and characters you read about in this unit:

Mafatu	"Babe" Didrickson Zaharias	Ida Tarbell
Nathan	Stevie Wonder	Geraldo Rivera
a Mother	Rachel Carson	Bob Woodward
Jill Kinmont	Nellie Bly	Carl Bernstein

Review the different kinds of courage that you discussed at the beginning of this unit. For each person or character listed above, identify which kind of courage he or she showed.

Following are some ideas about courage and cowardice. Decide which of the characters and people listed above would agree or disagree with each statement. Discuss the reasons for your decisions.

1. Acts do not have to have an audience to be courageous; courage can be quiet and private.
2. Courageous people don't necessarily plan to be; they just are when they have to be.
3. Courage involves being able to ask for help as well as being able to stand alone.

4. Courage involves both jumping into a situation and withdrawing from it as well as having the good sense to know when each is appropriate.
5. Courage is resistance to fear, mastery of fear—not the absence of fear.

Putting Your Knowledge to Work

Following are some ideas for activities that will give you opportunity to use what you have learned in this unit. Choose one or more that you would like to do alone or with a group.

1. Write your own biographical sketches about people who showed courage by coping with physical disabilities. Here are some people you might want to research: Helen Keller, Bob Mathias, Lou Gehrig, Ernie Davis, Wilma Rudolph, Rocky Bleier, Roy Campanella, Brian Piccolo, and others.
2. Read about other investigative reporters and the subjects of their investigations. Here is a good source:

   Levy, Elizabeth. *By-Lines: Profiles in Investigative Journalism.* New York: Four Winds Press, 1975.

3. Set up categories of courage based on the types of courage you discussed at the beginning of this unit. Then collect both fictional stories and factual articles from books, newspapers, and magazines which illustrate the various categories. If you wish, use the stories and articles to plan a series of TV programs about courage.
4. Do your own investigative reporting on some famous people in history. Your report should include important facts about the people, but it need not be objective. Include your own opinions on whether the people were courageous or cowardly. Analyze your subject's actions in terms of the kind of courage he or she displayed or the reasons he or she acted cowardly.

Here are some books about courage and cowardice you might enjoy:

Aiken, Joan. *Go Saddle the Sea.* Garden City, N.Y.: Doubleday and Co., Inc., 1977.
   Felix runs away to England to find his father.
Corcoran, Barbara. *The Faraway Island.* New York: Atheneum Publishers, 1977.
   Grandmother's senility allows Lynn to avoid school.
Gill, Derek L. T. *Tom Sullivan's Adventures in Darkness.* David McKay Co., Inc., 1976.
   Blind since birth, Tom becomes a successful composer-singer.
Haskins, James. *The Life and Death of Martin Luther King, Jr.* New York: Lothrop, Lee and Shepard Co., 1977.
   Real-life courage is needed in the civil rights movement.
Stambler, Irwin. *Women in Sports.* Garden City, N.Y.: Doubleday and Co., Inc., 1975.
   This book includes factual accounts of women who have struggled to excel in sports.

Winning and Losing

four

"The most important thing in the Olympic Games is not to win but to take part, just as the most important thing in life is not the triumph but the struggle. The essential thing is not to have conquered but to have fought well."

—Baron De Coubertin
Founder of the Modern Olympic Games

"Winning isn't everything; it's the only *thing."*

—Vince Lombardi
Coach, Green Bay Packers

"When the One Great Scorer comes to write against your name, he marks—not that you have won or lost, but how you played the game."

—Grantland Rice

These quotations express different viewpoints on the importance of winning and losing. Read the selections in this unit to see if you find expressions of these three viewpoints. You may find other viewpoints as well.

Key Concepts

winning   (a) gaining the victory in a contest or battle;   (b) succeeding by striving or effort;   (c) attaining or reaching a goal; (d) persuading.

losing   (a) failing to win a contest or battle;   (b) suffering the loss of something;   (c) failing to keep, preserve, or maintain; (d) bringing to destruction or ruin.

Getting in Touch with Your Experiences

The ideas of *winning* and *losing* are usually related to sports, but there are many other situations in which winning and losing are possible. Work with others in your group to list as many situations as you can think of from your own experience in which winning and/or losing might take place. Here are some ideas to get you started.

an election
a game of chess
? ? ?

Now that you have listed a variety of situations in which winning and/or losing may take place, read the following statements. Discuss each statement with other members of your group and decide whether or not you can agree with it on the basis of your own experiences.

- If you don't compete, you can't lose—but you can't win either.
- In order for there to be a winner, there must be a loser.
- Learning how to lose is as important as learning how to win.
- It's possible to win and lose at the same time.
- There are always more losers than winners.
- Winning is always positive; losing is always negative.
- What may seem like a win to one person may seem like a loss to someone else.
- Winning and losing can be predicted with a range of accuracy.
- There's a balance in nature, and winning and losing are part of that balance.

All the reading selections in this unit have something to do, either directly or indirectly, with winning and/or losing. As you read them, keep in mind the ideas you have just discussed to see how they relate to the various selections.

Winning and Losing in Literature

The story you are about to read tells about winning and losing from a personal point of view. The narrator, or storyteller, is a character in the story. Squeaky tells her own actions, thoughts, and feelings using *I*, the first-person pronoun. She seems very real because she uses her own conversational style.

Anticipate the Author's Point of View

There are several different *points of view* from which an author may choose to write a story.

In the *first-person point of view,* the narrator (storyteller) is a character in the story. The character tells his or her own actions, thoughts, and feelings using first-person pronouns, such as *I* and *me.* For example, in *Sing Down the Moon,* Bright Morning told her own story:

> "Running Bird and I crawled to our places near the piñon tree . . ." (pages 65–71)

In the *third-person point of view,* the narrator is an outsider, or third person, telling a story *about* the characters. The narrator calls the characters by name and/or uses third-person pronouns, such as *he* or *she*. For example, in "The Woods-Devil," the author wrote about Nathan:

> "Nathan fetched it and put a keen, shining edge on it with a whetstone. Then he ran a greased rag through each of the rifle barrels." (pages 161–173)

The third-person point of view can be treated in two ways. The narrator can be an *objective reporter* who simply describes the actions of the characters in the story, as in the example above from "The Woods-Devil." Or, the narrator can be an *omniscient* (all-knowing) *presence* who describes not only the actions, but also the thoughts and feelings of the characters. For example, in *Call It Courage,* the author described Mafatu's thoughts as well as his actions:

"This day as Mafatu climbed the rough trail through the jungle, he was preoccupied, lost in his thoughts . . . he was thinking about the rigging of his canoe, planning how he could strengthen it here, tighten it there." (pages 144–147)

As you read the stories in this book, consider the possible points of view:

- The narrator may be a story character telling his or her own story, or the narrator may be an outsider telling *about* the characters.
- The narrator may be an outsider, telling the story objectively (describing what the characters do) or omnisciently (describing what the characters think, feel, and do).

Raymond's Run
by Toni Cade Bambara

I don't have much work to do around the house like some girls. My mother does that. And I don't have to earn my pocket money by running errands and selling Christmas cards. George does that. And anything else that's got to get done, my father does. All I have to do in life is mind my brother Raymond, which is enough.

Sometimes I slip and say my little brother Raymond. But as any fool can see, he's much bigger and he's older too. But a lot of people call him my little brother 'cause he needs looking after 'cause he's not quite right. And a lot of smart mouths got lots to say about that too, especially when George was minding him. But now, if anybody has anything to say to Raymond, anything to say about his big head, they have to come by me. And I don't play the dozens or believe in standing around with somebody in my face doing a lot of talking. I much rather just knock you down and take my chances even if I am a little girl with skinny arms and a squeaky voice, which is how I got the name Squeaky. And if things get too rough, I run. And as anybody can tell you, I'm the fastest thing on two feet.

There is no track meet that I don't win the first-place medal. I use to win the twenty-yard (about eighteen meters) dash when I was a little kid in kindergarten. Nowadays it's the fifty-yard (about forty-five meters) dash. And tomorrow I'm subject to the quarter-mile (about 400 meters) relay all by myself and come in first, second, and third. The big kids call me Mercury 'cause I'm the swiftest thing in the neighborhood. Everybody knows that—except two people who know better, my father and me.

He can beat me to Amsterdam Avenue with me having a headstart of two fire hydrants and him running with his hands in his pockets and whistling. But that's private information. 'Cause can you imagine some thirty-five-year-old man stuffing himself into PAL shorts to race little kids? So far as everyone's concerned, I'm the fastest and that goes for Gretchen, too, who has put out the tale that she is going to win the first-place medal this year. Ridiculous. In the second place, she's got short legs. In the third place, she's got freckles. In the first place, no one can beat me, and that's all there is to it.

I'm standing on the corner admiring the weather and about to take a stroll down Broadway so I can practice my breathing exercises, and I've got Raymond walking on the inside close to the buildings 'cause he's subject to fits of fantasy and starts thinking he's a circus performer and that the curb is a tightrope strung high in the air. And sometimes after a rain, he likes to step down off the tightrope right into the gutter and slosh around getting his shoes and cuffs wet. Then I get hit when I get home. Or sometimes if you don't watch him, he'll dash across traffic to the island in the middle of Broadway and give the pigeons a fit. Then I have to go behind him apologizing to all the people sitting around trying

218

to get some sun and getting all upset with the pigeons fluttering around them, scattering their newspapers and upsetting the wax-paper lunches in their laps. So I keep Raymond on the inside of me, and he plays like he's driving a stagecoach which is OK by me so long as he doesn't run me over or interrupt my breathing exercises, which I have to do on account of I'm serious about my running and don't care who knows it.

Now, some people like to act like things come easy to them, won't let on that they practice. Not me. I'll high prance down 34th Street like a rodeo pony to keep my knees strong even if it does get my mother so uptight that she walks ahead like she's not with me, don't know me, is all by herself on a shopping trip, and I am somebody else's crazy child.

Now, you take Cynthia Procter, for instance. She's just the opposite. If there's a test tomorrow, she'll say something like, "Oh, I guess I'll play handball this afternoon and watch television to-night," just to let you know she ain't thinking about the test. Or like last week when she won the spelling bee for the millionth time, "A good thing you got *receive* Squeaky, 'cause I would have got it wrong. I completely forgot about the spelling bee." And she'll clutch the collar on her blouse like it was a narrow escape. Oh, brother.

But of course when I pass her house on my early morning

trots around the block, she is practicing the scales on the piano over and over and over and over. Then in music class, she always lets herself get bumped around so she falls accidently on purpose onto the piano stool and is so surprised to find herself sitting there and so decides just for fun to try out the ole keys, and what do you know—Chopin's waltzes just spring out of her fingertips, and she's the most surprised thing in the world. A regular prodigy. I could kill people like that.

I stay up all night studying the words for the spelling bee. And you can see me anytime of the day practicing running. I never walk if I can trot and shame on Raymond if he can't keep up. But of course he does, 'cause if he hangs back, someone's liable to walk up to him and get smart or take his allowance from him or ask him where he got that great big pumpkin head. People are so stupid sometimes.

So I'm strolling down Broadway breathing out and breathing in on counts of seven, which is my lucky number, and here comes Gretchen and her sidekicks—Mary Louise, who used to be a friend of mine when she first moved to Harlem from Baltimore and got beat up by everybody till I took up for her on account of her mother

and my mother used to sing in the same choir when they were
young girls, but people ain't grateful, so now she hangs out with
the new girl Gretchen and talks about me like a dog; and Rosie,
who is as fat as I am skinny and has a big mouth where Raymond
is concerned and is too stupid to know that there is not a big deal
of difference between herself and Raymond that she can't afford
to throw stones. So they are steady coming up Broadway, and I
see right away that it's going to be one of those Dodge City scenes
'cause the street ain't that big and they're close to the buildings
just as we are. First I think I'll step into the candy store and look
over the new comics and let them pass. But that's chicken, and I've
got a reputation to consider. So then I think I'll just walk straight
on through them or over them if necessary. But as they get to me,
they slow down. I'm ready to fight, 'cause, like I said, I don't feature
a whole lot of chitchat. I much prefer to just knock you down right
from the jump and save everybody a lotta precious time.

"You signing up for the May Day races?" smiles Mary Louise,
only it's not a smile at all.

A dumb question like that doesn't deserve an answer. Besides,
there's just me and Gretchen standing there really, so no use wasting
my breath talking to shadows.

"I don't think you're going to win this time," says Rosie, trying to signify with her hands on her hips all salty, completely forgetting that I have whupped her many times for less salt than that.

"I always win 'cause I'm the best," I say straight at Gretchen who is, as far as I'm concerned, the only one talking in this ventriloquist-dummy routine.

Gretchen smiles, but it is not a smile, and I'm thinking that girls never really smile at each other because they don't know how and don't want to know how and there's probably no one to teach us how 'cause grown-up girls don't know either. Then they all look at Raymond, who has just brought his mule team to a standstill. And they're about to see what kind of trouble they can get into through him.

"What grade you in now, Raymond?" asks Mary Louise.

"You got anything to say to my brother, you say it to me, Mary Louise Williams of Raggedy Town, Baltimore."

"What are you, his mother?" sasses Rosie.

"That's right, Fatso. And the next word out of anybody and I'll be their mother too." So they just stand there, and Gretchen shifts from one leg to the other and so do they. Then Gretchen puts her hands on her hips and is about to say something with her freckle-face self but doesn't. Then she walks around me, looking me up and down, but keeps walking up Broadway, and her sidekicks follow her. So me and Raymond smile at each other, and he says, "Gidyap" to his team, and I continue with my breathing exercises, strolling down Broadway toward 145th with not a care in the world 'cause I am Miss Quicksilver herself.

I take my time getting to the park on May Day because the track meet is the last thing on the program. The biggest thing on the program is the maypole dancing, which I can do without, thank you, even if my mother thinks it's a shame I don't take part and act like a girl for a change. You'd think my mother'd be grateful not to have to make me a white organdy dress with a big satin sash and buy me new white baby-doll shoes that can't be taken out of the box until the big day. You'd think she'd be glad her daughter ain't out there prancing around a maypole, getting the new clothes all dirty and sweaty and trying to act like a butterfly or a flower or whatever you're supposed to be when you should be trying to be yourself, whatever that is, which is, as far as I'm concerned, a poor black girl who really can't afford to buy shoes and a new dress you only wear once a lifetime 'cause it won't fit next year.

I was once a strawberry in a Hansel and Gretel pageant when I was in nursery school and didn't have no better sense than to dance on tiptoe with my arms in a circle over my head, doing umbrella steps and being a perfect fool just so my mother and father could come dressed up and clap. You'd think they'd know better than to encourage that kind of nonsense. I am not a strawberry. I do not dance on my toes. I run. That is what I am all about. So I always come late to the May Day program, just in time to get my number pinned on and lay in the grass till they announce the fifty-yard (about forty-five meters) dash.

I put Raymond in the little swing, which is a tight squeeze this year and will be impossible next year. Then I look around for Mr. Pearson, who pins the numbers on. I'm really looking for Gretchen, if you want to know the truth, but she's not around. The park is jam-packed. Parents in hats and corsages and breast-pocket handkerchiefs peeking up. Kids in white dresses and light-blue suits. The parkees unfolding chairs and chasing the rowdy kids from Lenox as if they had no right to be there. The big guys with their caps on backwards, leaning against the fence, swirling the basketballs on the tips of their fingers, waiting for all these crazy people to clear out of the park so they can play. Most of the kids in my class are carrying bass drums and glockenspiels and flutes. You'd think they'd put in a few bongos or something for real like that.

Then here comes Mr. Pearson with his clipboard and his cards and pencils and whistles and safety pins and fifty million other things he's always dropping all over the place. He sticks out in a crowd 'cause he's on stilts. We used to called him Jack and

the Beanstalk to get him mad. But I'm the only one that can out-run him and get away, and I'm too grown for that silliness now.

"Well, Squeaky," he says, checking my name off the list and handing me number seven and two pins. And I'm thinking he's got no right to call me Squeaky if I can't call him Beanstalk.

"Hazel Elizabeth Deborah Parker," I correct him and tell him to write it down on his board.

"Well, Hazel Elizabeth Deborah Parker, going to give some-one else a break this year?" I squint at him real hard to see if he is seriously thinking I should lose the race on purpose just to give someone else a break.

"Only six girls running this time," he continues, shaking his head sadly like it's my fault all of New York didn't turn out in sneakers. "That new girl should give you a run for your money." He looks around the park for Gretchen like a periscope in a sub-marine movie. "Wouldn't it be a nice gesture if you were . . . to ahhh . . ."

I gave him such a look he couldn't finish putting that idea into words. Grown-ups got a lot of nerve sometimes. I pin number seven to myself and stomp away—I'm so burnt. And I go straight for the track and stretch out on the grass while the band winds up with "Oh, the Monkey Wrapped His Tail Around the Flag Pole," which my teacher calls by some other name. The man on the loudspeaker is calling everyone over to the track, and I'm on my back looking at the sky trying to pretend I'm in the country, but I can't, because even grass in the city feels hard as sidewalk, and there's just no pretending you are anywhere but in a "concrete jungle" as my grandfather says.

The twenty-yard (about twenty meters) dash takes all of the two minutes 'cause most of the little kids don't know no better than to run off the track or run the wrong way or run smack into the fence and fall down and cry. One little kid, though, has got the good sense to run straight for the white ribbon up ahead, so he wins. Then the second graders line up for the thirty-yard (about thirty meters) dash, and I don't even bother to turn my head to watch 'cause Raphael Perez always wins. He wins before he even begins by psyching the runners, telling them they're going to trip on their shoelaces and fall on their faces or lose their shorts or something, which he doesn't really have to do since he is very fast, almost as fast as I am. After that is the forty-yard (about forty meters) dash, which I use to run when I was in first grade. Raymond is hollering from the swings 'cause he knows I'm about to do my thing 'cause the man on the loudspeaker has just announced the fifty-yard (about forty-five meters) dash, although he must just as well be giving a recipe for angel food cake 'cause you can hardly make out what he's saying for the static. I get up and slip off my sweat pants, and then I see Gretchen standing at the starting line kicking her legs out like a pro. Then as I get into place, I see that ole Raymond is in line on the other side of the fence, bending down with his fingers on the ground just like he knew what he was doing. I was going to yell at him, but then I didn't. It burns up your energy to holler.

Every time, just before I take off in a race, I always feel like I'm in a dream, the kind of dream you have when you're sick with a fever and feel all hot and weightless. I dream I'm flying over a sandy beach in the early morning sun, kissing the leaves of the trees as I fly by. And there's always the smell of apples, just like in the country when I was little and use to think I was a choo-choo train, running through the fields of corn and chugging up the hill to the orchard. And all the time I'm dreaming this, I get lighter and lighter until I'm flying over the beach again, getting blown through the sky like a feather that weighs nothing at all. But once I spread my fingers in the dirt and crouch over for the Get on Your Mark, the dream goes, and I am solid again and am telling myself, "Squeaky, you must win, you must win, you are the fastest thing in the world; you can even beat your father up Amsterdam if you really try." And then I feel my weight coming back just behind my knees, then down to my feet then into the earth, and the pistol shot explodes in my blood, and I am off and weightless again, flying past the other runners, my arms pumping up and down, and the whole world is quiet except for the crunch as I zoom over the gravel in the track. I glance to my left, and there is no one. To the right a blurred Gretchen who's got her chin jutting out as if it would win the race all by itself. And on the other side of the fence is Raymond with his arms down to his side and the palms tucked up behind him, running in his very own style, and the first time I ever saw that I almost stop to watch my brother Raymond on his first run. But the white ribbon is bouncing toward me, and I tear past it, racing into the distance till my feet with a mind of their own start digging up footfuls of dirt and brake me

short. Then all the kids standing on the side pile on me, banging me on the back and slapping my head with their May Day programs, for I have won again and everybody on 151st Street can walk tall for another year.

"In first place . . ." the man on the loudspeaker is clear as a bell now. But then he pauses, and the loudspeaker starts to whine. Then static. And I lean down to catch my breath, and here comes Gretchen walking back for she's overshot the finish line too, huffing and puffing with her hands on her hips, taking it slow, breathing in steady time like a real pro, and I sort of like her a little for the first time. "In first place . . ." and then three or four voices get all mixed up on the loudspeaker, and I dig my sneaker into the

grass and stare at Gretchen, who's staring back, we both wondering just who did win. I can hear old Beanstalk arguing with the man on the loudspeaker and then a few others running their mouths about what the stopwatches say.

Then I hear Raymond yanking at the fence to call me, and I wave to shush him, but he keeps rattling the fence like a gorilla in a cage like in them gorilla movies. But then like a dancer or something, he starts climbing up, nice and easy but very fast. And it occurs to me, watching how smoothly he climbs hand over hand and remembering how he looked running with his arms down to his side and with the wind pulling his mouth back and his teeth showing and all, it occurred to me that Raymond would make a very fine runner. Doesn't he always keep up with me on my trots? And he surely knows how to breathe in counts of seven 'cause he's always doing it at the dinner table, which drives my brother George up the wall. And I'm smiling to beat the band 'cause if I've lost the race, or if me and Gretchen tied, or even if I've won, I can always retire as a runner and begin a whole new career as a coach with Raymond as my champion. After all, with a little more study I can beat Cynthia and her phony self at the spelling bee. And if I bugged my mother, I could get piano lessons and become a

star. And I have a big rep as the baddest thing around. And I've got a roomful of ribbons and medals and awards. But what has Raymond got to call his own?

So I stand there with my new plan, laughing out loud by this time, as Raymond jumps down from the fence and runs over with his teeth showing and his arms down to the side, which no one before him has quite mastered as a running style. And by the time he comes over, I'm jumping up and down so glad to see him—my brother Raymond, a great runner in the family tradition. But of course everyone thinks I'm jumping up and down because the men on the loudspeaker have finally gotten themselves together and compared notes and are announcing, "In first place— Miss Hazel Elizabeth Deborah Parker." (Dig that.) "In second place— Miss Gretchen P. Lewis." And I look over at Gretchen, wondering what the *P* stands for. And I smile. 'Cause she's good, no doubt about it. Maybe she'd like to help me coach Raymond; she obviously is serious about running, as any fool can see. And she nods to congratulate me, and then she smiles. And I smile. We stand there with this big smile of respect between us. It's about as real a smile as girls can do for each other, considering we don't practice real smiling every day, you know, 'cause maybe we too busy being flowers or butterflies or strawberries instead of something honest and worthy of respect . . . you know . . . like being people.

Read the statements below. Discuss each statement with other members of your group and decide if it gives you the same information that you find in the story. Be ready to discuss the evidence to support your choices.

1. Squeaky, Mercury, Miss Quicksilver, and Hazel Elizabeth Deborah Parker are all the same person.
2. Raymond is older than his sister but needs care because of a disability.
3. Squeaky seems ready to pick a fight at any time.
4. All friendships are lasting.
5. Raymond runs with Squeaky while she practices.
6. Raymond drives a mule team.
7. Mr. Pearson makes a suggestion that Squeaky considers nervy.
8. Squeaky is more excited by Raymond's run than by her own win.
9. Squeaky realizes that Raymond needs success more than she does.
10. Squeaky decides not to help Raymond in the future.
11. Squeaky discovers the importance of mutual respect.

Interpret and Apply the Ideas

First, decide whether or not each of the following statements expresses an idea that can be supported by information in the story. Then, decide if you agree with the statement on the basis of your own experiences.

1. You can care *for* a person without really caring *about* that person.
2. Girls don't respect each other as people.
3. There's more to life than winning.
4. Every person can achieve in his or her own way if given the chance.
5. Losers can be winners if conditions are right.

Winning and Losing in Poetry

The poem "The Sprinters" is about persons struggling against time. Can a person beat time? Will time always be faster? What feelings come as people struggle against time?

Expand Your Vocabulary

Before you read the poem, note the definitions of these words:

pummeling   pounding rapidly
pistoning   pumping up and down
outpace   to move faster than someone or something else
mock   to make fun of something or someone

Knowing the vocabulary in a poem is just part of the total understanding. First read the poem silently to get the sense of it. Then read the poem aloud to get the feeling of it. See if reading the poem aloud gives you a feeling of speed.

The Sprinters

by Lillian Morrison

The gun explodes them.
Pummeling, pistoning they fly
In time's face.
A go at the limit,
A terrible try
To smash the ticking glass,
Outpace the beat
That runs, that streaks away
Tireless, and faster than they.

Beside ourselves
(It is for us they run!)
We shout and pound the stands
For one to win,
Loving him, whose hard
Grace-driven stride
Most mocks the clock
And almost breaks the bands
Which lock us in.

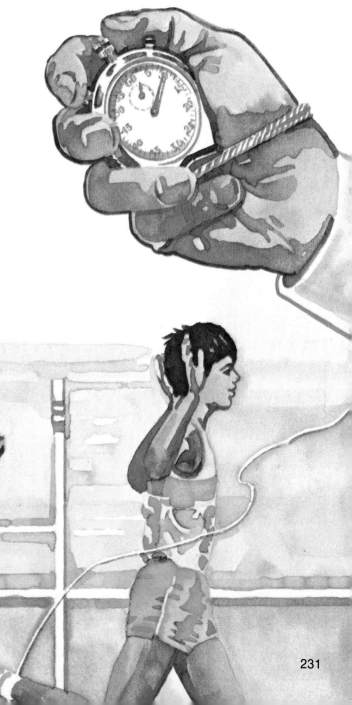

Analyze the Imagery

Some of the items listed below refer to runners, others refer to watchers, and others refer to time. Read each item and decide whether it refers to runners, watchers, or time. Discuss your decisions with your group.

1. the gun explodes them
2. they fly in time's faces
3. the ticking glass
4. try to smash
5. the beat that runs
6. the beat that streaks away
7. tireless
8. pound the stands
9. loving him
10. grace-driven stride
11. mocks the clock
12. the bands which lock us in

Apply the Ideas

First, decide whether or not each of the following statements expresses an idea that can be supported by information in the poem. Then, decide if you agree with the statement on the basis of your own experiences.

1. Time is a barrier to be broken.
2. No matter how fast a person moves, time is always faster.
3. People love winners more than losers.
4. Records are made to be broken.
5. All human beings, not only runners, have limits to what they can do.

The Motion Factor
in Winning and Losing

Know the Background

Almost three hundred years ago, Isaac Newton discovered a scientific law that explains why these things happen:

1. You release the air from a balloon. The air shoots one way, and the balloon flies the opposite way.
2. You swim in a pool. You push forward with your hands against the side of the pool. You move backwards toward the center of the pool.
3. You ride a scooter. You push backward with one foot while the other foot is on the scooter. You move forward.

The scientific principle that Newton discovered is called the Third Law of Motion. This says: For every action there is an equal and opposite reaction.

Let's see how that law operates in the three experiences listed above.

1. Having filled a balloon with air, you release the nozzle. The air escapes, moving out and away from the balloon. That is the *action.* The balloon shoots through the air in the opposite direction. That is the *reaction,* equal and opposite to the action.
2. Floating in a pool, you reach out and push forward against the side. That is the *action.* Your body moves backwards toward the center of the pool. That is the *reaction,* equal and opposite to the action.
3. Standing on the scooter with one foot, you push back against the ground with the other foot. That backward push is the *action.* You and the scooter move forward. That is the *reaction.* The reaction is equal to the action and is in the opposite direction.

Remember Newton's Third Law of Motion: For every action there is an equal and opposite reaction. In each of these experiences, *action* brought *reaction* and together they produced *motion.*

Set Your Purposes

The article you will read next explains how scientists use Newton's Third Law of Motion to produce rockets and how those rockets work. Some technical words are used in the article. Study the diagram that follows and see how many of the technical words you or other members of your group already know. The diagram shows how the words relate to one another in the article. Use the glossary to find the meanings of any unfamiliar words. Then read the article to find out how rockets work. While you're reading, consider how Newton's Third Law of Motion relates to winning and losing.

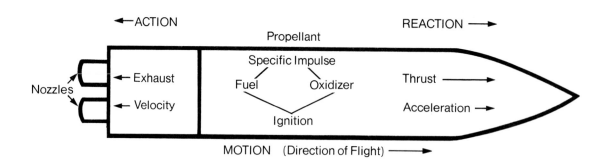

ROCKET TALK

by Harold L. Goodwin

1   Rockets come in all sizes, from the giant Saturn V to tiny jets hardly bigger than a drinking straw. Any rocket is interesting and often exciting, but there is one that also promises to be wonderful fun for the pilot. This rocket is designed to carry one person through the air for short distances.

2   Imagine a person able to rise higher than the treetops, to soar like a wingless bird over hills, streams, even buildings. Then, just by turning a handle, he or she can settle gently to earth again. All this is possible with a fascinating invention, hardly larger than a life jacket, called a rocket belt.

3   The rocket belt looks like a padded vest with heavy rings for armholes and two wide belts that lash around the waist. There are two steel tanks on the back and a handgrip extending over each shoulder. Turning the left handgrip lets the pilot rise into the air, higher than the tops of trees. Turning the right handgrip lets him or her speed ahead, like a wingless bird. By controlling the right grip and body motions, the

pilot can come to a stop in the air. Then, by regulating the thrust with the left hand, the pilot can come back to earth gently.

1 To understand how such a rocket belt works, it is necessary to know a little about the principles common to all rockets, whatever their size.

2 A rocket engine may be thought of as a special kind of furnace in which fuels are burned very rapidly at very high temperatures. The burning fuel creates hot gases. The hot gases then expand and push against the inside of the engine.

3 Imagine a steel cylinder with no openings except two tiny ones where fuel and oxygen enter. The fuel burns and gas is formed. This gas expands, pushing equally in all directions. Pressure becomes so great that, unless it is relieved, the cylinder will burst.

4 But before the steel cylinder can burst, the end opposite the fuel intake is suddenly opened and the hot gases rush out. More gases are formed instantly as the fuel continues to burn. The gases push against all parts of the cylinder except for the open end. This causes the cylinder to move away from the open end where there is no pressure.

5 The cylinder has become a reaction engine: the gases rushing out are the action, and the movement of the cylinder in the opposite direction is the reaction. This demonstrates Newton's Third Law of Motion: For every action there is an equal and opposite reaction.

6 All vehicles work according to the Third Law of Motion. The tires of an automobile push back against the earth, and the car moves forward. An airplane propeller drives back masses of air. A ship's propeller pushes water opposite the direction of travel.

7 In a rocket engine, the push of the gases is called thrust. Since all the thrust is inside the rocket engine, and no air or water must be moved to propel the vehicle, it can operate in the vacuum of space. The rocket actually works better in space, where there is no air to get in the way of its exhaust, than it does in the earth's atmosphere.

8 To operate at highest efficiency, the rocket engine is designed so that as much thrust as possible moves in a forward direction and the exhaust gases can move freely as they leave the rocket. This means the best designs are created for thrust chambers and exhaust nozzles.

Look back over "Rocket Talk I" to answer the following questions. The numbers after each question refer to the page and paragraph with helpful information.

1. How must fuels be burned in a rocket engine? (236, 2)
2. What is produced by burning fuel? (236, 2)
3. What happens when a cylinder under pressure is suddenly opened? (236, 4)
4. How does the release of pressure from the cylinder illustrate Newton's Third Law of Motion? (236, 5)
5. In rocket engines, what is *thrust* and in what direction should it move? (236, 8)

Decide which of the following statements correctly interpret the information in "Rocket Talk I." Use the diagram as well as the article to support your decisions. Be ready to identify your supporting evidence.

1. In rocket engines, the exhaust of the gases is the action, and the thrust of the rocket is the reaction.
2. The rocket moves in the same direction as that of the hot gases rushing out of the engine.
3. A rocket moves in the direction of its thrust.
4. For the rocket to have all possible thrust in a forward direction, there must be all possible exhaust in a backward direction.

Set Your Purposes

"Rocket Talk II" explains the fuel system of a rocket. As you read the article, keep in mind Newton's Third Law of Motion: For every action there is an equal and opposite reaction.

more ROCKET TALK

1   Air and ground vehicles burn fuel by combining it with the oxygen in the air. But a rocket cannot depend on atmospheric oxygen. Even pure oxygen gas would not be suitable because it would take up too much room. Furthermore, it couldn't be pumped into the engine fast enough to keep the fuel burning.

2   The rocket engineer solves the problem by using pure oxygen which has been compressed into liquid form. It takes a great amount of oxygen gas to form a small amount of the liquid, which is called lox.

3   Lox has a temperature of $-297°F$ ($-147°C$). It is expensive and difficult to store, so

when engineers do not need the high efficiency of pure oxygen they select another oxidizer. There are several chemical compounds rich in oxygen from which to choose. Some popular ones are called nitrogen tetroxide and white and red fuming nitric acids.

1   Rocket engineers choose their fuel and oxidizer to fit the engine. Each rocket engine is most efficient when using the fuel-oxidizer combination, called a bipropellant, for which it was designed. The term is often shortened to just propellant.

2   The efficiency of a propel-lant is measured by its specific impulse, which is the same kind of measurement as miles per gallon (kilometers per liter) in an automobile. It means: the force of thrust produced for each pound (kilogram) of propellant burned per second.

3   The higher the specific impulse, the faster the exhaust gases rush out of the rocket nozzle—the higher the exhaust velocity. The higher the exhaust velocity, the speedier the rocket. Another way to say the same thing is: The faster the action, the faster the reaction.

Locate Some Information

Look back over ''Rocket Talk II'' to answer the following questions. The numbers after each question refer to the page and paragraph with helpful information.

1. Is pure oxygen gas a suitable rocket fuel? Why or why not? (238, 1)
2. What is lox? (238, 2)
3. What are some drawbacks to the use of lox? (238, 3)
4. What is a bipropellant and how is it measured? (239, 1)
5. How does the rate at which the propellant burns affect the speed at which the rocket travels? (239, 3)

Interpret the Information

Decide which of the following statements correctly interpret the information in this section. Be ready to identify your supporting evidence.

1. A little lox goes a long way as an oxidizer.
2. Lox is the only oxidizer available.

3. Efficiency costs money: the most efficient oxidizers cost the most money.
4. Fuel alone can propel a rocket.
5. The faster the exhaust gases leave a rocket, the slower the rocket will move.
6. Specific impulse relates not only to whether the rocket moves, but also to how far and how fast it goes.

Apply the Ideas

Using what you learned from "Rocket Talk I and II" and other scientific knowledge you have, decide which of the following statements you can support. Be ready to explain the reasons for your decisions.

1. Scientific laws are discoveries, not inventions. They are descriptions of things that always have occurred and always will occur in the same way for the same reason.
2. You don't have to know about a scientific law for it to have an effect on you.
3. Following are two examples of Newton's Third Law of Motion in operation: (a) A car moves forward as its wheels push backward on the ground; (b) A scooter moves forward when you push backward with your foot. Can you think of other examples?

Make Some Generalizations

Have you considered how Newton's Third Law of Motion relates to winning and losing? Discuss the following statements with others in your group to see if a relationship is suggested.

1. Winning is to losing as gain is to loss.
2. In rockets, thrust is gained as fuel is burned.
3. In rockets, the higher the exhaust velocity, the speedier the rocket.
4. For every action there is an equal and opposite reaction.

The Humor of Winning and Losing

To appreciate a cartoon, you have to understand the cartoonist's humorous way of expressing an idea. Do you remember the three steps you should follow to do this? Here they are again, to refresh your memory.

1. Study the drawing to notice as much of the detail as you can.
2. Search your memory to see if you have read, heard, or seen anything that is related in some way to the cartoon.
3. Decide what ideas related to the people or the events in the cartoon the cartoonist is trying to communicate.

Now "read" the following cartoon, using the steps above.

"Would you be interested to know that it broke all records for coast-to-coast flight?"

Read the statements below and decide which ones are important to your understanding of the cartoon. Discuss the reasons for your choices with other members of your group.

1. Airplanes that fly at very high speeds may break the sound barrier.
2. Greenhouses are made of glass.
3. One of the men owns a nursery.
4. Nurseries grow plants in greenhouses.
5. Breaking the sound barrier creates a sonic boom.
6. Newspapers report important events.
7. When the shock wave created by a sonic boom hits the ground, it may cause glass to break.
8. Broken glass is messy.

Answer the following questions about the message of the cartoon. Discuss your answers with others in your group.

1. How does the cartoon relate to winning and losing? Who is the winner? Who is the loser?
2. Which of the following statements express ideas that the cartoonist is presenting?
   a. Winning or losing depends on point of view.
   b. One person's loss may be another person's gain.
   c. Always look on the bright side of things.

More Winning and Losing in Literature

The story you will read next is about two boys, Steve and Randy, who are friends at home but rivals on the football field. One more touchdown and Randy's old friend Steve would win a college scholarship. But this was football—what could Randy do? Read to find out the problem Randy faces and what he does about winning and losing.

by Cheryl Curtis

He slowly shut the locker door, pulling up on the handle. The sound of scraping metal rang throughout the abandoned room, echoing off the brick walls and the rows of beige lockers. Randy's mind felt like the sound of the locker door—hollow, empty, echoing on and on. Sighing loudly, he turned and stepped outside onto the gravel parking lot behind the high school.

Both hands in his pockets, he walked toward Main Street. The sky had a wild, stormy look, and the November wind hummed

eerily in the electrical wires above the tree-lined street. It was a lonesome sound; right now he felt very much alone. It was not a feeling he permitted himself often.

Why was he always the last person to leave football practice? He actually didn't like practice all that well. Who could truthfully say he enjoyed the monotonous drilling day after day? But Randy had lived and breathed football ever since he was a child, playing with his older brothers. Even then, he'd dreamed of the day when he could play on a real team with the stands full of cheering crowds.

Yes, Randy thought, football was football. Just a way of life. There wasn't too much else a guy could do in high school in a small town. Nothing else could compare to it. Football was the essence of the school, the source of its pride, and the life of all the people he knew. There was no choice when it came to football. It just was.

Leaves were blowing in front of him. They collected in bundles along the gutter. As he reached the corner, he debated whether to walk on home for dinner or to eat at Barry's Grill. His house was on the edge of town, half a mile (about 800 meters) away. Barry's Grill was on the corner. Randy chose the grill.

His fingers toyed with the napkin holder, and his eyes watched the steam form on the windowpane, where he saw his own reflection. Whenever he caught a glimpse of himself, he was shocked to see a man staring back, after having seen a boy for so long. His hair was dark and straight; his eyes were even darker. His muscular frame was large for his age. Often, he asked himself why he was born lucky. Like most questions he asked himself, he was afraid to know the answer.

"Hey, Randy?" The voice came from the back of the restaurant. "How's the team shaping up?"

He didn't respond right away but turned in his chair to face the man who asked the question. It was Mr. Ryder, the owner of the supermarket. "Good. We'll win tomorrow night," Randy said.

The man laughed and nodded. "You better win. I've got a bet on that game with a Hooverville grocer."

Randy really didn't care what Mr. Ryder had bet on the annual rival game between the Billings Bobcats and the Hooverville Pioneers. People shouldn't bet if they were worried about losing.

"Well, you don't have to worry," Randy assured him anyway. "They lost two first-string tackles in the Ashley game last week. We've got the offensive advantage."

"There's a lot more than just my money riding on it," Mr.
Ryder said. "Everyone in town's got someone in Hooverville to
bet with. Say, isn't Steve Carlson over in Hooverville this year?"

Randy nodded, his mouth full.

"Didn't you two buddy around before he moved?"

He nodded again.

"Is he still playing running back, now that he's with the
Pioneers?"

Randy felt obligated to answer this time, managing a "Yes"
between bites of French fries.

"That should be some game then—you two battling it out."

"Yes, sir." He wished people would stop making such a big
deal over it. It was going to be tough enough without the two
towns watching. He wondered how Steve felt about it. If he knew

his friend the way he thought he did, Steve probably couldn't care less. Even when he found out that it would be Randy who would be guarding him.

Randy finished his coffee and left a tip on the saucer. He was glad when at last he was out in the dark coldness, walking down the deserted street.

It was a small town, like many in northern Michigan. Most of the people had lived here all their lives. So had Steve, until last summer. His father had taken a new job in Hooverville, only eight miles (about twelve kilometers) away, and Steve had transferred to the rival school. He wasn't far away, but senior year just wasn't the same without him.

Later that night, in the darkness of his room, Randy couldn't sleep. When he closed his eyes, his mind marched through every formation, every play he'd ever memorized. When he dozed, he dreamed of football and the game Friday night. Finally, he gave up trying to sleep and sat up. He knew what was bothering him. It was seeing Steve yesterday afternoon—and that sense of foreboding.

Randy had stepped out of the door of Ryder's Market, two bags of groceries in his arms. Looking up, he saw Steve walking toward him.

"Hey, Randy. How've you been?"

"Great," Randy said. "What brings you over into enemy territory?"

Steve grabbed one of the bags, and the two walked toward Randy's car. "Oh, my folks still come over here for meat. They don't trust the hick Hooverville butcher."

"Oh, yeah, and Billings is true sophistication," Randy said, laughing.

"Well, after more than eighteen years, a person kind of gets attached to the old homestead."

For a moment, neither of them said anything. Randy's mind drifted back to last spring, when their plans had been nothing more than: "Next year, when we're finally seniors . . ."

"Hey, Randy." Steve suddenly brightened. "Ready for the battle on Friday? Hooverville is really fired up."

"Yeah? We can beat you guys any day."

"Aw, your offense is marshmallow without me."

They both laughed, knowing it was true. As they reached the car, Randy slid into the driver's seat. "Let's double to a movie some night, OK?"

"Sounds like a good idea," Steve said. "After this weekend, at least we're free from football." He suddenly looked serious and leaned through the open window. "There's a rumor going around that State will have a scout at the game Friday."

Randy's eyebrows raised. "For you?"

Steve nodded. "I guess so. And did you know, three more touchdowns, and I hold the district record?"

"That's great. Hey, good luck," Randy said. He started the engine of the car. The two said good-by. Randy hoped his friend did break the record. He knew how much it meant to him. Steve's future depended on a football scholarship. But as Randy left, he had a sick feeling of premonition.

Now, more than a day later, the feeling grew more intense. He glanced at his clock: 3:49 A.M. Why did he feel like this? Because he knew Steve so well, that's why. They had lived through first grade, first bicycles, and first love together. He knew Steve better than he knew himself. How many times had he stood on the sidelines during a game, watching Steve run with the ball,

taking in his every jump and weave? How many times, defense
replacing offense, had he rushed onto the field meeting a trium-
phant Steve running off? And in scrimmages, when he had tackled Steve, he could anticipate every move and match Steve in
agility and strength.

Yes, he knew Steve much too well to play a game of football
against him. Randy on defense, Steve on offense, just like always, only this time against each other, instead of with. Maybe
the coach would put Randy in a different position so at least he
wouldn't have to tackle Steve. But the idea was to win, wasn't
it? The team might have a chance if they were able to hold Steve
back, and he knew how to do that. After all, it was his last football game. It would be his night of glory, his chance to win the
game for Billings. It wasn't his fault that Steve was over there
while he was here. So why did he feel like this? Because of Steve,
his record, the scholarship, and the fact that it was Steve's last
night too.

Friday was a gray and chilly day with the smell of snow
in the air. At school, Randy moved among halls papered with
posters reminding him to support the Bobcats. Keeping near the
other members of the team, Randy was also trying very hard to
appear calm and casual. He got caught up in their excitement.
And the more he thought of the game, the more he knew he had
to win. As he left the school, he was filled, for the first time, with
a feeling of anticipation.

The crowd that night was the largest Randy had ever seen
at the annual rival game. The first three quarters had gone
smoothly enough. Now the score was 14-13, in Hooverville's
favor, with only three minutes left to play.

Randy watched the Bobcats' offense as it tried to gain
ground. It was a slow job, even against the weakened defense of
the Pioneers. He saw Steve on the far side of the field, pacing the
sideline. Yes, he was nervous too.

Steve had made both touchdowns. One more would give
him the record—and the Hooverville Pioneers the game. Randy
looked behind him. His father and three older brothers were in
the stands. Amy Johnson was there too, yelling, "Go, Randy!"
every time he moved.

Randy had let Steve get by him once, for the second touchdown. He hadn't done it on purpose; somehow he just hadn't
tried to stop him. But he had tackled him eleven times during the
game. Eleven times, singlehandedly, he had stopped a potential
goal. Wasn't that something? Wasn't it enough?

The next few plays were typical of the Pioneers' strategy.

They were barely able to make the ten yards in four downs but somehow managed. Steve ran several times, but each time, the Bobcats' front line stopped him before he gained more than a few yards. Finally, they were down to the Bobcats' twenty-yard line. Three times they attempted passes, and three times the quarterback was stopped.

Randy knew it was going to be now or never. There wouldn't be enough time on the clock for Hooverville to get this close again. Steve ran best in thirty- or forty-yard sprints, and it was easiest for him to receive from the left side of the field. As they moved into formation, Randy saw Steve's blue eyes narrow under his helmet, his jaw set.

The ball snapped. Randy moved forward and to his right. The Hooverville quarterback faked to the right, then passed to Steve, who had moved far to his left. Steve began sprinting forward, weaving past the Billings' defense, man after man. It was exactly like all the times before. Nothing had changed. Randy knew Steve would move back to the center, so he ran sideways, then backward.

He had to stop Steve. The team, his town, his brothers, and Amy were all watching him. He was the only one who even had a chance. There was no choice.

He could hear Steve's breath and the pounding of his feet. He saw Steve's eyes glaring steely blue. Steve had forgotten how well Randy knew him.

Steve leaped beyond Randy's reach. Yet both were equally matched in ability, and Steve had paused in surprise just a second too long. Randy made a final surge of speed and caught Steve around the waist. Both fell to the ground, and the football flew free into the air.

Randy was unaware of Brian behind him, scooping up the ball and running. He didn't hear the sudden crashing roar from the crowd as they cheered him. He only felt the cold ground beneath him, saw the green of Steve's jersey, and heard the rasping of their breath.

Randy stood up. "Steve," he said hoarsely. "I'm sorry." Randy wiped the sweat from his face. Steve rolled over on his back, slapping the forehead of his helmet with both fists. Randy held out a hand and helped Steve to his feet. They both paused a moment, gazing at each other.

Steve's face was shining with sweat; a trickle of blood ran from his nose. The blue eyes were vacant, except for a film that seemed to be collecting in the corners. His jaw was trembling ever so slightly as he said, "Good tackle." He looked at Randy,

his head tilted. His face was tired and blank. Steve shook his head, and turning, walked slowly off the field.

The crowd cheered as Randy approached the bench. His teammates met him with back slaps and victorious shouts. The coach patted his shoulder and congratulated him. Randy looked into the stands, where his father was grinning. Randy's brothers were celebrating loudly, and Amy yelled and waved to him.

Brian had run sixty yards with the ball after the tackle. There were forty-eight seconds left on the clock when Tom Cook made the winning touchdown for Billings. The crowd was ecstatic. The band played the school song, and the team stood proudly.

Hooverville had made a desperate attempt. But the clock ran out, and Billings had won for the fourth consecutive year— the score 20–14. The fans rushed onto the field in a frenzied mob.

Yes, this was true glory, this was what life was about, Randy thought, as he boarded the team bus. As it made its way down the street, traveling the three blocks to the school, the band marched in front, and cars followed behind, blowing their horns. The team waved out the windows, yelling as only the victorious can.

Randy leaned out his window into the night, watching the parade behind him. Down the street, just above the trees, he could see the lights of the field as they went out one by one, making a hole of darkness. He had met an old friend in a battle, and he had won. Was the prize of glory worth the price he had paid?

The bus stopped in front of the school, where the band and the fans had made a victory tunnel to the door of the locker room. He ran down it, smiling as if it were the most special night in his life. And yet, he could see nothing more than a pair of steel blue eyes staring tiredly back at him. Suddenly he realized that the film that had dulled his friend's eyes had been tears. He had never seen Steve cry before, not ever. He thought of that in wonder.

Football was football. It just was. There was no choice when it came to football. Stopping in front of his locker, Randy asked himself if he really believed that. He was afraid to find the answer. Once he had wondered what life would be like without football. Now he was glad to know he would soon find out.

Randy slowly opened the locker, pulling up on the handle. The scraping metal sounded the way his mind felt—hollow, empty, echoing on and on.

Analyze the Causes and Effects

This story is filled with actions and conditions (effects) brought about by a variety of causes. Listed below are partial statements that identify some of these effects. Following each are possible causes for the effect. Complete each statement by identifying the cause(s) which you can support with evidence from the story. Be ready to discuss the reasons for your decisions. You may identify more than one cause for each effect.

1. Randy felt depressed because
   a. football was becoming monotonous.
   b. he felt lonely.
   c. he was hungry and didn't want to walk home.
   d. he had seen his friend Steve and had experienced a sense of loss.
2. Football was important in Billings because
   a. it was the main spectator sport in the town in the fall.
   b. there were few other means of entertainment in the town.
   c. all the townspeople knew all the players.
   d. it was also important in Hooversville, a rival town.
3. Steve and Randy became rivals because
   a. Steve had moved from Billings to Hooversville.
   b. one played offense and the other defense.
   c. their teams were playing for the championship.
   d. each wanted his own team to win and could make it happen.

4. Randy's actions and feelings were confused because
   a. he felt he must support his team but didn't feel like cheering.
   b. he wanted to win the championship but wanted his friend to break the record.
   c. he wanted his friend to set a new record but not against him.
   d. he hoped Steve would play well but knew that he could stop Steve.
5. Billings won the game because
   a. Steve failed to set a new record.
   b. its cheerleaders were more spirited than Hooversville's.
   c. Brian was at the right place at the right time.
   d. Steve forgot how well Randy knew him.
6. Winning felt like losing to Randy because
   a. his friend lost a scholarship.
   b. he cared more about hurting his friend than helping his team.
   c. he couldn't win with divided loyalty.
   d. glory didn't make him feel glorious.

Apply the Ideas

Decide which of the following statements you can support by information and ideas from the story as well as from your own experiences. Be ready to give evidence in support of your decisions.

1. Winning doesn't come free; it always costs something.
2. Doing the right thing can trouble your conscience almost as much as doing the wrong thing.
3. It is never easy to live with doubt in your mind.
4. It's not always possible to please everyone.
5. It's possible to be more satisfied by not getting what you want than by getting it.

The Probability of Winning and Losing

"In this world nothing is certain but death and taxes."
—Benjamin Franklin

Did Franklin mean that nothing else can ever happen to you? No, of course not. He was exaggerating to make a point that people are taxed too much. There are, of course, things that are certain, such as Newton's Third Law of Motion: For every action there is an equal and opposite reaction.

In winning and losing, we have no certainty. Whatever we do, there is a chance that we will win; there is also a chance that we will lose. As a result, we are always talking in terms of chances or odds. Are any of these statements familiar to you?

1. The probability that a president will be re-elected for a second term is very high.
2. Our team probably will win the championship.
3. There is a seventy percent chance of rain tomorrow.
4. I feel certain of ninety percent of my answers on the test.
5. The odds against your finding a needle in a haystack are great.

All these statements involve probability. Probability is the mathematical basis for predicting the chances that something will or will not happen.

1. A scientist uses probability to predict the outcome of an experiment.
2. People in government use probability to predict income and to plan a budget for a year.
3. People use probability when they play games, such as backgammon.

Whether you use the word *chance, odds,* or *probability* doesn't really matter; either word indicates that you are guessing the outcome of some event. Saying, "The probability of my passing the math test is good," is like saying, "The chances of my passing the math test are good." The statements mean the same thing!

Mathematics materials give a great deal of information in a compact form. While you are reading, have a pencil handy to jot down useful points. The material that follows contains a description of an experiment and an explanation of some computations involved in the experiment. It asks you to use what you learn in your reading to solve a problem. To solve the problem you have to understand:

1. what information is given in the material.
2. what the problem asks you to do.
3. how to interpret and apply the information to the solution of the problem.

PROBABILITY

by B. H. Gundlach

Probability is the branch of mathematics which is concerned with analyzing the chance that a given outcome will occur.

In a *probability experiment,* a die was tossed 36 times onto smooth, flat surface. After each toss, the number of spots on the top face was recorded. Each face is associated with one of the numbers 1, 2, 3, 4, 5, and 6. Each toss is called an *outcome.*

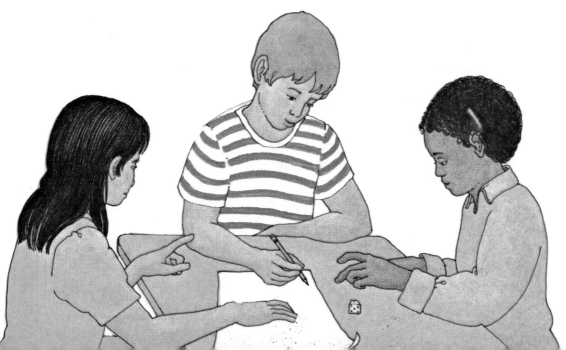

A frequency table for each of these outcomes follows.

Outcome (o)	Frequency (f)	
1	⊞⊞ II	7
2	⊞⊞ III	8
3	IIII	4
4	⊞⊞	5
5	⊞⊞ II	7
6	⊞⊞	5
	Sum (n)	36

Let f be the frequency of a given outcome. Let n be the sum of all the outcomes. Then the *probability* of any given outcome is $\dfrac{f \text{ (frequency)}}{n \text{ (sum)}}$.

Let $P(1)$ denote "the probability of getting a 1 on the die." Therefore:

$$P(1) = \frac{7}{36} \frac{\text{(frequency of outcome 1)}}{\text{(sum of the outcomes)}}$$

Now verify the probabilities from the table. What is the sum of all six probabilities?

$$P(1) = \frac{7}{36} \qquad P(3) = \frac{4}{36} = \frac{1}{9} \qquad P(5) = \frac{7}{36}$$

$$P(2) = \frac{8}{36} = \frac{2}{9} \qquad P(4) = \frac{5}{36} \qquad P(6) = \frac{5}{36}$$

A die has six faces, and each face is supposed to be as likely to come up as any other. That means you can expect the probability of each face to be $\dfrac{1}{6}$.

In an actual experiment you cannot expect to obtain probabilities of $\dfrac{1}{6}$ unless you make a very great number of tosses.

Suppose you toss 6,000 times; then each face will come up about 1,000 times.

To analyze the information, decide which of the following statements is correct according to the article. Be ready to give evidence to support your choices.

1. Probability is concerned with analyzing the chance that a particular outcome will occur.
2. A probability experiment is described.
3. In the experiment, a pair of dice was thrown 36 times.
4. In the experiment, one die was thrown 36 times.
5. The die used in the experiment had six faces, each with a different number of spots.
6. The number of spots on the die used in the experiment ranged from 1 to 10.
7. The number of spots on the top face of the die is called the outcome.
8. The top face of the die was read 36 times.
9. A frequency table shows the number of times each outcome occurred.
10. In this experiment, the sum of the frequencies of all the outcomes was 36.
11. The sum of the frequencies is equal to the number of times the die was tossed.
12. f = the number of times a given outcome occurred.
13. n = the total number of outcomes.
14. Probability $= \dfrac{f}{n}$
15. The more times a die is tossed, the more likely it is that each outcome will occur on $\dfrac{1}{6}$ of the tosses.

Some Probability Problems

Following are problems related to three different die-tossing experiments. Use the frequency tables below to help you find the answer to each problem.

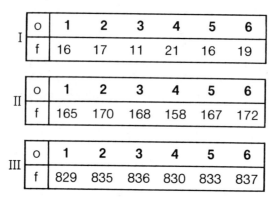

I	o	1	2	3	4	5	6
	f	16	17	11	21	16	19

II	o	1	2	3	4	5	6
	f	165	170	168	158	167	172

III	o	1	2	3	4	5	6
	f	829	835	836	830	833	837

1. How would you find the probability of each outcome for each experiment?
2. What is the sum of the probabilities of the outcomes for each experiment?

Analyze a Problem

Decide which of these statements correctly express what the problem asks you to do. Discuss the reasons for your choices. Use information you found in the material on probability.

a. Find the sum of the frequencies in each distribution table.
b. Find the probability for each outcome in Tables I, II, and III.
c. Find $\frac{f}{n}$ for each outcome in all three tables.
d. Find the sum of the probabilities of the six outcomes in each table.

Interpret the Ideas

Decide which of the following items correctly identify or describe mathematical operations that might be used in solving the problem.

1. $\dfrac{\text{outcome frequency} \quad (f)}{\text{sum of all the frequencies (n)}} = \text{outcome probability}$

2. $\dfrac{f}{n} = \dfrac{n}{f}$

3. $P(1) + P(2) + P(3) + P(4) + P(5) + P(6) = 1$

4. $\dfrac{f(1)}{n} + \dfrac{f(2)}{n} + \dfrac{f(3)}{n} + \dfrac{f(4)}{n} + \dfrac{f(5)}{n} + \dfrac{f(6)}{n} = 1$

Apply the Ideas

Now that you understand the information in the problem, try to do what the problem asks you to do. Decide which of the following are correct answers. Discuss each answer with other members of your group to make a decision.

Question 1

a. Table I: $P(3) = \dfrac{11}{100}$

b. Table II: $P(2) = \dfrac{170}{1000}$

c. Table II: $P(3) = 168$

d. Table III: $n = 5000$

e. Table III: $P(1) = \dfrac{829}{5000}$

Question 2

a. Table I: $\dfrac{16}{100} + \dfrac{17}{100} + \dfrac{11}{100} + \dfrac{21}{100} + \dfrac{16}{100} + \dfrac{19}{100} = \dfrac{100}{100} = 1$

b. Table II: $165 + 170 + 168 + 158 + 167 + 172 = 1000$

Make Some Generalizations

Decide which of the following statements reflect the relationship between probability and wining and losing. Explain how and why.

1. In a win-lose situation, you have a fifty-fifty chance for both winning and losing.
2. Losing half the time is really not unusual—just disappointing.
3. An optimist would expect to win half the time; a pessimist would expect to lose half the time.

More Winning and Losing in Poetry

In the poem that follows, the poet's point of view is very important to the question of winning or losing.

BATTLE WON IS LOST
by Phil George

They said, "You are no longer a lad."
    I nodded.
They said, "Enter the council lodge."
    I sat.
They said, "Our lands are at stake."
    I scowled.
They said, "We are at war."
    I hated.
They said, "Prepare red war symbols."
    I painted.
They said, "Count coups."
    I scalped.
They said, "You'll see friends die."
    I cringed.
They said, "Desperate warriors fight best."
    I charged.
They said, "Some will be wounded."
    I bled.
They said, "To die is glorious."
    They lied.

Give evidence from the poem to support your answers to the following questions.

1. Who is the ''I'' in the poem? What does he represent?
2. Who are ''they''? What do they represent?
3. Would you agree that in the poem:
   a. the elders talk and the young men listen.
   b. the elders talk and the young men act.
   c. the elders talk and the young men fight.
   d. the elders talk and the young men die.
   e. the elders think winning is everything.
   f. the young men know the battle won is lost in dying.
   g. the narrator speaks from beyond the grave.

More Winning and Losing in Literature

Most people think of competitive events, such as races and football games, when they think of winning and losing. In the next selection, however, a young woman is faced with a very different kind of win-lose situation. As you read, think about what the young woman has to lose in order to win something she wants very badly and how she resolves her problem.

The History Test

by Shirley Petersen

Carmelita sat tapping her pencil on the desk next to her history book. She rubbed her eyes and stretched her arms over her head.

"I can't look at you another second," she growled at the book as she slammed it shut.

Carmelita got up and paced back and forth, hoping to clear her head. History was her worst subject, but she needed a B in it to qualify for a college scholarship.

"I've got to get that scholarship," she said as she forced herself to sit back down at her desk. She picked up the reams of paper containing the notes she had been taking for hours.

"Outlines . . . diagrams . . . timelines . . . ," she muttered as she flipped the pages of neatly printed notes. "It doesn't matter what I do, I can't get this stuff into my head. I mean . . . who cares what happened two hundred years ago?"

She got up and paced again, then forced herself to sit down again. "I care," she told herself. "I care because my mother and brothers have worked hard so that I could stay in school. I care because if I get that scholarship, I'll be the first Mexican-American girl to win an academic scholarship to the university. That scholarship to the university means a lot to my family, my people, and me."

Carmelita opened the book and began taking notes again. The next thing she knew, her mother was calling her for breakfast. She had fallen asleep at the desk.

"*Caray*[1]!" she said, realizing what she had done. "I'll never be able to pass that test at this rate."

After washing and dressing quickly, Carmelita arrived in the kitchen just as her mother was putting her breakfast on the table.

"*Buenos días*,[2] Mama," she said, stopping to kiss her mother.

"*Buenos días*," replied Mrs. Martinez. "Or, maybe I should say '*buenos noches*.'[3] Your light was on awfully late last night. Were you studying hard for your history test?"

"I was studying, but not hard enough, Mama," Carmelita answered. "I fell asleep."

[1] *caray* (ka rā′)   Spanish for "ha" or "oh, my."
[2] *buenos días* (bwā′nōs dē′əs)   Spanish for "good morning" or "good day."
[3] *buenos noches* (bwā′nōs nō′chəs)   Spanish for "good night."

"That's all right," Mrs. Martinez said, "You have to have some sleep, or you won't be able to stay awake for the test."

"I need facts and dates more than I need sleep to get a B in history," said Carmelita despondently.

Mrs. Martinez patted her daughter's cheek and said, "Don't worry. You're a good girl—and very smart. You'll get the scholarship and make all of us very proud."

Smiling at the pride in her mother's face, Carmelita said, "I wish I had as much confidence in me as you do."

As Carmelita ate her breakfast, she admired the deft way in which her mother mixed the enchilada batter. Mrs. Martinez took great pride in making enchiladas the traditional way.

Frying the first enchilada, Mrs. Martinez asked, "Lita, will you have time to make the enchilada sauce after school? I may have to work late tonight. I was asked to make my special enchiladas for the big Mexican-American festival at church tomorrow."

"Sure, Mama," answered Carmelita with her mouth full. "For your enchiladas, even history can wait."

Just then a horn honked outside. "Oh, no! Carlos already," Carmelita said, jumping up and rinsing her plate.

"You tell your brother to come visit us once in a while. He gets married and forgets he has another family," Mrs. Martinez scolded.

"I will. *Vaya con Dios,*⁴" called Carmelita as she grabbed her books and ran down the steps. Her brother waited patiently as she struggled to open the car door that always stuck.

"Ugh," she said as she finally got the door open and climbed in next to her brother. "When are you going to get that fixed?"

Carlos flashed a teasing smile. "As soon as you get that scholarship. It will be my 'congratulations' gift to you."

"Oh, Carlos, don't tease about the scholarship!"

"*Que pasa, mi amiga*⁵?" he asked, still teasing. "Afraid you'll get an A minus instead of an A plus in something?"

Again wishing she had as much confidence in herself as others did, Carmelita answered, "I'd be happy with knowing just a few of the answers on the history test. I get good grades on my homework assignments, but I just can't keep the stuff straight in my head for the tests."

Realizing how serious his sister was, Carlos patted Carmelita's hand and said solemnly, "Don't get uptight, Lita, and you'll do fine."

⁴ *vaya con Dios* (vī'ə kōn dē'əs) Spanish for "farewell."
⁵ *que pasa, mi amiga* (kä'päs'ə mē ə mē'gə) Spanish for "What's the matter, my friend?"

Carmelita sank deeper into the seat as tears welled up in her eyes. She didn't know how she would ever be able to live up to the expectations her family had for her.

"Thanks, Carlos," Carmelita managed to squeak as the car stopped in front of the school.

"Go get 'em," Carlos said cheerfully as he drove away.

Carmelita walked up the deserted school steps, reviewing facts and dates. She was still reciting to herself when she passed her history teacher coming from the school office.

"Good morning, Carmelita," said Ms. Lewis. "Are you ready for the history test tomorrow?"

"Good morning, Ms. Lewis," Carmelita replied, trying to sound confident. "I'm ready if you ask the right questions."

"I'll see what I can do," Ms. Lewis said kindly. "It's too bad we can't include effort as part of the grade. I know history is difficult for you."

"Yeah," said Carmelita, embarrassed. "Thanks." She continued down the hall to the offices where she worked in the mornings and between classes to earn a little money. After dusting and arranging books, she started to clean the ditto machine.

"Darn," she said, trying to turn the cylinder. "Jammed again!" She removed the soleplate and found the culprit lying in a dozen tiny folds. Carefully, Carmelita pulled out the folds one at a time so that the paper wouldn't tear and jam more.

"There!" she exclaimed, triumphantly holding up the paper. Suddenly Carmelita's face turned red and her ears burned when she realized what she held in her hands: a copy of the history test!

Quickly she hid the paper behind her back and looked around to see if any teachers were nearby. No one was there. With her heart beating rapidly and her mouth going dry, Carmelita stooped down behind the machine so that she would not be seen. Her hands shook as she folded the paper into a tiny wad and stuck it in her shoe. She stood up and tried to finish cleaning the machine. But she was so nervous, she kept spilling the cleaning solution. She tried to make herself invisible as teachers began drifting in and out of the office.

Mrs. Czarniki, the school secretary, finally noticed Carmelita's peculiar behavior. "Lita, what's wrong with you this morning?" she asked. "You're all thumbs, and you've hardly said a word." When Carmelita didn't reply, Mrs. Czarniki looked at her intently. "Do you feel all right? You look a little flushed."

"I . . . I'm . . . I'm fine, M-Mrs. Czarniki," stammered Carmelita. "I just . . . I just didn't sleep well last night. Th-that's all."

"Studying for that history test, I bet," replied the older woman. "Lita, you take things too seriously. Relax a little. You'll do just fine." Misinterpreting the worried expression on Carmelita's face, Mrs. Czarniki continued, "Look, if you're that worried about the test, why don't you skip working during your free periods today? Take the time to study. You can make up the hours later in the week."

The bell rang, relieving Carmelita of having to give any detailed explanations. She grabbed her books and started backing out of the office, saying, "Thanks, Mrs. Czarniki. I-I think I'll do that. S-see you tomorrow after third period."

Walking down the hallway, Carmelita felt the test paper wadded up in the arch of her shoe. It felt like a hot coal, sending a burning sensation through her whole body. She wondered if she were limping. "What if someone asks me why I'm limping?" she asked herself. "What if I forget and take off my shoe . . ."

"Lita!"

Carmelita jumped at the sound of her name and dropped a book.

"You OK?" asked Sammy catching up with her. "I didn't mean to scare you," he said as he noticed the color drain from Carmelita's face. "I just wanted to know when you'll be able to go over the charts for the debate on Wednesday."

"I don't know, Sammy . . . ," began Carmelita.

"Listen, meet me here after class, and we'll talk about it," said Sammy as the second bell rang. Sammy hurried off to his class and Carmelita went to hers. When she got there, she was horrified to see that the only seat left was right in front of the room. But not today—not with the test burning a hole in her foot. She sat mute throughout the class. There had been so many ideas she had wanted to discuss about the story they had read, but now she couldn't think of a thing to say.

When the class was over, Carmelita was the first one out the door. She took the long way around to study hall so that she could avoid seeing Sammy or anyone else who might want to talk to her. She took a seat just as the bell rang again.

Carmelita opened her history book and began taking notes. She took notes the whole period without knowing one thing she wrote. A thousand thoughts fought with the facts for her attention. "I've worked hard for twelve years . . . I deserve that scholarship . . . The American Revolution began . . . How proud would Mama be if she knew I had to cheat to get a good grade in history . . . The Bill of Rights consists of . . . How would my teachers feel if they knew I took advantage of working in the office . . . The three branches of government . . . Everybody cheats once in a while just to keep up . . . The causes of the Civil War . . . It's just one silly history test in twelve years of hard work . . . The terms of the Versailles Treaty . . . I need that scholarship to pay back all the people who have helped me all these years. . . ."

The rest of the day passed like that for Carmelita. She couldn't concentrate on anything. She couldn't face anyone. She just kept frantically writing meaningless history notes. When the final bell rang, Carmelita ran out of the building. But she forced herself to slow down so that no one would notice her limp, which she was certain was getting more pronounced every minute.

Once safely at home, Carmelita took the folded test paper out of her shoe and placed it in the center of the table. Staring, she patted the paper and said, "You—you innocent-looking little piece of paper—you are going to get me a scholarship! But first, I must make Mama's enchilada sauce."

Opening the refrigerator, Carmelita took out the tomatoes and onions and other ingredients for the enchilada sauce. As she chopped the onions, she thought, "What a bother! Why can't Mama just buy enchilada sauce like everybody else? What's so special about homemade enchiladas? I'll bet if I stuck in canned enchilada sauce nobody would ever notice the difference." But Carmelita knew that her mother could tell the difference, and she could, too. So she kept chopping and adding ingredients to the big pot. And without even realizing it, she began humming an old Mexican folk song as her mother did when she was cooking.

When the sauce was ready, Carmelita lit the flame under the pot. Then she went to the table, unfolded the test paper, and re-folded it into a long, thin strip. Holding the paper by one end, she walked to the stove and set the paper on fire with the flame. She held the burning paper over the sink as it slowly burned away. Carefully, Carmelita washed the ashes down the sink. Then, with a sigh, she picked up her history book and her notes and started for her room.

Interpret the Character

The author of "The History Test" gave you many glimpses into Carmelita's mind. On the basis of those insights, determine which of the following statements describe Carmelita's character. Discuss the evidence from the selection that you find to accept or reject each statement.

1. Carmelita was ambitious and worked hard for everything she had.
2. Carmelita was selfish and took other people for granted.
3. Carmelita was proud of her family and her heritage.
4. Carmelita knew that she could do anything she set her mind to do.
5. Carmelita valued pride and self-respect more than anything.

Now work with your group to make up three or four additional statements that do and do not describe Carmelita. Exchange your statements with others in your group. Find evidence to accept or reject each statement.

Make Some Predictions

Now that you have analyzed Carmelita's character, can you predict what might happen to her in the future? Discuss the following questions and the reasons for your answers.

1. How will Carmelita do on the history test?
2. Will Carmelita get a college scholarship?
3. Will Carmelita go to college even if she doesn't get a scholarship?
4. If Carmelita doesn't get a scholarship, how do you think she will feel about what she did?

FOLLOW-THROUGH

Pulling It All Together

In this unit on winning and losing, you have read about:

1. a young woman who won more than a race;
2. the action of sprinters as they strive to beat the clock;
3. how winning and losing apply to rocket flights;
4. the humor of winning and losing;
5. two young men in competition, one winning and the other losing, with the winner uneasy about his victory;
6. how mathematics can be used to measure the chances of winning and losing;
7. how a young man's view of winning and losing contrasts with that of his elders; and
8. how a young woman risked losing something that was important to her to win something even more important.

Review the quotations at the beginning of this unit. Decide if some of the articles, stories, poems, and cartoon in this unit seem to illustrate any of those quotations and if some do not. Discuss your decisions with members of your group.

Now refer to the ideas about winning and losing listed under "Getting in Touch with Your Experiences." For each of the ideas, identify the story, article, cartoon, or poem that could be used as an example in support of that idea. Discuss your decisions with your group.

Putting Your Knowledge to Work

Following are some ideas for activities which give you the opportunity to use what you have learned about winning and losing and to demonstrate your understanding of the ideas. Choose one or more that you would like to do. Your group can work together on an activity, or you can work in pairs. It's usually more fun to share ideas.

1. Make a list of your sports heroes. Read about them in books from the library, in newspapers, or in magazines such as *Sports Illustrated*. Pay particular attention to athletes' views on winning and losing. Make a list of quotations that you can share with your classmates.

2. Make a collection of cartoons about winning and losing. Put them together to make a book to share with your classmates.

3. Newton discovered Three Laws of Motion. You have studied the third one. Find out about the other two and tell your classmates what they are and how they operate and then demonstrate or illustrate them with examples.

4. Make your own *Book of Records* on the greatest wins and the greatest losses in history. You can find such facts in the *Guinness Book of World Records.*

5. Do your own probability experiment and record the results. List your findings in a frequency distribution table.
   Possible experiments:
   a. Toss a die fifty times and find the probability of each outcome.
   b. Play odds and evens and find the probability of the outcomes *odds* and *evens.*
   c. Toss a coin fifty times and find the probability of the outcomes *heads* and *tails.*

6. Make up some win-lose situations similar to the one in "The History Test." Discuss each in terms of what the person involved stood to win and lose and what course of action he or she might take to resolve the problem.

Here are some books about winning and losing that you might enjoy:

Armstrong, William. *Sounder.* New York: Harper and Row, Publishers, 1969.
   This Newbery award-winning novel describes the struggles of a black family during the depression.

Bosworth, J. Allan. *Among Lions.* Garden City, N.Y.: Doubleday and Co., Inc., 1973.
   Jerry matches his will to survive against the elusive mountain lion that has been terrorizing his family's farm.

Fleming, Alice, comp. *Hosannah! the Home Run.* Boston: Little, Brown and Co., 1972.
   This anthology includes both humorous and thoughtful poems about sports.

Hunter, Mollie. *The Haunted Mountain.* New York: Harper and Row, Publishers, 1972.
   MacAllister pits his wit and stubbornness against the magical, unrelenting sidhe (or Good People).

Stambler, Irwin. *Speed Kings: World's Fastest Humans.* Garden City, N.Y.: Doubleday and Co., Inc., 1973.
   Each chapter consists of a biographical sketch of a person who tries to break a different speed record.

Sense and Nonsense

five

"The humor in nonsense comes from its apparent lack of sense or meaning. . . . On the surface it may seem completely without logic. But a second look usually shows it to be, if anything, super logical."

—Seymour Reit in *America Laughs*

Key Concepts

sense (a) the power to perceive by means of the sense organs; (b) an awareness, realization, or recognition; (c) sound, practical intelligence; (d) that which is reasonable or logical; (e) a feeling based on sensory impression.

nonsense (a) that which makes no sense; (b) words which convey absurd or silly ideas; (c) foolish conduct; (d) that which is unreasonable or illogical.

Getting in Touch with Your Experiences

You've heard the words *sense* and *nonsense* used to convey many different ideas. Look at the following sentences and decide which meaning above fits the meaning of the words as used in the sentences. Discuss your choices with other members of your group.

1. Having a light on in his room gives him a *sense* of security.
2. I will not put up with any more *nonsense* from them.
3. Juanita has a keen *sense* of smell.
4. The author of the story has a good *sense* of humor.
5. José's plan made very good *sense*.
6. The students made up *nonsense* rhymes for fun.
7. The pilot had a good *sense* of direction.
8. Your idea is pure *nonsense*.
9. The story was a combination of *sense* and *nonsense*.
10. Don't waste your allowance on *nonsense*.

Now that you have a sense of the different meanings of *sense* and *nonsense*, read the following statements. Discuss each statement with other members of your group and decide whether or not you can agree with it on the basis of your own experience.

1. Nonsense can be very sensible.
2. One person's sense can be another person's nonsense.
3. Sense and nonsense depend on one's point of view.
4. Sense and nonsense are always opposites.

Sense and Nonsense
in Poetry

The following short poems by Ogden Nash are a delightful mixture of sense and nonsense.

The Pig

The pig, if I am not mistaken,
Supplies us sausage, ham, and bacon.
Let others say his heart is big—
I call it stupid of the pig.

The Rhinoceros

The rhino is a homely beast;
For human eyes he's not a feast.
Farewell, farewell, you old rhinoceros,
I'll stare at something less prepoceros.

The Panther

The panther is like a leopard,
Except it hasn't been peppered.
Should you behold a panther crouch,
Prepare to say Ouch.
Better yet, if called by a panther
Don't anther.

The Seagull

Hark to the whimper of the sea-gull;
He weeps because he's not an ea-gull.
Suppose you were, you silly sea-gull,
Could you explain it to your she-gull?

The Cobra

This creature fills its mouth with venum
And walks upon its duodenum.
He who attempts to tease the cobra
Is soon a sadder he, and sobra.

Find and Interpret the Humor

Did you notice that in many of the poems the poet changed the
spelling of certain words to match that of the word he wanted it to
rhyme with? Which words did he change? Did the changes add to
the humor of the poems? Were the poems sense or nonsense or
both? Explain.

Sense and Nonsense
in Plays

Anticipate the Form

The plays you see on television and on stage are interpreted by the performers who act out the various parts. In order to play those parts, the performers must read the lines and imagine what their characters are like and how they will act.

Some plays are written to be read as well as to be performed. Before you read a play, go over the cast of characters and note the setting of the play. This will give you the background you need to understand the play. As you read the play "The Ugly Duckling," pay special attention to the stage directions, which are in parentheses. They will help you picture the action. Also watch for punctuation clues—dashes and ellipsis points—that let you know when a speaker is hesitating or when one is interrupting another.

Set Your Purposes

You may find this play quite humorous—full of nonsense. You may also find it confusing because some of the characters in the play also take part in another kind of play. Keeping track of who is really who can be difficult when you read the play. It is not so difficult when you see the play performed because you can see and hear the characters.

As you read the play—especially from lines 138 to 291, pay close attention to who the characters really are and who they are supposed to be in the eyes of other people in the play. To help you keep the characters straight, you should read the play as a whole, even though it is quite long. The speakers' lines are numbered to help you identify various sections of the play since it is not divided into acts and scenes as most plays are.

THE UGLY DUCKLING

BY A. A. MILNE

CHARACTERS

KING

CHANCELLOR

QUEEN

PRINCESS CAMILLA

DULCIBELLA

PRINCE SIMON

CARLO

SETTING: *The scene is the throne room of the palace—a room of many doors with thrones for the king, the queen, and the princess and a long seat on both sides of the thrones. As the curtain rises, the king is asleep on his throne with a handkerchief over his face.*

1 A VOICE (*announcing*): His Excellency the Chancellor! (*The Chancellor enters, bowing. The King wakes up with a start and removes the handkerchief from his face.*)

2 KING (*with simple dignity*): I was thinking.

3 CHANCELLOR (*bowing*): Never, Your Majesty, was greater need for thought than now.

4 KING: That's what I was thinking. (*He struggles into a more dignified position.*) Well, what is it? More trouble?

5 CHANCELLOR: What we might call the old trouble, Your Majesty.

6 KING: It's what I was saying last night to the queen. "Uneasy lies the head that wears a crown," was how I put it.

7 CHANCELLOR: An original thought, which may well go down to posterity.

8 KING: You mean it may go down well with posterity. I hope so. Remind me to tell you sometime of another little thing I said to Her Majesty: something about a fierce light beating on a throne. Posterity would like that too. Well, what is it?

9 CHANCELLOR: It is in the matter of Her Royal Highness's wedding.

10 KING: Oh . . . yes.

11 CHANCELLOR: As Your Majesty is aware, the young Prince Simon arrives today to seek Her Royal Highness's hand in marriage. He has been traveling in distant lands, and as I understand, has not—er—has not . . .

12 KING: You mean he hasn't heard anything?

13 CHANCELLOR: It is a little difficult to put this tactfully, Your Majesty.

14 KING: Do your best, and I will tell you afterwards how you got on.

15 CHANCELLOR: Let me put it this way. Prince Simon will naturally assume that Her Royal Highness has the customary—so customary as to be, in my own poor opinion, slightly monotonous—has what one might call the inevitable—so inevitable as to be, in my opinion again, almost mechanical—will assume, that she has the, as *I* think of it, faultily faultless, icily regular, splendidly . . .

16 KING: What you are trying to say in the fewest words possible is that my daughter is not beautiful. .

17 CHANCELLOR: Her beauty is certainly elusive, Your Majesty.

18 KING: It is. It has eluded you; it has eluded me; it has eluded everybody who has seen her. It even eluded the Court Painter. His last words were, "Well, I did my best." His successor is now painting the view across the water-meadows from the west turret. He says that his doctor has advised him to keep to landscape.

19 CHANCELLOR: It is unfortunate, Your Majesty, but there it is. One just cannot understand how it occurred.

20 KING: You don't think she takes after *me* at all? You don't detect a likeness?

21 CHANCELLOR: Most certainly not, Your Majesty.

22 KING: Good. . . . Your predecessor did.

23 CHANCELLOR: I have often wondered what happened to my predecessor.

24 KING: Well, now you know. (*There is a short silence.*)

25 CHANCELLOR: Looking at the bright side, although Her Royal Highness is not, strictly speaking, beautiful . . .

26 KING: Is not, truthfully speaking, beautiful . . .

27 CHANCELLOR: Yet she has great beauty of character.

28 KING: My dear Chancellor, we are not considering Her Royal Highness's character but her chances of getting married. You observe that there is a distinction.

29 CHANCELLOR: Yes, Your Majesty.

30 KING: Look at it from the suitor's point of view. If a girl is beautiful, it is easy to assume that she has, tucked away inside her, an equally beautiful character. But it is impossible to assume that an unattractive girl, however elevated in character, has, tucked away inside her, an equally beautiful face. That is, so to speak, not where you want it—tucked away.

31 CHANCELLOR: Quite so, Your Majesty.

32 KING: This doesn't, of course, alter the fact that the Princess Camilla is quite the nicest person in the kingdom.

33 CHANCELLOR (*enthusiastically*): She is indeed, Your Majesty. With the exception, I need hardly say, of Your Majesty—and Her Majesty.

34 KING: Your exceptions are tolerated for their loyalty and condemned for their stupidity.

35 CHANCELLOR: Thank you, Your Majesty.

36 KING: As an adjective for your king, the word *nice* is ill-chosen. As an adjective for Her Majesty, the word is—ill-chosen. (*Her Majesty comes in. The King rises. The Chancellor puts himself at right angles.*)

37 QUEEN (*briskly*): Ah, talking about Camilla? (*She sits down.*)

38 KING (*returning to his throne*): As always, my dear, you are right.

39 QUEEN (*to Chancellor*): This fellow, Simon—what's he like?

40 CHANCELLOR: Nobody has seen him, Your Majesty.

41 QUEEN: How old is he?

42 CHANCELLOR: Five-and-twenty, I understand, Your Majesty.

43 QUEEN: In twenty-five years, he must have been seen by somebody.

44 KING (*to Chancellor*): Just a fleeting glimpse?

45 CHANCELLOR: I meant, Your Majesty, that no detailed report of him has reached this country, save that he has the usual personal advantages and qualities expected of a prince and has been traveling in distant and dangerous lands.

46 QUEEN: Ah! Nothing gone wrong with his eyes? Sunstroke or anything?

47 CHANCELLOR: Not that I am aware of, Your Majesty. At the same time, as I was venturing to say to His Majesty, Her Royal Highness's character and disposition are so outstandingly. . .

48 QUEEN: Stuff and nonsense. You remember what happened when we had the Tournament of Love last year.

49 CHANCELLOR: I was not myself present, Your Majesty. I had not then the honor of—I was abroad and never heard the full story.

50 QUEEN: No, it was the other fool. They all rode up to Camilla to pay their homage. It was the first time they had seen her. The heralds blew their trumpets and announced that she would marry whichever prince was left master of the field when all but one had been unhorsed. The trumpets were blown again; they charged enthusiastically into the fight, and—(*The King looks at the ceiling and whistles a few bars.*) don't do that.

51 KING: I'm sorry, my dear.

52 QUEEN (*to Chancellor*): And what happened? They all simultaneously fell off their horses and assumed a posture of defeat.

53 KING: One of them was not quite so quick as the others. I was very quick. I proclaimed him the victor.

54 QUEEN: At the Feast of Betrothal held that night . . .

55 KING: We were all very quick.

56 QUEEN: The Chancellor announced that by the laws of the country the successful suitor had to pass a further test. He had to give the correct answer to a riddle.

57 QUEEN: I invented the riddle myself. Quite an easy one. What is it that has four legs and barks like a dog? The answer is "a dog."

58 KING (*to Chancellor*): You see that?

59 CHANCELLOR: Yes, Your Majesty.

60 KING: It isn't difficult.

61 QUEEN: He, however, seemed to find it so. He said an eagle. Then he said a serpent, a very high mountain with slippery sides, two peacocks, a moonlight night, the day after tomorrow . . .

62 KING: Nobody could accuse him of not trying.

63 QUEEN: *I* did.

64 KING: I *should* have said that nobody could fail to recognize in his attitude an appearance of doggedness.

65 QUEEN: Finally he said, "Death." I nudged the king . . .

66 KING: Accepting the word *death,* I clapped him on the shoulder and congratulated him on the correct answer. He disappeared under the table, and, personally, I never saw him again.

67 CHANCELLOR: It all seems so strange.

68 QUEEN: What does?

69 CHANCELLOR: That Her Royal Highness, alone of all the princesses one has ever heard of, should lack that distinctive feature of royalty, supreme beauty.

70 QUEEN (*to king*): That was your Great-aunt Malkin. She came to the christening. You know what she said.

71 KING: It was mysterious. Great-aunt Malkin's besetting weakness. She came to *my* christening. She was one hundred and one then and that was fifty-one years ago. (*to Chancellor*) How old would that make her?

72 CHANCELLOR: One hundred and fifty-two, Your Majesty.

73 KING (*after thought*): About that, yes. She promised me that when I grew up I should have all the happiness that my wife deserved. It struck me at the time—well, when I say, "at the time," I was only a week old—but it did strike me as soon as anything could strike me—I mean of that nature—well, work it out for yourself, Chancellor. It opens up a most interesting field of speculation. Though naturally I have not liked to go into it at all deeply with Her Majesty.

74 QUEEN: I never heard anything less mysterious. She was wishing you extreme happiness.

75 KING: I don't think she was *wishing* me anything. However . . .

76 CHANCELLOR (*to Queen*): But what, Your Majesty, did she wish Her Royal Highness?

77 QUEEN: Her other godmother—on my side—had promised her the dazzling beauty for which all the women in my family are famous . . . (*She pauses, and the King snaps his finger surreptitiously at the Chancellor.*)

78 CHANCELLOR (*hurriedly*): Indeed, yes, Your Majesty. (*The King relaxes.*)

79 QUEEN: Great-aunt Malkin said—(*to King*) what were the words?

80 KING: *I give you with this kiss*
            A wedding-day surprise.
            Where ignorance is bliss,
            'Tis folly to be wise.

I thought the last two lines rather neat. But what it *meant* . . .

81 QUEEN: We can all see what it meant. She was given beauty—and where is it? Great-aunt Malkin took it away from her. The wedding-day surprise is that there will never be a wedding day.

82 KING: Young men being what they are, my dear, it would be much more surprising if there *were* a wedding day. So how . . . (*The Princess comes in. She is young, happy, and healthy—but not beautiful.*)

83 PRINCESS (*to King*): Hullo, darling! (*seeing the others*) Oh, I say! Affairs of state? Sorry.

84 KING (*holding out his hand*): Don't go, Camilla. (*She takes his hand.*)

85 CHANCELLOR: Shall I withdraw, Your Majesty?

86 QUEEN: You are aware, Camilla, that Prince Simon arrives today?

87 PRINCESS: He has arrived. They're just letting down the drawbridge.

88 KING (*jumping up quickly*): Arrived! I must . . .

89 PRINCESS: Darling, you know what the drawbridge is like. It takes at *least* half an hour to let it down.

90 KING (*sitting down*): It wants oil. (*to Chancellor*) Have *you* been grudging it oil?

91 PRINCESS: It wants a new drawbridge, darling.

92 CHANCELLOR: Have I Your Majesty's permission . . .

93 KING: Yes, yes. (*The Chancellor bows and goes out.*)

94 QUEEN: You've told him, of course? It's the only chance.

95 KING: Er—no. I was just going to, when . . .

96 QUEEN: Then I'd better. (*She goes to the door.*) I'll explain to the girl. I'll have her sent to you. You've told Camilla?

97 KING: Er—no. I was just going to, when . . .

98 QUEEN: Then you'd better tell her now.

99 KING: My dear, are you sure . . .

100 QUEEN: It's the only chance left. (*dramatically to heaven*) My daughter! (*She goes out. There is a little silence when she is gone.*)

101 KING: Camilla, I want to talk seriously to you about marriage.

102 PRINCESS: Yes, Father.

103 KING: It is time that you learnt some of the facts of life.

104 PRINCESS: Yes, Father.

105 KING: Now, the great fact about marriage is that once you're married you live happily ever after. All our history books affirm this.

106 PRINCESS: And your own experience, too, darling.

107 KING (*with dignity*): Let us confine ourselves to history for the moment.

108 PRINCESS: Yes, Father, to history.

109 KING: Of course, there *may* be an exception here and there, which, as it were, proves the rule; just as—oh, well, never mind.

110 PRINCESS (*smiling*): Go on, darling. You were going to say that an exception here and there proves the rule that all princesses are beautiful.

111 KING: Well—leave that for the moment. The point is that it doesn't matter *how* you marry or *who* you marry as long as you

get married. Because you'll be happy ever after in any case. Do you follow me so far?

112 PRINCESS: Yes, Father.

113 KING: Well, your mother and I have a little plan . . .

114 PRINCESS: Was that it, going out of the door just now?

115 KING: Er—yes. It concerns your waiting maid.

116 PRINCESS: Darling, I have several.

117 KING: Only one that leaps to the eye, so to speak. The one with the—well, with everything.

118 PRINCESS: Dulcibella?

119 KING: That's the one. It is our plan that at the first meeting she should pass herself off as the princess—a harmless ruse, of which you will find frequent record in the history books—and allure Prince Simon to his—that is to say, bring him up to the—In other words, the wedding will take place immediately afterwards and as quietly as possible. Well, naturally, in view of the fact that your Aunt Malkin is one hundred and fifty-two, and since you will be wearing the family bridal veil—which is no doubt how the custom arose—the surprise after the ceremony will be his. Are you following me? Your attention seems to be wandering.

120 PRINCESS: I was wondering why you needed to tell me.

121 KING: Just a precautionary measure, in case you happened to meet the prince or his attendant before the ceremony; in which case, of course, you would pass yourself off as the maid . . .

122 PRINCESS: A harmless ruse, of which, also, you will find frequent record in the history books.

123 KING: Exactly. But the occasion need not arise.

124 A VOICE (*announcing*): The woman Dulcibella!

125 KING: Ah! (*to Princess*) Now, Camilla, if you will just retire to your own apartments, I will come to you there when we are ready for the actual ceremony. (*He leads her out as he is talking, and as he returns, he calls out.*) Come in, my dear! (*Dulcibella comes in. She is beautiful but dumb.*) Now don't be frightened; there is nothing to be frightened about. Has Her Majesty told you what you have to do?

126 DULCIBELLA: Y—yes, Your Majesty.

127 KING: Well now, let's see how well you can do it. You are sitting here, we will say. (*He leads her to a seat.*) Now imagine that I am Prince Simon. (*He curls his moustache. She giggles.*) You

are the beautiful Princess Camilla, whom he has never seen. (*She giggles again.*) This is a serious moment in your life, and you will find that a giggle will not be helpful. (*He goes to the door.*) I am announced: "His Royal Highness Prince Simon!" That's me being announced. Remember what I said about giggling. You should have a faraway look upon the face. (*She does her best.*) Farther away than that. No, that's too far. You are sitting there, thinking beautiful thoughts but with the mouth definitely shut. That's better. I advance and fall upon one knee. You extend your hand graciously— *graciously;* you're not trying to push him in the face. That's better, and I raise it to my lips—so—and I kiss it—no, perhaps not so ardently as that, more like this, and I say, "Your Royal Highness, this is the most—er —Your Royal Highness, I shall ever be—no—Your Royal Highness, it is the proudest . . ." Well, the point is that *he* will say it, and it will be something complimentary, and then he will take your hand in both of his and press it to his heart. (*He does so.*) And—what do *you* say?

128   DULCIBELLA: Coo!

129   KING: No, *not* Coo.

130   DULCIBELLA: Never had anyone do *that* to me before.

131   KING: That also strikes the wrong note. What you want to say is, "Oh, Prince Simon!". . . Say it.

132   DULCIBELLA (*loudly*): Oh, Prince Simon!

133   KING: No, no. You don't need to shout until he has said "What?" two or three times. Always consider the possibility that he *isn't* deaf. Softly, and giving the words a dying fall, letting them play around his head like a flight of doves.

134   DULCIBELLA: O-o-o-o-h, Prinsimon!

135   KING: Keep the idea in your mind of a flight of *doves* rather than a flight of panic-stricken elephants, and you will be all right. Now I'm going to get up, and you must, as it were, *waft* me into a seat by your side. (*She starts wafting.*) *Not* rescuing a drowning man, that's another idea altogether, useful at times, but at the moment inappropriate. Wafting. Prince Simon will put the necessary muscles into play—all you are required to do is to indicate by a gracious movement of the hand the seat you require him to take. Now! (*He gets up a little stiffly and sits next to her.*) That was better. Well, here we are. Now, I think you give me a look with an undertone of regal dignity, touched, as it were, with good comradeship. Now try that. (*She gives him a vacant look of bewilderment.*) Frankly, that didn't quite get it.

There was just a little something missing. An absence, as it were, of all the qualities I asked for and in their place an odd resemblance to an unsatisfied fish. Let us try to get at it another way. Dulcibella, have you a young man of your own?

136 DULCIBELLA (*eagerly seizing his hand*): Oo, yes, he's ever so smart; he's an archer, well not as you might say a real archer, and me being maid to Her Royal Highness and can't marry me till he's a real soldier, but ever so loving, and funny like, the things he says. I said to him once, "Eg," I said . . .

137 KING (*getting up*): I rather fancy, Dulcibella, that if you think of Eg all the time, *say* as little as possible, and, when thinking of Eg, see that the mouth is not more than partially open, you will do very well. I will show you where you are to sit and wait for His Royal Highness. (*He leads her out, saying,*) Now remember —*waft*—*waft*—not *hoick.*
(*Prince Simon wanders in from the back unannounced. He is a very ordinary-looking young man in rather dusty clothes. He gives a deep sigh of relief as he sinks into the King's throne . . . . Camilla, a new and strangely beautiful Camilla, comes in.*)

138 PRINCESS (*surprised*): Well!

139 PRINCE: Oh, hullo!

140 PRINCESS: Ought you?

141 PRINCE (*getting up*): Do sit down, won't you?

142 PRINCESS: Who are you, and how did you get here?

143 PRINCE: Well, that's rather a long story. Couldn't we sit down? You could sit here if you liked, but it isn't very comfortable.

144 PRINCESS: That is the king's throne.

145 PRINCE: Oh, is that what it is?

146 PRINCESS: Thrones are not meant to be comfortable.

147 PRINCE: Well, I don't know if they're meant to be, but they certainly aren't.

148 PRINCESS: Why were you sitting on the king's throne, and who are you?

149 PRINCE: My name is Carlo.

150 PRINCESS: Mine is Dulcibella.

151 PRINCE: Good. And now couldn't we sit down?

152 PRINCESS (*sitting down on the long seat to the left of the throne, and, as it were, wafting him to a place next to her*): You may sit here, if you like. Why are you so tired? (*He sits down.*)

153 PRINCE: I've been taking very strenuous exercise.

154 PRINCESS: Is that part of the long story?

155 PRINCE: It is.

156 PRINCESS (*settling herself*): I love stories.

157 PRINCE: This isn't a story really. You see, I'm attendant on Prince Simon, who is visiting here.

158 PRINCESS: Oh? I'm attendant on Her Royal Highness.

159 PRINCE: Then you know what he's here for.

160 PRINCESS: Yes.

161 PRINCE: She's very beautiful, I hear.

162 PRINCESS: Did you hear that? Where have you been lately?

163 PRINCE: Traveling in distant lands—with Prince Simon.

164 PRINCESS: Ah! All the same, I don't understand. Is Prince Simon in the palace now? The drawbridge *can't* be down yet!

165 PRINCE: I don't suppose it is. *And* what a noise it makes coming down!

166 PRINCESS: Isn't it terrible?

167 PRINCE: I couldn't stand it any more. I just had to get away. That's why I'm here.

168 PRINCESS: But how?

169 PRINCE: Well, there's only one way, isn't there? That beech tree and then a swing and a grab for the battlements, and don't ask me to remember it all . . . (*He shudders.*)

170 PRINCESS: You mean you came across the moat by that beech tree?

171 PRINCE: Yes. I got so tired of hanging about.

172 PRINCESS: But it's terribly dangerous!

173 PRINCE: That's why I'm so exhausted. Nervous shock. (*He lies back and breathes loudly.*)

174 PRINCESS: Of course, it's different for *me*.

175 PRINCE (*sitting up*): Say that again. I must have got it wrong.

176 PRINCESS: It's different for me because I'm used to it. Besides, I'm so much lighter.

177 PRINCE: You don't mean that *you* . . .

178 PRINCESS: Oh, yes, often.

179 PRINCE: And I thought I was a brave man! At least, I did until five minutes ago, and now I don't again.

180 PRINCESS: Oh, but you are! And I think it's wonderful to do it straight off the first time.

181 PRINCE: Well, *you* did.

182 PRINCESS: Oh, no, not the first time. When I was a child.

183 PRINCE: You mean that you crashed?

184 PRINCESS: Well, you only fall into the moat.

185 PRINCE: Only! Can you *swim?*

186 PRINCESS: Of course.

187 PRINCE: So you swam to the castle walls and yelled for help, and they fished you out and walloped you. And the next day you tried again. Well, if *that* isn't pluck . . .

188 PRINCESS: Of course I didn't. I swam back and did it at once; I mean I tried again at once. It wasn't until the third time that I actually did it. You see, I was afraid I might lose my nerve.

189 PRINCE: Afraid she might lose her nerve!

190 PRINCESS: There's a way of getting over from this side too; a tree grows out from the wall, and you jump into another tree—I don't think it's quite so easy.

191 PRINCE: Not quite so easy. Good. You must show me.

192 PRINCESS: Oh, I will.

193 PRINCE: Perhaps it might be as well if you taught me how to swim first. I've often heard about swimming, but never . . .

194 PRINCESS: You can't swim?

195 PRINCE: No. Don't look so surprised. There are a lot of other things that I can't do. I'll tell you about them as soon as you have a couple of years to spare.

196 PRINCESS: You can't swim, and yet you crossed by the beech tree! And you're *ever* so much heavier than I am! Now who's brave?

197 PRINCE (*getting up*): You keep talking about how light you are. I must see if there's anything in it. Stand up! (*She stands obediently, and he picks her up.*) You're right, Dulcibella. I could hold you here forever. (*He looks at her.*) You're very lovely. Do you know how lovely you are?

198 PRINCESS: Yes. (*She laughs suddenly and happily.*)

199 PRINCE: Why do you laugh?

200 PRINCESS: Aren't you tired of holding me?

201 PRINCE: Frankly, yes. I exaggerated when I said I could hold you forever. When you've been hanging by the arms for ten minutes over a very deep moat, wondering if it's too late to learn how to swim—(*He puts her down.*) what I meant was that I should *like* to hold you forever. Why did you laugh?

202 PRINCESS: Oh, well, it was a little private joke of mine.

203 PRINCE: If it comes to that, I've got a private joke too. Let's exchange them.

204 PRINCESS: Mine's very private. One other woman in the whole world knows, and that's all.

205 PRINCE: Mine's just as private. One other man knows, and that's all.

206 PRINCESS: What fun. I love secrets. . . . Here's mine. When I was born, one of my godmothers promised that I should be very beautiful.

207 PRINCE: How right she was.

208 PRINCESS: But the other one said this:

> *I give you with this kiss*
> *A wedding-day surprise.*
> *Where ignorance is bliss,*
> *'Tis folly to be wise.*

And nobody knew what it meant. And I grew up very plain. And then, when I was about ten, I met my godmother in the forest one day. It was my tenth birthday. Nobody knows this—except you.

209 PRINCE: Except us.

210 PRINCESS: Except us. And she told me what her gift meant. It meant that I *was* beautiful—but everybody else was to go on being ignorant and thinking me plain until my wedding day. Because, she said, she didn't want me to grow up spoilt and willful and vain as I should have done if everybody had always been saying how beautiful I was; and the best thing in the world, she said, was to be quite sure of yourself but not to expect admiration from other people. So ever since then my mirror has told me I'm beautiful, and everybody else thinks me ugly, and I get a lot of fun out of it.

211 PRINCE: Well, seeing that Dulcibella is the result, I can only say that your godmother was very, very wise.

212 PRINCESS: And now you tell me *your* secret.

213 PRINCE: It isn't such a pretty one. You see, Prince Simon was going to woo Princess Camilla, and he'd heard that she was beautiful and haughty and imperious—all you would have been if your godmother hadn't been so wise. And being a very ordinary-looking fellow himself, he was afraid she wouldn't think much of him, so he suggested to one of his attendants, a man called Carlo, of extremely attractive appearance, that *he* should pretend to be the prince and win the princess's hand; and then at the last moment they would change places . . .

214 PRINCESS: How would they do that?

215 PRINCE: The prince was going to have been married in full armor—with his visor down.

216 PRINCESS (*laughing happily*): Oh, what fun!

217 PRINCE: Neat, isn't it?

218 PRINCESS: Oh, very . . . very . . . very.

219 PRINCE: Neat, but not so terribly *funny*. Why do you keep laughing?

220 PRINCESS: Well, that's another secret.

221 PRINCE: If it comes to that, *I've* got another one up my sleeve. Shall we exchange again?

222 PRINCESS: All right. You go first this time.

223 PRINCE: Very well. . . . I am not Carlo. (*He stands up and speaks dramatically.*) I am Simon! *Ow!* (*He sits down and rubs his leg violently.*)

224 PRINCESS (*alarmed*): What is it?

225 PRINCE: Cramp. I was saying that I was Prince Simon.

226 PRINCESS: Is your leg better?

227 PRINCE (*despairingly*): I am Simon.

228 PRINCESS: I know.

229 PRINCE: How did you know?

230 PRINCESS: Well, you told me.

231 PRINCE: But oughtn't you to swoon or something?

232 PRINCESS: Why? History records many similar ruses.

233 PRINCE (*amazed*): Is that so? I've never read history. I thought I was being very original.

234 PRINCESS: Oh, no! Now I'll tell you *my* secret. For reasons very much like your own, the Princess Camilla, who is held to be extremely plain, feared to meet Prince Simon. Is the drawbridge down yet?

235 PRINCE: Do your people give a faint, surprised cheer every time it goes down?

236 PRINCESS: Naturally.

237 PRINCE: Then it came down about three minutes ago.

238 PRINCESS: Ah! Then at this very moment your man Carlo is declaring his passionate love for my maid, Dulcibella. That, I think, is funny. (*The Prince laughs heartily.*) Dulcibella, by the way is in love with a man she calls Eg, so I hope Carlo isn't getting carried away.

239 PRINCE: Carlo is married to a girl he calls "the little woman," so Eg has nothing to fear.

240 PRINCESS: By the way, I don't know if you heard, but I said, or as good as said, that I am the Princess Camilla.

241 PRINCE: I wasn't surprised. History, of which I read a great deal, records many similar ruses.

242 PRINCESS (*laughing*): Simon!

243 PRINCE (*laughing*): Camilla! (*He stands up.*) May I try holding you again? (*She nods. He takes her in his arms.*) Sweetheart!

244 PRINCESS: You see, when you lifted me up before, you said, "You're very lovely," and my godmother said that the first person to whom I would seem lovely was the man I should marry; so I knew then that you were Simon and I should marry you.

245 PRINCE: I knew when I saw you that I should marry you even if you were Dulcibella. By the way, which of you *am* I marrying?

246 PRINCESS: When she lifts her veil, it will be Camilla. (*Voices are heard.*) Until then it will be Dulcibella.

247 PRINCE (*in a whisper*): Then good-by, Camilla, until you lift your veil.

248 PRINCESS: Good-by, Simon, until you raise your visor. (*The King and Queen come in arm in arm, followed by Carlo and Dulcibella, also arm in arm. The Chancellor precedes them, walking backwards at a loyal angle.*)

249 PRINCE (*supporting the Chancellor as an accident seems inevitable*): Careful! (*The Chancellor turns indignantly around.*)

250 KING: Who and what is this? More accurately, who and what are all these?

251 CARLO: My attendant, Carlo, Your Majesty. He will, with Your Majesty's permission, prepare me for the ceremony. (*The Prince bows.*)

252 KING: Of course, of course, *of course!*

253 QUEEN (*to Dulcibella*): Your maid, Dulcibella, is it not, my love? (*Dulcibella nods violently.*) I thought so. (*to Carlo*) *She* will prepare Her Royal Highness. (*The Princess curtsies.*)

254 KING: Ah, yes. Yes. *Most* important.

255 PRINCESS (*curtsying*): I beg pardon, Your Majesty, if I've done wrong, but I found the gentleman wandering . . .

256 KING (*crossing to her*): Quite right, my dear, quite right. (*He pinches her cheek and takes advantage of this kingly gesture to speak in a loud whisper.*) We've pulled it off! (*They sit down— the King and Queen on their thrones, Dulcibella on the princess's throne. Carlo stands behind Dulcibella, the Chancellor on the right of the Queen, and the Prince and Princess behind the long seat on the left.*)

257 CHANCELLOR (*consulting documents*): Hmm! Have I your Majesty's authority to put the final test to His Royal Highness?

258 QUEEN (*whispering to King*): Is this safe?

259 KING (*whispering*): Perfectly, my dear. I told him the answer a minute ago. (*over his shoulder to Carlo*) Don't forget. *Dog.* (*aloud*) Proceed, Your Excellency. It is my desire that the affairs of my country should ever be conducted in a strictly constitutional manner.

260 CHANCELLOR (*oratorically*): By the constitution of the country, a suitor to Her Royal Highness's hand cannot be deemed successful until he has given the correct answer to a riddle. (*conversationally*) The last suitor answered incorrectly and thus failed to win his bride. (*to Carlo*) I have now to ask Your Royal Highness if you are prepared for the ordeal?

261 CARLO (*cheerfully*): Absolutely.

262 CHANCELLOR: I may mention, as a matter, possibly, of some slight historical interest to our visitor, that by the constitution of the country the same riddle is not allowed to be asked on two successive occasions.

263 KING (*startled*): What's that?

264 CHANCELLOR: This one, it is interesting to recall, was propounded exactly a century ago; and we must take it as a fortunate omen that it was well and truly solved.

265 KING (*to Queen*): I may want my sword directly.

266 CHANCELLOR: The riddle is this: What is it that has four legs and mews like a cat?

267 CARLO (*promptly*): A dog.

268 KING (*still more promptly*): Bravo, bravo! (*He claps loudly and nudges the Queen, who claps too.*)

269 CHANCELLOR (*peering at his documents*): According to the records of the occasion to which I referred, the correct answer would seem to be . . .

270 PRINCESS (*to prince*): Say something, quickly!

271 CHANCELLOR: Not dog, but . . .

272 PRINCE: Your Majesty, have I permission to speak? Naturally, His Royal Highness could not think of justifying himself on such an occasion, but I think that with Your Majesty's gracious permission, I could . . .

273 KING: Certainly, certainly.

274 PRINCE: In our country we have an animal to which we have given the name "dog," or, in the local dialect of the more mountainous districts, "doggie." It sits by the fireside and purrs.

275 CARLO: That's correct. It purrs like anything.

276 PRINCE: When it needs milk, which is its staple food, it mews.

277 CARLO (*enthusiastically*): Mews like nobody's business.

278 PRINCE: It also has four legs.

279 CARLO: One at each corner.

280 PRINCE: In some countries, I understand, this animal is called a "cat." In one distant country that His Royal Highness and I visited, it was called by the curious name of "hippopotamus."

281 CARLO: That's right. (*to Prince*) Do you remember that ginger-colored hippopotamus, which used to climb on to my shoulder and lick my ear?

282 PRINCE: I shall never forget it, sir. (*to King*) So you see, Your Majesty . . .

283 KING: Thank you. I think that makes it perfectly clear. (*firmly to chancellor*) You are about to agree?

284 CHANCELLOR: Undoubtedly, Your Majesty. May I be the first to congratulate His Royal Highness on solving the riddle so accurately?

285 KING: You may be the first to see that all is in order for an immediate wedding.

286 CHANCELLOR: Thank you, Your Majesty. (*He bows and withdraws. The King, Queen, and Dulcibella rise.*)

287 KING (*to Carlo*): Doubtless, Prince Simon, you will wish to retire and prepare yourself for the ceremony.

288 CARLO: Thank you, sir.

289 PRINCE: Have I Your Majesty's permission to attend His Royal Highness? It is the custom of his country for princes of the royal blood to be married in full armor, a matter that requires a certain adjustment . . .

290 KING: Of course, of course. (*Carlo bows to the King and Queen and goes out. As the Prince is about to follow, the King stops him.*) Young man, you have a quality of quickness, which I admire. It is my pleasure to reward it in any way which commends itself to you.

291 PRINCE: Your Majesty is ever gracious. May I ask for my reward *after* the ceremony? (*He catches the eye of the Princess, and they give each other a secret smile.*)

292 KING: Certainly. (*The Prince bows and goes out. The King speaks to Dulcibella.*) Now, young woman, make yourself scarce. You've done your work excellently, and we will see that you and your— what was his name?

293 DULCIBELLA: Eg, Your Majesty.

294 KING: That you and your Eg are not forgotten.

295 DULCIBELLA: Coo! (*She curtsies and goes out.*)

296 PRINCESS: Wait for me, Dulcibella!

297 KING (*to Queen*): Well, my dear, we may congratulate ourselves. As I remember saying to somebody once, "You have not lost a daughter, you have gained a son." How does he strike you?

298 QUEEN: Stupid.

299 KING: They made a very handsome pair, I thought, he and Dulcibella.

300   QUEEN: Both stupid.

301   KING: I said nothing about stupidity. What I *said* was that they were both extremely handsome. That is the important thing. Or isn't it?

302   QUEEN: What do *you* think of Prince Simon, Camilla?

303   PRINCESS: I adore him. We shall be so happy together.

304   KING: Well, of course you will. I told you so. Happily ever after.

305   QUEEN: Run along now and get ready.

306   PRINCESS: Yes, Mother. (*She throws a kiss to them and goes out.*)

307   KING (*anxiously*): It seemed to me that Camilla wasn't looking quite so plain as usual just now.

308   QUEEN (*carelessly*): Just the excitement of the marriage.

309   KING (*relieved*): Ah, yes, that would account for it.

Analyze the Information

The sense and nonsense in "The Ugly Duckling" took many different forms. The following questions should help you focus on some of the humor in the sense and nonsense. Answer each question and discuss the reasons for your answers with your group. The numbers following the questions refer to the characters' lines in the play. They will help you find places to look for some related ideas.

1. Was Princess Camilla considered beautiful? (16–29)
2. How did the Princes react in the Tournament of Love? Why did they react that way? (48–52)
3. How did the Queen feel about being beautiful? (77)
4. Why did the King want Dulcibella to pretend she was the Princess? (113–123)
5. To whom were the Princess and the Prince speaking in lines 138 to 208? To whom did they think they were speaking? At what point do you think the Prince and Princess knew for sure to whom they were talking?
6. To whom was the King speaking in lines 250–291? To whom did he think he was speaking? (Watch out; this gets complicated!)
7. How did the King and the Queen feel about their plan to get the Princess married? (297)

Apply the Ideas

Look again at the cast of characters at the beginning of the play. Decide which of the characters would agree with the following statements. Be ready to share the reasons for your choices.

1. Things are not always what they seem to be.
2. You work to please those who can decide your future.
3. People believe what they want to believe; they see what they want to see.
4. You can fool some of the people all the time and all the people some of the time, but you can't fool all the people all the time.
5. There is a lot of sense in nonsense.

Sense and Nonsense in Folktales

Anticipate the Form

Folktales are stories that have been passed on by word of mouth from one generation to the next. When people started writing the stories down, they often included an introduction to help the reader understand the customs that were important at the time of the story. The folktale that you will read next has such an introduction.

Another characteristic of folktales is that they often teach a lesson. As you read the folktale in this section, watch for the way in which nonsense is made from sense and then how sense is made from nonsense to make a point.

Expand Your Vocabulary

Before you read the story, check your understanding of some words you'll find in it. For each word in the following list, there is another word in the list that has a similar meaning. On a separate paper, write the pairs of words that have similar meanings. Work with other members of your group to complete your list. One pairing is done for you in the example. Use the glossary if you need help.

Example: inheritance—legacy

lineage	inheritance	continuity
son-like	posterity	illiterate
magistrate	legacy	astute
ignorant	filial	scrutinized
inspected	persistence	devotion
dedication	judge	descendants
sagacious	family	

The Will

A Chinese Folktale by Louise and Yuan-hsi Kuo

*In ancient times worship of heaven, earth, and the ancestors was
very important. The desire for male posterity arose from practicing
ancestral worship in which the male head of a family performed the
rituals. When he died, the oldest son, or a male next of kin, took his
place. If there were only a married daughter, her husband assumed
this responsibility and was treated like a son, if he seemed devoted to
the family. In that case, property, money, or worldly goods were be-
queathed to him. There was much scheming and many tragic inci-
dents as a result.*

*Although the baby in this story was called Tai (Big) as the eldest,
his middle name Fai (Not, a negative) indicated that he was physically small. A Chinese had several names besides the given name: a
milk name—as an infant; a school name—on first attending school;
another on reaching adulthood; one for scholarship; a professional
name; a retirement name, etc.*

*Only after lengthy contact with the West was practicing law
recognized as a profession in China. Prior to that, a magistrate controlled law and order. Some were notorious for being corrupt and
lacking wisdom; others, like the one in this tale, were honest and
sagacious. The play on words and elimination of punctuation in the
old man's will enabled the son-in-law to interpret it in his favor. The
astute magistrate prevented what would have been a miscarriage of
justice.*

There was once a rich man, over seventy years of age, living in Ch'angchow. He had only a daughter, who helped manage his affairs. After she married, her husband managed the old
man's properties. At first, his son-in-law took good care of the
old man, but the son-in-law's attitude gradually changed to
indifference. At times, he treated the old man very badly.

One day, old man Chiang thought to himself, "After all, a
son-in-law is an outsider. Besides, he has his own parents to
consider. Naturally, he would be inclined to protect the interests of his immediate family above all. Although I'm elderly,
I'm still strong. Why not marry a second time? I might have a
son, and in that case, the Chiang lineage would be continued."

A matchmaker was sent to a family in a nearby village.
They consented to the marriage, and a wedding was subse-
quently arranged. After a while, old Chiang's wife bore a baby

boy. The old man's daughter and his son-in-law were very up-set. But after all, what could they do? Old Chiang was truly a happy man.

According to custom, a big celebration was held when the child was one month old and given a name. He was named Chiang Tai Fei (Chiang Big Not) but was known by his milk name, Chiang Tai (Chiang Big or the eldest son of Chiang).

Time passed quickly, and after two years, old Chiang be-came seriously ill. Knowing that his end was near, he wrote two wills. The first was given privately to his wife, and he coached her thus: "I realize that my son-in-law is lacking in filial devo-tion. With my ancestors' blessings, you, my wife, gave me a son, thereby ensuring the continuity of the Chiang family. I'm leaving my property entirely to you. However, our son is only three years old (as soon as a baby was born, he was considered a year old), and since you're an illiterate woman, I'm afraid that my son-in-law will take advantage of you. It may seem as though my properties are being given to him—but wait until our son comes of age. Then go immediately to a righteous magistrate, declare your legal status, and claim the properties. Always remember the child's given name is Chiang Big Not. That is of utmost importance."

She carefully hid the will. Then the old man called his son-in-law to his deathbed to give him a will. "I've treated you well," he said. "Hereafter, you must look after your mother-in-law and her baby son. Don't make any trouble for them. Promise me that so I'll be able to die in peace."

"Yes, yes," the son-in-law said respectfully, taking the will. But since there is no capitalization in Chinese character-writing and old Chiang had omitted punctuation, the son-in-law interpreted the will according to his own wishful thinking and read: "Chiang big—not my son—to whom all property belongs son-in-law—outsider forbidden inheritance." This pleased him, and for a time he was most considerate of his mother-in-law and the child. But gradually he neglected them.

The years elapsed quickly, and the young boy came of age. The mother remembered her husband's last words and the will, so she took her son and the will to a righteous magistrate to claim the properties.

The son-in-law was not worried about the dispute over the old man's will because he believed that he possessed the rightful will, which he promptly presented to the magistrate. The handwriting was indisputably the old man's. Yet the neighbors said that the will was unfair since the old man had written it when very ill and not in complete control of his faculties. Nonetheless, since it was a legal document, the magistrate scrutinized it without saying a word. He did likewise with the will presented by the second wife. After examining both wills and hearing the neighbors' explanations, he felt that something was wrong with the son-in-law's will and pondered the matter for some time.

"What is the name of your father-in-law's son?" he asked the son-in-law.

"Chiang Big," he answered. "Everyone knows him by that name and calls him that."

"What is the name of your son?" the magistrate asked the mother.

"His name is Chiang Big Not. Chiang Big is his milk name."

"Have you heard what was said? Is this statement correct?" he asked the son-in-law.

The son-in-law was thinking that everybody called the baby by the milk name of Chiang Big but that his true given name was Chiang Big Not. So he nodded in agreement.

With that, the magistrate openly declared before the son-in-law, the daughter, the mother, all the relatives and neighbors present, "Old man Chiang was very clever. If the will had not been written in this manner, all the property would belong to his son-in-law. Something unfortunate might even have happened to the mother and son. This will was purposely written without punctuation." Thereupon he gave the proper punctuation to the will and officially declared it in order. "A given name must be used in all legal documents." Then he read aloud, "Chiang Big Not, my son to whom all properties belong; son-in-law, outsider, forbidden inheritance." The hidden meaning was thus revealed.

Everyone praised the fairness of the magistrate and the wisdom of old Chiang.

The following questions deal with specific actions, conditions, or information presented in the story. Discuss the answers with your group. Use information from the selection to support your answers.

1. What did Chiang do to protect his property and preserve his name?
2. What were the two names given to Chiang's son?
3. How did Chiang prepare his wife for his death?
4. How did Chiang prepare his son-in-law for his death?
5. How did the son-in-law interpret the will?
6. How did the magistrate interpret the will?
7. What was the result of the magistrate's interpretation of the will?

Interpret the Ideas

The following questions deal with ideas presented in the story. Discuss the answers with your group. Use information from the selection to support your answers.

1. Did Chiang view women and men as equals?
2. What responsibilities did the son-in-law feel toward promises he made?
3. What clues did the magistrate give as to how the will should be interpreted?
4. How did the magistrate insure that the brother-in-law would agree with his decision about the will?

Apply the Ideas

On the basis of the folktale you've just read and your own experiences, decide if you agree or disagree with this statement: When you depend on other people for help, it can be difficult to get them to do what you want them to do.

Punctuating for Sense and Nonsense

Punctuation is the system of inserting marks in writing or printing to help make the meaning clear. When people speak, they use pauses and voice changes to make meaning clear. When people write, they insert commas, semicolons, colons, periods, or dashes to stand for pauses or voice changes. Punctuation gives the reader information about how print would sound if it were spoken. It makes meaning clear. The folktale ''The Will'' showed the importance of punctuation in making meaning clear.

Placing the correct punctuation where it belongs can make the difference between understanding and confusion, sense and nonsense. For example, read these two sentences aloud to someone. They both use the same words, but each states a different fact.

1. Eileen Henry is looking for you.
2. Eileen, Henry is looking for you.

Which Is It?

Following is a series of questions followed by two sentences that are made different by a change in punctuation. Decide which sentence provides the best answer to the question. Be ready to give the reasons for your choices.

1. Both are slang greetings, but which is insulting?
   a. What's the latest, dope?
   b. What's the latest dope?

2. In which sentence is Mr. Rogers likely to be bawled out?
   a. Mr. Rogers, the secretary, is two hours late.
   b. Mr. Rogers, the secretary is two hours late.

3. Which may result in an embarrassing situation?
   a. The butler stood by the door and called the guests' names as they arrived.
   b. The butler stood by the door and called the guests names as they arrived.

4. Which headline would please the governor more?
   a. COLLEGE HEAD QUITS, CRITICIZING GOVERNOR
   b. COLLEGE HEAD QUITS CRITICIZING GOVERNOR

5. Which expresses greater regret?
   a. I'm sorry you can't come with us.
   b. I'm sorry. You can't come with us.

6. Which officials should be dismissed for revealing secrets?
   a. Seven officials knew the secret; all told.
   b. Seven officials knew the secret, all told.

7. Which sign would be better on (or over) a receptacle for litter?
   a. You can help throw it here.
   b. You can help; throw it here.

8. Which sentence shows the writer's extraordinary powers of persuasion?
   a. I left him convinced he was a fool.
   b. I left him, convinced he was a fool.

9. Which is an invitation to some kind of exhibit?
   a. We'd like to have you see our students work.
   b. We'd like to have you see our students' work.

10. In which case has the speaker already changed his friends' attitude toward him?
    a. Now, my friends, listen to me!
    b. Now my friends listen to me!

11. Which is being said by the person who has been insulted?
    a. You're always saying I'm stupid.
    b. You're always saying, "I'm stupid."

12. Which is merely a repetition for emphasis?
    a. In other words, the accent is on the second syllable.
    b. In other words the accent is on the second syllable.

Here are some brainteasers in which to apply your understanding of punctuation.

1. A Lifesaver

A story, undoubtedly untrue, is told of a Czarina who saved a man's life by shifting a semicolon. On the Czar's desk lay the request for leniency and the order he had just signed: "Pardon impossible; to be sent to Siberia."

Where did the Czarina place the semicolon that saved a man's life?

2. Turnabout Is Fair Play

Another story tells us that Mrs. Fiske, returning to her dressing room one evening, found a note from Margaret Anglin which read, "Margaret Anglin says Mrs. Fiske is the greatest actress in America." Greatly pleased, Mrs. Fiske decided to return both the compliment and the note by merely adding two commas.

How did the note that Margaret Anglin received read?

3. Men and Women

Still another story tells of a man who wrote an uncomplimentary line about women. The line read, "Woman without her man is a savage." A woman who knew her punctuation inserted two commas to make the line uncomplimentary to men.

Where did she place the commas?

More Sense and Nonsense in Poetry

Below is a poem that seems to be pure and simple nonsense. Yet, with a little imagination, it can be seen as a very sensible story. The poem has form, rhyme, and rhythm. Although some of the words are nonsense, the lines follow normal sentence structure. Just as punctuation can make sense out of nonsense, sentence structure can make sense out of nonsense words.

It's great fun to read the poem aloud, once you figure out how to pronounce the nonsense words. Read each stanza aloud with other members of your group to figure out the pronunciations of the nonsense words. Then prepare an oral reading for your classmates.

JABBERWOCKY

by Lewis Carroll

'Twas brillig, and the slithy toves
    Did gyre and gimble in the wabe:
All mimsy were the borogoves,
    And the mome raths outgrabe.

"Beware the Jabberwock, my son!
    The jaws that bite, the claws that catch!
Beware the Jubjub bird, and shun
    The frumious Bandersnatch!"

He took his vorpal sword in hand;
    Long time the manxome foe he sought—
So rested he by the Tumtum tree,
    And stood awhile in thought.

And, as in uffish thought he stood,
    The Jabberwock, with eyes of flame,
Came whiffling through the tulgey wood,
    And burbled as it came!

One, two! One, two! And through and through
    The vorpal blade went snicker-snack!
He left it dead, and with its head
    He went galumphing back.

"And hast thou slain the Jabberwock?
    Come to my arms, my beamish boy!
O frabjous day! Callooh, Callay!"
    He chortled in his joy.

'Twas brillig, and the slithy toves
    Did gyre and gimble in the wabe:
All mimsy were the borogoves,
    And the mome raths outgrabe.

Find the Sense

Does the poem make sense? See if you can answer these questions. Be ready to provide evidence from the poem to support your answers.

1. What were the slithy toves doing?
2. What was the father's warning?
3. Did the son find the Jabberwock, or did it find him?
4. What happened to the Jabberwock?
5. What was the father's reaction to the son's accomplishment?
6. What is the sense and the nonsense of the poem?

Interpret and Apply the Ideas

The poem is designed to appeal to your imagination. From your own imaginings of the events in the poem, select a segment of the poem and illustrate it. Be sure to be ready to defend your illustrations, using the meaning of the poem.

Sense and Nonsense in Tall Tales

Anticipate the Form

The story you are about to read is a tall tale, a story that uses exaggeration in a humorous way. The characters in a tall tale do extraordinary things that could never take place in real life. These impossible events, told in a straightforward manner using realistic details, are made to seem as though they could actually take place.

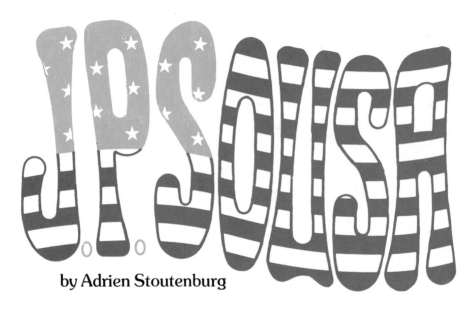

by Adrien Stoutenburg

Lots of folks around Killdugan Creek thought Uncle Jerry was crazy. Instead of selling his rickety little farm after years of dry weather and ruined crops, he stayed on and kept preaching about how there was going to be tons of rain soon. All the rest of the people, except those who stayed, sold their farms and moved to California. Old Jerry wouldn't budge. Day after day he'd sit on his porch playing his harmonica. "Old Jerry's a harmonica-playing fool," his neighbors said. But they admitted that he was very good at it.

One hot afternoon, along about sundown, Uncle Jerry was playing a concert for his bony chickens and his two or three skinny cows. He liked to play marching tunes, especially "The Stars and Stripes Forever," by the great bandmaster, John Philip Sousa. He was blowing away at that piece when suddenly he glanced down and saw a big, black, diamondback rattler coiled up at his feet. Uncle Jerry's false teeth almost fell out and the harmonica almost fell in, but he managed to keep on playing because that seemed the sensible thing to do. He played everything he knew and then started all over again. When he swung into "The Stars and Stripes Forever" once more, he noticed that the snake got kind of a happy look and swayed back and forth with the music.

Uncle Jerry kept playing until he ran out of breath. The sun had gone down and the moon was floating around overhead when, finally, he gave up. "You'll just have to go ahead and bite me," he told the snake, "if that's what you're hankerin' to do. I'll be blasted if I'm going to entertain you any more."

The snake seemed to nod as if it understood, and it looked completely satisfied. Then it gave its rattlers a few shakes, as if it were applauding, and crawled meekly away.

Every day after that, when Uncle Jerry came on the porch to play his harmonica, the snake showed up. It would sit there swaying in time to the music, its eyes glistening with pleasure. It wasn't long before Uncle Jerry liked that snake so much he'd play "The Stars and Stripes Forever" over and over. He even decided to call the snake J. P. Sousa, after his favorite composer. By the time a week or two had gone by, the snake had learned to shake his rattlers in time to the piece, and this made a really fine-sounding duet.

The days went on, getting hotter and dryer, and everybody said Uncle Jerry was double-crazy not to leave his farm and try raising crops somewhere else. Uncle Jerry just kept blowing his harmonica, while J. P. Sousa listened and rattled his tail in time. Then, one afternoon, the snake didn't come to the concert. He didn't show up the next day either, or the next. This shook Uncle Jerry so that he lost all his joy in music. Each day his concerts grew briefer until finally he put his harmonica away and sat silent, watching and waiting for J. P. Sousa to come back.

By July, Killdugan Creek was as dry as sandpaper, and Uncle Jerry's cows and chickens were standing around with their tongues hanging out, they were so thirsty. Then, on July 10, big, dark clouds started building up in the sky. It began to rain. It kept on raining for weeks on end. When the rain was over, the creek was full and all Uncle Jerry's crops were growing even faster than the weeds. People decided he wasn't as crazy as they thought—except for his talking about his pet snake and waiting for him to come back.

One day a neighboring farmer came along and said he'd like to graze a few of his cows on Uncle Jerry's land. He offered so much money for this that Uncle Jerry agreed. Uncle Jerry hitched up his two old horses to his broken-down wagon and drove the man around his land to show him the best grazing spots. All the time he kept watching for some glimpse of the musical snake.

Well, he and the neighbor were bouncing along in the squeaky, old buckboard wagon when all of a sudden Uncle Jerry heard a sound like drums rattling out a marching rhythm. The sound was coming from the top of a nearby hill. Uncle Jerry hollered "Whoa!" to the horses and jumped out of the wagon as fast as he could. He clambered up toward the top of the hill, his heart racing so fast his legs could hardly keep up with it.

There, at the top of the hill, was a large, flat rock. On the rock were three dozen fat diamondback rattlers in a circle. In the center of the circle was J. P. Sousa, his head high, his eyes shining with pride, waving his tail like the baton of an orchestra conductor. He was beating out the rhythm of "The Stars and Stripes Forever," while the rest of the snakes rattled along with him.

Fortunately, just that morning, Uncle Jerry had happened to put his harmonica in his hip pocket. Now he pulled it out and started blowing away. J. P. Sousa glanced around, stood up on the tip of his tail, and looked happy enough to faint. Then he went to work leading his snake orchestra again, and Uncle Jerry played along with them until the moon came up. The farmer who had come with him hated snakes, and he couldn't get away fast enough. He ran home and told everybody that Uncle Jerry was even crazier than they knew, that the snakes were going crazy, too, and that anybody with any sense would sell and get out of the country.

That's what everybody did, except Uncle Jerry. He stayed there with his fat cows and his green growing crops and plump chickens, and every day, around sundown, he'd go up to the hill and play his harmonica while the snake orchestra rattled time. Those

were the happiest hours of his life, and the happiest for J. P. Sousa too.

Those happy days are gone now, but the big, flat rock on the hill is still there (unless somebody has carried it away), and people say that on certain summer nights, the snakes still come there and form a circle and shake their rattlers to the tune of "The Stars and Stripes Forever." The snake in the middle, they say, is so old he has a beard. Whether it's really J. P. Sousa or not, no one knows. But they do say it makes sort of a pretty sound there in the Killdugan Creek country, if you happen to like marching tunes.

Analyze the Form

Tall tales, as you've just found out, are a combination of sense and nonsense. Decide whether the following statements from the story are examples of sense (what could actually take place) or nonsense (what is exaggerated). Be ready to defend your decisions.

1. Day after day he'd sit on his porch playing his harmonica.
2. When he swung into "The Stars and Stripes Forever" once more, he noticed that the snake got kind of a happy look and swayed back and forth with the music.
3. There, at the top of the hill, was a large, flat rock.
4. He (J. P. Sousa) was beating out the rhythm of "The Stars and Stripes Forever," while the rest of the snakes rattled along with him.
5. J. P. Sousa glanced around, stood up on the tip of his tail, and looked happy enough to faint.
6. Then he went to work leading his snake orchestra again, and Uncle Jerry played along with them until the moon came up.
7. The farmer who had come with him hated snakes, and he couldn't get away fast enough.
8. . . . on certain summer nights, the snakes still come there and form a circle and shake their rattlers to the tune of "The Stars and Stripes Forever."

Interpret and Apply the Ideas

In tall tales, the characters do extraordinary things. Humans can perform superhuman actions, and animals can do what only humans can do in real life. What did Uncle Jerry do that was a superhuman action? What did J. P. Sousa do that ordinarily only a human can do? What could the three dozen diamondback rattlers do that was extraordinary?

Sense and Nonsense in Cartoons

The humor in cartoons is usually based on a contrast between sense and nonsense. Some cartoons are based on a pun, the humorous use of a word that suggests its different meanings. The pun makes both sense and nonsense.

"Read" each of the cartoons on the following pages with two questions in mind:

1. In what way are the ideas presented in the cartoons sensible?
2. In what way are the ideas nonsense?

The Saturday Evening Post Company, 1975

"We can't afford to have you stay long—just discover Florida and come right back."

"Hello. Coast Guard? This is Johnson at the lighthouse."

Analyze and Apply the Ideas

Which statement can you relate to which cartoon? Can you relate some statements to more than one cartoon? Discuss your answers with your classmates.

1. Some rules and regulations do not apply to everyone.
2. Sometimes a rescuer needs rescuing.
3. One word may have several meanings.
4. History may have different interpretations.

Pulling It All Together

In this unit on sense and nonsense, you have read:

1. sense and nonsense about animals through poetry;
2. a play about a Princess who became beautiful at just the right moment, in spite of her parents' nonsense;
3. a Chinese folktale that teaches a lesson;
4. parallel sentences that illustrate how punctuation can convert sense to nonsense—or the reverse;
5. poetry made up of nonsense words;
6. about an extraordinary man and an extraordinary snake;
7. about sense and nonsense as shown through cartoons.

Refer to the definitions of sense and nonsense at the beginning of this unit. For each of the poems, stories, and cartoons and for the article and the play, identify the definitions of sense and nonsense that seem to fit it.

Also in this unit, you have read three different types of literature that combine sense and nonsense: a fairy tale, a folktale, and a tall tale. Decide whether each of the following statements describes a fairy tale, a folktale, or a tall tale. Some statements may describe more than one form of literature, so be sure you can give reasons for your answers.

1. The story uses exaggeration in a humorous way.
2. The setting of the story is usually an imaginary kingdom.
3. The story explains a custom or way of life of a people.
4. The story often teaches a lesson.
5. The main characters are usually members of royalty.
6. The characters are able to do extraordinary things.
7. The story may be a combination of sense and nonsense.

Following are some ideas about sense and nonsense. You discussed some of them earlier at the beginning of this unit. Other ideas have been added to that list. Decide which of the materials that you read in this unit are illustrations of these ideas. Be ready to discuss the reasons for your decisions.

1. Sense and nonsense depend on one's point of view.
2. Language does not make sense or nonsense; the user does.
3. If one person completely controls the actions of a second person, that second person cannot know if his or her action is sense or nonsense.

4. Sense and nonsense are always opposites.
5. If used in a certain way, words without meaning can show meaning.
6. Nonsense can be very sensible.

Now, go back to the quotation on the first page of this unit. Do you agree or disagree with the quotation? Explain your answer.

Putting Your Knowledge to Work

Here are some ideas for activities which give you the opportunity to use what you have learned in this unit. Choose one or more that you would like to do alone or with a group. Sometimes it makes more sense to work with others.

1. Put together a portfolio of cartoons that are based on puns. Ask some classmates to act as newspaper or magazine editors. Have them pick out the cartoons they think would work best in their publications.
2. Make a cartoon puzzle book as follows: Collect several cartoons. Remove the captions from the cartoons. Place three or four cartoons on the left-hand page of a notebook. On the opposite (facing) page, place the captions for those cartoons in a different order. Do several pages in the same way. Then ask classmates to match the captions to the cartoons and make sense out of nonsense!
3. Put together an anthology of nonsense poetry. Ask several different classmates to illustrate the poems so that you can get a variety of art styles into your anthology. Organize the poems and illustrations into a class book.
4. Do some research on such tall tale heroes as Paul Bunyan, Captain Stormalong, and John Henry. Share your findings with your classmates.
5. Find a one-act play that fits the theme of sense and nonsense. Rehearse the play with your group, and then perform it for your classmates.

Here are some books about sense and nonsense that you might enjoy:

Alexander, Lloyd. *The Town Cats and Other Tales*. New York: E. P. Dutton, 1977.
 These original stories describe magical cats, industrious cats, and wise cats.
Cummings, Richard. *Make Your Own Comics for Fun and Profit*. New York: Henry Z. Walck, Inc., 1976.
 This book describes how to create comics, complete with publication information.
Levin, Sonia. *The Mark of Conte*. New York: Atheneum Publishers, 1976.
 The school's computer lists one boy as ''Conte, Mark'' and ''Mark, Conte.'' Can he take both schedules and finish school early?
Rodgers, Mary. *A Billion for Boris*. New York: Harper and Row, Publishers, 1974.
 Boris wants to get rich by taking advantage of getting information a day early.
Silverstein, Shel. *Where the Sidewalk Ends*. New York: Harper and Row, Publishers, 1974.
 This anthology of poems includes zany illustrations by the author.

Lost and Found

six

"I have lost all and found myself."
—John Clarke

Lost and *found* are simple words, but you will find in your reading that they can have different meanings to different people or in different situations.

Key Concepts

lost (a) not used, won, or claimed; (b) unable to find the way or unable to be found; (c) ruined or destroyed; (d) no longer in possession.

found (a) met by chance; (b) discovered; (c) came upon by searching or studying; (d) recovered.

Getting in Touch with Your Experiences

Work with your group to make a list of all the words you can think of that have to do with the words *lost* and *found*: for example, compass, treasure, frighten. Then group your words under categories that make sense in terms of their meanings. You might group the word *frighten* with other words from your list that describe feelings about being lost. You might group the word *treasure* with other words that describe things that can be lost and found. Use as many categories as you need to group your words in ways that make sense. Be sure you can explain why certain words go together.

The statements below have something to do with the ideas of lost and found. Decide which of the statements you can agree with on the basis of your own experiences. You may agree with some or all of the statements or reject some or all of them. The important thing is to be able to give a reasonable explanation for your choices. Discuss your ideas with others in your group.

1. Finding takes more time and effort than losing.
2. It is possible not to know where you are located and yet not be lost; it is possible to know where you are located and yet be lost.
3. People are lost when they don't know how to get home from where they are.
4. Nothing is ever lost permanently; it will be found someday, somewhere, somehow, by someone.
5. As long as you know that you are alive and located somewhere, you aren't lost; you are lost only to those who happen to be looking for you.
6. As long as you can see the sun or the stars, you need not be lost.

Lost and Found
in Literature

Make Some Predictions

Suppose you were trapped in an old, abandoned mine with the only opening a hundred feet (about thirty meters) overhead. You had swum into the mine through an old underwater shaft, but that collapsed after you passed through it. All you have with you are your scuba equipment and a long steel pole. You can hear people outside the mine opening, but they don't know you are down there.

What would you do to help those people find you? Here's a checklist of ideas. Decide which ideas you might try, given the limitations of the situation. You may want to add ideas of your own. Discuss your choices—and your additions—with others in your group. Be ready to explain the reasons for your decisions.

Survival Checklist
1. Yell and scream a lot.
2. Light a fire and hope the smoke would drift out the opening.
3. Make a kite, write a message on its tail, and send the kite out the opening.
4. Build a large pyramid with rocks up to the opening and climb out.
5. Cut steps in the side of the shaft and climb out.
6. Practice your high jump.
7. Call for a helicopter to drop a line and pull you out.
8. Worry a lot.
9. Wish you had stayed home.
10. Find some way to send a message using your scuba equipment.

The story you are about to read describes one person's efforts to survive. As you read, note the sequence of the steps that were taken in the survival attempt.

The Message

by Raboo Rodgers

It was an incredible thing to have happen, but, more than
that, it was an awful way to die.

Ben leaned back and pushed idly at the pile of white bones
with his bare toes. So far he had identified the skulls of three deer
and two cattle. There were bones from smaller animals, too,
opossums or raccoons maybe, but he wasn't sure about those.

He heard the helicopter approach again, swinging wide to
make its turn and head back down river. This time he caught a
quick glimpse of it as it crossed the narrow shaft of light high
overhead, but he did not stand or wave or shout, because he
knew it was useless.

Less than a hundred yards (about ninety meters) away they
were looking for him, dragging the river for his body. The county
rescue department, along with a handful of volunteers, would
keep searching for him there.

"They might as well be looking for me in China," Ben said
aloud.

What had happened to Ben began three days earlier when
he and his good friend Carrie Burke donned their scuba gear and
descended into the deep waters of the Patawa River. They were
pursuing the big catfish which inhabited the numerous holes in
the face of the underwater portion of a cliff. Both divers carried
a long steel pole with a small gaff hook on one end.

It was a form of grabbling, modified by the use of scuba
gear. Using the blunt end of the poles, they poked in the holes or
beneath the overhangs and shelves until they felt the movement
of a catfish. Then, using the gaff end, they would work the fish
out until they could get their free hand in its mouth. It wasn't a
way to catch a lot of catfish, but it was a good way to catch the
big ones.

The water was murky, and it was difficult for the two divers
to keep each other in sight. Ben was trailing Carrie along the
face of the cliff near the bottom of the river, when suddenly he
saw a dark shape ghosting through a crevice. It was a big cat,
and he pursued it, hoping it would hole up where he could corner
it. The catfish glided under a huge overhang and disappeared.

Ben went under the rock after it and found himself in nearly
total darkness. He unsnapped the small underwater light from
his belt and switched it on. River plankton floated around him,

and through it he could see the dark gray rock which seemed to surround him. He had lost the catfish, but he was curious now about the underwater enclosure, and he began slowly kicking upward.

Expecting at any moment to meet solid rock, he suddenly broke through the surface of the water and found himself in a cavern the size of a small room. The rock ceiling arched overhead, dripping. The air was dank. Right then he should have turned back and gone after Carrie, but he didn't.

On one side of the cavern was a soft mud bank. Ben swam to it and pulled himself from the water. He stood and played the light around the rock, examining this strange phenomenon he had discovered. It was then that he felt the cold draft.

The side of the cavern where he stood was earthy and soft, and at knee level there was a hole in it, about two feet (about sixty centimeters) in diameter. The weight of his scuba tank still on his back, he knelt and examined it. On the other side of the hole was what appeared to be another cavernous area, but there was light in this one, though it seemed dim and far away. Excited, Ben dug at the hole with his hands, widening it. The soft, wet earth came away easily, until a large rock blocked any further digging. Grasping the edge of it, Ben leaned back and strained. The rock, too, fell away easily (too easily, he would realize later).

Ben stepped through the gaping hole into an adjoining tunnel, handmade and shored with ancient timbers. Briefly he thought of Carrie; then he removed his flippers and scuba tank. When diving in the Patawa, he and Carrie often became temporarily separated, and he knew Carrie wouldn't begin to worry for several more minutes.

The tunnel sloped up away from the river, and Ben walked quickly toward the light. But when he reached it, he found he had not come to the end of the shaft. Instead, the tunnel turned and rose vertically until it broke through the surface of the ground nearly a hundred feet (thirty meters) straight overhead. Ben saw the top of a fence post up there and a couple of strands of barbed wire, and then he realized where he was.

The entrance to a long-abandoned mine shaft was back about 350 feet (about one hundred meters) from the edge of Pinnacle Point in rough terrain, where few people ever went. Mildly disappointed, Ben turned and started back down the shaft toward the river.

A slurping, sucking noise was his first indication that something was wrong. When he reached the place where he had left his scuba gear, his suspicion turned to horror. Somehow, in digging into the mine shaft, he had disturbed something, releasing a massive mud flow. Already his exit was blocked as mud oozed and poured in from everywhere. In a matter of minutes, the end of the shaft was completely filled, and Ben was hopelessly trapped.

He had yelled. He had beaten his steel gaff pole against his scuba tank. He had even tried throwing rocks up out of the shaft in an effort to attract someone's attention (and had to dodge the rocks as they fell back down on him). But it was useless. It was all useless. Smoke rising from the shaft might have been effective, but in the wet tunnel, a fire was not possible.

The helicopter, as they searched the river for him, had excited him at first, but there was no way to signal it, and after three days he had given up hope. He would die in here.

Looking at his scuba tank, he thought it was too bad the shaft wasn't filled with water. Then he could swim out. "I've got a lot of air left," he mumbled. "I didn't use more than ten minutes of it. There's probably over 2,000 pounds (about 900 kilograms) still left in the tank."

Ben's mind wandered. He and Carrie had gotten their tanks filled at Diver's Den four days earlier. While waiting for the big, slow compressor, they read a couple of newspaper articles tacked to the bulletin board. One pictured an automobile in which a scuba tank had exploded, in the trunk. The car was demolished. Above the article was a reminder to have your tank inspected regularly.

The other article showed a picture of a concrete wall, one foot (about thirty centimeters) thick with a hole blown through it. A man had accidentally dropped his tank onto a concrete walk,

knocking off the valve. The tank became a missile and traveled three blocks before striking the wall. Above the article was a reminder to be careful. Two thousand to 2,500 pounds (about 900–1130 kilograms) of compressed air released suddenly could be devastating.

"Maybe I could blow up my tank somehow," Ben said, talking to himself. "Maybe they'd hear the explosion. Yeah, and maybe I'd just bring this whole shaft down on me, too," he added, dismissing the idea. Then another thought entered Ben's

head, this one even more absurd than blowing up the tank. He dismissed it, too, but it came back. He looked at his gaff pole and his flippers, and the ridiculous idea grew. Had he not been so desperate, he would have laughed it off. Instead, he got to his feet and went to work.

He removed the backpack from the tank, then removed the waist and shoulder straps from the backpack. Tossing the regulator aside, he placed his gaff pole against and parallel to the tank and cinched it there tightly with the straps. The gaff end of the pole now extended four feet (about 122 centimeters) beyond the tank's valve. He slipped a flipper over the gaff, pushing it up until the hook extended through the toe opening, preventing the flipper from sliding off. Now came the tricky part—setting it up.

Numerous rocks and boulders covered the floor of the mine shaft. Ben chose a large one with a hard, sharp edge about chest high. Using smaller rocks to prop it up, he placed the tank, valve down, on top of it with the gaff pole extending down and past the edge. The weight of the tank rested entirely on the valve, its weakest part. It would have been better for the rounded end of the tank to point straight up the shaft, but for what Ben had in mind, it was necessary to tilt it slightly, thereby aligning it with a point on the side of the shaft about twenty-five feet (seven-and-a-half meters) overhead.

Ben looked at what he had done. He had little hope it would actually work, but it was the only chance he had. He adjusted the rocks around the scuba tank, wedging one securely on the side of the acute angle of tilt. He checked the valve again. All of the weight was now on one side of its tip.

One final touch: using the buckle of his weight belt, Ben scratched a message in the yellow paint of the tank: LOOK IN OLD MINE SHAFT.

There it was, a Fourth-of-July and New-Year's-Eve rocket all rolled into one, its body of steel, its stabilizer a gaffpole and flipper, and its propulsion compressed air at 2,000 pounds (about 13,800 kilopascals) per square inch. Ben examined more of the rocks on the floor of the shaft, finally selected one of about forty pounds (eighteen kilograms) and placed it near the inverted scuba tank. Then he waited.

He waited for what seemed an eternity before he heard the faint sound of the chopper as it came back upriver. He picked up the rock and held it against his chest. The sound grew louder as the helicopter neared Pinnacle Point. Ben hoisted the rock high overhead and held it there.

If the tank exploded—well, it wouldn't matter.

Now! Ben thought. *Now!* With every ounce of strength he possessed, he brought the rock down and smashed it into the side of the scuba tank as near the valve as possible. The valve sheared against the hard stone, and the scuba tank took off as if shot from a cannon.

Ben was on his back, looking up. The tank slammed into the side of the shaft about where he had anticipated and glanced off, the stabilizer of gaff pole and flipper keeping the exhaust pointing downward. Rocks and dirt rained down as the rocket ricocheted from one side of the shaft to the other. Toward the top of the shaft the tank became more stable and traveled the last twenty-five feet (seven and a half meters) barely touching the sides.

Ben was amazed. The amount of thrust generated by the compressed air was incredible. Astonished, he watched the rocket blast out into the sunlight and shoot high into the sky before falling out of his field of view to one side. The last he saw of it was the sun glinting from the belt buckle of the strap which secured the gaff pole to the tank.

Within fifteen minutes, heads appeared at the top of the shaft. One of the heads was Carrie's. "Ben!" she shouted. "Ben!"

"You get my message, Carrie?" Ben yelled up at her.

Carrie laughed—the kind of relieved, hysterical laugh of someone whose best friend has come back from the dead. "We got your message all right, Ben. I was in the helicopter. You nearly shot us out of the sky."

Compare Your Predictions

Now you know how Ben managed to go from lost to found. Were any of his actions the same as what you thought you would do in the same situation? Go back to the Survival Checklist and see where Ben agreed with you.

Analyze the Sequence

Ben conducted an experiment in jet propulsion. It worked and saved his life. Did you follow clearly how Ben set up the equipment? Double-check your understanding by analyzing the following list. Compare the items listed to the description and the drawing in the story. Decide the order in which the items in this list should be placed to match Ben's experiment.

1. Ben discarded the air regulator.
2. Ben fastened one of his flippers to the hook on the gaff pole.
3. Ben removed the straps from his backpack.
4. Ben set the scuba tank on its valve on a rock ledge.
5. Ben struck the tank with a heavy rock to break the valve.
6. Ben propped up the tank with smaller rocks.
7. Ben fastened the gaff pole to the scuba tank with straps.
8. The tank shot up through the opening.
9. Ben scratched a message on the tank.

Analyze the Character

What was the character in this story really like? Listed below are statements which might describe Ben's character. Decide which of the statements apply to Ben, and be ready to give evidence from the story to support your decisions.

1. He had a good imagination.
2. He responded well in emergency situations.
3. He was willing to risk his life in order to live.
4. He was always careful.
5. He was curious about his surroundings.
6. He was physically strong.
7. He always used common sense.
8. He made good use of knowledge.
9. He was weak as well as strong.
10. He was a loner.

Apply the Ideas

On the basis of what you've read and your own experience, would you agree or disagree with the following statements? Be ready to defend your decisions.

1. It's better to act than to sit and worry.
2. Where there's a will, there's a way.
3. Even experienced scuba divers should never dive alone.
4. You can't always rely on others; sometimes only you yourself can solve a problem.
5. It's easier to make a mistake than it is to correct it.

Lost and Found Treasures

Throughout the ages, treasures have been hidden for safekeeping. In one ancient civilization, treasures were hidden not only for safekeeping, but also for use in an afterlife. The article you will read next tells of such treasures.

Expand Your Vocabulary

The pairs of words in column A are probably familiar to you. The pairs of words in column B, which are from the selection, may not be as familiar. Knowing these words will help you to read about the treasures of one ancient civilization.

Discuss the pairs in each column and consider in what ways the two words in each pair fit together. After you have discussed the pairs separately, try matching pairs. That is, match a pair from column B that has a certain relationship with a pair from column A that has the same kind of relationship. Match as many pairs as you can. Be ready to discuss the reasons for your matchings. Here's an example:

8. mass—humanity   i. hordes—people

Men, women, girls, and boys are thought of as humanity. When large numbers of them come together, it is thought of as a mass—of humanity. Large numbers of people also are thought of as hordes. Thus, *hordes of people* is an idea that is similar to *mass of humanity.*

Column A
1. scatter—mess
2. care—loss
3. grand—splendid
4. near—reach
5. corpse—coffin
6. church—reverent
7. riches—goods
8. mass—humanity
9. biologist—living things
10. search—dig
11. waiting room—room

Column B
a. archaeologist—ancient things
b. magnificent—wondrous
c. precaution—deterioration
d. antechamber—chamber
e. shrine—awestruck
f. verge—happen
g. strew—disarray
h. expedition—excavation
i. hordes—people
j. wealth—possessions
k. mummy—sarcophagus

Use the Headings

Authors of articles sometimes use headings to help their readers understand what they have written. These headings tell the reader what is coming next and also how the whole article is organized. The article you will read next has subheadings as well as main headings. Study the following outline to see how the subheadings relate to the main headings.

I. Lost
   A. The Pharaohs and Their Treasures
   B. The Tombs of the Kings
II. The Search
   A. The Davis Search
   B. The Carter Search
III. Found
   A. First Discoveries
   B. Antechamber
   C. Burial Chamber
   D. Treasury Chamber
   E. Side Chamber
IV. After the Lost Was Found
   A. Lord Carnarvon
   B. Howard Carter
   C. King Tutankhamen

Predict the Actions

Below are statements that describe some actions people might take if they were searching for something that had been lost for hundreds—or thousands—of years. First, read the statements and decide if you would take that action. Then read the article and see if the searchers would have agreed with you.

1. Study the problems you face and your chances of success.
2. Obtain permission for the search if permission is required.
3. Remain hopeful despite a lack of results.
4. Obtain the money necessary for doing the work.
5. Lay out a careful plan to avoid missing a spot and to avoid going over the same ground.
6. Share your discoveries with those who have helped you.
7. Record your findings carefully. Don't be so excited about their monetary value that you forget their historical value.

KING TUTANKHAMEN
AND HIS TREASURES

MEDITERRANEAN SEA

Cairo

RED
SEA

Thebes •

Nile River

EGYPT

**Egypt: At King Tuts Tomb, in the valley of the tombs
of the Kings, where twenty dynasties are buried.**

LOST

The Pharaohs and Their Treasures

More than five thousand years ago, a great and wealthy civilization grew up along the Nile River in Egypt. The ancient Egyptians had a strong belief in life after death. Whenever a pharaoh (a king or queen of Egypt) died, the body was embalmed and carefully wrapped to preserve it. This mummy was then put into a tomb with any possessions it might need in the next life. These possessions were usually gold or gold covered and encrusted with jewels. They included chariots, thrones, life-size statues, couches, caskets of jewelry, and preserved foods. The mummy itself, which took seventy days to prepare, was usually bedecked with jewels before it was placed in the sarcophagus.

The Tombs of the Kings

The pharaohs were buried in the remote Valley of the Tombs of the Kings. Because the treasures buried with each pharaoh were so valuable, the tombs had to be carefully hidden. They were usually dug deep into rock faces, and the entrances were covered with large rocks that were sealed. Dummy entrances leading to dead ends were even cut into the rock faces. Despite these precautions and a generally held belief that tomb robbers would be subject to a mummy's curse, the tombs were broken into and stripped of their treasures.

Of all the tombs uncovered in the valley, none was found in its original state. Each tomb had been looted and the mummy moved from its original resting place. It was the dream of every archaeologist in the valley to find a tomb that had remained untouched throughout the centuries.

THE SEARCH

The Davis Search

The Egyptian government allowed only one archaeological expedition at a time in the Valley of the Tombs of the Kings. In the early 1900's, the concession was given to Theodore Davis, a wealthy American. Davis believed that the tombs of all but three pharaohs had been uncovered. The three tombs yet to be found were those belonging to Tutankhamen,[1] Akhenaten,[2] and Horemheb.[3]

In the twelve years that Davis and his crew excavated in the valley, they made several finds. In 1908, they uncovered the granite sarcophagus of Horemheb; however, only the skull and a few bones remained inside. The remains of Akhenaten's tomb were also found. A shallow pit grave holding pottery jars bearing the seal of Tutankhamen lead Davis to believe that this was all that was left of Tutankhamen's burial site. Davis was convinced that there were no more tombs left to uncover in the valley.

[1] Tutankhamen   (tü'tang'käm'ən)
[2] Akhenaten   (ok'ə not'ən)
[3] Horemheb   (hō'rem heb)

342

The Carter Search

One member of the Davis expedition was Howard Carter, an English archaeologist and self-taught Egyptologist. Carter first visited Egypt in 1890. He wished to head his own expedition in the valley, but there were two drawbacks. First, Carter would have to get the concession from Davis; second, he would have to find a patron who would provide the money for the expedition.

In 1907, Carter found a patron in Lord Carnarvon, a wealthy earl and an amateur Egyptologist. For health reasons Lord Carnarvon traveled to Egypt to avoid the cold, damp winters in England. Lord Carnarvon and Carter began working together in Thebes.[4] When Davis gave up his concession in 1914, Carter and Carnarvon were given the concession to excavate in the Valley of the Tombs of the Kings.

Howard Carter was convinced that the tomb of Tutankhamen was yet to be found. He did not think that the shallow grave discovered by Davis could have been the tomb of a wealthy pharaoh. The pottery found in the grave was examined further. It was learned that the jars contained clay seals with Tutankhamen's name and floral collars like the ones worn at royal funerals. The site uncovered by Davis contained the items used during Tutankhamen's funeral but was not the actual burial site.

Carter began a systematic search of the valley. He drew a map of the area and divided it into carefully marked segments. He checked off each segment as it was excavated down to bedrock. By early 1922, Carter's search had yielded no clues to the whereabouts of Tutankhamen's tomb. Lord Carnarvon had already spent $250,000 on the search and was ready to call it off. Carter pleaded for one more year, and Lord Carnarvon agreed.

Only one triangular area near the entrance to the tomb of Rameses[5] VI was left. The area had been untouched because it contained the huts of ancient workers on the tomb of Rameses VI. This was a popular tourist site, and beginning a dig there meant closing off the tourist attraction.

FOUND

First Discoveries

In November 1922, tons of rubble were removed from the area near the tomb of Rameses VI. On November 4, a stone step cut into the bedrock was uncovered. The next day more rubble was removed to reveal the upper edge of a stairway leading deeper into the ground.

Carter could barely contain his enthusiasm. After almost twenty years of searching with no results, he was on the verge of a magnificent discovery. But in fairness to Lord Carnarvon, Carter re-covered the entrance and sent for Lord Carnarvon to be in on the search. When Lord Carnarvon and Lady Evelyn Herbert, his daughter, ar-

---

[4] Thebes (thēbz) [5] Rameses (ram′ə sēz)

rived from England, the excavation continued.

Soon sixteen stone steps were uncovered, along with a tomb door. On the door were several seals, some bearing the name of Tutankhamen. Examination of the door showed that it had been broken open at least twice by tomb robbers. The door and seals were photographed and then carefully removed. Behind the door was a passageway filled with rocks. It led to another door. This door led to an antechamber, but its seals showed that it, too, had been broken open.

Carter made a small hole in the doorway to the antechamber. He shone a light through the hole to determine if any of the original treasures remained. He was awe-struck by the wealth of the treasures contained there. But still Carter could not yet enter the antechamber. He closed it off and went to Cairo[6] to buy packing materials and preservatives. When he returned, he recleared the passageway and called together a group of archaeologists.

Antechamber

What excitement when the door to the antechamber was first opened! Hundreds of gleaming

[6] Cairo (kī′rō)

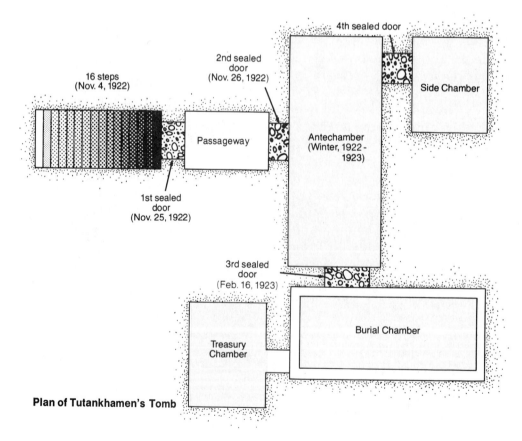

Plan of Tutankhamen's Tomb

treasures, beautifully designed and crafted, were piled one on top of another. The sight was dazzling. Two more doors were discovered in this room. But before what lay behind them could be explored, each of the items in the antechamber had to be carefully examined.

The slow, painstaking cataloguing of the seven hundred items began. Each item was photographed, and descriptive notes were made. Some necklaces and pectorals (chest ornaments) had to be restrung. Large pieces of furniture were disassembled and removed in sections. Among the items in the antechamber were boxes of flowers and preserved foods and alabaster jars and vases. There were golden couches decorated with the carved heads of animals, gold and alabaster statues, golden chariots, and a jewel-encrusted, gold-and-silver throne carved to show the images of King Tutankhamen and his young bride.

Each item had to be protected from deterioration, labeled, and carefully packed for shipment to the Cairo Museum. Archaeologists, botanists, chemists, anatomists, and photographers labored at the site. The work was made more difficult by the hordes of tourists, reporters, and officials who came to view the treasures.

Howard Carter, discoverer of the tomb of King Tutankhamen, at the entrance to the tomb

TURN TO PAGE 440

345

Burial Chamber

Only after the antechamber had been emptied in February of 1923 could the third door be examined. This led to the burial chamber of Tutankhamen. Two life-size statues of the king stood guard on each side of the door. This door, too, had been broken open and then resealed. Inside the door was a golden shrine—one with an unbroken seal. For the first time a tomb containing the sealed possessions and mummy of an ancient king had been uncovered. For 3,300 years the royal mummy of Tutankhamen had remained untouched by tomb robbers.

Three shrines were fitted snugly inside the main shrine. It took eighty-four days to remove the eighty parts of the four golden shrines. Finally, in November 1926, twelve years after the search had begun and four years after the uncovering of the first stone step, the coffins of Tutankhamen were uncovered.

Three coffins were found inside the fourth shrine, which was a stone sarcophagus. The inner-

Tomb of Tutankhamen showing the golden coffin

Miniature sarcophagus containing the internal organs of the king.

most coffin was of solid gold and weighed 2,500 pounds (about 1,130 kilograms). Inside lay the mummy of Tutankhamen. The face, shoulders, and heart were covered with a magnificent golden mask in the image of the young ruler. Within the folds of the linen bandages were 143 objects—gold rings, bracelets, finger sheaths, necklaces, and pectorals.

Treasury Chamber

Along one wall of the burial chamber was an entranceway to a treasury chamber. Inside this room was a chest containing the carefully preserved internal organs of the king. Four golden goddesses guarded the chest. Other statues, model ships, ornate chests, and golden furnishings filled the room.

Side Chamber

The fourth door of the tomb led to a side chamber filled with objects in disarray. This door had been broken open and the contents of the room strewn about by robbers. Archaeologists believe that the tomb had been broken into about twenty-five years after Tutankhamen's burial. The robbers probably broke in twice, the second time getting caught, as evidenced by the scattered loot left in the antechamber and this side room.

AFTER THE LOST WAS FOUND

Lord Carnarvon

Lord Carnarvon was never to know that Tutankhamen's untouched mummy was enshrined in the burial chamber. He died in April 1923, at the age of fifty-seven. His death started rumors of a mummy's curse; the rumors lasted for years.

Howard Carter

Carter continued working at the site until 1932. He searched carefully to see that not one bead or piece of broken pottery was overlooked. Throughout the years he engaged in various disputes with reporters, his patron Lord Carnarvon, government officials, and even nations. His find was so great that it aroused the interest and greed of people everywhere.

King Tutankhamen

Archaeologists learned that Tutankhamen reigned about 1400 B.C. His nine-year rule began when he was nine and ended with his death at eighteen. Carved images of his fourteen-year-old bride were found in his tomb.

King Tutankhamen ruled during the least glamorous period of Egypt's history. He was the youngest and least important of all the pharaohs buried in the Valley of the Tombs of the Kings. If his treasures were so great, how much greater the treasures of the well-known pharaohs must have been!

Tutankhamen treasures: Goddess of Serket

Mask of King Tutankhamen

Refer to the predictions you made on page 340. Decide which of them are supported by evidence from the article. Use the headings in the article to help you identify the evidence.

Apply the Ideas

Almost everyone has lost, found, or hidden something at some time in his or her life. Decide which of the following ideas you can support from your own experiences and which you can support with information from the article. Discuss each item and your evidence with others in your group.

1. If you want something badly enough, you will work until you get it—even though you may fail a few times along the way.
2. The more precious an object is, the more likely it is to be hidden.
3. A hidden object is more likely to be lost than an object that is just lying around.
4. Objects worth hiding are rarely enjoyed by those who own them or those who want them.
5. If something is lost, there is always someone who wants to find it.
6. If an object is hidden carefully and lost, not too many people will ever know that it needs to be found.
7. It is easier to interest people in trying to find lost money than to find lost history.

Lost and Found Geographically

Howard Carter was able to find a lost treasure by drawing an area map and carefully marking off segments as search areas. If you were lost at sea, drawing an area map would be impossible, since there would be no landmarks. But you could still figure out where you were. The next two articles will tell you how.

Anticipate the Ideas

Below are several questions that will help you focus on information and ideas contained in the next two articles. Work with others in your group to develop answers to the questions. If you are unfamiliar with a word, look it up in the glossary. Then, after you have read the articles, see if you should change any of your answers. Be ready to give evidence to support your ideas.

1. In what way are the following objects alike? In what way are they different?

    compass   sextant   chronometer

2. In what way are the following ideas alike? In what way are they different?

    north   south   east   west

3. In what way(s) are latitude and longitude alike? In what way(s) are they different?

4. What do the sun, the moon, and the stars have to do with the ideas of lost and found?

5. If you travel north on the earth, is there a time when you would automatically start traveling south? If you travel east on the earth, is there a time when you would automatically start traveling west? Demonstrate your answer by using a globe of the earth.

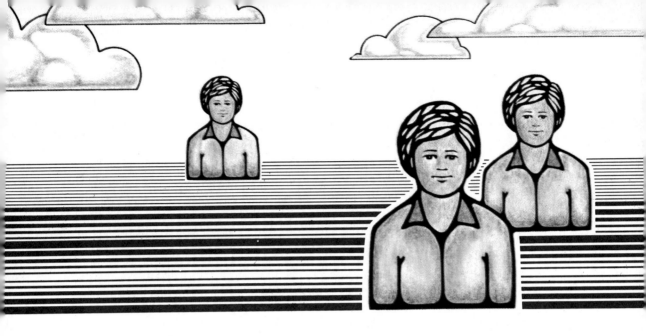

Where in the World Am I?: Latitude

by Beulah Tannenbaum and Myra Stillman

People have always been very curious about this world. The people of ancient Greece used their minds to find out things which their eyes could never see. They invented geometry to help them measure the earth. In fact, the word **geometry** comes from two Greek words meaning "to measure the earth."

All measurements must start somewhere. Any flat area, such as a field, has a beginning and an end, so that it is always possible to find an edge from which to start measuring. But a ball has no beginning and no end, and our earth is shaped somewhat like a ball.

MEASURING THE EARTH

Long ago the people of ancient Babylon* decided to divide the circle into 360 equal parts, and today we still use their system. Each of these parts is called a degree, so there are 360 degrees in a circle. This is often written as 360°. The mark ° means "degree." Each degree can be divided into 60 equal parts called minutes, written as 60′.

To measure the earth, the people of ancient times created two imaginary lines. One is a straight line running through the center of the earth from north to south. This line is called the earth's

---

* Babylon (bab ə ln)

axis and runs from the North Geographic Pole to the South Geographic Pole, the two points where all the earth's lines of longitude meet. (You will read about longitude in the next article.)

The second imaginary line they chose for measuring is a curved line that goes around the earth and is at all places halfway between the North and the South Poles. This line is called the equator because it is equally distant from both poles and therefore divides the earth exactly in half. The distance from every point on the equator to either pole is one fourth of a circle going completely around the earth and passing through each pole. Since a circle is divided into 360 degrees, the distance from any point on the equator to either pole is one fourth of 360 degrees, or 90 degrees. (See Figure 1.)

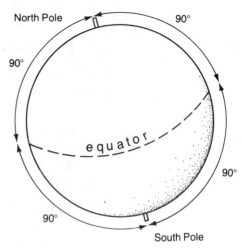

Fig 1: The distance from the equator to either pole is ¼ of a circle or 90°

LATITUDE

The distance in degrees north or south of the equator is called the latitude. A position north of the equator is always written as so many degrees North Latitude, and south of the equator as so many degrees South Latitude. For example, Cocos Island in the Pacific Ocean is about 5

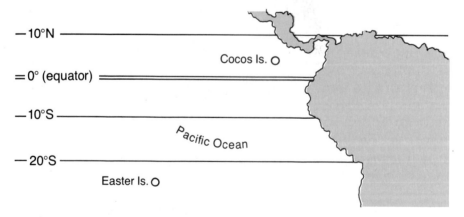

Fig 2: Position of Cocos and Easter Islands

degrees north of the equator and is noted on sea charts as 5°30' (5 degrees, 30 minutes) N. Lat. Easter Island is about 27 degrees south of the equator and is written 27°3' (27 degrees, 3 minutes) S. Lat. (See Figure 2.)

When two or more lines are the same distance apart for their entire length, they are called parallel lines. On a globe you will find a number of circles which are parallel to the equator. These are parallels of latitude. Notice that as you come closer to the poles, the distance around each parallel becomes shorter. (See Figure 3.) A parallel is a guide to help locate a spot on the globe.

If you want to find Bear Island, which is at 75° N. Lat. in the Arctic Ocean, you do not need to go all the way back to the equator to start measuring. You can look for it between the 70th and 80th parallels. (See Figure 4.)

Fig. 3: Globe Showing Parallels of Latitude

MEASURING LATITUDE

Sailors at sea cannot reach out across the water to the imaginary line called the equator when they need to measure the position of their ship. But they can use the North Star and the horizon to determine their latitude.

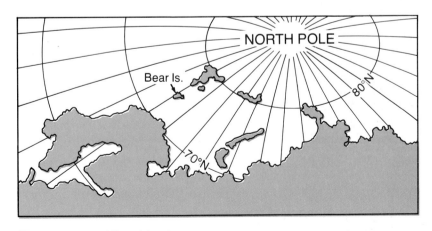

Fig. 4: Position of Bear Island

North Star To know how the North Star helps sailors, you must understand that the North Pole is almost directly under the North Star. (Actually, it is about one degree off-center.) As the earth spins around its axis, it appears as though the whole sky is turning, with only the North Star standing still. If you hold a large salad bowl upside down over a globe of the earth, you will have a very rough model of the universe. Imagine that the point in the center of the bowl is the North Star. Hold the center of the bowl directly over the pole and spin the globe slowly. It is easy to see that no matter where you stand on the earth, except at the North Pole itself, the North Star will always be north of you.

Horizon When sailors at sea look into the distance in any direction, the earth and the sky seem to be touching. As the sailors slowly turn around, the sky seems to meet the earth in every direction. The line where earth and sky appear to meet is called the horizon. On the open sea, you can see the horizon very easily. You also can see parts of the horizon at a beach or any place on land where there are no hills or buildings to block your view.

North Star and Horizon Ancient people, working with geometry, found a way to measure latitude. They discovered that the angle formed by two imaginary lines—one from the horizon to the observer's eye, the other from the observer's eye to the North Star—is equal to the latitude where the observer is located. Of course, the observer cannot draw these imaginary lines but must do what sharpshooters do when they aim a rifle. When sharpshooters line up the bull's-eye in the sights of their rifles, they are drawing an imaginary line from their eye to the target. In the same way, sailors can "shoot" both the North Star and the horizon. The size of the angle between these two lines is roughly equal to the sailors' latitude.

As sailors travel toward the equator, the North Star seems to move closer and closer toward the horizon. Of course, it is always to the sailors' north. But, as sailors travel toward the North Pole, the North Star seems to move higher and higher above the horizon. Still, the star is always to the sailors' north. So, the nearer sailors are to the equator, the smaller the angle between the two imaginary lines. As a ship sails north, the angle becomes larger.

When a ship is off the coast of St. Augustine, Florida, the angle is 30 degrees and the latitude is 30 degrees North. If the ship sails north to White Bay, Newfoundland, the angle will then be 50 degrees and the latitude will be 50 degrees North.

Sailors can measure this angle by using a sextant. (See Figure 5.) This instrument uses a system of mirrors and lenses on two arms so that the sailor can shoot the North Star and the horizon at the same time. It also has an accurate scale to measure the angle between the arms.

Find the Facts

This article gives you a lot of information which you have to keep straight in your mind if you are to understand the idea of latitude. This activity will help you sort through this information.

Below are incomplete sentences related to latitude. Each has blanks to be filled in with the words and phrases above it. On a separate paper, write the numbers *1* through *24*. Decide which word or phrase fits into each numbered blank so that each complete sentence presents accurate information about latitude. Write the word next to the correct number on your paper. Work with others in your group, and refer to the article to support your choices.

a. degree   degrees   minutes

A circle is divided into 360 __(1)__ , and each __(2)__ is divided into 60 __(3)__ .

b. earth's axis   imaginary   equator

Two ___(4)___ lines are used to measure the earth: the ___(5)___, which runs through the center of the earth from the North Geographic Pole to the South Geographic Pole; and the ___(6)___, which goes around the earth and divides it exactly in half.

c. 360 $\frac{1}{4}$ 90

The distance from any point on the equator to either pole is ___(7)___ of ___(8)___ degrees, or ___(9)___ degrees.

d. latitude   degrees   equator

The distance in ___(10)___ north or south of the ___(11)___ is called ___(12)___.

e. equator   latitude   parallels

Circles on the globe which are parallel to the ___(13)___ are called ___(14)___ of ___(15)___.

f. North Pole   North Star   horizon

A person can use the ___(16)___, which is almost directly over the ___(17)___, and the ___(18)___ to determine his or her latitude.

g. horizon   latitude   angle

The size of the ___(19)___ formed by two imaginary lines—one from the North Star to the observer's eye and the other from the ___(20)___ to the observer's eye—is equal to the observer's ___(21)___.

h. sextant   horizon   North Star

A ___(22)___ is used to shoot the ___(23)___ and the ___(24)___ to determine the observer's latitude.

Support Your Interpretations

Decide which of the following statements seem reasonable and can be supported by the article on latitude. Be ready to give evidence to support your decisions.

1. Since *hemisphere* means "half a sphere or globe," the equator can be thought of as dividing the earth into two hemispheres.
2. Any points of latitude north of the equator could be considered in the northern hemisphere; any points south of the equator could be considered in the southern hemisphere.

3. It is not possible to see the North Star from the southern hemisphere.
4. There must be a star in the southern hemisphere by which latitudes below the equator are determined.
5. To a sailor on a ship near the equator, a compass, as well as a sextant, would be useful for determining latitude.

Anticipate the Ideas

If you were lost at sea and you were able to figure out your ship's latitude, you still would not know exactly where you were. The next article will tell you why and also how to figure out your exact location.

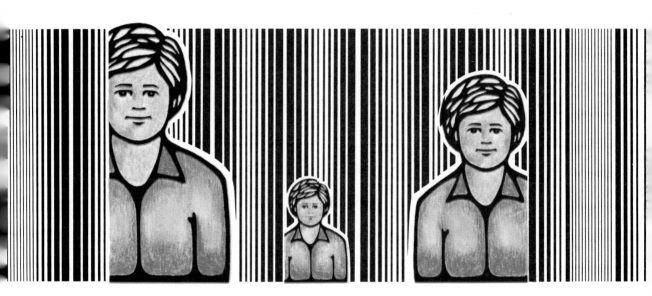

more Where in the World Am I?: Longitude

Sailors who know only a ship's latitude are in the same position you would be in if you and some friends wanted to meet and they told you, "Meet us on Main Street." Main Street might be several miles long. If they said, "Meet us on Maple Avenue," you might have the same problem. But if they told you to meet them at the corner of Main Street and Maple Avenue, you could find them easily. What you need to know in order to pinpoint your meeting place is two sets of information.

If you want to find an exact spot on a piece of paper, you must have two measurements: the distance from the top or bottom of the page and the distance from either of the sides. Suppose you want to start a drawing one inch (2½ centimeters) from the top and 1½ inches (4 centimeters) from the left side. In Figure 1, the line AB is one inch (2½ centimeters) from the top for its entire length. The line CD is 1½ inches (4 centimeters) from the left side for its entire length. No matter how long these lines are drawn, they will meet only at the point X.

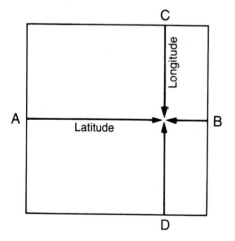

Fig 1: Finding your position using latitude and longitude

LONGITUDE

Sailors who want to give the location of their ship must give two measurements. One measurement is the distance north or south of the equator—the latitude. The other is the distance east or west of Greenwich, England —the longitude. A line drawn through a given latitude and a line through a given longitude will cross at only one point on a map.

MEASURING LONGITUDE

A line of longitude, or a meridian, is a half circle running along the surface of the earth from the North Pole to the South Pole. In order to measure distance, there must be a starting place. Choosing a starting place to measure latitude was easy. Parallels of latitude become smaller as they approach the poles, and the largest parallel, which is the equator, is exactly halfway between the poles. There is no such natural starting place for longitude. All the meridians are the same length. And, since there are no east-west poles, there can be no midpoint. But 45 degrees West Longitude has no meaning unless you know west of what, and so mapmakers had to choose a fixed starting place, or prime meridian.

Prime Meridian Old maps show the prime meridian passing through Paris, Rome, Washington, and many other cities. On English maps, it passed through Greenwich in southwest London. As England became the most important sea power, more and more maps were made in London. These maps were so good that sailors of many nations used them.

Since English maps measured longitude from the Greenwich meridian, it came to be widely used as the prime meridian. In 1884, most of the countries of the world agreed to its designation. All places along this meridian from the North Pole to the South Pole are located at 0° Longitude. Places west of the prime meridian are measured in degrees west; for example, New York City is 74° West Longitude. Places east of the Greenwich meridian are measured in degrees east. Berlin is 13°25′ East Longitude. (See Figure 2.) English mapmakers measured halfway around the earth westward and halfway eastward. That is why the 180th meridian is both 180 degrees East Longitude and 180 degrees West Longitude.

It is simple enough to find your longitude on land. Meridians are drawn on a map, and the degrees of longitude are printed across the top and bottom. You can find your lo-

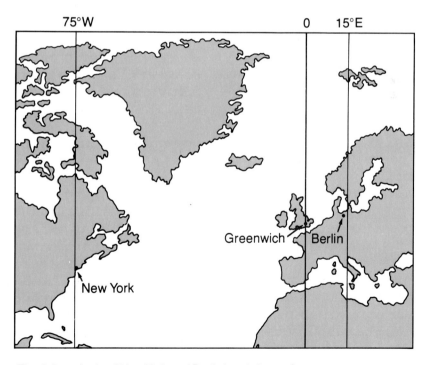

Fig. 2: Longitude of New York and Berlin in relation to Greenwich

cation on the map and read the longitude. But sailors far at sea, where there are no landmarks, cannot find their longitude so easily. Just as they look to the skies to find their latitude, sailors can determine their longitude from the sun and the stars.

People in ancient times learned many things about the earth by studying the heavens. Since the appearance of the sun in the sky divided day from night, it was natural for them to measure time according to the position of the sun. Time measured this way is called solar time.

Solar Time If you chart the position of the sun for one day, it seems to cross the sky in a great arc, rising out of the eastern horizon at dawn and sinking below the western horizon at dusk. The highest point in this path is called the zenith. When the sun reaches its zenith, it is noon solar time.

The earth spinning around its axis makes the sun appear to move across the sky. To visualize this, use a flashlight to represent the sun. Hold the light at the level of the equator several feet (at least a meter) from a globe of the earth. It is noon all along the meridian which passes through the center of the beam of light. Now turn the globe slowly from west to east,

the direction in which the earth spins. You can see that it is noon along only one meridian at a time and that as the earth turns, noon occurs farther and farther west. In one hour the earth turns 1/24 of a complete circle. Since there are 360 degrees in a circle, we know that with the passing of each hour the zenith of the sun will be over a meridian that is 1/24 of 360 degrees, or 15 degrees, farther west.

Sailors can use the spinning of the earth to measure longitude. By shooting the sun with their sextant, they can find the exact moment when the sun reaches its zenith. This is noon solar time all along the meridian on which the ship is located. They can compare this with Greenwich time, which is solar time along the prime meridian and is often written as G.T.

Greenwich Time Even in ancient times, people knew that longitude could be measured by comparing solar time with the time at the prime meridian. Unfortunately, this fact was of no use to sailors until they had an accurate way of knowing what time it was at the prime meridian.

In 1714, the chronometer was invented. This is a very accurate watch set to Greenwich time. No matter where a ship is, the sailors need only to look at the chronometer to find the exact time along the prime meridian.

Each hour before noon Greenwich time is equal to 15 degrees East Longitude, and each hour after noon Greenwich time means 15 degrees West Longitude. When it is noon on a ship at sea and 1:00 P.M. in Greenwich, the ship's longitude is 15° West. If it is 3:30 P.M. G.T., the ship's longitude is 3½ times 15 degrees, or 52°30′ West. At 11:00 A.M. G.T., the ship's longitude is 15° East. Earlier in the morning, at 8:30 A.M. G.T., the ship would be located somewhere along the meridian of 52°30′ East Longitude.

Most clocks and watches are not set to solar time. Since the earth is constantly spinning, solar noon is different for every spot on earth. For this reason, solar time cannot be used conveniently for everyday purposes. Imagine the confusion if watches were set by solar time. Time would change whenever you traveled a few miles east or west.

To avoid such confusion, the world has been divided into time zones. A time zone covers roughly 15 degrees of longitude. Standard Civil Time for the entire zone is the same as solar time along the meridian which runs through the center of the time zone. Each time zone extends from the North Pole to the South Pole. Lima, Peru, and New York City are in the same zone. (See Figure 3.)

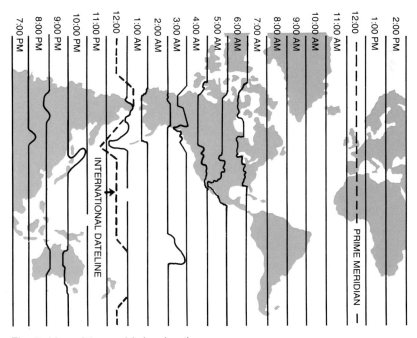

Fig. 3: Map of the world showing time zones.

When it is 3 A.M. in San Francisco, it is 6 A.M. in New York and 12 noon in Greenwich. Halfway around the world from Greenwich, along the 180th meridian, it is midnight. The 180th meridian is called the International Date Line, for when it is one minute after 12 noon on Monday in Greenwich, on the 180th meridian it is one minute after 12 midnight, and therefore it is already Tuesday.

Find the Facts

Like the article on latitude, this article contains a lot of information that you have to keep straight in your mind. This activity will help you sort through this information.

Below are incomplete sentences related to latitude and longitude. Each has blanks to be filled in with the words or phrases above it. On a separate paper, write the numbers 1 through 25. Decide which word or phrase fits into each numbered blank so that each complete sentence presents accurate information. Write the word next to the correct number on your paper. Work with others in your group, and refer to the article to support your choices.

a. latitude   longitude

____(1)____ is the distance north or south of the equator; ____(2)____ is the distance east or west of Greenwich, England.

b. longitude   meridian   pole

A ____(3)____ is a line of ____(4)____ running halfway around the world from one ____(5)____ to the other.

c. east or west   prime meridian   longitude

Map makers needed a starting point in order to measure ____(6)____. They created a ____(7)____ from which all distances ____(8)____ could be calculated.

d. 0° Longitude   prime meridian   Greenwich, England

In 1884, most countries agreed that the ____(9)____ would be located at ____(10)____, and would be called ____(11)____.

e. longitude   sun   zenith   solar noon

____(12)____ at a given ____(13)____ occurs when the ____(14)____ is at its ____(15)____.

f. difference   solar noon   Greenwich time

You can determine your longitude by comparing the __(16)__ where you are with __(17)__ and noting the __(18)__ between the two.

g. chronometer   solar noon   Greenwich time

To calculate your longitude using your __(19)__, you must have a __(20)__ set at __(21)__.

h. before   after   East   West

Each hour __(22)__ noon Greenwich time is equal to 15 degrees __(23)__ Longitude; each hour __(24)__ noon Greenwich time is equal to 15 degrees __(25)__ Longitude.

Support Your Interpretations

Read the following statements. Decide which of them seem reasonable and can be supported by information in the article on longitude. Be ready to give evidence to support your decisions.

1. To determine longitude, one needs a sunny day.
2. For purposes of comparing the time of day, the earth is divided into twenty-four time zones.
3. It is easier to be accurate in doing something when you have only one standard to follow rather than many standards.
4. Without a starting point, one cannot judge how far one has gone.
5. Unless two or more people use the same reference points, they cannot find a single location.

Lost and Found Numbers

Magic with numbers! It is fascinating what can be done with numbers when you find out how they work. The article "Finding Lost Numbers" is divided into two sections. The first section takes you through the "magic" step by step. Note carefully the sequence, or order, of the steps. You need to read this section very carefully, doing exactly what the directions tell you to do.

Review and Expand Your Vocabulary

The author uses the word *spectator* to indicate the person with whom you would work the "magic." How does this use of the word differ from ways in which it is usually used?

The word *comprise* also is used. In this usage the word should be defined as "to make up," in the sense of things being put together to make something.

Here are some other mathematics words used in the selection. Double-check in the glossary if you are uncertain about the definition of any.

computation	digit	multiplier
product	number	multiplicand

FINDING LOST NUMBERS: The Mechanics

by William Simon

An interesting and little known problem is to find a digit which has been "lost." Let us assume that your spectator selects a four- or five-place number. You then request that she "lose" one of the digits by simply drawing a line through it. After a few simple computations, you name the "lost" digit even though you had no knowledge of the original number used and did not see any of the computations!

Here are the mechanics:

(a) A spectator writes down any number she wishes of at least three digits. She does this while you are out of the room or in a position so that you could not possibly see what she writes. (Note: Any multidigit number may be used, but a four- or five-place number will take less time than a larger number and is thus more desirable.) Let us assume that your spectator chooses the number 7438 and writes this on a slip of paper.

(b) Request that she add together the digits which comprise the number she has chosen. "Add the digits together by adding the first to the second, this total to the third digit, and this total to the fourth. For example, if you choose the number 1234, you would add them for a total of 10: 1 + 2 + 3 + 4." If your spectator adds her digits (7 + 4 + 3 + 8) together correctly, she will arrive at a total of 22. Have this total placed to the right of the number she originally selected:

7438   22

(c) Request that she "lose" one of the digits from her original number by drawing a line through it. She may "lose" whichever digit she wishes. Let us assume that she draws a line through the 4:

7⁄438   22

(d) Have her place the remaining three-digit number (in this case, 738) directly above the number she placed to the right (22). Then ask her to subtract the smaller number from the larger. If your instructions have been carried out correctly, then your spectator will have written the following:

7⁄438
$\begin{array}{r} 738 \\ -\ 22 \\ \hline 716 \end{array}$

(e) You now say, "You have arrived at a number which I couldn't possibly know and which has no relation to either your original selected number or to the 'lost' number. What is that number?" In this example, your spectator will tell you that the number she has arrived at is 716. Using this number, you are able to discover the "lost" number!

(f) Upon learning the number, add the digits together to bring it down to a single digit. Using 716, you add 7 + 1 + 6 for a total of 14. You then add 1 + 4 (the remaining digits) for a total of 5.

(This is known as casting out the 9's.) To find the "lost" digit, you simply subtract 5 from 9. This would leave 4, and thus you know that 4 was the "lost" digit. Reveal this in a dramatic fashion and add to the effect. (Note: Always subtract the single-digit number from 9 to find the "lost" number.)

Let's do another example: Assume that the spectator has chosen the number 85129, which she secretly writes on the paper. She adds the five digits together (8 + 5 + 1 + 2 + 9) for a total of 25, and writes 25 to the right of the original five-digit number. Let us assume that she draws a line through ("loses") the 8. Thus, she writes the remaining four-digit number, 5129, above 25 and proceeds to subtract 25 from this number. The result of this subtraction, 5104, is then told to you. You add the digits together (5 + 1 + 0 + 4) for a total of 10, and bring this down to a single digit (1 + 0), which is 1. Upon subtracting 1 from 9, you get 8, the "lost" digit. If the result of this final addition is ever 9, then the "lost" digit is either a 0 or a 9.

Double-check your understanding of the mechanics of finding "lost" numbers, as presented in the examples. On a separate sheet of paper, rearrange the following steps so that they are in the same order as in the examples. Work with other members of your group.

a. You subtract from 9 the number you found by reducing to a single digit the number the spectator told you.

b. Spectator subtracts smaller number from the larger.

c. Spectator adds together the digits which make up the original number and records that sum.

d. You announce that you have found the lost number and what it is!

e. You reduce to a single digit the number the spectator tells you.

f. Spectator tells you the difference between the two numbers.

g. Spectator places remaining digits from the original number over the sum of the digits from the original number.

h. Spectator selects any number of at least three digits.

i. Spectator crosses out one digit from the original number.

Apply the Ideas

Now that you understand the procedure for finding lost numbers, try it out on other members of your group for practice. Then use the procedure with other people and see how it surprises them.

You are ready to find out about a practical use for "finding lost numbers." Apply the same kind of reading procedure to the following material as you did to the other section of the text. That is, analyze the information carefully as you read it, following each step along with the author. Then practice what you learn on numbers of your own.

more
FINDING LOST NUMBERS:
A Practical Application

When a number is reduced to a single digit, we are "casting out," or removing, all 9's and reducing the number to its simplest state minus all 9's and multiples of 9. For example, in a simple number such as 10, when we add the digits together (1 + 0), we reduce this to the single digit 1. We have actually cast out a 9. The number 30, for another example, can be reduced to the single digit 3 (3 + 0); 3 is 30 with three 9's cast out (three 9's = 27; 27 + 3 = 30). This works with numbers of any size. For example, the multidigit number 92672 adds up to 8 with the 9's cast out: 9 + 2 + 6 + 7 + 2 = 26 = 2 + 6 = 8.

Casting out the 9's can be used in many ways. One practical application is that used by many people to check figures on multiplication. Let us assume that you had to multiply 74361 by 83488. The correct product of this multiplication is 6,208,251,168. A quick way of checking the accuracy of this is to cast out the 9's.

Here are the mechanics:

(a) First, cast out the 9's of the multiplicand and the multiplier. Reduce 74361 to the single digit 3, and 83488 to the digit 4.
(b) Multiply the two digits (3 × 4 = 12). Then bring the product down to a single digit (12: 1 + 2 = 3). With the 9's cast out, the product of this multiplication is 3.
(c) Now reduce the product of the major number (6,208,251,168) to a single digit (6 + 2 + 8 + 2, etc.). You will find that with the 9's cast out the product comes down to 3! With this agreement, you can be fairly sure that the computation is correct if you have not reversed the digits in the product of the major number.

Double-check your understanding of the practical application of finding "lost" numbers or casting out 9's, as presented in the example. On a separate sheet of paper, rearrange the following steps so that they are in the same order as in the example.

a. Now reduce the product of the major number to a single digit.
b. Cast out the 9's of the multiplier until you have a single digit.
c. Multiply 560 by 269 and record the product.
d. Multiply the reduced digits from the multiplicand and the multiplier, and reduce the product to a single digit.
e. Cast out the 9's of the multiplicand until you have a single digit.
f. Match the single digits remaining from the two reduced products.

Apply the Ideas

On the basis of what you've read and your own computations, decide whether you agree or disagree with the following.

1. $842 \times 26 = 21892$
   $842 = 5$
   $26 = 8$
   $5 \times 8 = 40 = 4$
   $21892 = 4$
2. $945821 \times 721 = 681936941$
   $945821 = 2$
   $721 = 1$
   $2 \times 1 = 2$
   $681936941 = 2$
3. $89622 \times 4320 = 387167040$
   $89622 = 0$
   $4320 = 0$
   $0 \times 0 = 0$
   $387167040 = 0$

Lost and Found in Poetry

The following poem is written in a style called "free verse." That is, words do not rhyme, and stanzas do not end with a completed sentence. Yet, there is a form and an organization to the stanzas and to the poem. Follow the punctuation very carefully. Read the poem as though you were reading a regular story aloud.

The Secret
by Denise Levertov

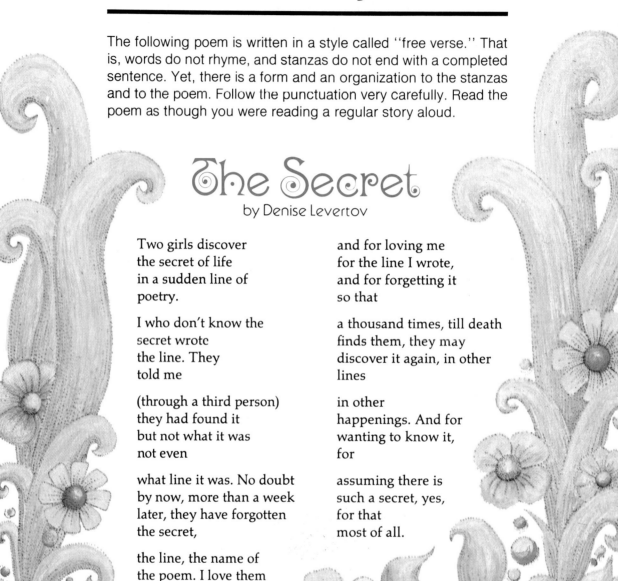

Two girls discover
the secret of life
in a sudden line of
poetry.

I who don't know the
secret wrote
the line. They
told me

(through a third person)
they had found it
but not what it was
not even

what line it was. No doubt
by now, more than a week
later, they have forgotten
the secret,

the line, the name of
the poem. I love them
for finding what
I can't find,

and for loving me
for the line I wrote,
and for forgetting it
so that

a thousand times, till death
finds them, they may
discover it again, in other
lines

in other
happenings. And for
wanting to know it,
for

assuming there is
such a secret, yes,
for that
most of all.

Read the following statements and decide which are correct according to the information given in the poem. Be ready to provide evidence from the poem to support your decisions.

1. Someone told the poet that two girls had discovered the secret of life in one of her poems.
2. The poet knows what the secret is and where to find it.
3. The poet thinks that the girls have probably forgotten the secret by now.
4. The poet is pleased with the reaction to her poetry.
5. The poet thinks that the secret will be rediscovered elsewhere.

Apply the Ideas

Which of the following ideas do you think the poet would agree to, based on what she expressed in the poem? Discuss your choices and the reasons for making them.

1. Beautiful ideas suddenly found are easily lost—to be found and lost again.
2. A reader can find a thought in a poem that the poet did not have in mind when he or she wrote it.
3. Beautiful ideas can be found by those who expect to find them.
4. Poetry is more than words and rhyme; poetry is the stuff of life and time.

More Lost and Found in Literature

So far in this unit, you have seen that losing can involve more loss than just the object that is lost. You also have seen that finding involves more than just the object that is found. See how both of these factors apply in the two-part story that follows. As you read, notice that this first part focuses on Sara.

The Summer of the Swans
by Betsy Byars

The Summer of the Swans is about a junior-high school girl named Sara. She lives in a small West Virginia town with her aunt Willie, her older sister Wanda, and her younger brother Charlie. Sara is fiercely protective of Charlie, who was left mentally disabled from an illness when he was three years old.

One day Sara takes Charlie to see the swans at a nearby lake. Charlie is fascinated by the swans and doesn't want to leave. That night, unable to sleep because of a missing button from his pajamas, Charlie leaves the house in search of the swans. He gets lost in the woods and tumbles into a ravine. When Charlie's disappearance is discovered the next day, all the townspeople join in the search. Sara enlists the help of her friend Mary in finding Charlie. This is where the story begins.

She and Mary were almost across the open field before Sara spoke. Then she said, "Guess who just stopped me and gave me the big sympathy talk about Charlie."

"I don't know. Who?"

"Joe Melby."

"Really? What did he say?"

"He wants to help look for Charlie. He makes me sick."

"I think it's nice that he wants to help."

"Well, maybe if he'd stolen your brother's watch you wouldn't think it was so nice."

Mary was silent for a moment. Then she said, "I probably shouldn't tell you this, but he didn't steal that watch, Sara."

"Huh!"

"No, he really didn't."

Sara looked at her and said, "How do you know?"

"I can't tell you how I know because I promised I wouldn't, but I *know* he didn't."

"How?"

"I can't tell. I promised."

"That never stopped you before. Now, Mary Weicek, you tell me what you know this minute."

"I promised."

"Mary, tell me."

"Mom would kill me if she knew I told you."

"She won't know."

"Well, your aunt went to see Joe Melby's mother."

"What?"

"Aunt Willie went over to see Joe Melby's mother."

"She didn't!"

"Yes, she did too, because my mother was right there when it happened. It was about two weeks after Charlie had gotten the watch back."

"I don't believe you."

"Well, it's the truth. You told Aunt Willie that Joe had stolen the watch—remember, you told everybody—and so Aunt Willie went over to see Joe's mother."

"She wouldn't do such a terrible thing."

"Well, she did."

"And what did Mrs. Melby say?"

"She called Joe into the room and she said, 'Joe, did you steal the little Godfrey boy's watch?' And he said, 'No.'"

"What did you expect him to say in front of his mother? 'Yes, I stole the watch?' Huh! That doesn't prove anything."

"So then she said, 'I want the truth now. Do you know who did take the watch?' and he said that nobody had *stolen* the watch."

"So where did it disappear to for a week, I'd like to know."

"I'm coming to that. He said some of the fellows were out in front of the drugstore and Charlie was standing there waiting for the school bus—you were in the drugstore. Remember it was the day we were getting the stamps for letters to those pen pals who never answered? Remember the stamps wouldn't come out of the machine? Well, anyway, these boys outside the store started teasing Charlie with some candy, and while Charlie was trying to get the candy, one of the boys took off Charlie's watch without Charlie noticing it. Then they were going to ask Charlie what time it was and when he looked down at his watch he would get upset because the watch would be gone. They were just going to tease him."

"Finks! *Finks!*"

"Only you came out of the drugstore right then and saw what they were doing with the candy and told them off and the bus came and you hurried Charlie on the bus before anybody had a chance to give back the watch. Then they got scared to give it back and that's the whole story. Joe didn't steal the watch at all. He wasn't even in on it. He came up right when you did and didn't even know what had happened. Later, when he found out, he got the watch back and gave it to Charlie, that's all."

"Why didn't you tell me before this?"

"Because I just found out about it at lunch. For four months my mother has known all about this thing and never mentioned it because she said it was one of those things best forgotten."

"Why did she tell you now?"

"That's the way my mom is. We were talking about Charlie at the dinner table, and suddenly she comes up with this. Like one time she casually mentioned that she had had a long talk with Mr. Homer about me. Mr. Homer, the principal! She went over there and they had a long discussion, and she never mentioned it for a year."

"That is the worst thing Aunt Willie has ever done."

"Well, don't let on that you know, or I'll be in real trouble."

"I won't, but honestly, I could just—"

"You promised."

"I know. You don't have to keep reminding me. It makes me feel terrible though, I can tell you that." She walked with her head bent forward. "Terrible! You know what I just did when I saw him?"

"What?"

"Accused him of stealing the watch."

"Sara, you didn't."

"I did too. I can't help myself. When I think somebody has done something mean to Charlie, I can't forgive them. I want to keep after them and keep after them just like Aunt Willie said. I even sort of suspected Joe Melby hadn't really taken that watch, and I still kept on—"

"Ssh! Be quiet a minute." Mary was carrying her transistor radio, and she held it up between them. "Listen."

The announcer was saying: "We have a report of a missing child in the Cass section—ten-year-old Charlie Godfrey, who has been missing from his home since sometime last night. He is wearing blue pajamas and brown felt slippers, has a watch on one wrist and an identification bracelet with his name and address on the other. He is a mentally disabled child who cannot speak and may become alarmed when approached by a stranger. Please notify the police immediately if you have seen this youngster."

The two girls looked at each other, then continued walking across the field in silence.

*　　　　　*　　　　　*

Mary and Sara were up in the field by the woods. They had been searching for Charlie for an hour without finding a trace of him.

"Charlie!" Sara called as she had been doing from time to time. Her voice had begun to sound strained, she had called so often. "Charlie!"

"Sara, do you know where we are?" Mary asked after a moment.

"Of course. The lake's down there and the old shack's over there, and you can see them as soon as we get up a little higher."

"*If* we get up a little higher," Mary said in a tired voice.

"You didn't have to come, you know."

"I wanted to come, only I just want to make sure we don't get lost."

"Come on, will you?"

"It seems useless, if you ask me, to just keep walking when we don't really know which way he went. Aunt Willie thinks he went in the old coal mine."

"I know, but she only thinks that because she associates the mine with tragedy because her uncle and brother were killed in that coal mine. But Charlie wouldn't go in there. Remember that time we went into the Bryants' cellar after they moved out, and he wouldn't even come in there because it was cold and dark and sort of scary."

"Yes, I do remember because I sprained my ankle jumping down from the window and had to wait two hours while you looked through old *Life* magazines."

"I was not looking through old magazines."

"I could hear you. I was down there in that dark cellar with the rats and you were upstairs and I was yelling for help and you kept saying, 'I'm going for help right now,' and I could hear the pages turning and turning and turning."

"Well, I got you out, didn't I?"

"Finally."

Sara paused again. "Charlie! Charlie!" The girls waited in the high grass for an answer, then began to walk again. Mary said, "Maybe we should have waited for the others before we started looking. They're going to have a regular organized posse with everybody walking along together. There may be a helicopter."

"The longer we wait, the harder it will be to find him."

They looked at each other without speaking. Between them the radio began announcing: "Volunteers are needed in the Cass area in the search for young Charlie Godfrey who disappeared from his home sometime during the night. A search of the Cheat woods will begin at three o'clock this afternoon."

Mary said, "Oh, I'll keep looking. I'll try to walk faster."

Sara shrugged, turned, and started walking up the hill, followed by Mary. They came to the old fence that once separated the pasture from the woods. Sara walked slowly beside the fence. "Charlie!" she called.

"Would he come if he heard you, do you think?"

Sara nodded. "But if they get a hundred people out here clomping through the woods and hollering, he's not going to come. He'll be too scared. I know him."

"I don't see how you can be so sure he came up this way."

"I just know. There's something about me that makes me understand Charlie. It's like I know how he feels about things. Like sometimes I'll be walking down the street and I'll pass the jeweler's and I'll think that if Charlie were here he would want to stand right there and look at those watches all afternoon, and I know right where he'd stand and how he'd put his hands up on the glass and how his face would look. And yesterday I knew he was going to love the swans so much that he wasn't ever going to want to leave. I know how he feels."

"You just think you do."

"No, I *know*. I was thinking about the sky one night and I was looking up at the stars and I was thinking about how the sky goes on and on forever, and I couldn't understand it no matter how long I thought, and finally I got kind of nauseated and right then I started thinking, 'Well, this is how Charlie feels about some things.' You know how it makes him sick sometimes to try to print letters for a long time and—"

"Look who's coming," Mary interrupted.

"Where?"

"In the trees, walking toward us. Joe Melby."

"You're lying. You're just trying to make me—"

"It is him. Look." She quickly began to tie her scarf over her head again. "And you talk about *me* needing eyeglasses."

"Out across the field, quick!" Sara said. "No, wait, go under the fence. Move, will you, Mary, and leave that scarf alone. Get under the fence. I am not going to face him. I mean it."

"I am not going under any fence. Anyway, it would look worse for us to run away than to just walk by casually."

"I cannot walk by casually after what I said."

"Well, you're going to have to face him sometime, and it might as well be now when everyone feels sorry for you about your brother." She called out, "Hi, Joe, having any luck?"

He came up to them and held out a brown felt slipper and looked at Sara. "Is this Charlie's?"

Sara looked at the familiar object and forgot the incident of the watch for a moment. "Where did you find it?"

"Right up there by the fence. I had just picked it up when I saw you."

She took the slipper and, holding it against her, said, "Oh, I *knew* he came up this way, but it's a relief to have some proof of it."

"I was just talking to Mr. Aker," Joe continued, "and he said he heard his dogs barking up here last night. He had them tied out by the shack and he thought maybe someone was prowling around."

"Probably Charlie," Mary said.

"That's what I figured. Somebody ought to go down to the gas station and tell the people. They're organizing a big search now, and half of the people are planning to go up to the mine."

There was a pause and Mary said, "Well, I guess I could go, only I don't know whether I'll have time to get back up here." She looked at Joe.

Sara cleared her throat and said, "Well, I think I'll get on with my search if you two will excuse me." She turned and started walking up the hill again. There seemed to be a long silence in which even the sound of the cicadas in the grass was absent. She thrashed at the high weeds with her tennis shoes and hugged Charlie's slipper to her.

"Wait a minute, Sara, I'll come with you," Joe Melby said.

He joined her and she nodded, still looking down at the slipper. There was a picture of an American Indian chief stamped on the top of the shoe and there was a loneliness to the man's profile, even stamped crudely on the felt, that she had never noticed before.

She cleared her throat again. "There is just one thing I want to say." Her voice did not even sound familiar, a tape-recorded voice.

He waited, then said, "Go ahead."

She did not speak for a moment but continued walking noisily through the weeds.

"Go ahead."

"If you'll just wait a minute. I'm trying to think how to say this." The words she wanted to say—I'm sorry—would not come out at all.

They continued walking in silence, and then Joe said, "You know, I was just reading an article about a guru over in India, and he hasn't spoken a word in twenty-eight years. *Twenty-eight years* and he hasn't said one word in all that time. And everyone has been waiting all those years to hear what he's going to say when he finally does speak because it's supposed to be some great wise word, and I thought about this poor guy sitting there and for twenty-eight years he's been trying to think of something to say that would be the least bit great and he can't think of anything and he must be getting really desperate now. And every day it gets worse and worse."

"Is there supposed to be some sort of message in that story?"

"Maybe."

She smiled. "Well, I just wanted to say that I'm sorry." She thought again that she was going to start crying and she said to herself, "You are nothing but a big soft snail. Snail!"

"That's all right."

"I just found out about Aunt Willie going to see your mother."

He shrugged. "She didn't mean anything by it."

"But it was a terrible thing."

"It wasn't all that bad. At least it was different to be accused of something I *didn't* do for a change."

"But to be called in like that in front of Aunt Willie and Mary's mother. No, it was terrible." She turned and walked into the woods.

"Don't worry about it. I'm tough. I'm indestructible. I'm like that coyote in 'Road Runner' who is always getting flattened and dynamited and crushed and in the next scene is strolling along, completely normal again."

"I just acted too hastily. That's one of my main faults."

"I do that too."

"Not like me."

"Worse probably. Do you remember when we used to get grammar-school report cards, and the grades would be on one part of the card, and on the other side would be personality things the teacher would check, like 'Does not accept criticism constructively'?"

Sara smiled. "I always used to get a check on that one," she said.

"Who didn't? And then they had one, 'Acts impetuously and without consideration for others,' or something like that, and one year I got a double check on that one."

"You didn't."

"Yes I did. Second grade. Miss McLeod. I remember she told the whole class that this was the first year she had ever had to give double checks to any student, and everyone in the room was scared to open his or her report card to see if they had got the double checks. And when I opened mine, there they were, two sets of double checks, on acting impetuously and on not accepting criticism, and single checks on everything else."

"Were you crushed?"

"Naturally."

"I thought you were so tough and indestructible."

"Well, I am"—he paused—"I think." He pointed to the left. "Let's go up this way."

She agreed with a nod and went ahead of him between the trees.

Interpret the Characters

Authors use many different techniques to let their readers know what their characters are like. They may describe the characters' actions and thoughts directly, or they may use dialogue. When authors use a great deal of dialogue, they leave it up to their readers to interpret the characters on the basis of what they say to each other and how they say it. Below are some phrases that describe what some of the characters in the first part of *Summer of the Swans* are like. Decide which of the characters—Sara, Mary, Joe, or Charlie—each describes. Discuss the evidence in the selection that you use to determine your answers as well as the technique the author used to reveal the traits.

1. doesn't keep secrets well
2. has difficulty expressing feelings
3. holds grudges
4. acts hastily
5. is unable to manage alone
6. believes in forgiving and forgetting wrongs
7. is protective of those who need help

Make Some Predictions

Before you read the next part of the story, see if you can predict what might happen. Answer the following questions on the basis of what you have learned about the characters and their actions so far. Some of your predictions will have to be based on your own experiences. Discuss your reasons for answering the questions as you do.

1. What will happen if a large search party reaches Charlie before Sara and Joe do?
2. What will Charlie do if he hears Sara calling him?
3. Are Sara and Joe heading in the right direction to find Charlie? How do you know?
4. Will Charlie be able to find his own way home? Why or why not?
5. Will Sara change her mind about Joe? If so, how and why?
6. What other predictions can you make about what might happen in the next part of the story?

Anticipate the Ideas

In the second part of the selection, the search for Charlie continues. As you read, notice how the focus shifts from Sara to Charlie and then back to Sara.

The Summer of the Swans

There was a ravine in the forest, a deep cut in the earth, and Charlie had made his way into it through an early morning fog. By chance, blindly stepping through the fog with his arms outstretched, he had managed to pick the one path that led into the ravine, and when the sun came out and the fog burned away, he could not find the way out.

All the ravine looked the same in the daylight, the high walls, the masses of weeds and wild berry bushes, the trees. He had wandered around for a while, following the little paths made by dirt washed down from the hillside, but finally he sat down on a log and stared straight ahead without seeing.

After a while he roused enough to wipe his hands over his cheeks where the tears and dirt had dried together and to rub his puffed eyelids. Then he looked down, saw his bare foot, put it on top of his slipper, and sat with his feet overlapped.

There was a dullness about him now. He had had so many scares, heard so many frightening noises, stared at so many shadows, been hurt so often that all his senses were worn to a flat hopelessness. He would just sit here forever.

It was not the first time Charlie had been lost, but never before had there been this finality. He had become separated from Aunt Willie once at the county fair and had not even known he was lost until she had come bursting out of the crowd screaming, "Charlie, Charlie," and enveloped him. He had been lost in school once in the hall and could not find his way back to his room, and he had walked up and down the halls, frightened by all the strange children looking out of every door, until one of the boys was sent out to lead him to his room. But in all his life there had never been an experience like this one.

He bent over and looked down at his watch, his eyes on the tiny red hand. For the first time, he noticed it was no longer moving. Holding his breath in his concern, he brought the watch closer to his face. The hand was still. For a moment he could not believe it. He watched it closely, waiting. Still the hand did not move. He shook his hand back and forth, as if he were trying to shake the watch off his wrist. He had seen Sara do this to her watch.

Then he held the watch to his ear. It was silent. He had had the watch for five months and never before had it failed him. He had not even known it could fail. And now it was silent and still.

He put his hand over the watch, covering it completely. He waited. His breathing had begun to quicken again. His hand on the watch was almost clammy. He waited, then slowly, cautiously, he removed his hand and looked at the tiny red hand on the dial. It was motionless. The trick had not worked.

Bending over the watch, he looked closely at the stem. Aunt Willie always wound the watch for him every morning after breakfast, but he did not know how she did this. He took the stem in his fingers, pulled at it clumsily, then harder, and it came off. He looked at it. Then, as he attempted to put it back on the watch, it fell to the ground and was lost in the leaves.

A chipmunk ran in front of him and scurried up the bank. Distracted for a moment, Charlie got up and walked toward it. The chipmunk paused and then darted into a hole, leaving Charlie standing in the shadows trying to see where it had gone. He went closer to the bank and pulled at the leaves, but he could not even find the place among the roots where the chipmunk had disappeared.

Suddenly something seemed to explode within Charlie, and he began to cry noisily. He threw himself on the bank and began kicking, flailing at the ground, at the invisible chipmunk, at the silent watch. He wailed, yielding in helplessness to his anguish, and his piercing screams, uttered again and again, seemed to hang in the air so that they overlapped. His fingers tore at the tree roots and dug beneath the leaves and scratched, animal-like, at the dark earth.

His body sagged and he rolled down the bank and was silent. He looked up at the trees, his chest still heaving with sobs, his face strangely still. After a moment, his eyelids drooped and he fell asleep.

*   *   *

"Charlie! Charlie!"

The only answer was the call of a bird in the branches overhead, one long tremulous whistle.

"He's not even within hearing distance," Sara said.

For the past hour she and Joe Melby had been walking deeper and deeper into the forest without pause, and now the trees were so thick that only small spots of sunlight found their way through the heavy foliage.

"Charlie, oh, Charlie!"

She waited, looking down at the ground.

Joe said, "You want to rest for a while?"

Sara shook her head. She suddenly wanted to see her brother so badly that her throat began to close. It was a tight feeling she got sometimes when she wanted something, like the time she had had the measles and had wanted to see her father so much she couldn't even swallow. Now she thought that if she had a whole glass of ice water—and she was thirsty—she probably would not be able to drink a single drop.

"If you can make it a little farther, there's a place at the top of the hill where the strip mining is, and you can see the whole valley from there."

"I can make it."

"Well, we can rest first if—"

"I can make it."

She suddenly felt a little better. She thought that if she could stand up there on top of the hill and look down and see, somewhere in that huge green valley, a small plump figure in blue pajamas, she would ask for nothing more in life. She thought of the valley as a relief map where everything would be shiny and smooth, and her brother would be right where she could spot him at once. Her cry, "There he is!" would ring like a bell over the valley and everyone would hear her and know that Charlie had been found.

She paused, leaned against a tree for a moment, and then continued. Her legs had begun to tremble.

It was the time of afternoon when she usually sat down in front of the television and watched game shows. She would sit in the doorway to the hall where she always sat and Charlie would come in and watch with her, and the living room would be dark and smell of the pine-scented cleaner Aunt Willie used.

Then the early movie would come on, and she would sit through the old movie, leaning forward in the doorway, making fun, saying things like, "Now, Charlie, we'll have the old Convict Turning Honest scene," and Charlie, sitting on the stool closer to the television, would nod without understanding.

She was good, too, at joining in the dialogue with the actors. When the cowboy would say something like, "Things are quiet around here tonight," she would join in with, "Yeah, *too* quiet," right on cue. It seemed strange to be out here in the woods with Joe Melby instead of in the living room with Charlie, watching *Flame of Araby*, which was the early movie for that afternoon.

Her progress up the hill seemed slower and slower. It was like the time she had won the slow bicycle race, a race in which she had to go as slow as possible without letting a foot touch the ground, and she had gone slower and slower, all the while feeling a strong compulsion to speed ahead and cross the finish line first. At the end of the race it had been she and T.R. Peters, and they had paused just before the finish line, balancing motionless on their bicycles. The time had seemed endless, and then T.R. lost his balance and his foot touched the ground and Sara was the winner.

She slipped on some dry leaves, went down on her knees, straightened, and paused to catch her breath.

"Are you all right?"

"Yes, I just slipped."

She waited for a moment, bent over her knees, then she called, "Charlie! Charlie," without lifting her head.

"Oh, Charleeeeee," Joe shouted above her.

Sara knew Charlie would shout back if he heard her, the long wailing cry he gave sometimes when he was frightened during the night. It was such a familiar cry that for a moment she thought she heard it.

She waited, still touching the ground with one hand, until she was sure there was no answer.

"Come on," Joe said, holding out his hand.

He pulled her to her feet and she stood looking up at the top of the hill. Machines had cut away the earth there to get at the veins of coal, and the earth had been pushed down the hill to form a huge bank.

"I'll never get up that," she said. She leaned against a tree whose leaves were covered with the pale fine dirt which had filtered down when the machines had cut away the hill.

"Sure you will. I've been up it a dozen times."

He took her hand and she started after him, moving sideways up the steep bank. The dirt crumbled beneath her feet and she slid, skinned one knee, and then slipped again. When she had regained her balance she laughed wryly and said, "What's going to happen is that I'll end up pulling you all the way down the hill."

"No, I've got you. Keep coming."

She started again, putting one foot carefully above the other, picking her way over the stones. When she paused, he said, "Keep coming. We're almost there."

"I think it's a trick, like at the dentist's when he says, 'I'm almost through drilling.' Then he drills for another hour and says, 'Now, I'm really almost through drilling,' and he keeps on and then says, 'There's just one more spot and then I'll be practically really through'."

"We must go to the same dentist."

"I don't think I can make it. There's no skin at all left on the side of my legs."

"Well, we're really almost practically there now, in the words of your dentist."

She fell across the top of the dirt bank on her stomach, rested for a moment, and then turned and looked down the valley.

She could not speak for a moment. There lay the whole valley in a way she had never imagined it, a tiny finger of civilization set in a sweeping expanse of dark forest. The black treetops seemed to crowd against the yards, the houses, the roads, giving the impression that at any moment the trees would close over the houses like waves and leave nothing but an unbroken line of black-green leaves waving in the sunlight.

Up the valley she could see the intersection where they shopped, the drugstore, the gas station where her mother had once won a set of twenty-four stemmed glasses which Aunt Willie would not allow them to use, the grocery store, the lot where the yellow school buses were parked for the summer. She could look over the valley and see another hill where white cows were all grouped together by a fence and beyond that another hill and then another.

She looked back at the valley and she saw the lake, and, for the first time since she had stood up on the hill, she remembered Charlie.

Raising her hand to her mouth, she called, "Charlie! Charlie! Charlie!" There was a faint echo that seemed to waver in her ears.

"Charlie, oh, Charlie!" Her voice was so loud it seemed to ram into the valley.

Sara waited. She looked down at the forest, and everything was so quiet it seemed to her that the whole valley, the whole world was waiting with her.

"Charlie, hey, Charlie!" Joe shouted.

"Charleeeeee!" She made the sound of it last a long time. "Can you hear meeeeee?"

With her eyes she followed the trail she knew he must have taken—the house, the Akers' vacant lot, the old pasture, the forest. The forest that seemed powerful enough to engulf a whole valley, she thought with a sinking feeling, could certainly swallow up a young boy.

"Charlie! Charlie! Charlie!" There was a waver in the last syllable that betrayed how near she was to tears. She looked down at the Indian slipper she was still holding.

"Charlie, oh, Charlie." She waited. There was not a sound anywhere. "Charlie, where are you?"

"Hey, Charlie!" Joe shouted.

They waited in the same dense silence. A cloud passed in front of the sun and a breeze began to blow through the trees. Then there was silence again.

"Charlie, Charlie, Charlie, Charlie, Charlie."

She paused, listened, then bent abruptly and put Charlie's slipper to her eyes. She waited for the hot tears that had come so often this summer, the tears that had seemed so close only a moment before. Now her eyes remained dry.

I have cried over myself a hundred times this summer, she thought, I have wept over my big feet and my skinny legs and my nose, I have even cried over my stupid shoes, and now when I have a true sadness there are no tears left.

She held the felt side of the slipper against her eyes like a blindfold and stood there, feeling the hot sun on her head and the wind wrapping around her legs, conscious of the height and the valley sweeping down from her feet.

"Listen, just because you can't hear him doesn't mean anything. He could be—"

"Wait a minute." She lowered the slipper and looked down the valley. A sudden wind blew dust into her face, and she lifted her hand to shield her eyes.

"I thought I heard something. Charlie! Answer me right this minute."

She waited with the slipper held against her chest, one hand to her eyes, her whole body motionless, concentrating on her brother. Then she stiffened. She thought again she had heard something—Charlie's long high wail. Charlie could sound sadder than anyone when he cried.

In her anxiety she took the slipper and twisted it again and again as if she were wringing water out. She called, then stopped abruptly and listened. She looked at Joe, and he shook his head.

She looked away. A bird rose from the trees below and flew toward the hills in the distance. She waited until she could see it no longer, and then slowly, still listening for the call that didn't come, she sank to the ground and sat with her head bent over.

Beside her, Joe scuffed his foot in the dust and sent a cascade

of rocks and dirt down the bank. When the sound of it faded, he began to call, "Charlie, hey, Charlie," again and again.

*   *   *

Charlie awoke, but he lay for a moment without opening his eyes. He did not remember where he was, but he had a certain dread of seeing it.

There were great parts of his life that were lost to Charlie, blank spaces that he could never fill in. He would find himself in a strange place and not know how he had got there. Like the time Sara had been hit in the nose with a baseball at the custard stand, and the blood and the sight of Sara kneeling on the ground in helpless pain had frightened him so much that he had turned and run without direction, in a frenzy, dashing headlong up the street, blind to cars and people.

By chance Mr. Weicek had seen him, put him in the car, and driven him home, and Aunt Willie had put him to bed, but later he remembered none of this. He had only awakened in bed and looked at the crumpled bit of ice-cream cone still clenched in his hand and wondered about it.

His whole life had been built on a strict routine, and as long as this routine was kept up, he felt safe and well. The same foods, the same bed, the same furniture in the same place, the same seat on the school bus, the same class procedure were all important to him. But always there could be the unexpected, the dreadful surprise that would topple his carefully constructed life in an instant.

The first thing he became aware of was the twigs pressing into his face, and he put his hand under his cheek. Still he did not open his eyes. Pictures began to drift into his mind. He saw Aunt Willie's cigar box which was filled with old jewelry and buttons and knickknacks, and he found that he could remember every item in that box—the string of white beads without a clasp, the old earrings, the tiny book with souvenir fold-out pictures of New York, the plastic decorations from cakes, the turtle made of sea shells. Every item was so real that he opened his eyes and was surprised to see, instead of the glittering contents of the box, the dull and unfamiliar forest.

He raised his head and immediately felt the aching of his body. Slowly he sat up and looked down at his hands. His fingernails were black with earth, two of them broken below the quick, and he got up slowly and sat on the log behind him and inspected his fingers more closely.

Then he sat up straight. His hands dropped to his lap. His head cocked to the side like a bird listening. Slowly he straightened until he was standing. At his side his fingers twitched at the empty air as if to grasp something. He took a step forward, still with his head to the side. He remained absolutely still.

Then he began to cry out in a hoarse excited voice, again and again, screaming now, because he had just heard someone far away calling his name.

*   *   *

At the top of the hill, Sara got slowly to her feet and stood looking down at the forest. She pushed the hair back from her forehead and moistened her lips. The wind dried them as she waited.

Joe started to say something, but she reached out one hand and took his arm to stop him. Scarcely daring to believe her ears, she stepped closer to the edge of the bank. Now she heard it un-mistakably—the sharp repeated cry—and she knew it was Charlie.

"Charlie!" she shouted with all her might.

She paused and listened, and his cries were louder and she knew he was not far away after all, just down the slope, in the direction of the ravine.

"It's Charlie, it's Charlie!"

A wild joy overtook her, and she jumped up and down on the bare earth, and she felt that she could crush the whole hill just by jumping if she wanted.

She sat and scooted down the bank, sending earth and pebbles in a cascade before her. She landed on the soft ground, ran a few steps, lost her balance, caught hold of the first tree trunk she could find, and swung around till she stopped.

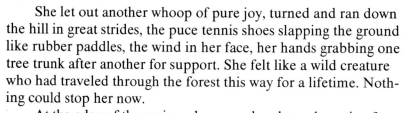

She let out another whoop of pure joy, turned and ran down the hill in great strides, the puce tennis shoes slapping the ground like rubber paddles, the wind in her face, her hands grabbing one tree trunk after another for support. She felt like a wild creature who had traveled through the forest this way for a lifetime. Nothing could stop her now.

At the edge of the ravine, she paused and stood gasping for breath. Her heart was beating so fast it pounded in her ears, and her throat was dry. She leaned against a tree, resting her cheek against the rough bark.

She thought for a minute she was going to faint, a thing she had never done before, not even when she broke her nose. She hadn't even believed people really did faint until this minute when she clung to the tree because her legs were as useless as rubber bands.

There was a ringing in her ears and another sound, a wailing sirenlike cry that was painfully familiar.

"Charlie?"

Charlie's crying, like the sound of a cricket, seemed everywhere and nowhere.

She walked along the edge of the ravine, circling the large boulders and trees. Then she looked down into the ravine where the shadows lay, and she felt as if something had turned over inside her because she saw Charlie.

He was standing in his torn pajamas, face turned upward, hands raised, shouting with all his might. His eyes were shut tight.

His face was streaked with dirt and tears. His pajama jacket hung in shreds about his scratched chest.

He opened his eyes and as he saw Sara a strange expression came over his face, an expression of wonder and joy and disbelief, and Sara knew that if she lived to be a hundred no one would ever look at her quite that way again.

She paused, looked down at him, and then, sliding on the seat of her pants, went down the bank and took him in her arms.

"Oh, Charlie."

His arms gripped her like steel.

"Oh, Charlie."

She could feel his fingers digging into her back as he clutched her shirt. "It's all right now, Charlie, I'm here and we're going home." His face was buried in her shirt and she patted his head, said again, "It's all right now. Everything's fine."

She held him against her for a moment, and now the hot tears were in her eyes and on her cheeks, and she didn't even notice.

"I know how you feel," she said. "I know. One time when I had the measles and my fever was real high, I got lost on my way back from the bathroom, right in our house, and it was a terrible feeling, terrible, because I wanted to get back to my bed and I couldn't find it, and finally Aunt Willie heard me and came and you know where I was? In the kitchen. In our kitchen and I couldn't have been more lost if I'd been out in the middle of the wilderness."

She patted the back of his head again and said, "Look, I even brought your bedroom slipper. Isn't that service, huh?"

She tried to show it to him, but he was still clutching her, and she held him against her, patting him. After a moment she said again, "Look, here's your slipper. Let's put it on." She knelt, put his foot into the shoe, and said, "Now, isn't that better?"

He nodded slowly, his chest still heaving with unspent sobs.

"Can you walk home?"

He nodded. She took her shirttail and wiped his tears and smiled at him. "Come on, we'll find a way out of here and go home."

"Hey, over this way," Joe called from the bank of the ravine. Sara had forgotten about him in the excitement of finding Charlie, and she looked up at him for a moment.

"Over this way, around the big tree," Joe called. "That's probably how he got in. The rest of the ravine is a mass of brier bushes."

She put one arm around Charlie and led him around the tree. "Everybody in town's looking for you, you know that?" she said. "Everybody. The police came and all the neighbors are out— there must be a hundred people looking for you. You were on the radio. It's like you were the President of the United States or something. Everybody was saying, 'Where's Charlie?' and 'We got to find Charlie'."

Suddenly Charlie stopped and held up his hand and Sara looked down. "What is it?"

He pointed to the silent watch.

She smiled. "Charlie, you are something, you know that? Here we are racing down the hill to tell everyone in great triumph that you are found, *found,* and we have to stop and wind your watch first."

She looked at the watch, saw that the stem was missing, and shook her head. "It's broken, Charlie, see, the stem's gone. It's broken."

He held it out again.

"It's *broken,* Charlie. We'll have to take it to the jeweler and have it fixed."

He continued to hold out his arm.

"Hey, Charlie, you want to wear my watch till you get yours fixed?" Joe asked. He slid down the bank and put his watch on Charlie's arm. "There."

Charlie bent his face close and listened.

"Now can we go home?" Sara asked, jamming her hands into her back pockets.

Charlie nodded.

Interpret the Ideas

Have you ever wondered sometimes if people say what they mean? Have you ever wondered if they mean what they say? Answer these questions about the characters in the story *The Summer of the Swans.*

1. Did these people say what they meant? Why do you think so?
    a. Joe: "I want to help."
    b. Mary: "He (Joe) didn't steal Charlie's watch."
    c. Mary: "I wanted to come."
    d. Sara: "I never want to see him (Joe)."
2. Did these people mean what they said?
    a. Joe: "I'm tough; I'm indestructible."
    b. Sara: "I just wanted to say I'm sorry."
    c. Sara: "I'm not going to face him."
    d. Sara: "I'll never get up that."
    e. Joe: "Charlie: you want to wear my watch?"
3. In the search for Charlie, many people were brought together. More was found than just Charlie. What were some of the things that were found? Who found them?
4. Would this be accurate to say about this story: When Charlie lost part of his world, Sara found part of a new world. When Charlie regained his old world, Sara retained her new world. Discuss your reasons for accepting or rejecting this statement.

FOLLOW-THROUGH

Pulling It All Together

In this unit on lost and found, you have read about:
1. a young man who kept his wits while lost and was then found;
2. an archaeologist's determination that led him to find a great treasure that everyone else believed was lost forever;
3. two ways to calculate your location if you ever seem lost;
4. a way to "lose" and "find" numbers that will mystify your friends;
5. a poet whose readers found an idea the poet didn't know she had but lost it before they could share it with her;
6. a girl, a boy, and a child—all who were lost, in their own way; all who were found, in their own way.

Do you remember the quotation at the beginning of this unit: "I have lost all and found myself"? How is it possible to lose everything and find yourself? What do you think the author meant by "lost all" and "found myself"? Based on what you have read and your own experiences, do you agree or disagree with the idea of lost and found as stated in the quotation?

At the beginning of this unit, you examined several definitions of the words *lost* and *found.* Now that you have read the selections in this unit, decide which of the definitions of the two words you would associate with each article, story, or poem. Discuss the reasons for your choices.

On page 329, you discussed several ideas that related to the ideas of lost and found. You decided whether or not you agreed with the ideas—and why. Now, decide if the authors of the selections would agree with you about those statements. Be ready to discuss your responses with others in the group. First, tell how you felt about each statement. Second, tell whether the author of one of the selections would agree with you. Third, give your reasons for your decision, based on the reading selection. Do this for each statement and each selection in the unit.

Putting Your Knowledge to Work

Following are some ideas for activities that will give you the opportunity to use what you have learned in this unit. Choose one or more that you would like to do alone or with a group.

1. Learn more about magic with numbers from the following books:

   Adler, Irving. *Logic for Beginners: Through Games, Jokes, and Puzzles.* New York: The John Day Co., 1964.
   _____. *The Magic House of Numbers.* New York: The John Co., 1974.

   Put on a magic number show for your classmates.

2. Make up "Where in the World Am I?" riddles for your classmates to solve. Find the latitude and longitude of interesting places in the world. Using information from an encyclopedia or from your own experiences, write short paragraphs describing the places and give the latitude and longitude of each. Ask your classmates to name the place from the information you've given. For example:

   I am visiting a place that is sometimes called the "City of the Angels." It is at approximately 34° North Latitude and 119° West Longitude. Where in the World Am I?

3. Find out more about lost and/or found treasures by reading one or more of the following:

   Aylesworth, Thomas G. *Mysteries from the Past.* Garden City, N.Y.: Natural History Press, 1971.
   Hall, Jennie. *Buried Cities,* rev. ed. New York: Macmillan Publishing Co., Inc., 1964.
   Hamblin, Dora J. *Buried Cities and Ancient Treasures.* New York: Simon and Schuster, Inc., 1973.
   Madison, Arnold. *Lost Treasures of America: True Stories of Hidden Riches.* Chicago: Rand McNally and Co., 1977.

Here are some other books about being lost and found you might enjoy:

Brandel, Marc. *The Mine of Lost Days.* Philadelphia: J. B. Lippincott Co., 1974.
   Henry finds four people living in a copper mine and learns that they have been there since the 1800's.
Christopher, John. *Wild Jack.* New York: Macmillan Publishing Co., Inc., 1974.
   In the 21st century, Clive has lost his sense of freedom in the city but finds it living with with "outlaws."
O'Dell, Scott. *Zia.* Boston: Houghton Mifflin Co., 1976.
   Zia's Aunt Karana (hero of *Island of the Blue Dolphins*) is rescued from her 18-year exile on the island.
Roth, Arthur. *The Iceberg Hermit.* New York: Four Winds Press, 1974.
   Based on a true story, this book describes a young man who is marooned on an iceberg for several years.

Freedom and Bondage

seven

FOCUS

"Freedom and bondage are always temporary. Bondage requires constant use of force. Freedom requires constant vigilance."

This quotation makes a statement about freedom and bondage. With your group, discuss whether you agree or disagree with it. Then read the selections in this unit to see if they support the ideas in the quotation.

Key Concepts

freedom (a) the state of being free; (b) civil or political liberty; (c) personal independence; (d) exemption from outside control or regulation; (e) absence of obligation; (f) the right to use something at will.

bondage (a) slavery or involuntary servitude; (b) bound or subject to outside control or regulation; (c) being under obligation to someone or something.

Getting in Touch with Your Experiences

Work with your group to make a list of all the words you can think of from your own experiences that have to do with the word *freedom.* Then decide with which of the definitions of *freedom* each of the words in your list is related. Be sure you can explain your answers.

Now do the same for the word *bondage.* First, list as many words as you can think of that have to do with bondage. Then decide with which definition each word relates.

Following is part of a poem by Wendell Berry. Think about what it means by relating it to your own ideas about freedom and bondage as well as to the quotation at the beginning of this unit.

from **"My Great-Grandfather's Slaves"**
by Wendell Berry

I have seen that freedom cannot be taken
    from one man and given to another,
    and cannot be taken and kept.

I know that freedom can only be given,
    and is the gift to the giver
    from the one who receives.

Below are some statements that have something to do with *freedom* and *bondage*. Decide which of the statements you can agree with on the basis of your own experience. Then decide with which of the statements the poet, Wendell Berry, might agree. Be sure to give evidence from the poem to support your decisions.

1. We insure our own freedom when we respect the freedom of others.
2. Freedom does not necessarily mean an absence of rules or regulations.
3. Neither master nor slave is really free; they are both in a kind of bondage.
4. Freedom is seldom appreciated unless it is lost or threatened.
5. Freedom and bondage are always temporary.

Freedom and Bondage in History

Anticipate the Ideas

Many of our country's most famous documents are written in a way that makes them difficult to read. There are two reasons for this. First, they are written in very formal language, and second, they are written in the language that people used during the early history of our country. As our language has changed over two centuries and become less formal, the documents have become more difficult to understand.

One way to make the documents easier to read is to restate their ideas in our present-day language. Then you can go back and read the original language and understand it better. The document you will be reading in this section is one that is more easily understood when stated in everyday language. Let's see how it works.

Pretend that you belong to a large organization of people. You and some others feel that the leader of the organization has treated you unfairly and violated your rights. You decide that you should break away from the organization and form your own group. You feel that you should write a statement explaining why you are doing so.

Which of the following ideas might you include in your statement? Make your own choices first, and then compare your responses with those of other members of your group. See where you have differences and discuss why.

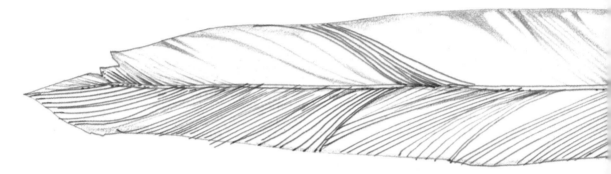

1. If one group decides to break away from the larger organization, it should give the reasons for its decision.
2. It is clear that all people are created equal and have the right to live, the right to be free, and the right to enjoy life.
3. To protect their rights, people form organizations and select leaders to protect the rights of the people and the organization.
4. A group should separate from the organization or change leaders only for the most serious reasons.
5. When organization leaders do not protect the rights of the people, the people should reorganize and select new leaders.
6. When it seems necessary to take such action, a group should do so.
7. The specific complaints of the group should be stated.

Now read the first part of the Declaration of Independence written in 1776. Decide whether the writers of the Declaration expressed ideas similar to those you have discussed. The Declaration is written in very long sentences, but don't let that confuse you. The sentences are well organized and understandable if you follow the argument being developed. At the end of each sentence, pause a moment to ask yourself how you would express that idea in modern, twentieth-century language. Then go on to the next sentence. The sentences in the Declaration are numbered to help you relate the ideas to the statements you discussed.

The Declaration of Independence

The unanimous Declaration of the thirteen united States of America.

1. When in the Course of human events, it becomes necessary for one people to dissolve the political bands which have connected them with another, and to assume among the powers of the earth, the separate and equal station to which the Laws of Nature and of Nature's God entitle them, a decent respect to the opinions of mankind requires that they should declare the causes which impel them to the separation. —

2. We hold these truths to be self-evident, that all men are created equal, that they are endowed by their Creator with certain unalienable Rights, that among these are Life, Liberty and the pursuit of Happiness. —

3. That to secure these rights, Governments are instituted among Men, deriving their just powers from the consent of the governed, — That whenever any Form of Government becomes destructive of these ends, it is the Right of the People to alter or to abolish it, and to institute new Government, laying its foundation on such principles and organizing its powers in such form, as to them shall seem most likely to effect their Safety and Happiness.

4. Prudence, indeed, will dictate that Governments long established should not be changed for light and transient causes; and accordingly all experience hath shown, that mankind are more disposed to suffer, while evils are sufferable, than to right themselves by abolishing the forms to which they are accustomed.

5. But when a long train of abuses and usurpations, pursuing invariably the same Object evinces a design to reduce them under absolute Despotism, it is their right, it is their duty, to throw off such Government, and to provide new Guards for their future security. —

6. Such has been the patient sufferance of these Colonies; and such is now the necessity which constrains them to alter their former Systems of Government.

7. The history of the present King of Great Britain is a history of repeated injuries and usurpations, all having in direct object the establishment of an absolute Tyranny over these States.

Anticipate More Ideas

The next part of the Declaration of Independence lists the specific acts of King George III that caused the American colonists to declare their independence. Listed below are some of the colonists' complaints against the King restated in present-day language. First, read the complaints as they are stated below. Then read the complaints in the original language of the Declaration. On a separate piece of paper, try to match the number of the complaint as stated below with the letter of the sentence in the Declaration that means the same thing.

1. He has increased the number of people in government, and they do nothing but bother the people and cost them money.
2. He is trying to prevent people from entering the colonies and obtaining new land.
3. He tries to blackmail large districts out of their right of representation.
4. He has refused to recognize and approve laws passed in the colonies.
5. He keeps armies in our midst without our permission, even though it is not wartime.
6. He has caused judges to be dependent on him for job and salary.
7. He won't let laws be passed unless agreement is made that they won't become effective until he approves them—then he doesn't bother to approve them.

8. He doesn't reorganize new legislative bodies after old ones have been dismissed, and the people, therefore, are taking the law into their own hands.
9. He has given the armies more power and control than the civilian government has.
10. He has aroused the Indians against us.
11. He keeps closing down the legislative bodies because they oppose his improper conduct.
12. He intentionally makes it hard for legislative bodies to meet.

more from **The Declaration of Independence**

8. To prove this, let Facts be submitted to a candid world.

a. He has refused his Assent to Laws, the most wholesome and necessary for the public good.

b. He has forbidden his Governors to pass Laws of immediate and pressing importance, unless suspended in their operation till his Assent should be obtained; and when so suspended, he has utterly neglected to attend to them.—

c. He has refused to pass other Laws for the accommodation of large districts of people, unless those people would relinquish the right of Representation in the Legislature, a right inestimable to them and formidable to tyrants only.—

d. He has called together legislative bodies at places unusual, uncomfortable, and distant from the depository of their public Records, for the sole purpose of fatiguing them into compliance with his measures.—

e. He has dissolved Representative Houses repeatedly, for opposing with manly firmness his invasions on the rights of the people.—

f. He has refused for a long time, after such dissolutions, to cause others to be elected; whereby the Legislative powers, incapable of Annihilation, have returned to the People at large for their exercise; the State remaining in the mean time exposed to all the dangers of invasion from without, and convulsions within.—

g. He has endeavoured to prevent the population of these States; for that purpose obstructing the Laws for Naturalization of Foreigners; refusing to pass others to encourage their migration hither, and raising the conditions of new Appropriations of Lands.—

h. He has obstructed the Administration of Justice, by refusing his Assent to Laws for establishing Judiciary powers.—

i. He has made Judges dependent on his Will alone, for the tenure of their offices, and the amount and payment of their salaries.—

j. He has erected a multitude of New Offices, and sent hither swarms of Officers to harass our people, and eat out their substance.—

k. He has kept among us in times of peace, Standing Armies without the Consent of our legislatures.—

l. He has affected to render the Military independent of and superior to the Civil power.—

m. He has combined with others to subject us to a jurisdiction foreign to our constitution, and unacknowledged by our laws; giving his Assent to their Acts of pretended Legislation:—

(1) For quartering large bodies of armed troops among us:—

(2) For protecting them, by a mock Trial, from punishment for any Murders which they should commit on the Inhabitants of these States:—

(3) For cutting off our Trade with all parts of the world:—

(4) For imposing Taxes on us without our Consent:—

(5) For depriving us in many cases, of the benefits of Trial by jury:—

(6) For transporting us beyond Seas to be tried for pretended offenses: —

(7) For abolishing the free System of English Laws in a neighbouring Province, establishing therein an Arbitrary government, and enlarging its Boundaries so as to render it at once an example and fit instrument for introducing the same absolute rule into these Colonies: —

(8) For taking away our Charters, abolishing our most valuable Laws, and altering fundamentally the Forms of our Governments: —

(9) For suspending our own Legislatures, and declaring themselves invested with power to legislate for us in all cases whatsoever. —

n. He has abdicated Government here, by declaring us out of his Protection and waging War against us. —

o. He has plundered our seas, ravaged our Coasts, burnt our towns, and destroyed the lives of our people. —

p. He is at this time transporting large Armies of foreign Mercenaries to compleat the works of death, desolation and tyranny, already begun with circumstances of Cruelty & perfidy scarcely paralleled in the most barbarous ages, and totally unworthy the Head of a civilized nation. —

q. He has constrained our fellow Citizens taken Captive on the high Seas to bear Arms against their Country, to become the executioners of their friends and Brethren, or to fall themselves by their Hands. —

r. He has excited domestic insurrections amongst us, and has endeavoured to bring on the inhabitants of our frontiers, the merciless Indian Savages, whose known rule of warfare, is an undistinguished destruction of all ages, sexes and conditions.

Restate the Ideas

The rest of the Declaration discusses the repeated pleas of the colonists to both the King and the British people to set right the wrongs that had been done. Finally, the last paragraph declares the separation of the colonies from Great Britain.

Read the rest of the Declaration. Then work with your group to write at least two statements that express in your own words what the colonists were declaring in the last paragraph of the Declaration.

more from **The Declaration of Independence**

9. In every stage of these Oppressions We have Petitioned for Redress in the most humble terms: Our repeated Petitions have been answered only by repeated injury.

10. A Prince, whose character is thus marked by every act which may define a Tyrant, is unfit to be the ruler of a free people.

11. Nor have We been wanting in attentions to our British brethren.

    a. We have warned them from time to time of attempts by their legislature to extend an unwarrantable jurisdiction over us.

    b. We have reminded them of the circumstances of our emigration and settlement here.

    c. We have appealed to their native justice and magnanimity, and we have conjured them by the ties of our common kindred to disavow these usurpations, which would inevitably interrupt our connections and correspondence.

12. They too have been deaf to the voice of justice and of consanguinity.

13. We must, therefore, acquiesce in the necessity, which denounces our Separation, and hold them, as we hold the rest of mankind, Enemies in War, in Peace Friends.—

14. WE, THEREFORE, the Representatives of the United States of America, in General Congress, Assembled, appealing to the Supreme Judge of the world for the rectitude of our intentions, do, in the Name, and by authority of the good People of these Colonies, solemnly publish and declare, That these United Colonies are, and of Right ought to be FREE AND INDEPENDENT STATES; that they are Absolved from all Allegiance to the British Crown, and that all political connection between them and the State of Great Britain, is and ought to be totally dissolved; and that as Free and Independent States, they have full Power to levy War, conclude Peace, contract Alliances, establish Commerce, and to do all other Acts and Things which Independent States may of right do. — And for the support of this Declaration, with a firm reliance on the protection of divine Providence, we mutually pledge to each other our Lives, our Fortunes and our Sacred Honor.

Apply the Ideas

You have just read the Declaration of Independence. Which of the following statements about freedom can you support with ideas from the Declaration as well as from your own experiences? Be ready to discuss the reasons for your choices.

1. Belief is as much a part of freedom as action is.
2. You may get freedom without working for it, but you can't keep it that way.
3. Freedom of people brings equality among them; bondage brings inequality.
4. Freedom and bondage have as much to do with your mind as with your body.

Freedom and Bondage in Plays

Anticipate the Ideas

You can enjoy a play by reading it as well as by seeing it performed on television or on the stage. As you read the play, pay special attention to stage directions so that you get a mental picture of the action and the actors.

In the unit on Fact and Fiction, you read about Bright Morning in *Sing Down the Moon,* which is historical fiction. Next you will read a play that is fictionalized history. In *Sing Down the Moon,* the events were real and the characters were fictional. In this play, the characters are real and the event is fictional.

The author makes up an event to summarize many things that did happen in early American history. She also uses the play to tell about what some of our early patriots did to help create this country and assure its independence. The characters make statements for which they are famous but in a situation that does not call for them to make such statements. The play makes you aware of the words and the actions of these famous people.

An Imaginary Trial of George Washington

by Diana Wolman

CHARACTERS

JUDGE, appointed by the King of England

BAILIFF

LORD NORTH, lawyer for the Crown

JOHN ADAMS, lawyer for the defense

GEORGE WASHINGTON, the defendant

JOHN HANCOCK

RICHARD HENRY LEE

THOMAS JEFFERSON

PATRICK HENRY

BENEDICT ARNOLD

PAUL REVERE

MARY HAYES (Molly Pitcher)

RACHEL SALOMON

DEBORAH GANNET

BENJAMIN FRANKLIN

CITIZENS

} witnesses

SCENE 1

SETTING: *A courtroom.*

AT RISE: *The Judge, wearing a wig in typical British fashion, sits at a large table at right of stage, facing the center. The British flag stands beside his chair. The witness stand, now empty, stands in the center of the stage. At left, there are several rows of chairs facing the center, and on these sit the witnesses and interested citizens. In the first row sits John Adams. George Washington sits beside Adams. Lord North stands right center, holding a document. Bailiff stands near Judge.*

BAILIFF (*striking floor with long wooden staff*): Hear ye, hear ye! The trial of George Washington for treason against the British Crown is now in session. (*He sits.*)

JUDGE (*striking gavel on table*): Lord North, as lawyer for the Crown, will you please read the bill of particulars?

NORTH (*reading from legal document*): "(1) After pledging loyalty to his country and his king, as subject and officer, George Washington has taken up arms against his government in an effort to overthrow it. (2) He has conspired with other subjects of His Majesty to overthrow the rightfully established government of England by force and violence. (3) He has surrounded himself with people of low character — anarchists, robbers, smugglers — who have incited the people to riot and made treasonous statements in public."

JUDGE: George Washington, step forward. (*Washington goes up steps to stage and faces Judge.*) How do you plead, guilty or not guilty?

WASHINGTON: Before God and man, as history is my witness, I am *not* guilty!

JUDGE: Take the stand.

NORTH: Your full name, please.

WASHINGTON: George Washington.

NORTH: Where and when were you born?

WASHINGTON: February 22, 1732, at Bridges Creek, Virginia.

NORTH: Occupation?

WASHINGTON: Farmer.

NORTH: A farmer, did you say?

WASHINGTON: To me there is nothing more rewarding than to

plant and watch living things grow. I would like above all to be able to return to my beloved Mt. Vernon.

NORTH (*with sarcasm*): And can you explain just how you, a lover of the land, became Commander-in-Chief of this handful of rebellious subjects?

WASHINGTON: This honor came to me by default, so to speak. *All* of us are farmers, or workers, or merchants. We are not soldiers by training or desire. I, at least, had some experience as an officer under General Braddock in the recent French and Indian War. In the spring of 1775, five years ago, the second Continental Congress appointed me Commander-in-Chief of the Continental Army, and this responsibility I undertook with great humility and a sense of duty.

NORTH (*interrupting angrily*): May I interpose here, Your Lordship, that this man is most responsible for all our troubles today. I can show that it was Washington and probably Washington alone who kept the Revolution alive. He was the only one among them who combined military experience with a sense of organization and an ability to deal with people. Oh, I am willing to admit his personal superiority of character and love for justice. But, in the year and a half from November 1776 to the spring of 1778, the Revolution would have collapsed had we killed or captured only this one man.

ADAMS (*rising*): I would like to ask the defendant some questions, if I may. (*He approaches the witness chair.*) General Washington, what duties have you performed in the past?

WASHINGTON: I have been a surveyor, a soldier, an officer . . .

ADAMS: And how did you carry on these activities?

WASHINGTON: Very faithfully, Mr. Adams. I have always been loyal to my work and to my superiors.

ADAMS: What was your attitude toward the conflict with the English government at first?

WASHINGTON: At first I never dreamt of separation from our mother country. Even after I became Commander-in-Chief, we officers would nightly toast King George's health. But now I am convinced that separation is the only possible solution.

ADAMS: Thank you. (*He nods to Washington, who leaves stand and returns to his seat.*)

NORTH: Your Honor, I intend to prove to you that Washington has surrounded himself with persons of low and treasonous character, and I have witnesses to prove it. I now call to the stand John Hancock. (*Hancock comes to witness stand.*) You are a smuggler by trade. That would be correct, would it not?

HANCOCK: No, sir, a merchant, a rather wealthy merchant, I am glad to say, but one who respectfully disregards the hated duties imposed on our imports.

JUDGE: I see. I shall write down—John Hancock, smuggler. (*He picks up pen.*)

HANCOCK (*angrily*): You may write what you please, but I, too, have written, knowing full well what the consequences might be. I was the first to sign the Declaration of Independence, and I signed it in large bold letters to make sure that George III could read it without his spectacles. (*A burst of laughter comes from audience.*)

JUDGE (*striking table with gavel*): Order in the court!

NORTH: That will be all, Mr. Hancock. (*Hancock leaves witness stand.*) Indeed, I wish to speak about this hateful document, which I now hold in my hand. Will Richard Henry Lee please take the stand? (*Lee, in dress of Southern gentleman of period, approaches.*) Mr. Lee, can you identify the document that I am now holding?

LEE: Certainly, that is the Declaration of Independence.

NORTH: And what was your connection with this piece of treachery?

ADAMS (*Jumping up*): I object, your Honor, to the prosecutor's use of such prejudiced language to describe this noble expression of the free spirit of man.

JUDGE (*dryly*): Objection overruled.

LEE: I am proud to state here that I am the one who made the original motion concerning independence, at the Continental Congress. May I read it to you? (*He takes paper from pocket and reads.*) "RESOLVED: That these United Colonies are, and of Right ought to be, FREE AND INDEPENDENT STATES; that they are Absolved from all Allegiance to the British Crown, and that all political connection between them and the State of Great Britain, is, and ought to be, totally dissolved . . ."

NORTH: You will live to regret this rash notion of yours.

LEE: On the contrary, I am glad that I said on that momentous occasion (*continuing reading*), "Let this happy day give birth to a new nation." In my opinion, July 4th will in the future be regarded as the birthday of these United States.

NORTH (*with disgust*): That is quite enough.

ADAMS (*stepping forward to witness chair as North sits down*):
Now I would like to ask the witness: What is your opinion of
General Washington?

LEE: Washington is more than a general. He is the embodiment
of all that is noblest and best in the American people. Not only
has he willingly served without any pay, but from his own
pocket he has bought clothing for his army and sent aid to the
destitute families of his companions in battle. I prophesy that
Washington will go down in history as first in war, first in
peace and first in the hearts of his countrymen. (*Spontaneous
applause comes from the audience as Lee leaves stand.*)

ADAMS: Thank you, Mr. Lee.

NORTH: I call Thomas Jefferson to the stand (*Jefferson walks up
to stand and sits down.*) I ask you, sir, whether you recognize
this paper.

JEFFERSON: Yes, I do.

NORTH: Will you read the opening words?

JEFFERSON (*reading*): "In Congress, July 4, 1776, Unanimous Declaration of the United States of America . . . "

NORTH: Would you please state briefly in your own words, Mr. Jefferson, the purpose of that declaration.

JEFFERSON: We wished to make known to the world why we moved to declare our independence from the government of Great Britain. We listed the reasons for our act, including the tyrannical action of the present British king. We presented also . . .

NORTH (*interrupting impatiently*): Would you say, Mr. Jefferson, that the words of the Declaration of Independence are, in truth, *your* very own words? Is it not true that *you*, in fact, are the author of this treacherous paper? (*He brandishes the paper in his hands.*)

JEFFERSON: Sir, I had the honor to be chosen by my colleagues at the Continental Congress to help in the writing of this document.

NORTH: Do you accept the doctrines announced in the paper?

ADAMS (*from seat*): Objection!

JUDGE: Lord North, this line of questioning should not be continued, since Mr. Jefferson is not now on trial.

NORTH (*to Judge*): I wish, sir, to submit this Declaration to be marked Exhibit A.

JUDGE: Is there evidence that the defendant, George Washington, signed this document?

NORTH: No, sir, he did not sign it, but we shall introduce conclusive evidence that the defendant in fact supported the views of the Declaration.

JUDGE: Admitted. (*North hands document to Judge.*)

NORTH (*to Jefferson*): I have no further questions for the witness. (*Jefferson leaves stand and returns to his seat.*)

JUDGE: Who is your next witness, Lord North?

NORTH: Patrick Henry, of Virginia.

JUDGE: Patrick Henry, step forth! (*Henry stands up at his seat.*) Take the stand. (*He goes to witness stand.*)

NORTH: You are a Virginian?

HENRY: The distinction between New Yorkers, New Englanders, Virginians, and Pennsylvanians is no more. I am not a Virginian, sir. I am an American.

JUDGE: Yes, I hear you've been inventing that word lately. And you have been making treasonous statements, haven't you?

HENRY: What I said is merely that Caesar had his Brutus, Charles the First his Cromwell, and George the Third . . .

JUDGE (*striking gavel on the table*): Treason!

HENRY (*calmly*): . . . may profit by their example. If *this* be treason, make the most of it.

JUDGE: Do you realize what you are saying, you bold young man? You shall hang for this!

HENRY: Is life so dear or peace so sweet as to be purchased at the price of chains and slavery? Forbid it, Almighty God. I know not what course others may take, but as for me, give me liberty or give me death!

JEFFERSON (*speaking from his seat*): He speaks the way Homer wrote.

JUDGE: You will hang, all right, you may be sure of that. (*to Jefferson*) And you, too, Mr. Jefferson.

FRANKLIN: (*from his seat, in a loud whisper*): We must all hang together, or assuredly we shall all hang separately. (*Applause from audience is heard.*)

JUDGE: Order in the court or I shall clear the room!

JUDGE: Who is your next witness, Lord North?

NORTH: The next witness will be someone who actually heard George Washington incite soldiers to fight their king, someone who saw him make plans to rebel against the rightful government of these colonies, one who can identify him as the chief ringleader of the rebellion — a man who only last week had breakfast with him . . . I now call to the stand — Benedict Arnold. (*Shouts come from audience — "Traitor," "Informer," etc. — as Benedict Arnold approaches witness stand.*)

JUDGE: Order in the court!

NORTH: What is your name?

ARNOLD: Benedict Arnold.

NORTH: Have you ever seen the defendant before?

ARNOLD: Many times.

NORTH: What do you know about him?

ARNOLD: I have heard him make plans for the defeat of the British Army. At a time when officers and troops had not been paid for a long period, and their families were close to starving, a number of Continental officers were ready to revolt. They were stopped from doing so by a letter from George Washington, asking them to act for the good of their cause and not according to their personal desires.

NORTH: Thank you. You have done a real service to His Majesty today.

ARNOLD: I am glad to have this chance to serve my king and to make amends for my former disloyalty.

ADAMS: *And* to get paid 6,000 British pounds.

JUDGE: You are out of order, Mr. Adams. Proceed, Lord North.

NORTH: Mr. Arnold, what was your position with Washington?

ARNOLD: I was a commanding officer. I took part in the famous battle of Saratoga and was largely responsible for Burgoyne's surrender.

NORTH: How do you feel about those activities now?

ARNOLD: I am willing to speak freely of the days when I erred. Truly I was a dupe. I now realize that I was wrong when I worked for the overthrow of His Majesty, King George III. I was blinded and full of false ideas. I wish to atone for those days and will eagerly identify any of the rebels you may wish me to point out.

NORTH: Thank you. That is all for now. (*Benedict Arnold returns to his seat.*)

WASHINGTON (*aside*): Whom can we trust now?

JUDGE: There will now be a short recess.

CURTAIN

This play has a unique way of presenting historical facts: it puts real people and real facts together in an imaginary situation. To determine some of the facts you learned from an imaginary situation, read each statement below and decide whether it is true or false. Find the page and line reference to support your decision. Then, rewrite each false statement so that it is true.

1. George Washington was born in Virginia in 1732.
2. George Washington was a soldier and politician by trade.
3. John Hancock was the first person to sign the Declaration of Independence.
4. Henry Lee was violently opposed to signing the Declaration.
5. Thomas Jefferson helped write the Declaration of independence.
6. George Washington signed the Declaration of Independence with pride.
7. Patrick Henry said, "Give me liberty or give me death."
8. Benedict Arnold was always a spy for the British.

Set Your Purposes

Now that you have examined some of the ways in which facts can be presented in an imaginary situation, look for additional facts in the next scene. Also notice how those facts are brought out by the various people on the witness stand.

SCENE 2

SETTING: *Same as Scene 1.*

AT RISE: *Same as Scene 1, but Lord North is seated in front row of seats where witnesses sit, at left. John Adams stands left center.*

BAILIFF (*striking staff on floor*): Hear ye, hear ye! The trial of George Washington for treason against the Crown will now be resumed. (*He sits.*)

JUDGE: As lawyer for the defense, you may now proceed, Mr. Adams. (*Adams walks toward table and addresses the Judge.*)

ADAMS: On trial today stands a man whose name will go down in history as the father of his country, whose picture will be revered throughout the civilized world as the image of liberty and freedom. He is guilty only of following the Lord's will that truth should be told and that freedom be proclaimed throughout the land. I will show you that the colonies suffered long and grievously before they took the extreme measure of armed rebellion, that they took this step only after all other measures failed because of the obstinacy of the British government, that the followers of Washington are men and women from all walks of life, from town and country, from north, south and even the frontier. They are Presbyterians, Jews, Frenchmen, Germans, Poles, Africans, and even pioneers.

First, allow me to present some character witnesses who will explain in their own words why they support George Washington and his struggle, of their own accord, without hope of award or glory. First I call to the stand that outstanding citizen of Boston, Paul Revere.

REVERE (*walking up to stand*): I am glad to appear here in Washington's behalf and also to correct a false impression that the court may be getting.

JUDGE: What impression is that, Mr. Revere?

REVERE: Perhaps you have assumed up to now that all of us in the Revolution are merchants—or smugglers, as you choose to call them—or even rich farmers. As a matter of fact, the majority of us are workers, and it is we—mechanics, carpenters, rope-makers, printers, and joiners—who organized the Sons of Liberty.

JUDGE: I have heard of you. What is your trade—that is, when you are not riding a horse?

REVERE: Silversmith, sir . . . and as for the incident you are referring to, well, I was acting for the North End Club of the Sons of Liberty, and I am proud to say that it was our organization that prevented your troops from capturing John Hancock at Lexington.

NORTH (*jumping up*): Your Lordship, this insurrection has been brewing for a long time. Before you is a member, nay, a leader of this mob, this mixed rabble of Scotch, Irish, and other foreign vagabonds.

ADAMS: I object, Your Honor. Paul Revere and his type are the very strength of our community. It is the firm patriotism of these workers that will save our country.

REVERE: Indeed it will. We are determined to fight up to our knees in blood rather than be ruled by tyrants, foreign or domestic. As our song goes (*chanting*),

> Come, rally, Sons of Liberty,
> Come all with hearts united,
> Our motto is "We Dare Be Free,"
> Not easily affrighted!

ADAMS: Thank you, Mr. Revere (*Revere leaves stand and returns to his seat.*) Allow me to present one such person who is not easily affrighted, Mrs. Mary Hayes! (*Molly Pitcher goes to witness stand.*) Please tell the court your full name.

PITCHER: Mary Ludwig Hayes, sir.

ADAMS: By what name are you better known?

PITCHER: Molly Pitcher.

ADAMS: And I am sure our grandchildren will remember you as Molly Pitcher. Tell me, how did you acquire this unusual nickname?

PITCHER: It was at the Battle of Monmouth, in New Jersey. As you may remember, the day of the battle was very hot. Our noble patriots, fighting for independence, naturally suffered from the heat. I moved among them, offering water from my pitcher.

ADAMS: And a brave thing that was, too. But I also know that you did even more. Tell the court about the rest of your action in that battle.

PITCHER: My husband was firing a cannon. Suddenly, he fell to the ground. Immediately, I ran to his cannon and continued to fire it. For this action George Washington gave me the rank of sergeant.

ADAMS: It was well deserved, and the cause must be a noble one to inspire a woman like you to take such drastic action. (*Molly Pitcher bows and leaves the stand, returning to her seat.*)

JUDGE: Have you more witnesses?

ADAMS (*to Judge*): Yes, Your Lordship. My next witness is a woman who came here of her own free will to explain how she and others like her feel about George Washington. I call to the stand Mrs. Rachel Salomon. (*Rachel Salomon approaches the witness stand.*)

SALOMON: Thank you, Mr. Adams.

ADAMS: Will you explain why you came here today?

SALOMON: My husband, Haym, is now in jail, but I know that he wants me to come to talk about Washington and to tell the world why we and other Jews, like Benjamin Nones, for instance, have gladly supported the Revolutionary cause.

ADAMS: Tell us something about yourself and your husband.

SALOMON: My husband and I were born in Poland. Ten years ago, we were forced to flee that country because of the large part he was taking in the struggle for Polish independence. In 1772 we came to New York, where Haym became a financier. Gradually we became wealthy. Then we became interested in the cause of independence. In 1776 Haym was arrested by the British and was supposed to be put to death, but he was released by the Hessians, whose language he could speak. Then, two years ago, he was put in jail again.

ADAMS: Then you and your husband believe in American independence?

SALOMON: Deeply. My husband and I are not fighting people, but we have helped the cause by giving of our own money and by helping to raise more. I'll never forget that Yom Kippur night. Yom Kippur, Mr. Adams, is the holiest of holidays for

us. Nothing in the world, I had always thought, would ever make my husband interrupt these services. But a messenger came right into the synagogue, informing us that Washington needed money desperately for his army. Right then and there, my husband took up a collection, and Washington had his needed funds to carry on longer.

ADAMS: Why has Mr. Salomon been willing to risk his life, his wealth, all he has worked so hard to attain?

SALOMON: Perhaps the court will understand better when I read a part of a letter that George Washington sent to the Jewish community of Newport, Rhode Island. In his own words, he has stated that "the government of the United States will give to bigotry no sanction, to persecution no assistance." He has pledged to make America, once it is independent, a haven for all people of different faiths. At last Jews will have one country in which they can live and bring up their children without fear of persecution and banishment.

ADAMS: I am sure that your sentiments are shared by thousands of our fellow Americans. You may step down, Mrs. Salomon. (*She returns to her seat.*)

JUDGE (*to Adams*): Who is your next witness?

ADAMS: I now call Miss Deborah Gannet to the stand. (*Deborah Gannet, a young black woman, comes to the witness stand.*) Will you give the court your full name, please?

GANNET: Deborah Gannet.

ADAMS: What is your occupation, Miss Gannet?

GANNET: Fighting for my country's freedom is my favorite one, sir, although I used to be a slave.

ADAMS: How do you know George Washington?

GANNET: He is my commanding officer.

ADAMS: How can that be possible for you, a woman?

GANNET: After the Governor of Virginia offered blacks their freedom and fifty dollars to serve in the King's army, the American army gave blacks the same chance. I then decided to enlist as a soldier under George Washington—in disguise, of course.

ADAMS: How long did you serve in the army?

GANNET: For seventeen months I was a member of the Massachusetts regiment without anyone suspecting my real identity or that I was a woman.

ADAMS: Do all the regiments have white and black troops?

GANNET: Most of them. Only Georgia and South Carolina bar slaves from signing up. As a Bostonian, you know that among the first to fall in the Boston Massacre was a former slave by the name of Crispus Attucks. And I am proud that it was one of my people, Peter Salem, who killed that boastful British Major John Pitcairn. And . . .

JUDGE: That is enough!

ADAMS: Just one more question. Why were you willing to lead a hard soldier's life for so long?

GANNET: I can't help thinking of the words of your wife, Abigail Adams, when she wrote: "I wish most sincerely there was not a slave in the province; it always appeared a most iniquitous scheme to me to fight ourselves for what we are daily robbing and plundering from those who have as good a right to freedom as we have."

ADAMS: Thank you, Miss Gannet. That's all. (*She returns to her seat.*)

JUDGE: Who is your next witness, Mr. Adams?

ADAMS: I call Mr. Benjamin Franklin. (*Franklin, wearing his bifocal glasses and leaning on a cane, comes up to stand.*) How old are you, Mr. Franklin?

FRANKLIN: Seventy-six.

ADAMS: And an interesting life it has been, too—as well as a useful one.

FRANKLIN: Well, you know what I say: Early to bed and early to rise makes a man healthy, wealthy, and wise.

ADAMS: Tell the court something of your background.

FRANKLIN: I was apprenticed to my older brother in Boston, but I ran away at the age of seventeen. Since then I have been a writer, the publisher of a newspaper, and an inventor of sorts.

ADAMS: You are very modest, but this assemblage knows that you are the author of *Poor Richard's Almanac*, that you started our first public library, that you are the inventor of the famous Franklin stove, bifocal glasses—the kind Lord North is wearing (*laughter*)—and a number of other household helps. But right now we are interested most in your official duties.

FRANKLIN: I represented the colonies in England in 1765. . .

ADAMS: What was your advice to the British Parliament concerning the Stamp Act?

FRANKLIN: I told them then that it could never work. It was my warning that if the British Army were sent to enforce it, a revolution might result.

ADAMS: Did you try in any other way to prevent this conflict?

FRANKLIN: Several times. The most recent was several years ago. I was negotiating with Lord Howe on Staten Island. I offered then that the matter be peacefully settled on the basis of independence. But all he was instructed to offer was the King's clemency if we would stop fighting, with no guarantee of future liberty within the Empire.

For years, Mr. Adams, I have striven to prevent just such a conflict as we are having now between brother and brother.

ADAMS: Despite your efforts, the conflict was not averted. What is your opinion of the situation today?

FRANKLIN: Once I wrote, "There never was a good war or a bad peace." Now I realize that rebellion against tyrants is obedience to God. (*The audience cheers.*)

ADAMS: Thank you, Mr. Franklin. Two continents value your opinion. (*Franklin returns to his seat.*)

JUDGE: Have you completed your case, Mr. Adams?

ADAMS: I have one final witness—the defendant, George Washington. Will you come forward, General Washington? (*George Washington goes to witness stand.*)

WASHINGTON: I appreciate this opportunity to thank the many friends of liberty who have spoken here today.

ADAMS: General Washington, you did not sign the Declaration of Independence. Is this an indication that you did not think it was justified?

WASHINGTON: When the Declaration of Independence was written, I was on the battlefield with my soldiers. But I believe with all my heart in the ideas expressed in the Declaration. This document specifically states (*reading*): "Governments long established should not be changed for light and transient causes; . . . experience hath shown that mankind are more disposed to suffer, while evils are sufferable, than to right themselves by abolishing the forms to which they are accustomed. But when a long train of abuses . . . evinces a design to reduce them under absolute Despotism, it is their right, it is their duty, to throw off such Government, and to provide new Guards for their future security."

JUDGE (*interrupting*): General Washington, consider for a moment to what chaos such a doctrine may lead. If a dissatisfied people can, of their own will, overthrow their established government, what rule of law and order could possibly prevail?

NORTH: If the court please, we can easily foresee the terrible consequences of this traitorous doctrine. The loyal colonies of Canada and the royal lands of India might also decide to secure this independence by declaration of supposed rights. Should this doctrine spread to other lands, the kingdom of Spain might lose the allegiance of Mexicans and of the Argentine. Brazilians might declare: Brazil for Brazilians! What would the world come to?

JUDGE: Indeed, this is the very heart of their treason.

ADAMS: You both forget that there is a right higher than the right of kings over their subjects. A government exists not for the sake of the rulers but only for the good of the people, and only by the consent of the governed. Governments exist to help the people secure the rights which are theirs as human beings.

JUDGE: What rights? And who gave these rights?

WASHINGTON: In answer to your question, allow me to quote what I think is the *heart* of that document: "We hold these truths to be self-evident, that all men [people] are created equal, that they are endowed by their Creator with certain unalienable Rights, that among these are Life, Liberty, and the pursuit of Happiness. — That to secure these rights, Governments are instituted among Men, deriving their just powers from the consent of the governed, — That whenever any Form of Government becomes destructive of these ends, it is the Right of the People to alter or to abolish it . . ."

JUDGE (*to Adams*): If you have no further witnesses, let the defendant, George Washington, come forward. (*George Washington rises and goes to Judge's table and stands facing the Judge.*) George Washington, as defendant in this trial, do you have anything further to say before we pass judgment?

WASHINGTON: Only history can pass judgment on our noble cause. But I believe firmly that history shall prove our cause was just, our path honorable, and that what we have started and fought for here and now will in the future lead this nation to greatness and leadership among the free peoples of the world. (*Curtains close.*)

THE END

432

Locate Some Details

In the play you learned how certain men and women were willing to risk their lives and their fortunes to win freedom and create a new nation. Tell what each of the following did in the struggle for freedom. Be ready to support your answers with evidence from the play.

1. Patrick Henry
2. Paul Revere
3. Molly Pitcher
4. Rachel Salomon
5. Deborah Gannet

Analyze the Characters and Contrasts

Opposing views are always part of a trial. Listed below in Part B are pairs of opposing descriptions. First, match each pair of descriptions with the person or thing it describes in Part A. Then, identify each opposing description in Part B as belonging, either to the American colonists' point of view or to the British Crown's point of view.

PART A

1. George Washington
2. John Hancock
3. Declaration of Independence
4. King George III
5. Thomas Jefferson
6. Benedict Arnold
7. Paul Revere

PART B

a. noble expression of the free spirit of humans/traitorous doctrine
b. author of the Declaration of Independence/author of a treacherous paper
c. traitor/loyal subject
d. outstanding citizen of Boston/leader of a mob
e. smuggler/merchant
f. tyrant/king
g. father of his country/ringleader of the rebellion

Apply the Ideas

Based on your reading, which of the following statements do you think the colonists would accept? Be ready to give reasons for your choices.

1. Fighting for freedom is better than living with tyranny.
2. Freedom is worth risking one's life for.
3. What is patriotism to some may be treason to others.
4. A common cause can unite men and women from all walks of life.

Freedom and Bondage in Biographies

Set Your Purposes

Even though the United States was founded on the principles of freedom that you read about in the Declaration of Independence, not all people were free. Some were slaves. Slavery existed in the United States for almost a hundred years—until 1861 when Abraham Lincoln abolished it. Before slavery was abolished, thousands of slaves escaped from the South, where slavery was widespread, to the North, where slavery was not so acceptable. They were helped in their escapes by both white and black people who were against slavery. Those people formed what was called the Underground Railroad, a system of connections to help runaway slaves.

Some of the slaves who were helped by the Underground Railroad were so grateful that they went on to help other slaves escape to freedom. One such person was Harriet Tubman. In this section, you will read a selection from Tubman's biography that describes her escape to the North. As you read the account of Tubman's escape, notice how various actions and events linked together to help her succeed. Notice also what Tubman accomplished by her own determination and by the bravery of others.

Harriet Tubman: Conductor on the Underground Railroad

by Ann Petry

During her early life as a slave on a Maryland plantation owned by Edward Brodas, Harriet was "rented out" to different families to do different chores. Harriet rebelled against household work because she preferred being outdoors. Although very tiny, Harriet developed her strength and was frequently applauded for being able to chop trees and carry heavy loads on her back.

Once she tried to prevent the capture of a runaway slave and was hit on the head with an iron bar. Afterward, she started to have visions and uncontrollable sleeping spells. Harriet lived in constant fear of being sold, especially after the Brodas plantation was taken over by Doc Thompson. She married a free man named John Tubman and tried to convince him to run away to the North with her. John refused and told Harriet that he would turn her in if she attempted to run away.

The following selection covers Harriet's own escape from bondage to freedom.

One day, in 1849, when Harriet was working in the fields, near the edge of the road, a white woman wearing a faded sunbonnet went past, driving a wagon. She stopped, and watched Harriet for a few minutes. Then she spoke to her, asked her what her name was, and how she had acquired the deep scar on her forehead.

Harriet told her the story of the blow she had received when she was a girl. After that, whenever the woman saw her in the fields, she stopped to talk to her. She told Harriet that she lived on a farm, near Bucktown. Then one day she said, not looking at Harriet, but looking instead at the overseer, far off at the edge of the fields, "If you ever need any help, Harriet, ever need any help, why you let me know."

That same year the young heir to the Brodas estate died. Harriet mentioned the fact of his death to the white woman in the faded sunbonnet, the next time she saw her. She told her of the panic-stricken talk in the quarter, told her that the slaves were afraid that the master, Dr. Thompson, would start selling them. She said that Doc Thompson no longer permitted any of them to hire their time. The woman nodded her head, clucked to the horse, and drove off, murmuring, "If you ever need any help—"

The slaves were right about Dr. Thompson's intention. He began selling slaves almost immediately. Among the first ones sold were two of Harriet Tubman's sisters. They went South with the chain gang on a Saturday.

When Harriet heard of the sale of her sisters, she knew that the time had finally come when she must leave the plantation. She was reluctant to attempt the long trip North alone, not because of John Tubman's threat to betray her, but because she was afraid she might fall asleep somewhere along the way and so would be caught immediately.

She persuaded three of her brothers to go with her. Having made certain that John was asleep, she left the cabin quietly, and met her brothers at the edge of the plantation. They agreed that she was to lead the way, for she was more familiar with the woods than the others.

The three men followed her, crashing through the under- brush, frightening themselves, stopping constantly to say, "What was that?" or "Someone's coming."

She thought of Ben and how he had said, "Any old body can go through a woods crashing and mashing things down like a cow." She said sharply, "Can't you boys go quieter? Watch where you're going!"

One of them grumbled, "Can't see in the dark. Ain't got cat's eyes like you."

"You don't need cat's eyes," she retorted. "On a night like this, with all the stars out, it's not black dark. Use your own eyes."

She supposed they were doing the best they could but they moved very slowly. She kept getting so far ahead of them that she had to stop and wait for them to catch up with her, lest they lose their way. Their progress was slow, uncertain. Their feet got tangled in every vine. They tripped over fallen logs, and once one of them fell flat on his face. They jumped, startled, at the most ordinary sounds: the murmur of the wind in the branches of the trees, the twittering of a bird. They kept turning around, looking back.

They had not gone more than a mile when she became aware that they had stopped. She turned and went back to them. She could hear them whispering. One of them called out, "Hat!"

"What's the matter? We haven't got time to keep stopping like this."

"We're going back."

"No," she said firmly. "We've got a good start. If we move fast and move quiet—"

Then all three spoke at once. They said the same thing, over and over, in frantic hurried whispers, all talking at once:

They told her that they had changed their minds. Running away was too dangerous. Someone would surely see them and recognize them. By morning the master would know they had "took off." Then the handbills advertising them would be posted all over Dorchester County. The patrollers would search for them. Even if they were lucky enough to elude the patrol, they could not possibly hide from the bloodhounds. The hounds would be baying after them, snuffing through the swamps and the underbrush, zigzagging through the deepest woods. The bloodhounds would surely find them. And everyone knew what happened to a runaway who was caught and brought back alive.

She argued with them. Didn't they know that if they went back they would be sold, if not tomorrow, then the next day, or the next? Sold South. They had seen the chain gangs. Was that what they wanted? Were they going to be slaves for the rest of their lives? Didn't freedom mean anything to them?

"You're afraid," she said, trying to shame them into action. "Go on back. I'm going North alone."

Instead of being ashamed, they became angry. They shouted at her, telling her that she was a fool and they would make her go back to the plantation with them. Suddenly they surrounded her, three men, her own brothers, jostling her, pushing her along, pinioning her arms behind her. She fought against them, wasting her strength, exhausting herself in a furious struggle.

She was no match for three strong men. She said, panting, "All right. We'll go back. I'll go with you."

She led the way, moving slowly. Her thoughts were bitter.

Not one of them was willing to take a small risk in order to be free. It had all seemed so perfect, so simple, to have her brothers go with her, sharing the dangers of the trip together, just as a family should. Now if she ever went North, she would have to go alone.

Two days later, a slave working beside Harriet in the fields motioned to her. She bent toward him, listening. He said the water boy had just brought news to the field hands, and it had been passed from one to the other until it reached him. The news was that Harriet and her brothers had been sold to the Georgia trader, and that they were to be sent South with the chain gang that very night.

Harriet went on working but she knew a moment of panic. She would have to go North alone. She would have to start as soon as it was dark. She could not go with the chain gang. She might die on the way, because of those inexplicable sleeping seizures. But then she—how could she run away? She might fall asleep in plain view along the road.

But even if she fell asleep, she thought, the Lord would take care of her. She murmured a prayer, "Lord, I'm going to hold steady on to You and You've got to see me through."

Afterward, she explained her decision to run the risk of going North alone, in these words: "I had reasoned this out in my mind; there was one of two things I had a *right* to, liberty or death; if I could not have one, I would have the other; for no man should take me alive; I should fight for my liberty as long as my strength lasted, and when the time came for me to go, the Lord would let them take me."

At dusk, when the work in the fields was over, she started toward the Big House. She had to let someone know that she was going North, someone she could trust. She no longer trusted John Tubman and it gave her a lost, lonesome feeling. Her sister Mary worked in the Big House, and she planned to tell Mary that she was going to run away, so someone would know.

As she went toward the house, she saw the master, Doc Thompson, riding up the drive on his horse. She turned aside and went toward the quarter. A field hand had no legitimate reason for entering the kitchen of the Big House—and yet—there must be some way she could leave word so that afterward someone would think about it and know that she had left a message.

As she went toward the quarter she began to sing. Dr. Thompson reined in his horse, turned around and looked at her. It was not the beauty of her voice that made him turn and watch her, frowning, it was the words of the song that she was singing, and something defiant in her manner, that disturbed and puzzled him.

> When that old chariot comes,
>   I'm going to leave you,
> I'm bound for the promised land,
>   Friends, I'm going to leave you.
>
> I'm sorry, friends, to leave you,
>   Farewell! Oh, farewell!
> But I'll meet you in the morning,
>   Farewell! Oh, farewell!
>
> I'll meet you in the morning,
>   When I reach the promised land;
> On the other side of Jordan,
>   For I'm bound for the promised land.

That night when John Tubman was asleep, and the fire had died down in the cabin, she took the ashcake that had been baked for their breakfast, and a good-sized piece of salt herring, and tied them together in an old bandanna. By hoarding this small stock of food, she could make it last a long time, and with the berries and edible roots she could find in the woods, she wouldn't starve.

She decided that she would take the quilt with her, too. Her hands lingered over it. It felt soft and warm to her touch. Even in the dark, she thought she could tell one color from another, because she knew its pattern and design so well.

Then John stirred in his sleep, and she left the cabin quickly, carrying the quilt carefully folded under her arm.

Once she was off the plantation, she took to the woods, not following the North Star, not even looking for it, going instead toward Bucktown. She needed help. She was going to ask the white woman who had stopped to talk to her so often if she would help her. Perhaps she wouldn't. But she would soon find out.

When she came to the farmhouse where the woman lived, she approached it cautiously, circling around it. It was so quiet. There was no sound at all, not even a dog barking, or the sound of voices. Nothing.

She tapped on the door, gently. A voice said, "Who's there?" She answered, "Harriet, from Dr. Thompson's place."

When the woman opened the door she did not seem at all surprised to see her. She glanced at the little bundle that Harriet

Turn to page 345

440

was carrying, at the quilt, and invited her in. Then she sat down at the kitchen table, and wrote two names on a slip of paper, and handed the paper to Harriet.

She said that those were the next places where it was safe for Harriet to stop. The first place was a farm where there was a gate with big white posts and round knobs on top of them. The people there would feed her, and when they thought it was safe for her to go on, they would tell her how to get to the next house, or take her there. For these were the first two stops on the Underground Railroad—going North, from the Eastern Shore of Maryland.

Thus Harriet learned that the Underground Railroad that ran straight to the North was not a railroad at all. Neither did it run underground. It was composed of a loosely organized group of people who offered food and shelter, or a place of concealment, to fugitives who had set out on the long road to the North and freedom.

Harriet wanted to pay this woman who had befriended her. But she had no money. She gave her the patchwork quilt, the only object she had ever owned.

That night she made her way through the woods, crouching in the underbrush whenever she heard the sound of horses' hoofs, staying there until the riders passed. Each time she wondered if they were already hunting for her. It would be so easy to describe her, the deep scar on her forehead like a dent, the old scars on the back of her neck, the husky speaking voice, the lack of height, scarcely five feet tall. The master would say she was wearing rough clothes when she ran away, that she had a bandanna on her head, that she was muscular and strong.

She knew how accurately he would describe her. One of the slaves who could read used to tell the others what it said on those handbills that were nailed up on the trees, along the edge of the roads. It was easy to recognize the handbills that advertised runaways, because there was always a picture in one corner, a picture of a black man, a little running figure with a stick over his shoulder, and a bundle tied on the end of the stick.

Whenever she thought of the handbills, she walked faster. Sometimes she stumbled over old grapevines, gnarled and twisted, thick as a man's wrist, or became entangled in the tough, sinewy vine of the honeysuckle. But she kept going.

In the morning, she came to the house where her friend had said she was to stop. She showed the slip of paper that she carried to the woman who answered her knock at the back door of the farmhouse. The woman fed her, and then handed her a broom and told her to sweep the yard.

Harriet hesitated, suddenly suspicious. Then she decided that with a broom in her hand, working in the yard, she would look as though she belonged on the place, certainly no one would suspect that she was a runaway.

That night the woman's husband, a farmer, loaded a wagon with produce. Harriet climbed in. He threw some blankets over her, and the wagon started.

It was dark under the blankets, and not exactly comfortable. But Harriet decided that riding was better than walking. She was surprised at her own lack of fear, wondered how it was that she so readily trusted these strangers who might betray her. For all she knew, the man driving the wagon might be taking her straight back to the master.

She thought of those other rides in wagons, when she was a child, the same clop-clop of the horses' feet, creak of the wagon, and the feeling of being lost because she did not know where she was going. She did not know her destination this time either, but she was not alarmed. She thought of John Tubman. By this time he must have told the master that she was gone. Then she thought of the plantation and how the land rolled gently down toward the river, thought of Ben and Old Rit, and that Old Rit would be inconsolable because her favorite daughter was missing. "Lord," she prayed, "I'm going to hold steady onto You. You've got to see me through." Then she went to sleep.

The next morning when the stars were still visible in the sky, the farmer stopped the wagon. Harriet was instantly awake.

He told her to follow the river, to keep following it to reach the next place where people would take her in and feed her. He said that she must travel only at night, and she must stay off the roads because the patrol would be hunting for her. Harriet climbed out of the wagon. "Thank you," she said simply, thinking how amazing it was that there should be white people who were willing to go to such lengths to help a slave get to the North.

When she finally arrived in Pennsylvania, she had traveled roughly ninety miles from Dorchester County. She had slept on the ground outdoors at night. She had been rowed for miles up the Choptank River by a man she had never seen before. She had been concealed in a haycock, and had, at one point, spent a week hidden in a potato hole in a cabin which belonged to a family of free Negroes. She had been hidden in the attic of the home of a Quaker. She had been befriended by stout German farmers, whose guttural speech surprised her and whose well-kept farms astonished her. She had never before seen barns and fences,

farmhouses and outbuildings, so carefully painted. The cattle and horses were so clean they looked as though they had been scrubbed.

When she crossed the line into the free state of Pennsylvania, the sun was coming up. She said, "I looked at my hands to see if I was the same person now I was free. There was such a glory over everything, the sun came like gold through the trees, and over the fields, and I felt like I was in heaven."

Analyze the Sequence and Causes and Effects

Harriet Tubman ran away from the plantation where she was a slave and escaped to freedom. This was made possible by a whole series of interrelated events. One event caused another event which, in turn, caused other events.

Listed below are sentences which represent events in the story. Rearrange the events in the order in which they actually occurred. Then go back over the rearranged list and decide what cause-and-effect relationships exist among them. For example: "The heir to the estate dies" caused "The slaves fear Dr. Thompson will sell them," which, in turn, caused "Panic breaks out in the slave quarters." Look at all the events in this way.

a. The heir to the estate dies.
b. Harriet's sisters are sold.
c. A white woman offers help to Harriet.
d. The master sells Harriet and her two brothers.
e. Her brothers panic.
f. Harriet trusts people to help her, though she doesn't know them.
g. Harriet receives the names of others who will help her.
h. Harriet finally reaches Pennsylvania and freedom.
i. Harriet runs away alone.
j. Harriet persuades her brothers to join her in an escape attempt.
k. The slaves fear Dr. Thompson will sell them.
l. Harriet asks the white woman for help.
m. Harriet's first escape attempt fails.
n. Panic breaks out in the slave quarters.

Apply the Ideas

Which of the following statements are supported by ideas from the story about Harriet Tubman and also from your own experiences? Be ready to give reasons from both sources for your choices.

1. There are times when the only way to be successful is to be helped by someone else.
2. Desperate actions are caused by desperate conditions.
3. For every cause there is an effect; for every effect there is a cause.
4. Sometimes it is easier to trust strangers than relatives.
5. To experience success after a long struggle is a glorious feeling.

Expand Your Reading

To find out more about Harriet Tubman and the work she did to help slaves escape to freedom, read *Harriet Tubman: Conductor on the Underground Railroad* by Ann Petry (New York: Thomas Y. Crowell Company or Archway Paperbacks, 1955).

Freedom Speaks

Anticipate the Form

The idea of freedom has been the inspiration for many famous speeches throughout history. One of the most famous speeches in recent American history was the speech given by Dr. Martin Luther King, Jr., on August 28, 1963, at a freedom rally at the Lincoln Memorial in Washington, D.C. Part of this speech, called his "I have a dream" speech, is given here for you to enjoy.

Speeches are created to be heard, not read. But famous speeches are almost always put into print so that more people can be reached. As you read the speech, imagine Dr. King delivering it in person. In that way you can share in the feelings as well as the ideas of the speech.

Anticipate the Author's Purpose

Remember that different speeches have different purposes. Some are meant to inform an audience about certain matters. Some are meant to persuade the audience to accept certain ideas or actions. Some are meant to challenge the audience to take on new responsibilities or to do a difficult job. And some are meant to inspire the audience to give them new hope for success in doing what they must do. Dr. King's speech was designed to inspire his audience, to help them face their difficulties as they worked for integration. As you read the speech, look for two things: (1) the ideas he shared with his audience to inspire them; (2) the words and phrases he used repeatedly to inspire his audience.

Dr. Martin Luther King, Jr.

"I Have a Dream"

I have a dream today!

I have a dream that one day "every valley shall be exalted and every hill and mountain shall be made low. The rough places will be made plain and the crooked places will be made straight, and the glory of the Lord shall be revealed, and all flesh shall see it together."

This is our hope. This is the faith that I go back to the South with. With this faith, we shall be able to transform the jangling discords of our nation into a beautiful symphony of brotherhood. With this faith, we will be able to work together, to pray together, to struggle together, to go to jail together, to stand up for freedom together, knowing that we will be free one day. And this will be the day. This will be the day when all of God's children will be able to sing with new meaning: "My country 'tis of thee, sweet land of liberty, of thee I sing. Land where my fathers died, land of the pilgrim's pride, from every mountainside, let freedom ring." And if America is to be a great nation, this must become true.

So let freedom ring from the prodigious hilltops of New Hampshire. Let freedom ring from the mighty mountains of New York. Let freedom ring from the heightening Alleghenies of Pennsylvania. Let freedom ring from the snowcapped Rockies of Colorado. Let freedom ring from the curvaceous slopes of California. But not only that. Let freedom ring from Stone Mountain of Georgia. Let freedom ring from Lookout Mountain of Tennessee. Let freedom ring from every hill and molehill of Mississippi. From every mountainside, let freedom ring.

And when this happens, and when we allow freedom to ring, when we let it ring from every village and every hamlet, from every state and every city, we will be able to speed up that day when all God's children, black men and white men, Jews and gentiles, Protestants and Catholics, will be able to join hands and sing in the words of the old Negro spiritual: "Free at last. Free at last. Thank God Almighty, we are free at last."

Identify Some Literary Devices

An author frequently uses quotations to emphasize a point. Dr. King quoted from an Old Testament psalm (song), a patriotic song, and a religious song during his speech. Answer the following questions on the basis of what you've read and your own experiences.

1. What did each of the songs contribute to the speech?
2. How do you think the audience was affected by each of the songs?

An author also frequently uses repetition to emphasize a point. Dr. King repeated several phrases in his speech. Answer the following questions on the basis of what you've read and your own experiences.

3. Why do you think this speech is called the "I have a dream" speech?
4. How did the phrase make you feel as you read it?
5. What do you think Dr. King's purpose was in repeating "I have a dream"?
6. What other phrases did Dr. King repeat in his speech?

Apply the Ideas

Below are some ideas that may relate to the speech and to similar kinds of experiences. Decide which ideas you can support from your own experiences and from the speech. Be ready to share the reasons for your choices.

1. Wishing won't make a dream come true; action is necessary.
2. A memorable phrase from a speech can become a rallying cry.
3. Dreams can become reality.
4. A dream may be shared by many people.
5. A nation cannot be truly great unless all its people are free.

Freedom and Bondage in Space

The article that follows deals with a very different kind of freedom and bondage—the freedom and bondage of objects in space.

You have heard the saying "What goes up must come down." Right? Not always. What goes up may stay up—forever—if the conditions are right. This article tells you why and how that can be.

Expand Your Vocabulary

There are several words that you should be sure to know before you read the article. You may know them already, but read through the list to make certain. If there are any you don't know, look them up in the glossary. Then continue the activities in this section.

balance	force	mass	resistance
constant	gravity	motion	satellite
distance	inertia	orbit	speed

The words above fit together in a structured overview that explains the relationship between gravity and orbiting objects:

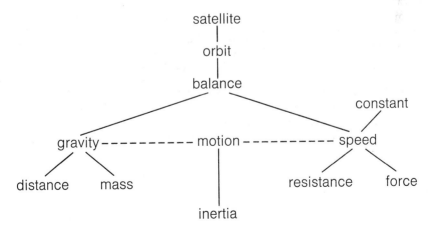

When you read the article, watch for these words and see how they relate to each other. Does the author seem to connect them in this—or a similar—way?

Anticipate the Ideas

When you read science material, it is useful to look for specific information. As you read, you are then able to develop ideas and relate them to information from other sources. Questions like the following ones will help you anticipate. Before you read the article, study the questions so that you'll know what information to look for.

1. What two relationships are there among a baseball, a satellite, and the moon?
2. What is the influence of gravity upon two objects or bodies?
3. According to Newton's First Law of Motion, how does a body in motion tend to "behave"?
4. How does gravity influence the motion of a satellite or the moon?
5. How can a satellite continually fall and yet never hit the earth's surface?
6. How does the curve of the earth's surface relate to the way a satellite curves when it falls out of orbit, when it stays in orbit, and when it flies out into space?
7. How fast does an earth-orbiting satellite travel?
8. How fast must a body travel to break away from the earth's gravitational pull?

Gravitation and Orbiting Objects

by George K. Stone

Think of the moon, an orbiting weather satellite, and a dropped baseball. What do they have in common? You can probably think of many things that these three objects have in common, but there is one thing that not too many people include in their lists—all three objects are falling!

It is easy to think of a baseball falling, or maybe even a satellite—once it drops out of orbit. But the moon? If it's falling, why doesn't it get closer to the earth? If an orbiting satellite is falling, why doesn't it hit the earth's surface? Our minds are just not used to thinking of objects falling without also thinking of them hitting the earth's surface sometime. Even so, they are all falling because they have something in common. All three of them are being pulled toward earth by gravity, the force of attraction between objects.

Scientists don't yet know what causes gravity. However, they do know what gravity does. Gravity is so predictable and certain that a scientific law written by Isaac Newton describes it. "Every particle in the universe attracts every other particle with a force that varies directly as the product of their masses and inversely as the square of the distance between their centers." In other words, this law says that the attraction between any two bodies is determined by the quantity of matter in them. It also says that as the two bodies move away

from each other, the attraction between them decreases as the distance between them increases. For our purposes, we can concentrate on the first part of the law: "Every particle in the universe attracts every other particle . . . "

Why don't the moon and the weather satellite hit the earth's surface if they are falling, just as the baseball does when it is dropped? One other law is influencing the moon and the satellite, the First Law of Motion—also written by Newton.

Newton's First Law of Motion states that "a body at rest stays at rest and a body in motion continues in motion at a constant speed in a straight line unless acted on by an external force." The tendency of a body at rest to stay at rest, or for a body in motion to continue in motion, is called *inertia*. In other words, inertia is lack of change of condition or constancy of condition; whatever is, stays the way it is unless acted upon by something else.

These two laws, the Law of Universal Gravitation and the First Law of Motion, contribute to keeping objects, like the moon and a satellite, from crashing onto the earth's surface, even though they are falling. Here's how they work.

Let's say that the "body" that is in motion is the weather satellite up in space. Newton's law says that it should travel in a straight line, but it doesn't. It keeps curving back toward the earth—"falling," if you please. Since it is not traveling in a straight line, there must be some "external force" to keep it from doing so. That external force is gravity—the attraction between the earth and the satellite. When the speed of the satellite in space is balanced by the pull of gravity, the satellite travels in an orbit around the earth.

The moon is also a satellite of the earth. It is a body in motion, tending to remain in motion at a constant speed. The pull of gravity between the earth and the moon acts on the moon as an external force. The gravity of the earth's greater mass pulls the moon out of a straight line of motion and into an orbit around the earth—where it has been for millions of years. (Figure 1)

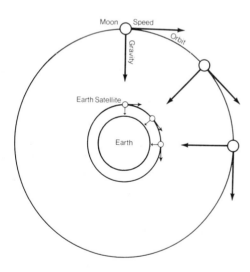

Fig. 1

Perhaps you are wondering why some space missiles fall back to earth, some go into orbit, and others escape from the earth entirely. Figures 2, 3, and 4 will help you to understand:

Imagine a mountain 300 miles (about 500 kilometers) high with a cannon mounted on top. If the cannon is fired horizontally with an ordinary charge of explosive, the cannonball will travel outward in a wide curve. The curve of its path, however, will be greater than the curve of the earth's surface, so it will eventually strike the earth. (Figure 2)

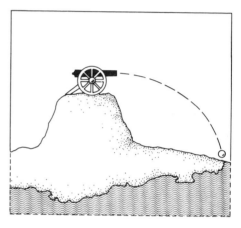

Fig. 2

Now suppose the explosive in the cannon is increased to make the curve of the cannonball's fall exactly equal to the curve of the earth's surface. At a height of 300 miles (about 500 kilometers), the cannonball will not meet enough air molecules to slow its forward motion. It should now travel around the earth indefinitely in a circular orbit. Gravity will pull the cannonball away from a straight path just enough to keep it at the same height above the earth's surface. (Figure 3)

A third possibility would be to increase the explosive in the cannon so that the curve of the cannonball's fall is less than the curve of the earth's surface. It will therefore travel farther

Orbit of Satellite

Fig. 3

and farther from the earth and finally escape into space. If the cannon is fired at exactly the right time and in exactly the right direction, the cannonball might strike some other heavenly body or go into orbit around it. (Figure 4)

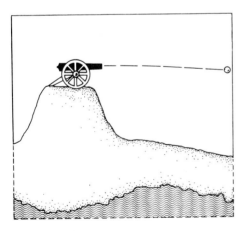

Fig. 4

A rocket carries the weather satellite to a preset altitude above the earth's atmosphere. At that altitude, the rocket increases the speed of the satellite until it is traveling about 5 miles (about 8 kilometers) per second. Without encountering friction, its speed remains constant. Gravity pulls it toward the earth, but the curve of its fall is the same as the curve of the earth's surface. It does not fall steeply enough to reach the earth. It remains in orbit because of the perfect balance among the pull of gravity, the speed of the satellite's motion, and the satellite's inertia.

Probably you have already related all of this to sending space capsules to other planets. You know that scientists place a space capsule into orbit around the earth just like a weather satellite. Then when they are ready to send it to the moon or to another planet, they "blast it" out of earth orbit. They use Newton's First Law of Motion. They apply an external force (a rocket) and increase its speed. As the speed increases, the capsule travels in a straighter and straighter line away from the earth. The increased speed overcomes the pull of gravity so that the capsule no longer falls toward the earth. When the capsule's speed reaches approximately 7 miles (about 11 kilometers) per second, the capsule breaks free from the earth's gravitational pull and heads out into space.

And what of the moon? It stays in orbit for the same reasons that the weather satellite does—the balance between its speed and the pull of gravity. That balance remains constant. Somewhere, somehow in the distant past, some force set the moon in motion around the earth. It has been falling for millions of years—bound by gravity but remaining free because of its speed.

Locate the Information

Reread the questions that appear before the article. Make certain that you can answer all of them. Double-check your answers by talking them over with other members of your group. Be ready to locate the information in the text that supports your answers to the questions.

Interpret the Overview

Refer to the structured overview at the beginning of this section on page 449. Using the words and relationships indicated there, see if you can talk your way through it, explaining how satellites stay in orbit.

Support Your Interpretations

The statements below relate to what you have read. Decide which of them you can support with evidence from the article.

1. The speed of 5 miles (about 8 kilometers) per second can balance the pull of gravity on an orbiting body.
2. Any object that falls is a satellite.
3. Without adequate speed a satellite would fall to the earth's surface; without gravitational attraction a satellite would fly out into space.
4. A satellite is both bound and free.
5. For man-made objects, causes of initial motion are easily discovered; for bodies in space, causes of initial motion are more of a mystery.
6. As the moon is a satellite of the earth, so is the earth a satellite of the sun, with inertia, speed, and gravity working the same way for both.
7. Nature is so dependable that descriptions of that dependability can be written as laws.

Apply the Ideas

In your group, discuss this question: How does gravity in space relate to freedom and bondage? Use ideas from what you have read so far in the unit as well as from other experiences you have had.

Freedom and Bondage in Math

CALCULATING SPEED

Science and mathematics are interrelated in many ways. The article you have just read contains mathematical information which may be more meaningful for you when translated into more familiar terms. Here's the information that was given:

1. The speed of approximately 5 miles per second is the speed necessary to balance the pull of gravity and maintain a satellite in orbit.
2. If the speed of a satellite increases to approximately 7 miles per second, the satellite will overcome the pull of gravity and fly out into space.

Do you have any real sense of how fast 5 miles per second or 7 miles per second really is? Would you have a better sense of the speed if it were in the more familiar measure of miles per hour? How would you change miles per second to miles per hour?

Confirm the Facts

Read the following statements and decide which contain information needed to change miles per second to miles per hour.

1. There are 60 seconds in a minute.
2. There are 60 minutes in an hour.
3. There are 24 hours in a day.
4. In order to change miles per second to miles per minute, you multiply miles per second by the number of seconds in a minute.
5. In order to change miles per minute to miles per hour, you multiply miles per second by minutes per hour.
6. In order to change miles per minute to miles per hour, you multiply miles per minute by minutes per hour.

Interpret and Apply the Ideas

Which of the following statements express mathematical operations needed to solve the problem of changing from miles per second to miles per hour?

1. Miles per second multiplied by seconds per minute multiplied by minutes per hour
2. $5 \times 60 \times 60$
3. $5(60 \times 60)$
4. $7 \times 60 \times 60$
5. (60×60)

Now answer the following questions:

1. How many miles per hour must a weather satellite be traveling to remain in earth orbit?
2. How many miles per hour must a weather satellite be traveling to escape earth orbit and fly out into space?

456

Freedom and Bondage in Literature

In this unit you have been reading about different kinds of freedom and bondage: political, social, physical, and scientific. The story you are about to read deals with personal freedom and bondage. As you read, try to discover why Marcie did not feel free, what she thought freedom was, and whether she changed her views.

The Runaway

by Felice Holman

Sometimes I thought loving care was suffocating. I wrote a verse about it, but I didn't show it to my mother because she would have been deeply hurt. All the same, she would have said, "It's wonderful, Marcie . . . just wonderful! I don't know how you do it, Marcie!" And it *wasn't* wonderful. It was full of flaws, but they always said everything was wonderful.

> "Loving care
> Too much to bear
> Leave me alone! . . ." That's how it started.

But even so, I didn't want to be all alone . . . not all alone. Just not so tight. Sometimes I wanted to go away from it. Everything outside was different and exciting, but it was awfully . . . spread out. And then sometimes my mother and father would say, "Why don't you do this?" "Why don't you do that?" "Be like this." "Be like that." But I didn't want to be like that. And then, sometimes, I might want to be like that very much, but I just *couldn't* be. What did they WANT!

And then, when it seemed just unbearable, I would plan to run away. I would lie awake watching a place on the bedroom wall where the streetlight picked out the pale peach pattern of the blue wallpaper. It was a bright hole in the dark wall. I made marvelous plans, but mostly they were impractical. I only passed over stowing away and usual things like that. I liked one plan where I dressed up to look much older, got a job as a tutor with a rich family, where the husband was widowed, and he fell in love with me. I did that plan over and over. But, really, the plan that was most attractive was the one that was most possible—I thought about going to Aunt Bea.

Aunt Bea was not my real aunt, but she was even better than my real aunts. She was the mother of my best friend, Hilda, and Hilda's younger brother Jamie, and two other kids. Their house was so different from ours. When I came by in the morning to pick up Hilda on the way to school, they were all in such a mad scramble—nothing like our quiet morning, our whispered morning. Hilda was always grabbing cold milk from the refrigerator with one hand, and grabbing her books from the bench with the other. Her mother, sitting peacefully over her coffee, never made her eat hot oatmeal before going out into the cold mornings, nor told her to wear a hat and scarf. And Hilda was much sturdier than I, and that certainly proved something. And Aunt Bea loved Hilda, I know. She loved all the children. She loved me, too. She loved everyone. And that's why I felt that Aunt Bea would always give me a home if I ever needed it. Their family was fun. It was a really comfortable plan, and just far enough away. And not too far.

I acted the whole thing out lots of times, watching the bright spot on the wall; how they would welcome me—casually, but with the real warmth underneath—and how I would be at home there. But I skipped very quickly over the part where my parents suffered, and missed me, and wasted away. And just before they did . . . well, sometimes, I came back. And that was rather wonderful. But sometimes, too, I'd fall asleep before I had to do anything about it at all.

And then one day when the world seemed tighter than ever, I did it. I came home from my Saturday afternoon gymnastics class and there was a new dress on my bed. My mother wasn't home, but there was a note on the dress in Mother's lovely handwriting. "To wear to Julie's party. Love, Mother." But I had told her and told her I didn't want to go to Julie's party . . . where everybody was such . . . such . . . old friends. I had always known them, but I was not like old friends. I didn't want to go. I *wasn't* going to go.

I did it all in a rush, crying the whole time. I packed valuable things—my ivory brush, my diary, a small bottle of L'aimant perfume, a large book of modern American poetry, a snapshot of Mother and Daddy and me in a rowboat, and a change of clothes. Maybe a few other things. I tied them all up in my pajama coat and rushed out of the house crying very hard. But,

by the time I had run three blocks, I was out of breath and my crying was more gasping, and when I got to Aunt Bea's, only a dozen blocks away, I was quite weak and felt I had walked fifty miles.

My friend Hilda opened the door. "Shhhhh!" was her first word to me. "Shhhhh! They're listening to *Das Rheingold* straight from the Metropolitan Opera."

"Listen, Hilda . . ." I started.

"I tell you, shhhh! They'll hack us in little pieces if we make another sound."

"But I want to talk to your mother," I hissed. "I *have* to talk to your mother." I put down my pack. Hilda gave it only a passing, incurious glance, kicked it lightly, and whispered, "Well, you can't talk to her until the opera is over. Come on in and play Parcheesi."

"I don't feel like playing Parcheesi," I said, but Hilda had the board out and onto the dining table as if I hadn't spoken. Hilda got to go first, as usual, and put a man into play straight off. I jiggled the dice about in the snug little black cylinder without much enthusiasm. It took me three throws before I got a player into action, and the moment I did, there came this absolutely awful sharp pain in my leg. I cried out and grabbed my leg. At the same time, Jamie rolled out from under the table, laughing in the manner of movie fiends, and sped into the kitchen with Hilda in screaming pursuit. I rubbed my bitten calf.

"I told you to be quiet in there," came Aunt Bea's furious voice, pitched well above the strains of *Das Rheingold*. "I am going to wallop you as soon as this is over!"

"It wasn't me. It was Marcie," my friend Hilda yelled on the return chase from the kitchen. She delivered a good kick at Jamie, and that settled that.

"I don't care who it was. I'm going to wallop the lot of you," yelled Aunt Bea.

"Your turn," said Hilda, returning to the table. "Wait a minute! You *moved* while I was gone," she said examining the Parcheesi board.

"I didn't," I protested. "I've just been sitting here, rubbing my leg."

"Your leg, my foot!" said Hilda. "You *moved*. It's my turn." She began to shake the dice.

"But it's my turn," I complained, and with some heat.

"Cheater!" cried Hilda. "Cheater! Cheater!"

"I'm not going to play," I said, getting up.

"Spoil sport!" yelled Hilda.

461

"Shut up!" shouted Aunt Bea. "I said, shut up!"

My eyes burned from crying, my leg hurt, and now a sort of chill was all over me. It seemed to take me so long to stand up. I kept rising and rising and rising. But finally, I was on my feet. Then I went out into the hall and looked for my pack. It was over in a corner where Hilda had kicked it. I opened the heavy front door and walked down the red brick stairs, down the red brick walk, but my feet seemed to sink into it as if it were made of great heavy extra-soft pillows. And I walked twelve blocks through thick feather pillows . . . back to unbearable love.

Support Your Ideas

Based on your understanding of the story, answer the following questions. Be ready to support your answers with evidence from the story. Discuss your answers and your evidence with your classmates.

1. How much freedom did Marcie want?
2. In what ways did Marcie feel bound?
3. What did Marcie find attractive at Aunt Bea's?
4. What did Marcie take with her when she ran away that showed how she felt about leaving her home?
5. What did she discover at Aunt Bea's that surprised her?
6. Why did Marcie return home?
7. Were the two households really different? Explain.

Interpret and Apply the Ideas

Discuss the following statements with other members of your group to decide which you can agree with based on ideas from the story and your own experiences. Be ready to give reasons for your decisions.

1. People show their love in different ways.
2. Different families have different life-styles; what is good for one family is not necessarily good for all families.
3. Something new may seem better than something old and familiar.
4. You can't run away from your problems.
5. Sometimes even best friends may disappoint you.
6. There's no place like home.
7. It is possible to love someone too much.

FOLLOW-THROUGH

Pulling It All Together

In this unit on freedom and bondage, you have read:

1. a statement which declares that people should be and are free, a statement which founded a new nation;
2. a play which communicates history while imagining an incident that never happened;
3. the story of a young black woman's escape to freedom and out of slavery;
4. a speech by a famous civil rights leader in which he appeals for equal rights for all people;
5. an article that tells how freedom and bondage relate to gravity and space vehicles;
6. an article that tells how the mathematics of the freedom of speed can be computed;
7. a story about a young woman who believes that love causes bondage but discovers that love also creates its own freedoms.

Refer to the definitions of *freedom* and *bondage* at the beginning of this unit. Then, identify the definitions of *freedom* and *bondage* that fit the selections in this unit.

Reread the quotation at the beginning of the unit. Discuss how the quotation relates to each of the selections in the unit.

Below are some ideas about freedom and bondage. Decide which of the selections you read are illustrations of these ideas. Reasons for your decisions should be discussed with other members of your group.

1. It is possible to have your body bound but your mind free.
2. It is also possible to have your body free but your mind bound.
3. Most forces that bind are invisible.
4. Freedom is more easily lost than bondage.
5. Millions have died to escape bondage and find freedom; few have done the opposite.
6. Nature and people have much in common.
7. Bondage is gained by neglect; freedom is gained by hard work.
8. Freedom requires trust; bondage doesn't need it.

Putting Your Knowledge To Work

Here are some ideas for activities that give you an opportunity to use what you have learned in this unit. Choose one or more that you would like to do. Your group may prefer working together on an activity.

1. Another famous document in American history is the Constitution. Read the preamble to the Constitution and/or the Bill of Rights and state the ideas presented in your own words.

2. Reread the play "An Imaginary Trial of George Washington" to see how many famous quotations you can find in it. Then see if you can find out to what event in history each quotation is related. Don't be afraid to ask people about the sources. Asking friends, parents, teachers, librarians, and others is a very good way of finding things out. Check the information yourself, however, to be sure it is correct.

3. Make a study of persons who have struggled to win or to preserve the freedoms of others: Joan of Arc, Edith Cavell, Martin Luther King, Jr., Frederick Douglass, Alexander Solzhenitsyn, Toussaint L'Ouverture, José de San Martín, John Peter Zenger, Simón Bolívar, Luis Muñoz Rivera, Eleanor Roosevelt, Sojourner Truth.

4. Contrast the freedom fighters with some infamous people who have tried to deprive others of their freedoms: Adolf Hitler, Joseph Stalin, Attila the Hun, Mao Tse-tung, Napoleon Bonaparte, Antonio de Oliveira Salazar.

5. Make a study of the influence of gravity on falling objects. Does a heavy object fall faster than a light object? Does the velocity of an object increase the longer it falls?

Here are some books about freedom and bondage you might enjoy:

Henderson, Nancy. *Walk Together: Five Plays on Human Rights.* New York: Julian Messner, 1972.
Included in this collection are plays about the Underground Railroad, migrant workers, American Indians, etc.

Jordan, June. *Who Look at Me.* New York: Thomas Y. Crowell Co., Inc., 1969.
Poems and paintings trace the history of blacks in America.

Merriam, Eve. *Independent Voices.* New York: Atheneum Publishers, 1968.
Long narrative poems describe people who had the courage to work for the rights of others.

O'Brien, Robert C. *Mrs. Frisby and the Rats of NIMH.* New York: Atheneum Publishers, 1972.
Intelligent laboratory rats escape and create their own civilization underground.

Sterne, Emma Gelders. *The Slave Ship.* New York: Scholastic Book Services, 1975.
This true story describes a successful slave ship mutiny.

HELP WITH WORDS
(Glossary)

How to Use HELP WITH WORDS

HELP WITH WORDS is your glossary. It was written to help you understand certain words found in the stories and articles in this book. It is shorter than a full dictionary. However, it has many of the helps you will find in other dictionaries.

The pronunciation of each word is shown just after the word, in this way:
ab·bre·vi·ate (ə brē′vē āt).
The letters and signs used are pronounced as in the words below.
The mark ′ is placed after a syllable with primary or heavy accent, as in the example above.
The mark ′ after a syllable shows a secondary or lighter accent, as in **ab·bre·vi·a·tion** (ə brē′vē ā′shən).

Full pronunciation key

a	hat, cup	i	it, pin	p	paper, cup	v	very, save
ā	age, face	ī	ice, five	r	run, read	w	will, woman
ä	father, far			s	say, yes	y	young, yet
		j	jam, enjoy	sh	she, rush	z	zero, breeze
b	bad, rob	k	kind, seek	t	tell, it	zh	measure, seizure
ch	child, much	l	land, coal	th	thin, both		
d	did, red	m	me, am	ᴛʜ	then, smooth		
		n	no, in			ə	represents:
e	let, best	ng	long, bring	u	cup, butter		a in about
ē	equal, be			u̇	full, put		e in taken
ėr	term, learn	o	hot, rock	ü	rule, move		i in pencil
		ō	open, go				o in lemon
f	fat, if	ô	order, all				u in circus
g	go, bag	oi	oil, voice				
h	he, how	ou	house, out				

Grammatical key

adj.	adjective	*n.*	noun
adv.	adverb	*prep.*	preposition
conj.	conjunction	*pron.*	pronoun
interj.	interjection	*v.*	verb
sing.	singular	*pl.*	plural

A a

ab·a·tis (ab'ə tis) *n.* **ab·a·tis** (ab'ə tēz') *or* **ab·a·tis·es** (ab'ə tēz'ēz) a defense made of cut-down trees with sharpened branches facing outward

ab·di·cate (ab'də kāt) *v.* **ab·di·cat·ed; ab·di·cat·ing** to formally give up sovereign power, office, or responsibility

abol·ish (ə bol'ish) *v.* to put an end to; do away with completely (*abolish* slavery)

abrupt·ly (ə brupt'lē) *adv.* suddenly; unexpectedly

ab·solve (ab solv' *or* ab zolv') *v.* **ab·solved; ab·solv·ing** to free from guilt, punishment, or obligation

ab·surd (ab sėrd') *adj.* ridiculous; ridiculously unreasonable

abun·dance (ə bun'dəns) *n.* **1** an overflowing quantity; more than enough **2** wealth

abun·dant (ə bun'dənt) *adj.* plentiful

abuse (ə byüs') *n.* a corrupt practice or custom; misuse

ac·cel·er·ate (ak sel'ə rāt) *v.* **ac·cel·er·at·ed; ac·cel·er·a·t·ing** to speed up

ac·cel·er·a·tion (ak sel'ə rā'shən) *n.* **1** the act or process of hastening or moving faster **2** the rate of change of speed

ac·claim (ə klām') *v.* **1** to praise or applaud **2** to proclaim

ac·com·mo·da·tion (ə kom'ə dā'shən) *n.* the satisfaction of a need or desire

ac·qui·esce (ak'wē es') *v.* **ac·qui·esced; ac·qui·esc·ing** to give consent by not raising objections

ac·tion (ak'shən) *n.* the working of one thing on another so as to produce a change

acute angle (ə kyüt' ang'gəl) an angle measuring less than ninety degrees

ad·e·quate (ad'ə kwit) *adj.* **1** as much as is necessary **2** barely sufficient

ad·mi·ra·tion (ad'mə rā'shən) *n.* **1** an object of high regard **2** a feeling of delighted approval

adz *or* **adze** (adz) *n.* a cutting tool somewhat like an ax, used for shaping wood

af·fec·tion (ə fek'shən) *n.* fondness

af·fright (ə frīt') *v.* to frighten; alarm

agent (ā'jənt) *n.* one who acts for or in the place of another and by his or her authority (government *agent*)

agil·i·ty (ə jil'ə tē) *n.* **agil·i·ties** the ability to move quickly and easily; nimbleness

ail·ment (āl'mənt) *n.* a bodily disorder; sickness

al·a·bas·ter (al'ə bas'tər) *n.* a fine-textured, usually white and translucent mineral used for carving

al·ba·tross (al'bə trôs) *n.* **al·ba·tross** *or* **al·ba·tross·es** a large web-footed seabird related to the petrel

al·der (ôl'dər) *n.* a toothed-leaved tree or shrub related to the birch

al·ga (al'gə) *n.* **al·gae** (al'jē) any plant of a group that forms the lowest division of the plant kingdom, mostly growing in water, lacking a vascular system, and having chlorophyll often masked by brown or red coloring matter

alien¹ (ā'lyən *or* ā'lē ən) *adj.* foreign; strange

alien² *n.* a foreigner; a person from another country

align (ə līn') *v.* to bring into line or adjust to a line

al·le·giance (ə lē'jəns) *n.* the loyalty and obedience owed a ruler or government by a subject or citizen

al·lure (ə lùr') *v.* **al·lured; al·lur·ing** to tempt, fascinate, or attract

al·ly¹ (ə lī') *v.* **al·lied; al·ly·ing** to join in an alliance; unite

ally² (al'ī *or* ə lī') *n.* **al·lies** one united or associated with another for some common purpose

al·ter (ôl'tər) *v.* to partly change or make different

am·big·u·ous (am big'yü əs) *adj.* not clear because of having more than one meaning

amends (ə mendz') *n. sing. or pl.* payment or satisfaction for a loss or an injury

an·ar·chist (an'ər kist) *n.* one who rebels against an established government and wants to overthrow it

anat·o·mist (ə nat'ə mist) *n.* one who deals with the structure of animals or plants

an·ces·tor (an'ses'tər) *n.* one from an earlier period from whom one is descended

an·cient (ān'shənt) *adj.* belonging to times long past

an·guish (ang'gwish) *n.* extreme pain or distress

an·ni·hi·la·tion (ə nī'ə lā'shən) *n.* complete destruction

an·tag·o·nis·tic (an tag'ə nis'tik) *adj.* hostile; showing opposition

an·te·cham·ber (an'ti chām'bər) *n.* a room used as an entrance to a main room

anx·i·e·ty (ang zī'ə tē) *n.* **anx·i·e·ties** uneasiness; worried concern

ap·pall·ing (ə pô'ling) *adj.* shocking; terrifying

ap·pend·age (ə pen'dij) *n.* something attached to a larger or more important part

ap·proach (ə prōch') *v.* to come near or nearer

ap·pro·pri·a·tion (ə prō'prē ā'shən) *n.* **1** the act of taking for one's own **2** something, especially a sum of money, formally set aside for a specific use

ar·bi·trary (är'bə trer'ē) *adj.* tyrannical (*arbitrary* rule)

ar·chae·ol·o·gist (är'kē ol'ə jist) *n.* one who studies the life of ancient peoples as shown by relics, artifacts, and ruins

ar·dent·ly (ärd'nt lē) *adv.* with enthusiastic feeling; passionately

as·sent (ə sent') *n.* agreement; acceptance

as·tute (ə stüt' *or* ə styüt') *adj.* clever; able to act successfully in one's own interests

asy·lum (ə sī'ləm) *n.* **1** a place of safety; shelter **2** protection given political refugees **3** an institution for the care of those unable to care for themselves

atone (ə tōn') *v.* **atoned; aton·ing** to make amends; to make up for a wrongdoing

at·tack¹ (ə tak') *v.* **1** to fight physically **2** to use bitter words against **3** to act upon injuriously **4** to set to work on

attack² *n.* **1** the act of setting upon forcefully **2** a start **3** a fit of sickness

at·tain (ə tān') *v.* to achieve, obtain, or reach

---

hat, āge, fär; let, ēqual, tèrm; it, īce; hot, ōpen, ôrder; oil, out; cup, pùt; rüle; ch, child; ng, long; sh, she; th, thin; ᴛʜ, then; zh, measure;

ə represents *a* in about, *e* in taken, *i* in pencil, *o* in lemon, *u* in circus.

at·trac·tion (ə trak′shən) *n.* a force acting mutually between particles of matter, tending to draw them together

au·then·tic (ô then′tik) *adj.* genuine; true or correct

au·tho·rize (ô′thə rīz′) *v.* **au·tho·rized; au·tho·riz·ing 1** to empower **2** to approve legally or officially

avert (ə vėrt′) *v.* to prevent from happening

awe¹ (ô) *n.* **1** a humble, reverent attitude **2** great fear inspired by authority or power

awe² *v.* **awed; aw·ing 1** to inspire with awe **2** to control by inspiring with awe

awe·struck (ô′struk′) *adj.* filled with wonder

ax·is (ak′sis) *n.* **ax·es** (ak′sēz′) a straight line about which something rotates

B b

bai·liff (bā′lif) *n.* **1** a minor officer of some United States courts, usually serving as a messenger or an usher **2** in Great Britain, one who manages an estate; lord

bal·ance¹ (bal′əns) *n.* a condition in which opposing forces offset each other

balance² *v.* **bal·anced; bal·anc·ing** to make equal

bane (bān) *n.* **1** something deadly **2** a source of injury or ruin

ban·ish·ment (ban′ish mənt) *n.* the act or state of being driven out or away, as from a home or a country

bar·bar·ic (bär bar′ik) *adj.* uncivilized; savage

bar·bar·ous (bär′bər əs) *adj.* uncivilized

ba·salt (bə sôlt′ *or* bā′sôlt) *n.* a dark-colored dense to fine-grained igneous rock

bat·tle·ment (bat′l mənt) *n.* a low wall built for defense, usually at the top of a tower, with openings to shoot through

bawl out (bôl out) *v.* to scold loudly or severely

be·queath (bi kwēŦĦ′) *v.* **1** to give or leave, usually personal property, by will **2** to hand down

be·seech (bi sēch′) *v.* **be·sought** *or* **be·seeched; be·seech·ing** to ask earnestly for; beg

be·set·ting (bi set′ing) *adj.* constantly present

be·tray (bi trā′) *v.* **1** to give over to an enemy **2** to tell in violation of a trust

be·troth·al (bi trô′thəl) *n.* an engagement to be married

be·wil·der·ment (bi wil′dər mənt) *n.* uncertainty; confusion

big·ot·ry (big′ə trē) *n.* **big·ot·ries** the act or state of being intolerant of the beliefs of others; prejudice

bill of particulars a detailed statement of the items in a legal action or counterclaim

bi·ol·o·gist (bī ol′ə jist) *n.* a scientist who studies living organisms and life processes

Bluecoat a Union soldier during the American Civil War

bog (bog) *n.* swampland; wet, spongy ground

bold·ness (bōld′nis) *n.* the state of showing courageous daring, to the extent of being scornful of danger

bol·ster (bōl′stər) *v.* **bol·stered; bol·ster·ing** to provide support; to reinforce

bot·a·nist (bot′n ist) *n.* one who studies plant life

boun·ty (boun′tē) *n.* **boun·ties 1** generosity **2** money given as a reward

brave·ly (brāv′lē) *adv.* courageously

brav·er·y (brā′vər ē) *n.* **brav·er·ies** fearlessness; courage

bra·vo (brä′vō *or* brä′vō) *n.* **bra·vos** a shout of approval, often used to applaud a performance

bron·chi·al (brong′kē əl) *adj.* relating to or involving either of the main divisions of the trachea, each leading to a lung

brood¹ (brüd) *n.* a family of young animals or children

brood² *v.* **1** to sit on eggs to hatch them **2** to cover young with wings **3** to think moodily

bulge¹ (bulj) *n.* an outward bend or swelling

bulge² *v.* **bulged; bulg·ing** to swell or bend outward

buoy·ant (boi′ənt *or* bü′yənt) *adj.* **1** able to rise and float in the air or on water **2** able to hold something up **3** lighthearted; cheerful

bur·den (bėrd′n) *v.* **bur·dened; bur·den·ing** to load or weigh down

bus·tle (bus′əl) *v.* **bus·tled; bus·tling** to move busily or noisily

C c

cache¹ (kash) *n.* **1** a storage or hiding place **2** hidden supplies or food

cache² *v.* **cached; cach·ing** to place, hide, or store

cam·ou·flage (kam′ə fläzh *or* kam′ə fläj) *n.* concealment by disguise—**camouflage,** *v.*

cam·paign (kam pān′) *n.* **1** a series of military operations **2** a planned series of actions for a particular result (election *campaign*)—**campaign,** *v.*

can·did (kan′did) *adj.* marked by honesty; frank

ca·nine¹ (kā′nīn) *adj.* relating to dogs or to the family that includes dogs, wolves, jackals, and foxes

canine² *n.* dog

can·yon (kan′yən) *n.* a deep valley with high steep slopes and often with a stream flowing through it

car·ni·vore (kär′nə vôr) *n.* **1** a flesh-eating animal **2** an insect-eating plant

ca·su·al·ly (kazh′ü əl lē) *adv.* **1** happening by chance; accidentally **2** unconcernedly

cat·a·log (kat′l ôg) *v.* **cat·a·loged; cat·a·log·ing** to make a list of; to enter in a list

caulk (kôk) *v.* to make a seam watertight by filling with waterproofing material

cer·tain·ty (sėrt′n tē) *n.* **cer·tain·ties 1** sureness **2** the state of being or feeling free of doubt

cer·vi·cal (sėr′və kəl) *adj.* of or relating to the neck, especially the back part of the neck

chal·lenge¹ (chal′ənj) *v.* **chal·lenged; chal·leng·ing 1** to claim as due **2** to demand a countersign **3** to dispute **4** to dare someone to take part in a game or contest

challenge² *n.* **1** an exception taken **2** a sentry's demand for identification **3** an invitation to compete

cham·ber (chām′bər) *n.* a room

chan·cel·lor (chan′sə lər) *n.* a very high government official

cha·os (kā′os) *n.* a confused, disorganized state

character writing writing that uses symbols that stand for ideas rather than an alphabet

chiv·al·ry (shiv′əl rē) *n.* **chiv·al·ries 1** the qualities (as bravery, honor, protection of the weak) which characterized the ideal knight **2** the ways or spirit of medieval knighthood

chro·nom·e·ter (krə nom′ə tər) *n.* an instrument for measuring time with great accuracy

ci·ca·da (sə kā′də) n. a large insect with a stout body, a short, wide head, and four thin wings, the male of which makes a buzzing sound

cinch (sinch) v. to put a strap or band on; to bind firmly

civ·il (siv′əl) adj. relating to citizens or their rights

civil war a war between opposing groups of citizens of the same country or nation

Civil War the war between the North and the South (1861–1865)

clem·en·cy (klem′ən sē) n. **clem·en·cies** mercy; an act or instance of being merciful

coarse (kôrs) adj. **1** common **2** made of large parts or particles **3** rough or harsh **4** crude in behavior

co·in·ci·dence (kō in′sə dəns) n. events that happen by chance at the same time or place and seem to have some connection

col·li·sion (kə lizh′ən) n. **1** crash **2** clash or conflict

col·lo·di·on (kə lōd′ē ən) n. a solution, used especially as a coating for wounds or for photographic films

col·o·nel (kėr′nl) n. a commissioned officer ranking just below a brigadier general

com·mend (kə mend′) v. **1** to praise **2** to give to another for safekeeping

com·mu·nion (kə myü′nyən) n. communication; fellowship

com·pass (kum′pəs) n. a device for determining directions by means of a magnetic needle pointing to the magnetic north

com·pas·sion·ate (kəm pash′ə nit) adj. sympathetic; filled with sorrow or pity by the suffering of others

com·pli·ance (kəm plī′əns) n. the act or process of yielding to a request or demand

com·pli·men·ta·ry (kom′plə men′tər ē) adj. **1** expressing praise **2** given free (a *complimentary* ticket)

com·pound (kom′pound) n. a substance formed by a union of elements

com·pre·hen·sion (kom′pri hen′shən) n. the act or power of understanding

com·press (kəm pres′) v. **1** to press or become pressed together **2** to reduce in size or volume by pressure

com·pres·sor (kəm pres′ər) n. a piece of equipment that contains air under pressure greater than that of the atmosphere

com·prise (kəm prīz′) v. **com·prised; com·pris·ing** to be made up of; include

com·pro·mise¹ (kom′prə mīz) n. **1** a settlement of a dispute whereby each party gives up some demands **2** surrender

compromise² v. **com·pro·mised; com·pro·mis·ing 1** to settle differences by mutual concessions **2** to expose to discredit or danger

com·pul·sion (kəm pul′shən) n. force; strong impulse

com·pu·ta·tion (kom′pyə tā′shən) n. the process of determining by mathematical means

com·put·er (kəm pyü′tər) n. an automatic electronic machine that performs calculations

con·ceal·ment (kən sēl′mənt) n. hiding; hiding place

con·ces·sion (kən sesh′ən) n. a grant or a right given by a government

con·demn (kən dem′) v. **1** to declare to be wrong **2** to convict or sentence **3** to declare to be unfit for use or consumption

con·di·tion¹ (kən dish′ən) n. **1** the state a person or thing is in **2** a provision **3** a qualification

condition² v. **con·di·tioned; con·di·tion·ing 1** to put into a desired state of being **2** to change behavior to get a desired response

con·fine (kən fīn′) v. **con·fined; con·fin·ing 1** to restrict or limit **2** to imprison or keep indoors

con·jure (kon′jər) v. **con·jured; con·jur·ing** to plead earnestly

con·san·guin·i·ty (kon′sang gwin′ə tē) n. **con·san·guin·i·ties 1** descent from the same ancestor **2** a close relation or connection

con·sent (kən sent′) n. approval; permission

con·spir·a·tor (kən spir′ə tər) n. one who joins in a plot

con·spire (kən spīr′) v. **con·spired; con·spir·ing** to plot; scheme

con·stan·cy (kon′stən sē) n. **con·stan·cies** freedom from change

con·stant (kon′stənt) adj. unchanging; uniform

con·strain (kən strān′) v. to force

con·struc·tive·ly (kən struk′tiv lē) adv. helpfully developing, improving, or reinforcing something

con·verge (kən vėrj′) v. **con·verged; con·verg·ing** to move toward one point or one another; meet

con·vey (kən vā′) v. **con·veyed; con·vey·ing 1** to carry from one place to another **2** to communicate **3** to transfer to another

con·vic·tion (kən vik′shən) n. **1** a decision that a person is guilty of a crime or offense **2** the state of being convinced **3** a strong belief or opinion

con·vul·sion (kən vul′shən) n. violent disturbance

con·vul·sive (kən vul′siv) adj. **1** violently disturbing **2** shaking with irregular spasms; fitful

cope (kōp) v. **coped; cop·ing** to deal with a problem or difficulty, usually with some chance of success

cor·dial·i·ty (kôr′jē al′ə tē) n. **cor·dial·i·ties** warm friendliness; sincere affection and kindness

cor·re·spond (kôr′ə spond′ or kor′ə spond′) v. **1** to agree **2** to be connected by means of a mathematical relationship **3** to communicate by exchanging letters

cor·ru·gate (kôr′ə gāt) v. **cor·ru·gat·ed; cor·ru·gat·ing** to form or shape into wrinkles or folds or into ridges and grooves

cor·rupt (kə rupt′) adj. characterized by improper conduct; dishonest (a *corrupt* official)

coup (kü) n. **coups** (küz) a sudden, successful action

cov·ert (kuv′ərt or kō′vərt) n. **1** a hiding place or shelter **2** a thicket giving cover

cov·et (kuv′it) v. to desire what belongs to another

cow·ard·ly (kou′ərd lē) adj. lacking courage; not brave —**cowardly,** adv.

cred·i·bil·i·ty (kred′ə bil′ə tē) n. the quality or state of being believable

cringe (krinj) v. **cringed; cring·ing** to shrink or cower in fear

---

hat, āge, fär; let, ēqual, tėrm; it, īce; hot, ōpen, ôrder; oil, out; cup, pùt, rüle; ch, child; ng, long; sh, she; th, thin; ŦH, then; zh, measure;

ə represents *a* in about, *e* in taken, *i* in pencil, *o* in lemon, *u* in circus.

crit·i·cize (krit′ə sīz) *v.* **crit·i·cized; crit·i·ciz·ing 1** to judge **2** to express criticism, usually unfavorable **3** to find fault with

crys·tal (kris′tl) *n.* a clear glass of superior quality

cud·gel (kuj′əl) *n.* a short heavy club

cul·prit (kul′prit) *n.* **1** one accused of a crime **2** one guilty of a crime or an offense

cul·ti·vate (kul′tə vāt) *v.* **cul·ti·vat·ed; cul·ti·vat·ing 1** to prepare the soil for planting **2** to aid in the growth of **3** to encourage **4** to seek friendship with

cus·tom (kus′təm) *n.* **1** a practice common to many or habitual with an individual **2** customers

cus·tom·ary (kus′tə mer′ē) *adj.* usual; commonly practiced

cyl·in·der (sil′ən dər) *n.* a long, round, solid or hollow body shaped like a roller

czar (zär) *n.* the ruler of Russia until the 1917 revolution

cza·ri·na (zä rē′nə) *n.* the wife of a czar

D d

dank (dangk) *adj.* unpleasantly damp or wet

dar·ing¹ (dar′ing *or* der′ing) *adj.* courting danger; bold and adventurous

daring² *n.* fearless boldness

daub (dôb) *v.* **1** to plaster **2** to smear or smudge **3** to paint unskillfully

ded·i·cat·ed (ded′ə kāt′əd) *adj.* devoted to a cause or an ideal

deem (dēm) *v.* to believe or suppose

de·fault¹ (di fôlt′) *n.* failure to do something required by law or duty

default² *v.* to fail to carry out a contract or obligation

de·feat¹ (di fēt′) *v.* to win a victory over; beat

defeat² *n.* **1** the prevention of success of **2** the overthrow of an army in battle **3** the loss of a contest

def·er·ence (def′ər əns) *n.* respectful regard for another's wishes

de·fi·ant (di fī′ənt) *adj.* disobedient; boldly resistant

de·fi·cient (de fish′ənt) *adj.* lacking in completeness (*deficient* in vitamins)

de·lu·sion (di lü′zhən) *n.* a false belief that persists despite the facts

de·mol·ish (di mol′ish) *v.* to tear down; destroy

de·nounce (di nouns′) *v.* **de·nounced; de·nounc·ing** to accuse, especially publicly

de·par·ture (di pär′chər) *n.* **1** the act of going away **2** the starting of a course of action **3** a change

de·pos·i·to·ry (di poz′ə tôr′ē) *n.* **de·pos·i·to·ries** a place where something is stored for safekeeping

de·prive (di prīv′) *v.* **de·prived; de·priv·ing** to take something away from or to keep from having

de·rive (di rīv′) *v.* **de·rived; de·riv·ing** to receive or obtain

de·scend·ant (di sen′dənt) *n.* a person born of a certain family; offspring

de·spond·ent·ly (di spon′dənt lē) *adv.* feeling extremely dejected, discouraged, or depressed.

des·po·tism (des′pə tiz′ əm) *n.* rule by a tyrant, someone with absolute power

des·ti·ny (des′tə nē) *n.* **des·ti·nies 1** fortune **2** a predetermined course of events; fate

des·ti·tute (des′tə tüt *or* des′tə tyüt) *adj.* lacking the necessities; suffering extreme want

de·tail (di tāl′ *or* dē′tāl) *v.* to assign to a task (*detailed* to kitchen duty)

de·te·ri·o·ra·tion (di tir′ē ə rā′shən) *n.* a worsening condition

de·ter·rent (di tėr′ənt) *adj.* serving to discourage or prevent—**deterrent,** *n.*

dev·as·tate (dev′ə stāt) *v.* **dev·as·tat·ed; dev·as·tat·ing** to ruin, destroy, or lay waste

de·vo·tion (di vō′shən) *n.* great love, affection, or dedication

di·a·lect (dī′ə lekt) *n.* a form of language used in a certain area or by a certain group of people

di·a·logue (dī′ə lôg) *n.* a conversation between two or more persons

dic·tate (dik′tāt) *v.* **dic·tat·ed; dic·tat·ing** to give orders; to speak with authority

dig·it (dij′it) *n.* **1** any of the Arabic numerals 1 to 9 and usually the symbol 0 **2** a finger or toe

di·late (dī lāt′) *v.* **di·lat·ed; di·lat·ing** to make or grow larger or wider; swell

dirge (dėrj) *n.* a mournful song or hymn; a funeral song

dis·ar·ray (dis′ə rā′) *n.* a lack of order; confusion

dis·avow (dis′ə vou′) *v.* to refuse to acknowledge

dis·cord (dis′kôrd) *n.* conflict; lack of agreement

dis·count (dis′kount *or* dis kount′) *v.* **1** to reduce or deduct from an amount **2** to minimize **3** to allow for

dis·pose (dis pōz′) *v.* **dis·posed; dis·pos·ing** to make willing; to be inclined toward

dis·po·si·tion (dis′pə zish′ən) *n.* temperament; a habitual way of acting and thinking (a cheerful *disposition*)

dis·so·lu·tion (dis′ə lü′shən) *n.* an ending or breaking up of

dis·solve (di zolv′) *v.* **dis·solved; dis·solv·ing 1** to break up **2** to liquefy **3** to bring to an end **4** to fade away **5** to resolve itself as if by dissolution

dis·tance (dis′təns) *n.* the amount of space between two points or objects

dis·tinct (dis tingkt′) *adj.* **1** different **2** unmistakable

dis·tinc·tion (dis tingk′shən) *n.* something that makes a difference

dis·tract (dis trakt′) *v.* to draw attention away from

di·verge (də vėrj′ *or* dī vėrj′) *v.* **di·verged; di·verg·ing 1** to move in different directions from a common point **2** to turn aside from a course

doc·trine (dok′trən) *n.* a principle or the principles of a system of belief

dog·ged·ness (dô′gid nis) *n.* persistence; stubbornness

dole¹ (dōl) *n.* **1** a giving out of food, money, or clothing to the needy **2** something given out to the needy

dole² *v.* **doled; dol·ing 1** to distribute as a charity **2** to give out in small portions

dope (dōp) *n.* **1** a stupid person **2** information

dor·sal (dôr′səl) *adj.* of, on, or near the back, as of an animal (*dorsal* fin)—**dorsal,** *n.*

draw (drô) *n.* **1** the act or process of drawing **2** a lot drawn at random **3** a tie in a contest **4** a gully shallower than a ravine

dread·ful (dred′fəl) *adj.* **1** frightening **2** extremely unpleasant or shocking

dream (drēm) n. **1** a series of thoughts or images occurring during sleep **2** a daydream **3** something especially enjoyable **4** a goal or ideal

du·ly (dü′lē or dyü′lē) adv. properly (duly signed)

du·o·de·num (dü′ō dē′nəm or dyü′ō dē′nəm) n. **du·o·de·na** (dü′ō dē′nə or dyü′ō dē′nə) or **du·o·de·nums** the first part of the small intestine

dupe (düp or dyüp) v. **duped; dup·ing** to deceive; cheat—**dupe,** n.

dur·a·ble (dür′ə bəl) adj. able to last a long time (durable material)

dusk (dusk) n. **1** the darker part of twilight **2** gloom

E e

ebb (eb) v. **1** to flow or pass from a high to a low point **2** to grow less or weaker

ed·dy (ed′ē) n. **ed·dies** a circular current, as of air or water, running contrary to the main current

ef·fi·cien·cy (ə fish′ən sē) n. **ef·fi·cien·cies 1** the quality or degree of being productive; not wasteful **2** the ratio of the useful energy delivered by a machine to the energy supplied to it

Egyp·tol·o·gist (ē′jip tol′ə jist) n. one who specializes in the study of Egyptian relics and monuments of ancient times

eke (ēk) v. **eked; ek·ing** to live by scanty or laborious means

elapse (i laps′) v. **elapsed; elaps·ing** to slip away; pass

ela·tion (i lā′shən) n. great joy or gladness

elim·i·na·tion (i lim′ə nā′shən) n. removal; the getting rid of or driving out of

elude (i lüd′) v. **elud·ed; elud·ing** to avoid or escape by skill, quickness, or trickery

elu·sive (i lü′siv) adj. **1** tending to escape **2** hard to understand or define

em·balm (em bäm′ or em bälm′) v. to preserve a dead body by treating it with special preparations

em·bar·rass (em bar′əs) v. to cause to be upset; to make feel uncomfortable or self-conscious

em·bod·i·ment (em bod′ē mənt) n. a symbol or representation of an idea or quality

em·i·gra·tion (em′ə grā′shən) n. leaving a country or region to settle elsewhere

emo·tion·al (i mō′shə nəl) adj. relating to a mental and bodily reaction (as anger, joy, hate, or fear) marked by strong feeling

em·u·late (em′yə lāt) v. **em·u·lat·ed; em·u·lat·ing** to strive to equal or excel; to imitate

en·chi·la·da (en′chi lä′də) n. a rolled, meat-filled tortilla covered with chili-seasoned tomato sauce

en·coun·ter (en koun′tər) v. **en·coun·tered; en·coun·ter·ing 1** to meet in a conflict or fight **2** to come face to face with **3** to meet unexpectedly

en·deav·or (en dev′ər) v. **en·deav·ored; en·deav·or·ing** to try; make a serious effort

en·dow (en dou′) v. to provide

en·dur·ance (en dür′əns) n. **1** the ability to withstand hardship, misfortune, or stress **2** permanence

en·dure (en dür′ or en dyür′) v. **en·dured; en·dur·ing 1** to last **2** to bear patiently **3** to tolerate or permit

en·gulf (en gulf′) v. **1** to flow over and enclose **2** to swallow up

en route (än rüt′ or en rüt′) adv. on or along the way (en route from Houston to Dallas)

en·shrine (en shrīn′) v. **en·shrined; en·shrin·ing** to enclose in a sacred place; to preserve or cherish as sacred

en·ti·tle (en tī′tl) v. **en·ti·tled; en·ti·tling 1** to give a title to **2** to give a legal right to; qualify

eon (ē′ən or ē′on) n. [variant of **aeon**] a vast period of time

err (ėr or er) v. to make a mistake or do wrong

er·rat·ic (ə rat′ik) adj. showing a lack of regularity

es·pi·o·nage (es′pē ə näzh or es′pē ə nij) n. the practice of spying; the use of spies

etch (ech) v. to impress or mark sharply (a face etched with wrinkles)

evade (i vād′) v. **evad·ed; evad·ing** to avoid by cleverness

event (i vent′) n. **1** a happening **2** a result or outcome **3** any of the contests in a program of sports

evil¹ (ē′vəl) adj. **evil·er; evil·est 1** wicked; sinful **2** harmful **3** unlucky

evil² n. **1** something distressful **2** harmful conduct or nature **3** misfortune; disaster

evince (i vins′) v. **evinced; evinc·ing** to show clearly; reveal

ex·ag·ger·ate (eg zaj′ə rāt′) v. **ex·ag·ger·at·ed; ex·ag·ger·at·ing** to enlarge a fact or statement beyond the truth

ex·alt (eg zôlt′) v. to raise high

ex·am·ine (eg zam′ən) v. **ex·am·ined; ex·am·in·ing** to look closely at, investigate, or question

ex·ca·va·tion (ek′skə vā′shən) n. a hole made by digging

ex·e·cu·tion·er (ek′sə kyü′shə nər) n. one who carries out a death sentence

ex·haust (eg zôst′) n. the escape or means of escape of used steam or gasoline from an engine

ex·o·dus (ek′sə dəs) n. a mass departure

ex·pe·di·tion (ek′spə dish′ən) n. **1** a journey for a special purpose, such as exploring **2** the group making such a journey

ex·tend (ek stend′) v. **1** to stretch out in distance, space, or time **2** to exert **3** to offer to someone (extend a welcome)

ex·ter·nal (ek stėr′nl) adj. of or relating to the outside; acting from outside

ex·tinct (ek stingkt′) adj. **1** no longer active (an extinct volcano) **2** no longer existing (an extinct species)

F f

fac·tor (fak′tər) n. **1** an agent **2** an ingredient **3** any of the numbers or symbols in mathematics that when multiplied together form a product

fac·ul·ty (fak′əl tē) n. **fac·ul·ties 1** ability or power of the mind or body **2** the teachers in a school

---

hat, āge, fär; let, ēqual, tėrm; it, īce; hot, ōpen, ôrder; oil, out; cup, pùt, rüle; ch, child; ng, long; sh, she; th, thin; ᵺ, then; zh, measure;

ə represents a in about, e in taken, i in pencil, o in lemon, u in circus.

fail·ure (fā′lyər) *n.* **1** a lack of success **2** a falling short **3** one who has failed

false·hood (fôls′hŏod) *n.* lie; untruthfulness

fal·ter (fôl′tər) *v.* **fal·tered; fal·ter·ing 1** to move unsteadily **2** to stammer **3** to hesitate

fal·ter·ing·ly (fôl′tə ring lē) *adv.* waveringly; hesitatingly

fan·ta·sy (fan′tə sē) *n.* **fan·ta·sies 1** something produced by a person's imagination **2** illusion

fate (fāt) *n.* **1** a power beyond human control that is held to determine what happens; destiny **2** fortune **3** outcome **4** disaster, especially death

fa·tigue (fə tēg′) *v.* **fa·tigued; fa·tigu·ing** to tire; to make or become weary

fer·ment (fər ment′) *v.* **1** to undergo or produce a gradual chemical change **2** to excite or cause intense activity

fer·ret[1] (fer′it) *n.* a mammal related to the weasel, used for hunting rodents

ferret[2] *v.* **1** to drive out from hiding **2** to hunt or search

fi·del·i·ty (fə del′ə tē *or* fī del′ə tē) *n.* **fi·del·i·ties 1** faithfulness; loyalty **2** accuracy

fiend (fēnd) *n.* a devil; a cruel person

flail (flāl) *v.* to move or swing as if wielding a flail, a hand-threshing tool consisting of a wooden handle with a short, stout stick fastened at one end by a thong

flaw (flô) *n.* a fault; a slight defect

fleet·ing (flē′ting) *adj.* passing quickly; not lasting

flinch (flinch) *v.* to draw back from or as if from physical pain; to wince

fo·li·age (fō′lē ij) *n.* the leaves of a plant

force (fôrs) *n.* an influence (such as a push or pull) that results chiefly in acceleration

fore·bod·ing (fôr bō′ding) *n.* a feeling that something bad is going to happen

for·mi·da·ble (fôr′mə də bəl) *adj.* **1** fearsome **2** imposing difficulties or hardships **3** awe-inspiring

for·mu·la (fôr′myə lə) *n.* **for·mu·las** *or* **for·mu·lae** (fôr′myə lē) **1** a set form of ceremonial words **2** a recipe or prescription **3** a general rule or principle expressed in symbols **4** a set form or method

for·ti·tude (fôr′tə tüd) *n.* strength of mind that enables a person to meet danger or bear pain with courage

frag·ment (frag′mənt) *n.* a part broken off, detached, or incomplete

fraud (frôd) *n.* **1** something dishonest **2** a trick **3** an impostor or cheat

frond (frond) *n.* a leaf or leaflike shoot

fru·gal (frü′gəl) *adj.* characterized by living simply and economically; not wasteful

fu·el (fyü′əl) *n.* a material used to produce heat or power by burning

func·tion[1] (fungk′shən) *n.* **1** the action for which someone or something exists **2** the specific contribution of a bodily part to the living organism **3** a formal ceremony or social gathering

function[2] *v.* **func·tioned; func·tion·ing 1** to have a use **2** to operate

fur·tive·ly (fėr′tiv lē) *adv.* secretly; slyly

fu·ture[1] (fyü′chər) *adj.* that which is going to happen

future[2] *n.* **1** time that is to come **2** an expectation of development **3** a stock or commodity sold for delivery at a future time **4** a verb form in the future tense

G g

gaff (gaf) *n.* a handled hook for holding or lifting heavy fish

gal·lant·ly (gal′ənt lē) *adv.* **1** nobly **2** bravely **3** chivalrously

gal·lant·ry (gal′ən trē) *n.* **gal·lant·ries** bravery that is showy and attracts attention

ga·lore (gə lôr′) *adj.* plentiful; in abundance (toys *galore*)

gape (gāp) *v.* **gaped; gap·ing 1** to open wide **2** to open the mouth wide; yawn **3** to stare openmouthed

gaunt (gônt) *adj.* **1** thin and bony; starved-looking **2** desolate

gen·tile (jen′tīl) *n.* a person who is not Jewish

ges·ture (jes′chər) *n.* **1** any action for effect or as a formality (a *gesture* of friendship) **2** a movement of the body or limbs to express an idea or feeling

ghast·ly (gast′lē) *adj.* **ghast·li·er; ghast·li·est 1** shocking; horrible **2** like a ghost

girth (gėrth) *n.* **1** the measure around something **2** a band around an animal's body to keep a saddle in place

gland (gland) *n.* a cell or group of cells that prepares and secretes a product (as saliva or sweat) for further use in the body or for elimination from the body

gnarled (närld) *adj.* knotted; twisted

goad (gōd) *n.* **1** a pointed rod used to urge an animal on **2** anything that urges or drives one on—**goad,** *v.*

goods (gŏodz) *n. pl.* property, such as clothing, furniture, autos, etc.; wares

gov·ern (guv′ərn) *v.* to control, direct, or influence the actions of

grab·ble (grab′əl) *v.* **grab·bled; grab·bling** to grope or search with the hand

grav·i·ty (grav′ət ē) *n.* **grav·i·ties 1** seriousness **2** weight **3** the attraction of the earth's mass for bodies near its surface toward the center of the earth

Graycoat a Confederate soldier during the American Civil War

grid (grid) *n.* **1** a grating **2** an electrode that controls the flow of current **3** a network of horizontal and perpendicular lines, as for locating points on a map

grim·ace (grim′is) *n.* a twisted facial expression, usually of disgust or disapproval

griz·zled (griz′əld) *adj.* mixed with gray

gun·wale *or* **gun·nel** (gun′l) *n.* the upper edge of a ship's or boat's side

gu·ru (gü′rü *or* gŏo rü′) *n.* **gu·rus** a personal religious teacher and spiritual guide

guts (guts) *n.* **1** courage; pluck; endurance **2** the intestines of an animal **3** the inner essential parts

gut·tur·al (gut′ər əl) *adj.* relating to an unpleasantly harsh sound formed or pronounced in the throat

H h

hab·i·ta·tion (hab′ə tā′shən) *n.* **1** occupancy **2** dwelling

ham·let (ham′lit) *n.* a small village

han·ker (hang′kər) *v.* **han·kered; han·ker·ing** to wish or desire strongly

ha·rass (hə ras′ *or* har′əs) *v.* to worry, tire, or annoy with repeated attacks

hark (härk) *v.* listen

hath (hath) *v. archaic* has

haugh·ty (hô′tē) *adj.* **haugh·ti·er; haugh·ti·est** overly proud; arrogant

ha·ven (hā′vən) *n.* a place of safety; shelter

her·ald (her′əld) *n.* official messenger; one who makes announcements

her·i·tage (her′ə tij) *n.* **1** property that descends to an heir **2** something acquired from a predecessor **3** birthright

he·ro·i·cal·ly (hi rō′ə kəl lē) *adv.* courageously; daringly; nobly

her·o·ism (her′ō iz′əm) *n.* bravery and boldness in accepting risk or sacrifice for a noble purpose

hew (hyü) *v.* **hewed; hewed** or **hewn; hew·ing 1** to cut up **2** to make or shape by cutting with an ax

hinge¹ (hinj) *n.* a jointed piece on which a swinging part turns

hinge² *v.* **hinged; hing·ing 1** to attach with hinges **2** to hang or turn on a hinge **3** to depend on

his·to·ry (his′tər ē) *n.* **his·to·ries 1** a record of factual events, arranged according to time, with an explanation of their causes **2** tale; story

hith·er (hiTH′ər) *adv.* to this place

hoick (hoik′) *v.* to yank

hom·age (hom′ij or om′ij) *n.* **1** respect; honor **2** formal allegiance pledged to a lord by a vassal

home·ly (hōm′lē) *adj.* **home·li·er; home·li·est** plain; not handsome

horde (hôrd) *n.* a large number of people

hor·i·zon·tal (hôr′ə zon′tl) *adj.* **1** parallel to the horizon or a base line **2** level or flat

hor·mone (hôr′mōn) *n.* a product of living cells that circulates in body fluids or sap and produces a specific effect on cells at a distance from its point of origin

hum·ble (hum′bəl) *adj.* **hum·bler; hum·blest 1** meek in spirit or manner; not proud **2** low in rank or status

hu·mil·i·ty (hyü mil′ət ē) *n.* the quality or state of being modest or meek in spirit or manner

hys·te·ria (hi ster′ē ə or hi stir′ē ə) *n.* **1** a nervous disorder marked by emotional excitability **2** senseless excitement

I i

ig·nit·er (ig nīt′ər) *n.* something that causes a fuel mixture to burn

ig·ni·tion (ig nish′ən) *n.* the act or process of setting a fuel mixture afire

ig·no·rant (ig′nər ənt) *adj.* not educated

il·lit·er·ate (i lit′ər it) *adj.* having little or no education; unable to read or write—**illiterate,** *n.*

im·age (im′ij) *n.* **1** a likeness or imitation of someone or something **2** a likeness of an object produced by photography, a lens, or a mirror **3** a mental picture **4** a person strikingly like another person

imag·ine (i maj′ən) *v.* **imag·ined; imag·in·ing 1** to form a mental picture of something not present **2** think; guess

im·mi·nent (im′ə nənt) *adj.* about to take place (an *imminent* collapse)

im·pact (im′pakt) *n.* **1** a striking together of two bodies; collision **2** forceful effect

im·pale (im pāl′) *v.* **im·paled; im·pal·ing** to pierce with or as if with something pointed

im·pel (im pel′) *v.* **im·pelled; im·pel·ling** to urge or drive forward or into action; force

im·per·a·tive (im per′ə tiv) *adj.* not to be avoided or evaded; urgent

im·pe·ri·ous (im pir′ē əs) *adj.* commanding; domineering

im·pet·u·ous·ly (im pech′ü əs lē) *adv.* impulsively; acting hastily or rashly

im·plac·a·ble (im plak′ə bəl or im plā′kə bəl) *adj.* unyielding; unable to be appeased or soothed

im·ple·ment (im′plə mənt) *n.* a tool or piece of equipment for work (farm *implements*)

im·pose (im pōz′) *v.* **im·posed; im·pos·ing** to establish by force or apply as a charge or penalty (*impose* a tax)

im·pres·sion (im presh′ən) *n.* an image imprinted on the senses or the mind

in·ac·ces·si·ble (in′ak ses′ə bəl) *adj.* not easily reached

in·cite (in sīt′) *v.* **in·cited; in·cit·ing** to stir up to action (*incite* a riot)

in·cline (in klīn′) *v.* **in·clined; in·clin·ing** to be favorably disposed toward

in·con·sol·a·ble (in′kən sō′lə bəl) *adj.* not to be comforted

in·cred·i·ble (in kred′ə bəl) *adj.* unbelievable; too extraordinary to be believed

in·def·i·nite·ly (in def′ə nit lē) *adv.* not fixed or limited; vaguely

in·de·struc·ti·ble (in′di struk′tə bəl) *adj.* incapable of being destroyed

in·dif·fer·ence (in dif′ər əns) *n.* lack of interest

in·dig·nant·ly (in dig′nənt lē) *adv.* scornfully or righteously angry

in·dis·put·a·bly (in′dis pyü′tə blē) *adv.* with no doubt; unquestionably

in·dom·i·ta·bil·i·ty (in dom′ə tə bil′ə tē) *n.* the state or act of being unconquerable or unyielding

in·er·tia (in ėr′shə) *n.* the tendency of matter to remain at rest or in uniform motion in the same straight line unless acted on by some outside force

in·es·ti·ma·ble (in es′tə mə bəl) *adj.* too great in excellence or value to be measured or appreciated

in·ev·i·ta·ble (in ev′ə tə bəl) *adj.* sure to happen; certain

in·ex·o·ra·bly (in ek′sər ə blē) *adv.* relentlessly; not yielding

in·ex·plic·a·ble (in′ik splik′ə bəl or in ek′splə kə bəl) *adj.* unable to be explained or accounted for

in·fir·mi·ty (in fėr′mə tē) *n.* **in·fir·mi·ties 1** the quality or state of being feeble or frail **2** ailment

in·for·ma·tion (in′fər mā′shən) *n.* **1** the communication of knowledge **2** facts; data **3** news

in·her·it·ance (in her′ə təns) *n.* something that is received by legal right from an ancestor at his or her death

in·iq·ui·tous (in ik′wə təs) *adj.* something completely unjust or wicked

---

hat, āge, fär; let, ēqual, tėrm; it, īce; hot, ōpen, ôrder; oil, out; cup, pút, rüle; ch, child; ng, long; sh, she; th, thin; ŦH, then; zh, measure;

ə represents *a* in about, *e* in taken, *i* in pencil, *o* in lemon, *u* in circus.

in·sa·tia·ble (in sā′shə bəl) *adj.* greedy; incapable of being satisfied

in·sur·rec·tion (in′sə rek′shən) *n.* rebellion; a rising against established authority

in·te·ger (in′tə jər) *n.* a natural number (the number *1* or any number obtained by repeatedly adding *1* to it), the negative of a natural number, or zero

in·tense (in tens′) *adj.* **1** existing in an extreme degree **2** deeply felt **3** considerable

in·ter·con·ti·nen·tal (in′tər kon′tə nen′tl) *adj.* **1** capable of traveling between continents **2** carried on between continents

in·te·ri·or¹ (in tir′ē ər) *adj.* **1** inner; on the inside **2** inland

interior² *n.* **1** the inner part **2** the inland part **3** the internal affairs of a state or nation

in·ter·mit·tent·ly (in′tər mit′nt lē) *adv.* starting, stopping, and starting again

in·ter·nal (in tėr′nl) *adj.* **1** inner **2** relating to the interior of the body

in·ter·pose (in′tər pōz′) *v.* **in·ter·posed; in·ter·pos·ing** **1** to interrupt **2** to be or come between

in·ter·pret (in tėr′prit) *v.* **1** to explain the meaning of **2** to understand **3** to translate

in·ter·vene (in′tər vēn′) *v.* **in·ter·vened; in·ter·ven·ing** **1** to come or be between **2** to come between in order to settle or stop

in·var·i·a·ble (in ver′ē ə bəl *or* in var′ē ə bəl) *adj.* not changing; constant

in·vert (in vėrt′) *v.* to turn upside down

iron·i·cal·ly (ī ron′ik lē) *adv.* showing a difference between an actual and an expected result

J j

jeer (jir) *v.* to mock, scoff at, or taunt—**jeer,** *n.*

jour·nal·ist (jėr′nl ist) *n.* a writer or an editor for a periodical or news medium

judge (juj) *n.* one who is authorized to decide questions brought before a court

judg·ment *or* **judge·ment** (juj′mənt) *n.* **1** an opinion or decision formed after evaluating a situation **2** a formal court decision

ju·di·ci·ary (jü dish′ē er′ē) *n.* **ju·di·ci·ar·ies** **1** a system of courts of law **2** a branch of government that administers justice—**judiciary,** *adj.*

jur·is·dic·tion (jür′is dik′shən) *n.* the authority to interpret and apply the law; control

jus·ti·fy (jus′tə fī) *v.* **jus·ti·fied; jus·ti·fy·ing** to show or prove to be just or right

K k

kid·ney (kid′nē) *n.* **kid·neys** either of a pair of organs located in the back part of the abdomen near the spine that pass off waste products in the form of urine.

kin·dred (kin′drid) *n.* a group of related individuals

L l

la·goon (lə gün′) *n.* a shallow body of water near or connected with a larger body of water

lance (lans) *n.* a long-shafted weapon with a sharp steel head used by knights or light cavalry

landmark decision a decision that marks an important turning point

lat·i·tude (lat′ə tüd *or* lat′ə tyüd) *n.* distance north or south from the equator measured in degrees

leg·a·cy (leg′ə sē) *n.* **leg·a·cies** something left to a person by will; inheritance

leg·i·ble (lej′ə bəl) *adj.* easily read; plain

leg·is·la·tion (lej′ə slā′shən) *n.* **1** the action of making laws **2** the laws made by a law-making body

leg·is·la·tive (lej′ə slā′tiv) *adj.* of or relating to a law or a law-making body

leg·is·la·ture (lej′ə slā′chər) *n.* an organized body of persons having the authority to make laws

le·git·i·mate (lə jit′ə mit) *adj.* rightful; within rightful standards (a *legitimate* excuse for being late)

le·ni·en·cy (lē′nyən sē) *n.* **le·ni·en·cies** the quality or act of showing mercy; a mild disposition

levy (lev′ē) *v.* **lev·ied; levy·ing** to impose or collect by legal authority

li·bel (lī′bəl) *n.* the action or crime of injuring someone's reputation in print or writing, slander

li·cense¹ *or* **li·cence** (lī′sns) *n.* **1** freedom of action **2** official permission **3** an artist's freedom from rules **4** too much liberty of action

license² *or* **licence** *v.* **li·censed; li·cens·ing** to permit or authorize by license

lin·sey-wool·sey (lin′zē wül′zē) *n.* a strong, coarse fabric of wool and linen or cotton

live·stock (līv′stok′) *n.* farm animals kept or raised for use and profit

lo·gy (lō′gē) *adj.* **lo·gi·er; lo·gi·est** sluggish, slow

lon·gi·tude (lon′jə tüd′ *or* lon′jə tyüd) *n.* distance measured by degrees or time east or west from the prime meridian

lox (loks) *n.* [*liquid* oxygen] liquid oxygen

lu·mi·nous (lü′mə nəs) *adj.* **1** brightly shining **2** lighted **3** clear

lurk (lėrk) *v.* **1** to stay about secretly **2** to lie in wait, as in ambush

lux·u·ri·ant (lug′zhŭr′ē ənt *or* luk′shŭr′ē ənt) *adj.* **1** showing lush growth **2** lavish; luxurious

M m

mag·is·trate (maj′ə strāt) *n.* **1** a local judge **2** an official with executive powers

mag·na·nim·i·ty (mag′nə nim′ə tē) *n.* **mag·na·nim·i·ties** **1** generosity **2** nobility of character

mag·nif·i·cent (mag nif′ə sənt) *adj.* grand; splendid

mal·ice (mal′is) *n.* ill will; spite

ma·neu·ver (mə nü′vər) *v.* **ma·neu·vered; ma·neu·ver·ing** **1** to move (as troops) according to plan **2** to carry out such a movement **3** to manage skillfully **4** to scheme

Manifest Destiny **1** the mid-nineteenth-century expansion to the Pacific **2** (lowercase *m* and *d*) imperialistic expansion considered inevitable and necessary

mar·ten (märt′n) *n.* **mar·ten** *or* **mar·tens** a slender flesh-eating mammal larger than the related weasel, valued for its fur

mass (mas) *n.* the quantity of matter in a body as measured by its inertia

mas·sa·cre¹ (mas′ə kər) *v.* **mas·sa·cred; mas·sa·cring** to kill; slaughter

massacre² *n.* the violent, merciless killing of a number of persons or animals

mat·ter (mat'ər) *n.* something that occupies space and has weight

mer·ce·nary (mėr'sə ner'ē) *n.* **mer·ce·nar·ies** a soldier hired by a foreign country to fight in its army

mere·ly (mir'lē) *adv.* only; simply

me·sa (mā'sə) *n.* a flat-topped hill with steep sides

me·thod·i·cal·ly (mə thod'ə kəl lē) *adv.* acting in a habitual manner

mid·thwart (mid'thwort) *n.* the middle of a rower's seat in a boat

mi·grate (mī'grāt) *v.* **mi·grat·ed; mi·grat·ing 1** to move from one place to another **2** to move periodically from one region or climate to another **3** to extend the habitat into a new region

mi·gra·tion (mī grā'shən) *n.* the move from one country or locality to another

min·i·mum (min'ə məm) *n.* **min·i·ma** *or* **min·i·mums 1** the least quantity possible **2** the lowest degree or amount reached—**minimum,** *adj.*

mis·car·riage (mis kar'ij) *n.* a failure in the administration of justice

moat (mōt) *n.* a water-filled trench around the walls of a castle or fortress

mo·bi·lize (mō'bə līz) *v.* **mo·bi·lized; mo·bi·liz·ing 1** to make ready for action **2** to put into movement or circulation

mock (mok) *v.* to ridicule; to make fun of by imitating

mod·est (mod'ist) *adj.* not vain or boastful

mol·e·cule (mol'ə kyül) *n.* the smallest portion of a substance having all the properties of the substance in a mass (a *molecule* of water)

mo·men·tous (mō men'təs) *adj.* very important

mon·arch (mon'ərk) *n.* one who rules over a kingdom or empire

mo·nop·o·ly (mə nop'ə lē) *n.* **mo·nop·o·lies 1** the exclusive ownership or control of a commodity or supply **2** a commodity controlled by one party **3** a person or group having a monopoly

mo·not·o·nous (mə not'n əs) *adj.* **1** unvaryingly dull and boring **2** continuing in the same tone

mon·stros·i·ty (mon stros'ə tē) *n.* **mon·stros·i·ties 1** the state of being monstrous **2** a monster

moor¹ (mür) *n.* an open wasteland, usually wet and peaty

moor² *v.* to fasten with cables or lines (*moor* a boat)

mope (mōp) *v.* **moped; mop·ing 1** to be in a dull, dejected state **2** to dawdle

mo·tion (mō'shən) *n.* an act, process, or instance of changing place or position; movement

muck (muk) *n.* **1** dirt; filth **2** moist manure **3** mud **4** defamatory remarks or writings

mul·ti·pli·cand (mul'tə plə kand') *n.* the number that is to be multiplied by another (In 10 times 100, *100* is the *multiplicand.*)

mul·ti·pli·er (mul'tə plī'ər) *n.* a number by which another number is multiplied (In 10 times 100, *10* is the *multiplier.*)

mul·ti·tude (mul'tə tüd *or* mul'tə tyüd) *n.* a great number of things or people

mum·my (mum'ē) *n.* **mum·mies** a dead body of a human being or animal embalmed for burial in the manner of the ancient Egyptians

murky (mėr'kē) *adj.* **murk·i·er; murk·i·est** dark and gloomy

mute (myüt) *adj.* **mut·er; mut·est** silent; marked by an absence of speech

myth (mith) *n.* **1** a legend or story, usually attempting to account for something in nature **2** something having only an imaginary existence **3** an unsupported belief

N n

nat·u·ral·i·za·tion (nach'ər ə lə zā'shən) *n.* the act of conferring the rights and privileges of citizenship on

naught (nôt) *n.* **1** nothing; nothingness **2** zero

nau·se·ate (nô'zē āt *or* nô'shē āt) *v.* **nau·se·at·ed; nau·se·at·ing** to affect or become affected with a sick feeling

nerve (nėrv) *n.* **1** a stringy band of nervous tissue connecting the nervous system with other organs and conducting nerve impulses **2** boldness; daring; power of endurance or control **3** a sore or sensitive point **4** the sensitive pulp of a tooth

ni·tro·glyc·er·in *or* **ni·tro·glyc·er·ine** (nī'trə glis'ər ən) *n.* an oily, explosive, poisonous liquid used chiefly in dynamite and in medicine

no·mad (nō'mad) *n.* **1** a member of a people that has no fixed home but wanders from place to place **2** a person who roams about aimlessly

no·to·ri·ous (nō tôr'ē əs) *adj.* **1** widely talked about and known, especially something unfavorable **2** famous

noz·zle (noz'əl) *n.* a projecting part with an opening that serves as an outlet

num·ber (num'bər) *n.* a word or symbol used to represent a numeral

O o

ob·jec·tive (əb jek'tiv) *adj.* **1** treating facts as they are, without bias; fair **2** relating to a goal

ob·li·ga·tion (ob'lə gā'shən) *n.* something one is bound to do; duty

oblique (ə blēk') *adj.* slanting

ob·sti·na·cy (ob'stə nə sē) *n.* **ob·sti·na·cies** being fixed or unyielding in a course or purpose; stubbornness

omen (ō'mən) *n.* a sign of things that supposedly will happen in the future

opin·ion (ə pin'yən) *n.* **1** a belief not as strong as knowledge **2** a judgment **3** a formal statement by an expert

op·pres·sive (ə pres'iv) *adj.* unjust; cruel; hard to bear

op·ti·cal (op'tə kəl) *adj.* **1** relating to the properties of light and the effects that light produces **2** relating to vision or the eye

or·a·tor·i·cal·ly (ôr'ə tôr'ə kəl lē) *adv.* in the manner of an effective public speaker

or·bit (ôr'bit) *n.* a patch of one body or object in its revolution about another

---

hat, āge, fär; let, ēqual, tėrm; it, īce; hot, ōpen, ôrder; oil, out; cup, pùt, rüle; ch, child; ng, long; sh, she; th, thin; ᵀH, then; zh, measure;

ə represents *a* in about, *e* in taken, *i* in pencil, *o* in lemon, *u* in circus.

or·deal (ôr dêl′) *n.* a difficult or painful experience

or·nate (ôr nāt′) *adj.* elaborately decorated

out·look (out′lŭk′) *n.* **1** a place offering a view or a view from a particular place **2** a point of view **3** the prospect for the future

out·pace (out′pās′) *v.* **out·paced; out·pac·ing** to outdo in speed

ox·i·dize (ok′sə dīz) *v.* **ox·i·dized; ox·i·diz·ing** to combine with oxygen

ox·i·diz·er (ok′sə dī′zər) *n.* an oxidizing agent, especially one used to support the combustion of a rocket propellant

P p

pae·an (pē′ən) *n.* a song of joy, praise, or triumph

pains·tak·ing (pānz′tā′king) *adj.* marked by extreme care and effort

par·al·lel¹ (par′ə lel) *adj.* **1** extending in the same direction, everywhere equally distant and not meeting **2** similar

parallel² *n.* **1** a parallel line, curve, or surface **2** one of the imaginary circles on the earth's surface paralleling the equator and marking latitude **3** similarity

parallel³ *v.* **1** compare **2** match **3** move in a direction parallel to

par·don¹ (pärd′n) *n.* the forgiveness of an offense without a penalty

pardon² *v.* **par·doned; par·don·ing** to forgive or free from penalty

par·tial·ly (pär′shəl lē) *adv.* partly

par·ti·cle (pär′tə kəl) *n.* one of the minute subdivisions of matter, as a molecule

pas·sion·ate (pash′ə nit) *adj.* having, showing, or expressing strong feeling

pas·to·ral (pas′tər əl) *adj.* **1** of or relating to rural life **2** of or relating to the pastor of a church

pa·tron (pā′trən) *n.* one who generously supports the work of another

peat (pēt) *n.* a dark substance formed when certain plants partly decay in water; turf

pelt (pelt) *n.* the skin of an animal before it is tanned

per·ceive (pər sēv′) *v.* **per·ceived; per·ceiv·ing** to become aware of; observe

per·cep·tion (pər sep′shən) *n.* **1** observation **2** the act or power of perceiving **3** understanding or insight

per·fi·dy (pėr′fə dē) *n.* **per·fi·dies** treachery; faithlessness; disloyalty

per·il·ous (per′ə ləs) *adj.* dangerous; involving risk

peri·scope (per′ə skōp) *n.* a tubular optical instrument containing lenses and mirrors by which an observer obtains an otherwise obstructed field of view (a submarine *periscope*)

per·ish (per′ish) *v.* **1** die **2** become destroyed or ruined

per·se·cu·tion (pėr′sə kyü′shən) *n.* the act or practice of causing others to suffer because of their beliefs

per·se·ver·ance (pėr′sə vir′əns) *n.* the condition of keeping at something; steadfastness

per·sist (pər sist′) *v.* to go on in spite of opposition; persevere

per·sist·ent (pər sis′tənt) *adj.* **1** continuing for a long or longer than usual time **2** lasting

per·spec·tive (pər spek′tiv) *n.* **1** the art of drawing or painting so that objects seem to have depth and distance **2** the power to understand things in their true relationship to each other **3** the true relationship of objects to one another **4** the appearance to the eye of objects in respect to their relative distance and positions

phe·nom·e·non (fə nom′ə non) *n.* **phe·nom·e·na** *or* **phe·nom·e·nons** something remarkable, rare, or exceptional

phos·pho·res·cent (fos′fə res′nt) *adj.* having a substance that, when excited by radiation, gives out light without seeming to give out heat (*phosphorescent* fireflies)

pin·ion (pin′yən) *v.* to restrain by binding the arms

pis·ton (pis′tən) *n.* a sliding piece, usually a short cylinder, moving within a larger cylinder by fluid pressure

pit·tance (pit′ns) *n.* a small portion, amount, or allowance, especially of money

pi·tu·i·tary gland (pə tü′ə ter′ē gland′) *n.* a small oval organ attached to the base of the brain that produces secretions that regulate growth and reproduction

plan·e·toid (plan′ə toid) *n.* a body resembling a planet; an asteroid

plank·ton (plangk′tən) *n.* the minute animal and plant life of a body of water

plan·tain (plan′tən) *n.* a banana plant with large greenish, starchy fruit that is eaten cooked

play the dozens a game of exchanging insults, usually about the opponent's family

plun·der (plun′dər) *v.* to rob openly and forcefully, as in a raid; loot

political hack a politician who serves a cause merely for reward

pon·der (pon′dər) *v.* **pon·dered; pon·der·ing** to consider carefully

pos·ses·sion (pə zesh′ən) *n.* something held as one's own property

pos·ter·i·ty (po ster′ə tē) *n.* **1** descendants **2** all future generations

pound (pound) *n.* **pounds** *or* **pound** [*also,* **pound sterling**] the basic monetary unit of the United Kingdom

prac·ti·cal (prak′tə kəl) *adj.* **1** having to do with action or practice rather than thought **2** capable of being put to use; useful

pre·cau·tion (pri kô′shən) *n.* something done in advance to ward off trouble or to guarantee good results; safeguard

pre·cau·tion·ary (pri kô′shə ner′ē) *adj.* using care and forethought

pred·e·ces·sor (pred′ə ses′ər) *n.* one who has held a position or office before another

prej·u·diced (prej′ə dist) *adj.* having a strong feeling for or against something without any good reason

pre·mo·ni·tion (prē′mə nish′ən *or* prem′ə nish′ən) *n.* a forewarning or feeling that something will happen

pres·ent·ly (prez′nt lē) *adv.* **1** before long; soon **2** now

pres·ti·dig·i·ta·tion (pres′tə dij′ə tā′shən) *n.* a magical trick requiring skill and dexterity; sleight of hand

pre·vail (pri vāl′) *v.* **1** to win a victory **2** to urge successfully **3** to persist

pre·vail·ing (pri vā′ling) *adj.* **1** most frequent or common (*prevailing* winds) **2** having superior force or influence

pri·or (prī′ər) *adj.* earlier in time

pro·claim (prə klām′) v. to announce publicly, declare

pro·di·gious (prə dij′əs) adj. **1** huge in size, quantity, or degree; enormous **2** wonderful

prod·i·gy (prod′ə jē) n. **prod·i·gies** a highly talented child

prod·uct (prod′əkt) n. the numeral resulting from the multiplication of two or more numerals

pro·file (prō′fīl) n. the side view of a head or face

pro·found (prə found′) adj. **1** scholarly **2** deeply felt **3** very deep

pro·long (prə lông′) v. to continue or lengthen in time, extent, or range

pro·pel·lant (prə pel′ənt) n. fuel plus an oxidizing agent used to propel a rocket engine

proph·e·sy (prof′ə sī) v. **proph·e·sied; proph·e·sy·ing** to tell what will happen; predict

pro·pound (prə pound′) v. to propose or put forward for consideration

pro·pul·sion (prə pul′shən) n. the action or process of pushing or driving forward or onward

pros·pect (pros′pekt) n. **1** a wide view **2** the act of looking forward; anticipation **3** something awaited or expected **4** a potential buyer or candidate

pros·per·ous (pros′pər əs) adj. **1** successful; thriving **2** favorable

pro·trude (prō trüd′) v. **pro·trud·ed; pro·trud·ing** to stick out; project

pru·dence (prüd′ns) n. good judgment

psy·cho (sī′kō) n. **psy·chos** [short for **psychoneurotic**] a person with a severe mental or emotional disorder

puce (pyüs) n. a dark red

pum·mel (pum′əl) v. **pum·meled** or **pum·melled; pum·mel·ing** or **pum·mel·ling** to pound, beat, or thump

pur·sue (pər sü′) v. **pur·sued; pur·su·ing 1** to chase **2** to seek **3** to follow **4** to practice

Q q

qual·i·fy (kwol′ə fī) v. **qual·i·fied; qual·i·fy·ing** to fit or be fit for a special purpose (to *qualify* for a scholarship)

quar·ter (kwôr′tər) v. to provide with or occupy a lodging or shelter

R r

ra·di·ate (rā′dē āt) v. **ra·di·at·ed; ra·di·at·ing 1** to send out rays, as of light **2** to proceed in a line from or toward a center **3** to send out

rash (rash) adj. too hasty in speech or action or in making decisions; reckless

rat·i·fy (rat′ə fī) v. **rat·i·fied; rat·i·fy·ing** to confirm; to approve formally (*ratify* a treaty)

ra·vine (rə vēn′) n. a deep, narrow valley or gorge

re·ac·tion (rē ak′shən) n. the force that a body subjected to the action of a force from another body exerts in the opposite direction

read·i·ly (red′l ē) adv. speedily; willingly

re·al·i·ty (rē al′ə tē) n. **re·al·i·ties 1** actual existence **2** someone or something real or actual **3** the characteristic of being a real thing or fact

realm (relm) n. **1** a kingdom **2** a particular field of influence or activity

re·call (ri kôl′) v. to remember or bring back to mind

re·cede (ri sēd′) v. **re·ced·ed; re·ced·ing 1** to move back or away **2** to grow less or smaller

re·cep·ta·cle (ri sep′tə kəl) n. something used to contain smaller objects; container

rec·ti·tude (rek′tə tüd or rek′tə tyüd) n. moral soundness; righteousness

rec·to·ry (rek′tər ē) n. **rec·to·ries** the residence of a person in charge of a church or parish

re·dress (ri dres′ or rē′dres) n. compensation for a wrong or loss; a setting right

reef (rēf) n. a narrow ridge of rocks or sand at or near the surface of water

re·flect (ri flekt′) v. **1** to bend or throw back waves of light, sound, or heat **2** to give back an image or likeness of **3** to bring as a result **4** to cast blame or discredit **5** to meditate

re·gal (rē′gəl) adj. royal; splendid

re·gard[1] (ri gärd′) n. **1** a feeling of respect and affection **2** a steady look **3** consideration or attention

regard[2] v. **1** to pay attention to **2** to respect or hold in high esteem **3** to look at steadily **4** to take into consideration **5** to think of

reg·i·ment (rej′ə mənt) n. a military unit composed of smaller units, as battalions

reign (rān) v. to possess or exercise authority over; rule

re·lin·quish (ri ling′kwish) v. to release a claim to or possession of; to give up

re·luc·tant (ri luk′tənt) adj. unwilling

re·mote (ri mōt′) adj. **re·mot·er; re·mot·est** far off in time or place; out-of-the-way

ren·der (ren′dər) v. to cause to be or become

res·er·va·tion (rez′ər vā′shən) n. **1** an arrangement to have something held for one's use **2** something reserved for a special use, especially public lands (an Indian *reservation*) **3** something held or kept back; an exception

re·sist·ance (ri zis′təns) n. an opposing force

re·solve (ri zolv′) v. **re·solved; re·solv·ing 1** to clear up **2** to decide; to make up one's mind **3** to declare by formal resolution and vote

re·spect[1] (ri spekt′) n. **1** the state of being highly regarded or honored **2** esteem **3** reference to **4** detail or particular

respect[2] v. **1** to consider worthy of high regard **2** to concern

re·tal·i·ate (ri tal′ē āt) v. **re·tal·i·at·ed; re·tal·i·at·ing** to get revenge; return like for like

re·tire (ri tīr′) v. **re·tired; re·tir·ing 1** to retreat or withdraw **2** to give up one's position or occupation **3** to go to bed

re·tort (ri tôrt′) v. to answer back angrily or sharply

re·treat[1] (ri trēt′) n. **1** an act of withdrawing **2** a place of safety; refuge

retreat[2] v. to withdraw

---

hat, āge, fär; let, ēqual, tėrm; it, īce; hot, ōpen, ôrder; oil, out; cup, put, rüle; ch, child; ng, long; sh, she; th, thin; ₮H, then; zh, measure;

ə represents *a* in about, *e* in taken, *i* in pencil, *o* in lemon, *u* in circus.

re·trieve (ri trēv′) v. **re·trieved; re·triev·ing 1** to get and bring back **2** to recover, repair, or make good

re·veal (ri vēl′) v. **1** to make known **2** to display

re·vere (ri vir′) v. **re·vered; re·ver·ing** to show devoted honor and respect to

rev·er·ent (rev′ər ənt) adj. very respectful

re·volt[1] (ri vōlt′) v. to rebel or rise against a government

revolt[2] n. a rebellion against a government or other authority

rich·es (rich′iz) n. pl. things that make one rich; wealth

ric·o·chet (rik′ə shā′) v. **ric·o·cheted** (rik′ə shād′) or **ric·o·chet·ted** (rik′ə shet′d); **ric·o·chet·ing** (rik′əshā′ing) or **ric·o·chet·ting** (rik′ə shet′ing) to spring off upon hitting a flat surface

right·eous (rī′chəs) adj. acting justly or rightly; honest

rit·u·al (rich′ü əl) n. an act or series of acts performed at a special time for a solemn purpose; ceremony

rout (rout) n. **1** the state of disorderly retreat **2** a disastrous defeat

rub·ble (rub′əl) n. rough broken stones or bricks

ru·mor[1] (rü′mər) n. hearsay; talk having no known source

rumor[2] v. **ru·mored; ru·mor·ing** to tell or spread by rumor

ru·ral (rür′əl) adj. of or relating to the country or country life

ruse (rüs or rüz) n. trick or scheme

S s

sa·ga·cious (sə gā′shəs) adj. having keen and far-sighted understanding; shrewd

salt (sôlt) n. sharp, biting wit

sanc·tion[1] (sangk′shən) n. official permission or approval

sanction[2] v. to approve or permit

sap·ling (sap′ling) n. a young tree

sar·coph·a·gus (sär kof′ə gəs) n. **sar·coph·a·gi** or **sar·coph·a·gus·es** a stone coffin

sat·el·lite (sat′l īt) n. a heavenly body or a man-made object that orbits the earth or another heavenly body

sav·age (sav′ij) adj. **1** wild **2** ferocious **3** uncivilized

scar·ci·ty (sker′sə tē or skar′sə tē) n. **scar·ci·ties** the quality or condition of being in very small supply; rarity

scorch (skôrch) v. **1** to burn on the surface **2** to wither or dry up

score (skôr) n. **scores** or **score** twenty; a group of twenty things

scru·ti·nize (skrüt′n īz) v. **scru·ti·nized; scru·ti·niz·ing** to examine very closely

scut (skut) n. a short erect tail

se·crete (si krēt′) v. **se·cret·ed; se·cret·ing** to produce or give off

seek (sēk) v. **sought; seek·ing 1** to go in search of **2** to request **3** to try to acquire **4** to attempt

seg·ment (seg′mənt) n. a section or division; a part marked off

self-as·sured (self′ə shùrd′) adj. self-confident

self-pos·sessed (self′pə zest′) adj. calm; composed in mind or manner

ser·ried (ser′ēd) adj. marked by ridges

sex·tant (sek′stənt) n. an instrument used at sea to measure the altitude of a heavenly body in order to determine latitude and longitude

shag·bark (shag′bärk′) n. a hickory tree with a rough gray outer bark that peels off in long strips

shear (shir) v. **sheared; sheared** or **shorn; shear·ing** to cut off

sheathe (shēᴛʜ) **sheathed; sheath·ing** to cover with something (snow-*sheathed* log)

shoal (shōl) n. **1** a shallow place in a body of water **2** a sandbar or sandbank that makes the water shallow

shore (shôr) v. **shored; shor·ing** to prop or support

shrine (shrīn) n. a holy or sacred place

shunt (shunt) v. to turn off to one side; shift or switch

Si·be·ria (sī bir′ē ə) n. a region in northern Asia from the Ural Mountains to the Pacific belonging to the Union of Soviet Socialist Republics

si·mul·ta·ne·ous·ly (sī′məl tā′nē əs lē) adv. occurring at the same time

sin·ewy (sin′yü ē) adj. tough; strong

skulk (skulk) v. **1** to sneak **2** to hide or conceal oneself out of cowardice or fear or for a treacherous purpose

sla·lom (slä′ləm or slal′əm) n. a ski race or run having a zigzag or wavy course between upright poles

slang (slang) n. an informal language usage considered nonstandard—**slang,** adj.

slew (slü) v. **slued; slu·ing** [variant of **slue**] to turn, twist, or swing about; skid

snipe (snīp) n. **snipes** or **snipe** a game bird that lives in marshy areas

sole·plate (sōl′plāt′) n. **1** the undersurface of a flatiron **2** the plate that comes into contact with something during pressing

sol·i·tary (sol′ə ter′ē) adj. **1** all alone **2** lonely

som·ber (som′bər) adj. **1** dark and gloomy **2** melancholy **3** dull or dark colored

so·nar (sō′när) n. [sound navigation ranging] equipment that detects the presence and location of an underwater object by means of sound waves reflected back to it from the object

sough·ing (suf′ing or sou′ing) n. a moaning, sighing sound; rustling

specific impulse the thrust produced by a propellant that is a measure of a rocket engine's efficiency

spec·u·la·tion (spek′yə lā′shən) n. thinking or theorizing about something

speed (spēd) n. the rate of motion; velocity

spir·i·tu·al (spir′ə chü əl) n. a Negro religious song, especially of the South, and usually of a deeply emotional character

splay (splā) v. to flatten and spread out

spleen (splēn) n. a ductless organ located near the stomach or intestine concerned with final destruction of blood cells, storage of blood, and production of lymphocytes

spon·ta·ne·ous (spon tā′nē əs) adj. occurring naturally, of itself

spor·tive (spôr′tiv) adj. playful; merry

sta·bi·liz·er (stā′bə lī′zər) n. a device that steadies

stan·za (stan′zə) n. a division of a poem

sta·ple (stā′pəl) adj. principal; chief (staple food)

stim·u·late (stim′yə lāt) v. **stim·u·lat·ed; stim·u·lat·ing** to arouse or make active

stol·id (stol′id) *adj.* showing little emotion; not easily excited

sto·ry (stôr′ē) *n.* **sto·ries 1** an account of events **2** the plot of a narrative **3** a rumor or lie **4** a news article or broadcast

stow away (stō′ə wā′) *v.* to hide on board a vehicle as a means of getting transportation

strain (strān) *n.* tune; a passage of musical expression

strand (strand) *n.* **1** one of the threads, strings, or wires twisted to make a rope or cable **2** something long and twisted resembling a rope (a *strand* of hair)

stren·u·ous (stren′yü əs) *adj.* **1** energetic **2** requiring stamina

stress (stres) *n.* **1** a factor that causes bodily or mental tension **2** emphasis; weight

strew (strü) *v.* **strewed; strewed** *or* **strewn; strew·ing** to spread by scattering

strive (strīv) *v.* **strove** *or* **strived; striv·en** *or* **strived; striv·ing 1** to struggle in opposition **2** to try hard

strobe (strōb) *n.* [**stroboscope**] a device that uses a flashtube for high-speed lighting

stu·pen·dous (stü pen′dəs *or* styü pen′dəs) *adj.* amazing because of great size or height; tremendous

sub·mit (səb mit′) *v.* **sub·mit·ted; sub·mit·ting** to yield to power or authority; surrender

sub·stan·tive (sub′stən tiv) *adj.* **1** being real or independent **2** considerable in number **3** creating and defining rights and duties

suc·ces·sion (sək sesh′ən) *n.* **1** the order of succeeding to a throne, title, or property **2** the following of one person or thing after another

suc·ces·sive (sək ses′iv) *adj.* following in order; consecutive

suc·ces·sor (sək ses′ər) *n.* one who follows or succeeds another in office, position, or ownership

suc·cu·lent¹ (suk′yə lənt) *adj.* juicy

succulent² *n.* a succulent plant, such as a cactus

suf·fer (suf′ər) *v.* **suf·fered; suf·fer·ing 1** to feel or endure pain **2** to experience **3** to permit or allow

suf·fi·cient (sə fish′ənt) *adj.* enough to meet the needs of a situation

suf·fo·cate (suf′ə kāt) *v.* **suf·fo·cat·ed; suf·fo·cat·ing** to strangle; suffer, as from a lack of breathable air

suit·or (sü′tər) *n.* one who courts a woman or seeks to marry her

sul·len (sul′ən) *adj.* **1** resentfully silent **2** dull or somber **3** gloomy

su·per·in·tend·ent (sü′pər in ten′dənt) *n.* a person who oversees or manages some operation

su·per·vi·sor (sü′pər vī′zər) *n.* an administrative officer in charge of a business, government, or school operation

sup·pres·sion (sə presh′ən) *n.* **1** the act of putting down by force or authority **2** the act of keeping in or holding back

surge¹ (sėrj) *v.* **surged; surg·ing 1** to rise and fall, as in waves **2** to rise suddenly in current or voltage

surge² *n.* **1** a swelling or rolling, as of a wave **2** a large wave **3** a sudden rise in electrical current

sur·ren·der (sə ren′dər) *v.* **sur·ren·dered; sur·ren·der·ing 1** to give up power, control, or possession to another upon demand **2** to give oneself up into another's power

surrender² *n.* the giving up of oneself or something into the power of another

sur·rep·ti·tious·ly (sėr′əp tish′əs lē) *adv.* secretly; stealthily

sus·tain (sə stān′) *v.* **1** to support or relieve **2** to nourish **3** to endure **4** to confirm or prove

swell¹ (swel) *v.* **swelled; swelled** *or* **swol·len; swell·ing 1** to expand or increase **2** to fill or become filled with pride, arrogance, or emotion

swell² *n.* **1** the condition of being increased in amount, size, or intensity **2** a huge wave or succession of waves **3** a person of high fashion, position, or competence

swell³ *adj.* **1** stylish **2** excellent

swoon¹ (swün) *v.* to faint or become dazed

swoon² *n.* a dazed, enraptured state

symp·tom (simp′təm) *n.* an indication or sign

syn·a·gogue (sin′ə gôg) *n.* the house of worship and communal center of a Jewish congregation

T t

tact·ful·ly (takt′fə lē) *adv.* dealing skillfully with others without offending them

te·dious (tē′dē əs *or* tē′jəs) *adj.* tiresome; boring

ten·ure (ten′yər) *n.* the act, right, manner, or term of holding something, as an office

ter·rain (tə rān′) *n.* the physical features or a tract of land (mountainous *terrain*)

ter·ri·to·ry (ter′ə tôr′ē) *n.* **ter·ri·to·ries 1** a geographical area belonging to or under the authority of a government **2** an assigned area (neutral *territory*)

throat·latch (thrōt′lach′) *n.* the area around the head of a valley, similar to the throat of an animal

thrust (thrust) *n.* a reaction force directed forward, produced by a high-speed jet of fluid discharged backwards from a nozzle

to·ken (tō′kən) *n.* **1** a sign, symbol, act, or gesture (a *token* of peace) **2** a keepsake **3** a piece resembling a coin, used as money

tol·er·a·bly (tol′ər ə blē) *adv.* **1** capable of being borne or endured **2** passably; moderately

tol·er·ate (tol′ə rāt′) *v.* **tol·er·at·ed; tol·er·at·ing 1** to put up with **2** to allow to be done without hindrance **3** to endure

tra·di·tion·al (trə dish′ə nəl) *adj.* having to do with a belief or custom handed down from one generation to another

trag·e·dy (traj′ə dē) *n.* **trag·e·dies 1** a serious drama with a sad or disastrous ending **2** a very sad or disastrous happening

trag·ic (traj′ik) *adj.* **1** having to do with tragedy **2** sorrowful

trance (trans) *n.* **1** a state of partly suspended animation **2** a sleeplike state **3** a state of deep absorption

---

hat, āge, fär; let, ēqual, tėrm; it, īce; hot, ōpen; ôrder; oil, out; cup, pùt; rüle; ch, child; ng, long; sh, she; th, thin; ᴛʜ, then; zh, measure;

ə represents *a* in about, *e* in taken, *i* in pencil, *o* in lemon, *u* in circus.

trans·form (tran sfôrm′) v. to change in character or condition

tran·sient (tran′shənt) adj. not lasting; changing in form or appearance

trans·port (tran spôrt′) n. a highly pleasurable emotion

treach·er·ous (trech′ər əs) adj. unreliable; guilty of deceiving

treach·ery (trech′ər ē) n. **treach·er·ies** a violation of trust; treason

trea·son (trē′zn) n. the offense of attempting to overthrow the government to which one owes allegiance or to bring about its defeat in war

treasure trove 1 a discovery of things to be treasured **2** treasure of unknown ownership found hidden away

trea·ty (trē′tē) n. **trea·ties** an agreement or arrangement between two or more parties

trem·u·lous (trem′yə ləs) adj. trembling; timid

trep·i·da·tion (trep′ə dā′shən) n. fear

tri·fling (trī′fling) adj. **1** frivolous **2** unimportant; trivial

truce (trüs) n. an interruption of warfare by mutual agreement; a temporary peace or cease-fire

trust (trust) n. a combination of firms or corporations, formed by a legal agreement, that controls much of a certain kind of business and threatens to reduce competition

truth (trüth) n. **truths 1** honesty **2** something that is accepted as true **3** a fact; actuality

tur·ret (tėr′it) n. a small tower, often at a corner of a building

ty·ran·ni·cal (tə ran′ə kəl) adj. of or relating to a tyrant or tyranny; cruel and unjust

tyr·an·ny (tir′ə nē) n. **tyr·an·nies** a government in which a single ruler has absolute power; arbitrary and oppressive government

U u

un·alien·a·ble (un ā′lyə nə bəl) adj. not capable of being taken away or given away

unan·i·mous (yü nan′ə məs) adj. agreed to by all

un·com·pli·men·tary (un′kom plə men′tər ē) adj. unfavorable; not flattering

un·de·fin·a·ble (un′di fīn′ə bəl) adj. not distinct in form, outline, or meaning

un·du·ly (un dü′lē or un dyü′lē) adv. **1** improperly **2** excessively

uni·son (yü′nə sən) n. **1** sameness in pitch or sound **2** exact agreement

un·ques·tion·a·bly (un kwes′chə nə blē) adv. beyond doubt

un·war·rant·a·ble (un wôr′ən tə bəl) adj. inexcusable; not justifiable

usur·pa·tion (yü′sər pā′shən or yü′zər pā′shən) n. the act or state of seizing and holding power or authority by force or without right

uten·sil (yü ten′səl) n. a useful instrument or article (a cooking utensil)

ut·ter·ly (ut′ər lē) adv. completely; absolutely

V v

vac·u·um (vak′yü əm or vak′yüm) n. a perfectly empty space

vag·a·bond (vag′ə bond) n. a homeless wanderer or tramp with no visible means of support

va·grant[1] (vā′grənt) n. a wanderer; tramp

vagrant[2] adj. **1** wandering aimlessly **2** random

val·or (val′ər) n. personal bravery in combat; courage

var·mint (vär′mənt) n. an animal or bird considered a pest, especially those classed as vermin and unprotected by game law

veg·e·tar·i·an (vej′ə ter′ē ən) n. one who eats vegetables but no meat

ve·loc·i·ty (və los′ə tē) n. **ve·loc·i·ties** rate of motion; speed

ven·ture (ven′chər) v. **ven·tured; ven·tur·ing** to dare; to dare to say or do

verge (vėrj) n. on the edge or brink (on the *verge* of discovery)

ver·i·ta·ble (ver′ə tə bəl) adj. actual; real

ver·te·bra (vėr′tə brə) n. **ver·te·brae** (vėr′tə brē) or **ver·te·bras** one of the bony or cartilaginous segments of the spinal column

ver·ti·cal (vėr′tə kəl) adj. **1** perpendicular to a base line; upright **2** directly overhead

ves·sel (ves′əl) n. a tube (as an artery or a vein) in which a body fluid is contained and conveyed or circulated

ves·tige (ves′tij) n. a visible sign or trace

vi·cin·i·ty (və sin′ə tē) n. **vi·cin·i·ties** a nearby area; neighborhood

view·point (vyü′point′) n. outlook; point of view

vig·il (vij′əl) n. **1** the act of keeping awake when sleep is customary **2** the act of watching or guarding **3** the day before a religious feast observed as a day of spiritual preparation

vi·o·late (vī′ə lāt) v. **vi·o·lat·ed; vi·o·lat·ing 1** to break or disregard **2** to do harm **3** to treat disrespectfully **4** to disturb

vi·sor (vī′zər) n. a movable upper piece of a helmet that covers the face

vi·su·al (vizh′ü əl) adj. **1** relating to sight **2** visible **3** producing mental images

W w

waft (waft) v. to move lightly by, as if on a breeze

wal·lop (wal′əp) v. to beat or hit with force

wealth (welth) n. **1** all property that has a money or an exchange value **2** abundant supply

wealthy (wel′thē) adj. **wealth·i·er; wealth·i·est** having an abundance of possessions; rich

whet·stone (hwet′stōn′) n. a stone for sharpening edged tools

whole·some (hōl′səm) adj. healthful; promoting health or well-being

wind·fall (wind′fôl′) n. **1** something, as a tree, blown down by the wind **2** an unexpected advantage or piece of good luck

woe (wō) n. **1** deep suffering or grief **2** misfortune

wol·ve·rine (wul′və rēn′) n. a blackish shaggy-furred mammal of northern North America noted for its thievishness, strength, and cunning

won·drous (wun′drəs) adj. wonderful

wry·ly (rī′lē) adv. cleverly or ironically humorous

Z z

zeal (zēl) n. eagerness; enthusiasm